CONTRACT LAW IN RUSSIA

The book explains Russian contract law in a form understandable to lawyers qualified in other countries, especially common law countries. The introduction gives a concise overview of the Russian legal system in general and contract law in particular, as well as a brief insight into the history of contract law in Russia. Then the main concepts of Russian contract law are explained, using the conceptual framework of English contract law to make them accessible to someone not familiar with the codified Russian system.

The book not only considers the legislation regulating Russian contractual relations but also includes appropriate case law to show how the legislation is interpreted. The focus is on contract law in Russia as it actually operates, rather than merely the legislative texts, so that it will be directly relevant to legal practitioners and others who wish to acquire knowledge of the practical application of an important element of the Russian legal system, as well as those seeking an insight into the realities of codified law in action.

The target readership therefore includes legal practitioners who have to deal with Russian law, academics and students with an interest in Russian law, the law of contract and comparative civil law, as well as scholars of comparative legal systems and Russian area studies.

Contract Law in Russia

Maria Yefremova
Svetlana Yakovleva
and
Jane Henderson

HART
PUBLISHING
OXFORD AND PORTLAND, OREGON
2014

Hart Publishing
An imprint of Bloomsbury Publishing Plc

Hart Publishing Ltd
Kemp House
Chawley Park
Cumnor Hill
Oxford OX2 9PH
UK

Bloomsbury Publishing Plc
50 Bedford Square
London
WC1B 3DP
UK

www.hartpub.co.uk
www.bloomsbury.com

Published in North America (US and Canada) by
Hart Publishing
c/o International Specialized Book Services
920 NE 58th Avenue, Suite 300
Portland, OR 97213-3786
USA

www.isbs.com

British Library Cataloguing-in-Publication Data
A catalogue record for this book is available from the British Library.

ISBN: 978-1-84946-299-0

Typeset by Hope Services, Abingdon
Printed and bound in Great Britain by
Lightning Source UK Ltd

To find out more about our authors and books visit www.hartpublishing.co.uk. Here you will find extracts, author information, details of forthcoming events and the option to sign up for our newsletters.

Contents

Table of Legislation

Russian and Soviet Legislation

UK legislation

International law

Table of Informational Circulars

Table of Plenum Resolutions

Introduction

The aim of this book is to explain Russian contract law to the English reader. It seeks to do this not in the usual way of Russian books on contract law, which is more or less to follow the order of the Russian Civil Code.[1] Instead, our substantive chapters follow the trajectory of the formation, existence and discharge of a contract, which is the approach which would be more familiar to an English lawyer (or other lawyers from non-codified legal systems).

We also bring to our explanation of the rules of Russian contract law illustration from cases even though case law is only rather controversially emerging as a source of law in Russia. The text of the Civil Code is rather dry in itself and the use of actual cases, we believe, makes it easier for the reader to feel the way Russian law works in real life (we have simplified the parties' names, for convenience). Case law gives useful clues to the precise meaning of legal rules, and when the cases have been cited by the topmost Russian courts as examples of the correct interpretation of the Civil Code, then irrespective of whether that is law creation or law interpretation, the example will be respected. Both lawyers advising clients and judges will take note.

Not all cases used as illustrations in the book can be called case law, that is, as setting examples for the resolution of similar cases in future. We also use decisions of lower level courts where we believe they are the best way to illustrate how a particular rule might be applied. These cases, in our opinion, are no less valuable than decisions of higher courts; they help us to understand the actual logic of judges and the way they think.

The collective authorship of this book is comprised of two Russian lawyers with both academic and practical experience, and an English academic comparative lawyer who also teaches English contract law to undergraduate students. Their combined expertise brings you the opportunity to appreciate the complexity of Russian contract law, including, in some cases, its very different approach to making contractual relations in comparison to English law.

The structure of the book is the following: the first chapter gives the institutional context in which contract law works, so should be essential reading for

[1] For examples in English see WE Butler (ed and trans) VP Mozolin and AI Masliaev, *Russian Civil and Commercial Law Volume 2 Law of Obligations: General Provisions and Individual Types* (London, Wildy, Simmonds & Hill, 2011); V Moudrykh, *Russian Contract Law* (Moscow, RDL Publishers, 2000).

those unfamiliar with the Russian legal system. Then different aspects of contract law are dealt with in chapters which will stand alone (suitable cross-referencing is included), but may be read in the following sequence: an explanation of the Russian approach to Terms of a Contract (Chapter 2); Requirements of Form (Chapter 3); Formation of Contracts (Chapter 4); the Russian analogy to Consideration (Chapter 5); Factors Tending to Defeat Contractual Liability (Chapter 6); the position of Third Parties (Chapter 7); Assignment (Chapter 8); Performance (Chapter 9); Remedies for Breach (Chapter 10); and Discharge (Chapter 11), followed by Chapter 12, Conclusion.

The law is stated as at 1 September 2013.

I A NOTE ABOUT LANGUAGE

This book is aimed at the English-speaking reader who does not have any knowledge of Russian, so all Russian words and phrases have been translated. The extracts from the Civil Code have been taken from WE Butler, *The Civil Code of the Russian Federation Parts 1, 2 and 3: Parallel Russian and English Texts* (Moscow, JurInfoR-Press, 2008). Professor Butler was kind enough to supply the authors with copies of this extremely useful parallel text and we acknowledge our thanks to him. Occasionally we have preferred a different translation, for example, 'legal entity' rather than 'juridical person', in which case we have included the alternative in square parentheses. All other translations, including those of recent amendments to the Civil Code, are by the authors.

We decided to use the more familiar expressions of promisor and promisee in our discussions about contractual parties, rather than the more literal translations of кредитор (*kreditor*) and должник (*dolzhnik*) as creditor and debtor, because most English readers associate those terms with situations of money owed, rather than any type of contractual obligation. The exception is in Chapter 8 on Assignment, where creditor and debtor have been retained; although it does not have to be, assignment is almost invariably of a right to claim money, that is, a debt.

In some instances we have included the Russian phrase in our text, and its transliteration using the American Library Association-Library of Congress convention.

Those who read Russian may be interested to know our standard translation conventions (in Cyrillic alphabetical order):

- Высший Арбитражный Суд Российской Федерации; Vysshii Arbitrazhnyi Sud Rossiiskoi Federatsii; Supreme Commercial Court
- Информационное письмо; *Informatsionnoe pis'mo*; Informational Circular
- неосновательное обогащение; *neosnovatelnoe obogashchenie*; unfounded enrichment
- Определение; *Opredelenie*; Ruling

- Постановление; *Postanovlenie*; Resolution
- физическое лицо; *fizicheskoe litso*; individual
- юридическое лицо; *iuridicheskoe litso*; legal entity

1

Useful Information

I INTRODUCTION

This chapter gives information which the reader needs to understand the institutional and legal context within which Russian contract law operates. It begins with an account of the development of Russian contract law from prerevolutionary times to the present day, followed by an overview of the relevant Russian state agencies, particularly the court system. We then explain sources of law and the legal profession, before rounding off with some important general principles about contract law. We have clearly been selective; if the reader wishes to learn more about the Russian legal system as a whole, there are reference works available in English.[1] We have also tried to include in our footnotes here some suggestions for further reading on specific topics.

II A HISTORY OF RUSSIAN CONTRACT LAW

A Prerevolutionary Law

Russia's current law of contract has developed from her own legal heritage, with the addition of features based on the experience of other legal systems, particularly continental European codified systems which followed the Roman law tradition. Russia's law is traditionally based on legislation, not case law, but prior to the nineteenth century it was disorderly and unsystematised. The first major compilation of Russian law, the 48 volume chronological Complete Collected Laws of the Russian Empire (Полное собрание законов Российской империи; *Polnoe sobranie zakonov Rossiiskoi imperii*) was published in 1830, followed in 1832 by the more systematised 15 volume Code of Laws (Свод законов; *Svod zakonov*).[2] The *Svod* came into force on 1 January 1835, with new editions in

[1] For example, WE Butler, *Russian Law*, 3rd edn (Oxford, Oxford University Press, 2009); W Burnham and PB Maggs, *Law and Legal System of the Russian Federation*, 5th edn (Huntington, NY, Juris Publishing Inc, 2012), or more generally, R Sakwa, *Russian Politics and Society*, 4th edn (London and New York, Routledge, 2008).

[2] See T Borisova, 'Russian National Legal Tradition: *Svod versus Ulozhenie* in Nineteenth-century Russia' (2008) 33 *Review of Central and East European Law* 395.

1881 and 1905.[3] Contract law, as part of civil law, was dealt with in Volume X, which 'owed much to the French civil code in its general style and method, although it was adapted to a social-economic system in which the state played a leading role and in which property rights still depended on class status'.[4]

In the 1880s a commission to draft a new Civil Code was established.[5] There was extensive preparatory work between 1910 and 1913 on a draft Civil Code which 'reflected the highest legal traditions',[6] but it was stillborn. The Complete Collected Laws and smaller Code of Laws (albeit with new editions) remained in force until the reforms after the 1917 October Bolshevik Revolution. Although Tsarist courts were abolished by one of the first post-revolutionary laws,[7] reference to prerevolutionary law was not. Only in November 1918 did the Law on the People's Court[8] specifically forbid 'reference in judgments and decisions to the laws of overthrown governments',[9] although as Butler points out 'prohibiting a "reference" is not the same as prohibiting application of those laws'[10] and, for example, compensation rights accrued to workers before the Revolution were preserved by the courts in their interpretation of the particular legislation.[11]

B 1922: First Soviet Civil Code

In the period immediately following the Bolshevik Revolution, there was no immediate hurry to introduce new Soviet civil law, for two main reasons. On the one hand, the revolutionaries were busy fighting a civil war against monarchist Russian forces and their foreign supporters; on the other, the revolutionaries' ideology, Marxist theory, postulated that when society had fully evolved, there would be neither a formal state apparatus nor law.[12]

By the early 1920s the civil war had been won, but at the cost of economic and agricultural crisis and pending famine. Pragmatism trumped ideology in

[3] JN Hazard, 'The Future of Codification in the USSR' (1954–55) 29(2) *Tulane Law Review* 239 at 240.

[4] HJ Berman, *Justice in the USSR* (Cambridge, MA, Harvard University Press, 1963) 209.

[5] Hazard, above n 3, at 240.

[6] Berman, above n 4, at 216.

[7] Decree No 1 on Courts of 22 November (December 5) 1917, revised by Decree No 2 on Courts of 15 February 1918.

[8] *Polozhenie o narodnom sude*, SU RSFSR 1918 No 85 item 889, § 22 (note) (cited in J Quigley, 'The Romanist Character of Soviet Law' in FJM Feldbrugge (ed), *The Emancipation of Soviet Law* (Dordrecht, Boston and London, Martinus Nijhoff Publishers, 1992) 35.

[9] Cited in Butler, above n 1, at 646.

[10] Ibid 646.

[11] See Z Zile, *Ideas and Forces in Soviet Legal History* (New York and Oxford, Oxford University Press, 1992) extract 134 at 177.

[12] Eg 'Society, which will reorganise production on the basis of a free and equal society of producers, will put the whole machinery of state where it will then belong: into the museum of antiquities, by the side of the spinning-wheel and the bronze axe'. F Engels, *The Origins of Family, Private Property and the State* (Moscow, Progress Publishers, 1968) 170.

Lenin's decision to allow market forces to be resurrected to stimulate the economy. On 14 March 1921, he persuaded the Fourteenth session of the Tenth Congress of the Russian Communist Party (Bolsheviks) to allow market freedom so that 'exchange shall be permitted within the limits of the local market'.[13] On 21 March 1921, the Congress adopted the New Economic Policy, as it was termed.[14]

As a direct result of this *volte face* encouraging entrepreneurial activity, the decision was taken to enact Codes in the main areas of law, including civil law. One of the main draftsmen of the new Civil Code was Aleksandr Grigor'evich Goikhbarg (1883–1962), who had previously been heavily involved in drafting the Imperial Russian Civil Code which failed to be adopted in 1913. Goikhbarg was given only four months to prepare a new Soviet Code. It is therefore not unsurprising that aspects of the prerevolutionary draft law were evident in the new Code, as well as elements of continental European Codes, particularly the German and Swiss.[15]

On 31 October 1922, the Civil Code of the Russian Socialist Federated Soviet Republic (RSFSR)[16] was adopted by the Central Executive Committee, to come into force on 21 January 1923.

The Civil Code was not expected to be durable. 'Consequently the code resembles a barracks more than a solid building.'[17] The assumption was 'that law was a temporary expedient, borrowed for specific purposes from the defunct bourgeois order of society, and destined to die away as soon as socialism became a reality'.[18] A revision, promised by 1 January 1925, did not appear. The Code was not significantly amended until the Fundamental Principles of Civil Law of 1961, and not repealed until the latter was expanded into the 1964 Civil Code of the RSFSR.[19]

Although bourgeois in form, the 1922 Civil Code (CC) did include some significant revolutionary elements. The exclusion of prerevolutionary law was reasserted (CC article 6).[20] Under CC article 4, judges were encouraged to be

[13] Zile, above n 11, extract 115, 144 at 145, quoting discussion of section 8 of the Resolution 'On the Economic Policy'. Other sections in Extract 117, 'Resolution of May 27, 1921 "On the Economic Policy"' 154.

[14] BN Mamlyuk, *Russia and Legal Harmonization: An Historical Inquiry into IP Reform as Global Convergence and Resistance*, Cornell Law Faculty Working Paper 71 (2010) 10–11, available at www.scholarship.law.cornell.edu/clsops_papers/71, in note 49 points to an audio file of Lenin's speech 'On Foodstuff Tax and/or Free Exchange of Excess Wheat Production', available at www.upload.wikimedia.org/wikipedia/commons/e/eb/Lenin_-_About_Natural_Tax.ogg.

[15] H Freund, 'Civil Law of the Soviet Union' (1928) 22 *Illinois Law Review* 699 at 716.

[16] RSFSR stood for Russian Socialist Federated Soviet Republic until 1936, when it changed to the Russian Soviet Federated Socialist Republic to emphasise Stalin's stated view that socialism had been achieved; see J Henderson, *The Constitution of the Russian Federation: A Contextual Analysis* (Oxford, Hart Publishing, 2011) 38.

[17] Ibid 712.

[18] EH Carr, *A History of Soviet Russia* (London, Macmillan, 1958) vol 5, 67, cited in M Head, 'The Passionate Legal Debates of the Early Years of the Russian Revolution' (2001) 14(3) *Canadian Journal of Law and Jurisprudence* 11.

[19] B Rudden, 'Soviet Tort Law' (1967) 42 *New York University Law Review* 583 at 586.

[20] Zile, above n 11, at 176.

'guided by the general principles of Soviet legislation and the general policy of the workman's and peasant's government'.[21] Custom was not recognised as a source of law.

Notoriously, CC article 1 specified that 'Civil-law rights shall be protected by law except in those instances when they are exercised in contradiction with their socioeconomic purpose'.[22] 'By this overriding principle (subsequently copied, as was the doctrine of analogy, by the Nazis) an attempt was made to counteract the absolutist and conceptual character of the private rights granted in other sections of the code.'[23] The end of the New Economic Policy era in the late 1920s brought an end to the application of article 1; its use was not recorded after 1930.[24]

CC article 30 declared contracts made contrary to law, made in evasion of law, or directed to the detriment of the state to be invalid. The sting in the tail is that under CC article 147, in the event of invalidity under CC article 30, neither party could reclaim restitution. Any benefits were regarded as unfounded enrichment and forfeited to the state.[25] A contract concluded in violation of the state planning system (discussed below) could be caught by this provision, although court practice imported a requirement of bad faith.[26] A similar 'bonus' for the state was given by legislation of 27 July 1923 on State Contracts for Services and Deliveries, which imposed asymmetric rights. The law only permitted unilateral forfeit clauses; a private contractor could never extract a forfeit from a state agency.[27]

Article 17 of the 1922 Civil Code restricted foreign commercial transactions preserving the state monopoly on foreign trade transactions established since 1918. This monopoly remained in place until 1986 when reforms introduced direct trade and foreign investment through joint ventures. Until then, foreign trade was deliberately used as one aspect of state foreign policy.[28]

C Era of State Planning

In 1927 the New Economic Policy was brought to an end.[29] The introduction of a centralised state planned economy from 1928 devalued the role of the Civil Code in general, and contract law in particular. 'Many parts of the Civil Code,

[21] Freund, above n 15, at 714.
[22] Zile, above n 11, at 173. See also JN Hazard, *Communists and their Law* (Chicago, IL, University of Chicago Press, 1969) 72.
[23] Berman, above n 4, at 36.
[24] Hazard, above n 22, at 78.
[25] Berman, above n 4, at 141.
[26] Ibid 142.
[27] Zile, above n 11, at 190; commentary at 193.
[28] See J Quigley, *The Soviet Foreign Trade Monopoly* (Columbus, OH, Ohio State University Press, 1974).
[29] O Ioffe, 'Law and Economy in the USSR' (1982) 95 *Harvard Law Review* 1591 at 1619.

especially the part on contracts, became obsolete and the whole of it was treated with considerable disdain.'[30]

Then Stalin reintroduced a role for law, even if mainly instrumental. The promulgation of the 1936 Union of Soviet Socialist Republics (USSR) Constitution marked this shift in emphasis to 'stability of laws'.[31] Even with this resurrection of law, it was rule by law not rule of law. Although contracts were used between different state enterprises, organisations and institutions, their role within the state planned economy was very different to contract as conceived in a market economy.[32] In short, there was no contractual freedom.

In its developed form, the centralised state planned economy was organised by the State Planning Commission, Gosplan (Госплан)[33] which (on the basis of policy enunciated at the five-yearly Communist Party Congress) worked out successive Five-Year Economic Plans for the whole of the USSR. Each Five-Year Plan set the activities of each individual unit in the economy, including the agricultural sector after forced collectivisation from late 1929.[34] As a result, 'By the mid 1930s, planning had become so detailed that there was nothing about which to contract'.[35]

It was noted above that special rules had been enacted in 1923 for state contracts for service and delivery. Under the planned economy, the importance of performance in the state sector was given increased emphasis. In 1931 a Decree on Liability for Nonperformance of Contracts within the Socialist Sector imposed criminal liability for nonperformance or improper performance of services and deliveries to the state sector. It also made it 'obligatory on economic organisations to put their commitment to services and deliveries in the form of written contracts' (article 1).[36] Contract law was thus used, but only as yet another means of control.

D Post-Stalin Fundamental Principles and the 1964 Russian (RSFSR) Civil Code

Stalin's death in March 1953 allowed reassessment of the Soviet legal system. Article 14 of the 1936 USSR Constitution had assigned jurisdiction to enact codes of law to the USSR, but no USSR Civil Code had been adopted.

However, a change in policy ushered in at the Twentieth Congress of the Communist Party set the stage for decentralisation. By a Law of 11 February

[30] Berman, above n 4, at 45.

[31] Phrase used by Stalin in his Report on the Draft Constitution in 1936. Berman, above n 4, at 53.

[32] See some details of 'planned' and 'unplanned' economic contracts in Ioffe, above n 29, at 1613.

[33] Acronym of the State Committee for Planning (Государственный комитет по планированию; *Gosudarstvennyi Komitet po Planirovaniiu*) first established 22 February 1921.

[34] For an overview of Soviet economy, see Ioffe, above n 29.

[35] Ioffe, above n 29, at 1620.

[36] Decree of the Central Executive Committee and the Council of People's Commissars of the USSR, 18 February 1931, in Zile, above n 11, at 239.

1957, the Constitution was amended to give the 15 Union Republics which made up the USSR at that time jurisdiction to enact codes on civil and criminal law, civil and criminal procedure, and the court structure. The USSR retained power to lay down Fundamental Principles (Основы законодательства; *Osnovy zakonodatel'stva*) for each of these branches, which would be the basis for the Union Republics' codes.

The Fundamental Principles of Civil Law of USSR and Union Republics ('1961 Fundamental Principles') were adopted on 8 December 1961 and entered into force on 1 May 1962. The 1961 Fundamental Principles are a short document of only 129 articles. Two-thirds of its provisions were not previously in the 1922 Civil Code.[37]

In Russia, the provisions of the 1961 Fundamental Principles became the basis of the 1964 RSFSR Civil Code, which was adopted on 11 June 1964 and entered into force on 1 October 1964. The Code consisted of 568 articles which further added detail to the provisions of the 1961 Fundamental Principles. Civil Codes in the other Union Republics were adopted between 1963–1965 and to a large extent resembled the 1964 RSFSR Civil Code. All of them would include the 1961 Fundamental Principles' provisions. Thus a complicated two-layer system of codification was established. Makovskii notes that this is reminiscent of a tandem bicycle in the fact that only one of the riders is steering.[38]

The 1961 USSR Fundamental Principles continued the system of economic relations of 'command and control' established in the era of state planning and enshrined in the 1936 USSR Constitution when the 1922 RSFSR Civil Code (and similar codes of the other Union Republics) were still applied.

The Preamble to the 1961 USSR Fundamental Principles holds that the 'economy of the period of extensive construction of communism is based on socialist property of the means of production in the form of state (nationwide) and collective farm-cooperative ownership [колхозно-кооперативная собственность; *kolkhozno-kooperativnaia sobstvennost'*]'. This continued the exclusive state ownership of land and other natural resources, established in 1918.[39] Under the system which had been introduced, land did not have any monetary value and could only be transferred for use to organisations and individuals on the basis of administrative acts (административно-правовой акт; *administrativno-pravovoi akt*). All natural resources were outside the scope of civil law and instead were the subject matter of specific branches of administrative law (1961 USSR Fundamental Principles article 2).

Legal entities (that is, state-owned enterprises, institutions and organisations), their buildings, equipment and other property still formally had monetary value and were within the scope of civil law. However, in practice

[37] AL Makovskii, *О кодификации гражданского права* [O kodifikatsii grazhdanskogo prava; *On Codification of Civil Law*] *(1922–2006)* (Moscow, Statut, 2010) 39.

[38] Ibid at 30.

[39] See J Henderson, 'The Politics of the Emergence of Private Landholding in Russia' (2012) 7(2) *Journal of Comparative Law* 157 at 161.

there were no commercial dealings with such property. Transfer of property between one socialist organisation and another was carried out by redistribution without compensation on the basis of decrees of the executive governmental authorities.[40]

The 1961 Fundamental Principles article 2(2) for the first time in Soviet legislation strictly divided all economic relations regulated by civil law into three sectors: (1) relations between organisations (almost all of which belonged to the state); (2) relations between individuals and organisations; and (3) relations between individuals. Makovskii points out that 'this led to a three sector division of all economic relations in Soviet society with inevitable principal differences in the nature of such relations and their regulation'.[41] It has some echoes in the current Civil Code where there is a different approach to regulating business contractual relationships and consumer relationships, as shown below at p 42 and in other places throughout this book.

Under the system of state economic planning, all relations between socialist organisations, the majority of which were state-owned, were predetermined by the state. 'Acts of planning' (акты планирования; *akty planirovaniia*) became the main basis for rights and obligations of socialist organisations.[42] Under the 1961 Fundamental Principles article 34, the content of a contract concluded on the basis of an 'act of planning' must comply with that act. Administrative acts further regulated contractual relations in detail. This resulted in a reduction in both the 1961 USSR Fundamental Principles and 1964 RSFSR Civil Code of the section regulating contractual relations between organisations. The number of contracts relevant to organisations was reduced to main five types (contracts of delivery, agricultural procurement contracts, contracts of independent construction work, contracts of transfer of cargo and credits contracts).[43]

In other parts of the Code, the opposite occurred. Whereas the part relating to social organisations was simplified, regulation of contractual relations between individual citizens became very detailed, even excessive. The idea behind this was to leave as little freedom of contract as possible. Existing contracts were divided into subtypes tailored towards citizens' day-to-day needs.[44] For example, within the contract of purchase-sale the following subtypes were created: contract of retail purchase-sale on credit (договор розничной продажи в кредит; *dogovor roznichnoi prodazhi v kredit*; USSR Fundamental Principles article 43; 1964 CC article 252) and contract of purchase-sale of a dwelling house with maintenance of the seller for life (договор купли-продажи жилого дома с условием пожизненного содержания продавца; *dogovor kupli-prodazhi zhilogo doma s usloviem pozhiznennogo soderzhaniia prodavtsa*; 1964 CC articles 253, 254). New contracts aimed at regulating day-to-day relation-

[40] Makovskii, above n 37, at 33.
[41] Ibid 35.
[42] Ibid.
[43] Ibid 36.
[44] Ibid 37.

ships between individuals appeared: the contract of uncompensated use (договор ссуды (безвозмездного пользования); *dogovor ssudy (bezvozmezd-nogo pol'zovaniia*); 1964 CC chapter 29) and contract of keeping (1964 CC chapter 37).[45] These contracts have been retained in the current Civil Code; but now individuals can also make business contracts, unlike in the early 1960s.

E *Perestroika* (Перестройка)

The *perestroika* (restructuring) era (circa 1985 to 1991) saw a number of hugely important developments in relation to the Russian legal system. The reform process was motivated by a desire to get the stagnating Soviet planned economy to function. Mikhail Gorbachev had made a success of agricultural reform in his home region of Stavropol, and by 1985 was prepared to take up the role of General Secretary to the Communist Party of the Soviet Union (CPSU) ('the Party') with a reform agenda. He presided over the Twenty-seventh Party Congress in February–March 1986, at which a new Party Programme was adopted, and the principle of economic reform (at this stage, still within a planned system) was agreed. Shortly after, groundbreaking legislation began the economic transformations: the USSR Laws on Individual Enterprise of 19 November 1986; on the State Enterprise of 30 June 1987; on Cooperative Societies in the USSR of 26 May 1988; of Ownership in the USSR of 6 March 1990; on Enterprises in the USSR of 4 June 1990; and the RSFSR Laws on Property in the RSFSR of 14 July 1990; on Enterprises and Entrepreneurial Activity of 25 December 1990, and others.

The rapidity of the change during this period meant that civil law in Russia in the early 1990s was characterised by a high degree of uncertainty. There was a lack of unification and coordination between legal rules while a new platform was being created for novel types of civil relations, in the developing conditions of a market economy based on economic principles completely new to Russia.

One of the main foundations of a market economy is private property, so the process of denationalisation of state property, including state-owned enterprises, began. It had already started spontaneously at the end of the 1980s without any prior legal foundation. The first laws regulating privatisation appeared in July 1991: the USSR Law on the Basic Foundations of Denationalisation and Privatisation of Enterprises of 1 July 1991; and the RSFSR Law on Privatisation of State and Municipal Enterprises of 3 July 1991.

Those driving for the changes were mainly economists and as a result many of the laws adopted during the *perestroika* period were of poor quality. The legal rules within them were mutually inconsistent and fragmentary. To a large extent contract law was still regulated by the 1961 USSR Fundamental Principles and 1964 RSFSR Civil Code. However, serious legal scholars were working to

[45] Ibid 37–8.

update the civil law to make it appropriate to the new conditions of a developing market economy.

On 31 May 1991, just a few months before the USSR ceased to exist (26 December 1991)[46] new Fundamental Principles of Civil Law of the USSR and Union Republics[47] ('1991 USSR Fundamental Principles') (FP) were adopted in the USSR. The 1991 USSR Fundamental Principles were to enter into force from 1 January 1992. Unfortunately, by that date the USSR no longer existed, so the new law could not come into effect. However, it was realised in newly-independent Russia that the 1991 USSR Fundamental Principles were more appropriate to the current conditions than the 1964 RSFSR Civil Code, so by a Decree adopted on 14 July 1992, the Russian Supreme Soviet brought them into use in Russia:

> Until the passing of a new Civil Code of the Russian Federation, the Fundamental of Civil Legislation of the USSR and Republics promulgated on 31 May 1991 shall be applied on the territory of the Russian Federation, with the exception of those provisions establishing the jurisdiction of the USSR in the area of civil legislation, and in instances where they do not conflict with the Constitution of the Russian Federation and legislative acts of the Russian Federation, passed after 12 June 1990 [the date of Russia's Declaration of State Sovereignty].[48]

The decree went on to say that the 1964 RSFSR Civil Code would be applied residually, if there was a gap in the law despite any new legislation passed since 12 June 1990 and the provisions of the 1991 USSR Fundamental Principles.

As Makovskii puts it, the preparation of 1991 USSR Fundamental Principles 'was largely reminiscent of the restoration of old masterpieces'.[49] The draftsmen were challenged by the task of reconstructing legal instruments and institutions which had not been used for over 60 years. During this long period generations of lawyers had been raised on the basis of Soviet civil law which had merely served as a façade for numerous acts of planning and other administrative orders. As a minimum it would be necessary for the draughtsmen to remove from the existing civil law all extraneous elements introduced by the 'command and control' system which had governed the Soviet planned economy.

1991 USSR Fundamental Principles broadened the range of legal entities which could participate in the new market economy. FP article 18(2) set out a broad but exhaustive list of types of commercial legal entities, the main ones being economic partnerships and societies (хозяйственные товарищества и общества; *khoziaistvennye tovarishchestva i obshchestva*) – voluntary associations of individuals and legal entities. Unlike socialist organisations under the

[46] On 26 December 1991 the Supreme Soviet of the USSR (Верховный Совет СССР, *Verkhovnyi Soviet SSSR*) (supreme legislative body in the USSR from 1938), on the last day of its existence declared that in connection with the creation of the CIS the Supreme Soviet of the USSR ceased its activities. This declaration denotes the end of the USSR.

[47] USSR Law No 2211-1.

[48] On this Declaration and its significance, see J Henderson, *The Constitution of the Russian Federation: a Contextual Analysis* (Oxford, Hart Publishing, 2011) 61.

[49] Makovskii, above n 37, at 241.

1961 USSR Fundamental Principles and 1964 RSFSR Civil Code, all legal entities mentioned in FP article 18(2) would be liable for their own debts to the extent of their own property. State enterprises did not completely become old history; they were still mentioned in FP article 22. However, the extent of their liability for debts to counterparties rose; they became liable to pay debts from the property transferred to their use by the state.[50] State-owned enterprises continue to exist even now in the form of state (and municipal) enterprises; see eg Chapter 1 at p 19.

The 1991 Fundamental Principles declared two very important principles of the market economy which for obvious reasons had been absent in the preceding legislation from the 1960s: equality of participants in the commercial market (FP article 1(1)) and free disposition of property rights (имущественные права; *imushchestvennye prava*) (FP article 5(1)). The 1991 Fundamental Principles did not explicitly mention the principle of freedom of contract. However, at least they did ensure more freedom of contract to participants in the commercial market by reducing the amount of administrative regulation of contractual relations. Also, all mention of acts of planning, planning tasks and administrative acts was eliminated.

Makovskii observes that the limitation of state interference into contractual relations led to a much wider use than before in the 1991 Fundamental Principles of evaluative expressions such as 'usually presented requirements' (обычно предъявляемые требования; *obychno pred"iavliaemye trebovaniia*, article 57(2)); 'normally necessary time' (нормально необходимое время; *normal'no neobkhodimoe vremia*, article 58(5), (7)); 'practice of relations between the parties' (практика взаимоотношений сторон; *praktika vzaimootnoshenii storon*, article 59(2)); 'customs of business turnover' (обычаи делового оборота; *obychai delovogo oborota*, articles 59, 63, 64, 74, 75).[51] All of these phrases are still used in the current Russian Civil Code, although recent reforms to have simplified the last to 'customs'.[52]

The transformation from the command and control system required the development of contracts suitable for market relations. Hence, the 1991 Fundamental Principles included at least 10 types of contracts which were not known to the 1961 Fundamental Principles. These include a contract of bank account (договор банковского счета; *dogovor bankovskogo scheta*, article 110); contract of bank deposit (договор банковского вклада; *dogovor bankovskogo vklada*, article 111); contract of loan (договор займа; *dogovor zaima*, article 113); contract of commission agency (договор комиссии; *dogovor komissii*, chapter 17) and others.[53] These too have been incorporated into the Russian Civil Code.

[50] USSR Law on the State Enterprise of 30 June 1987.
[51] Makovskii, above n 37, at 251.
[52] Federal Law of 30 December 2012 No 302-FZ.
[53] Makovskii, above n 37, at 254.

F Russia's Current Civil Code

Following the adoption of the 1991 USSR Fundamental Principles as an interim measure, work proceeded in earnest to draft a new Russian Civil Code appropriate to contemporary conditions. Eventually the Code was produced in four parts, taking over a decade.[54] Part One was adopted as a federal law by the State Duma (first chamber of the legislature) on 21 October 1994 and came into force on 1 January 1995. It deals with General Provisions, Ownership and the General Part of the Law of Obligations. Part Two was passed by the Duma on 22 December 1995 and came into effect on 1 March 1996. It deals with specific types of Obligations. Part Three was adopted on 26 November 2001 and came into force on 1 March 2002. It deals with Law of Succession and Private International Law. Part Four, on Intellectual Property, was passed on 24 November 2006 and came into force on 1 January 2008. That is the date when the RSFSR 1964 Civil Code and the 1991 Fundamental Principles finally lost force on the territory of Russia. Until then intellectual property issues had been regulated, among other rules, by these two pieces of legislation.

Osakwe characterises the first two Parts of the Civil Code (which contain the rules on contract law) as 'in part Soviet and in part Western . . . The Code is modern, but it does not represent a revolutionary break with the past'.[55]

The Civil Code certainly seeks to establish the legal foundations of a market economy as known in the West: freedom of economic activity, free movement of goods, services and financial assets, sanctity of private property, freedom of contract, equality of all participants of economic turnover (CC article 1). Also, in comparison to its predecessors, the Civil Code includes a greater variety of contracts.

At the same time, the Civil Code still contains a number of provisions which may not be helpful in a market economy, for example, different standards for business and consumer relations. The regulation of contractual relationships is still rather formal and detailed, and governmental authorities in the course of their supervisory functions (such as tax or customs authorities) have and actively use the possibility of interfering in contractual relations by claiming in court that a contract is void. As noted, the state enterprise as a form of legal entity and some other institutions inherited from the Soviet civil legislation still persist.

[54] This was still impressively quick compared with the Netherlands, where their new Civil Code was decades in the making; see W Snijders, 'Lessons from St Petersburg: Commerce and Civil Law' (2009) 34 *Review of Central and East European Law* 107.

[55] C Osakwe, *Russian Civil Code Annotated* (Moscow, Moscow State University, 2000) 27.

G Reform of Civil Law in the Twenty-first Century

In 2008, in one of his first moves after being elected, the then President, Dmitrii Medvedev, set up a presidential task force of leading civil law experts to review the Civil Code.

As announced by Medvedev, the main ideas behind the reform are: developing the rules of the Civil Code to a level to meet the new stage of development of market relations; reflection of the experience of the application and interpretation of the Civil Code by courts; harmonisation of the Civil Code with European law and using positive recent European experience of modernisation of civil legislation; and ensuring the stability of civil legislation.[56]

The experts on the presidential task force produced a 'Conception on Perfecting the Russian Civil Code' which was adopted and endorsed by the President.[57] On 8 February 2012 there was a report that the Russian Justice Minister Alexander Konovalov had said that a draft law to amend the Civil Code was ready for submission to the State Duma.[58] On 27 April 2012 the draft law amending the Civil Code passed the first of its three readings in the State Duma.[59] Then without explanation it was divided into a number of separate laws. As of 1 September 2013 three of these have been adopted. These are:

(1) Federal Law of 30 December 2012 on Amending Chapters 1, 2, 3 and 4 of Part One of the Civil Code (in force 1 March 2013, except for individual provisions).[60] The Law explicitly introduces the principle of good faith into Russian civil law (discussed below at p 46), and amends provisions on the legal status of individuals and organisations and formation of contracts.
(2) Federal Law of 7 May 2013 on Amending Subsections 4 and 5 of Section I of Part One and Article 1153 of the Civil Code (in force 1 September 2013, except for individual provisions).[61] The Law mainly amends provisions concerning invalidity and formation of contracts.
(3) Federal Law of 2 July 2013 on Amending Subsection 3 of Section I of Part One of the Civil Code (in force 1 October 2013).[62] The Law amends provisions of property law.

Although there was a public discussion at the stage of preparation of the Conception and adoption of the initial draft law by the State Duma, since it was subdivided there has been no public discussion of the new draft laws. It is not

[56] Decree (Указ; *Ukaz*) of the President of the Russian Federation of 18 July 2008 No 1108 on the Perfection of Civil Legislation, para 1.
[57] Available at www.privlaw.ru/index.php?section_id=24.
[58] Interfax Business Law Review for 31 January–7 February 2012, translated by and available on Westlaw: World News Connection (Newswire).
[59] Draft Federal Law on Amendments to Parts One, Two, Three and Four of the Civil Code No 47538-6.
[60] No 302-FZ.
[61] No 100-FZ.
[62] No 142-FZ.

even clear how many small separate draft laws will yet be passed and what they will contain. They might not necessarily have exactly the same provisions as in the initial draft law which gained its first reading in the Duma in April 2012.

As far as contract law is concerned, analysis of the amendments so far shows that to a certain extent they change the Civil Code positively in line with the court practice that has developed in response to some practical problems. However, there is still a risk that too many amendments will cause uncertainty in the Civil Code's application and disrupt market relations which have become accustomed to the Civil Code's imperfect but (until recently) fairly stable provisions. Throughout this book we draw attention as appropriate to the most important Civil Code amendments (and draft amendments) in the light of the current application of the Civil Code rules.

III THE RUSSIAN STATE AND ITS AGENCIES

We have given an overview of contract law and its historical development. We now examine the country in which it operates.

A Russia's Federal Structure

Russia is a federal state. There are currently 83 subjects of the Federation: 21 republics (республики; *respubliki*, singular республика; *respublika*); nine territories (края; *kraia*, singular край; *krai*); 46 regions (области; *oblasti*, singular область; *oblast'*, sometimes translated as 'province'); two cities of federal status (Moscow and St Petersburg); one autonomous region (автономная область; *avtonomnaia oblast'*), and four autonomous areas (автономные округа; *avtonomnye okruga*, singular автономный округ; *avtonomnyi okrug*, sometimes translated as 'district').[63] The division of powers between the central federal authorities and the subjects of the Federation is set out in articles 71–73 of the current Constitution, which dates from December 1993. Amongst other things, Constitution article 71 allocates court organisation, civil law and civil procedure, including procedure in the commercial (Арбитраж; *Arbitrazh*) courts, to the jurisdiction of the federal authorities, while Constitution article 72 specifies that the federal authorities share jurisdiction with the subjects of the Federation over judicial personnel, the *advokatura* (адвокатура) and the *notariat* (нотариат) (see below for explanation of these sectors of the legal profession), as well as legislation on housing, land, water, forests and subsoil, and environmental protection. Constitution article 73 entrusts any residual power to the subjects of the Federation. It follows that any legislation regulating contractual relations is adopted at the federal level, so is uniform throughout Russia.

[63] Full list in Henderson, above n 48, at 3.

B Relevant State Agencies

According to Constitution article 10, separation of powers is one of the core principles on which the Russian state system is based: 'Agencies of legislative, executive, and judicial power shall be autonomous'.[64]

The President is the Head of State. One of the main functions of the President is to 'ensure the coordinated functioning and interaction of agencies of State power'.[65] The President also leads the executive branch, although the Constitution actually says that 'executive power in Russia is exercised by the Government'[66] which consists of the Chairman of the Government (the Prime Minister), Deputy Chairman and federal ministries.[67]

The structure of executive agencies below government level is set by the President. Some executive agencies are controlled directly by him (the so-called Presidential Bloc),[68] and the rest are controlled by the Government. Executive bodies can be divided into three categories:

(1) Federal Ministries (Федеральные Министерства; *Federal'nye Ministerstva*, singular федеральное министерство; *Federalnoe Ministerstvo*);
(2) Federal Services (Федеральные службы; *Federal'nye Sluzhby*, singular Федеральная служба *Federal'naia Sluzhba*); and
(3) Federal Agencies (федеральные агентства; *Federa'lnye Agentstva*, singular Федеральное агентство; *Federalnoe Agentstvo*).

Federal Ministries are agencies responsible for development of policy in a particular sphere. They also have regulatory powers and can issue normative legal acts which regulate relations within their particular area of responsibility. The legal effects of this subordinate legislation is discussed below at p 25. The Ministries also control the Federal Services and Federal Agencies that are subordinate to them.[69] For example, the Ministry of Finance defines the general direction of policy and is responsible for regulation of budgetary matters, tax, insurance, currency, banking and similar.[70] The Ministry of Finance controls the Federal Service for Financial Budget and Supervision (Федеральная служба Финансово-Бюджетного Надзора; *Federal'naia Sluzhba Finansovo-Biudzhetnogo*

[64] WE Butler, *Russian Public Law*, 3rd edn (London, Wildy, Simonds & Hill Publishers, 2013) 6.

[65] Constitution art 80(2); Butler, above n 64, at 18.

[66] Constitution art 110(2).

[67] Constitution art 110(1). See Henderson, above n 48, ch 4 for further discussion of the relationship between President and Prime Minister in Russia.

[68] See Henderson, above n 48, 124–7.

[69] Указ Президента РФ of 21 May 2012 No 636 (redaction of 29 June 2013) О структуре федеральных органов исполнительной власти [*Ukaz Prezidenta RF O structure federal'nykh organov ispolnitel'noi vlasti*; Decree of the President of the Russian Federation of 21 May 2012 No 636 on the System and Structure of Federal Executive Bodies].

[70] Part 1 of Постановление Правительства РФ of 30 June 2004 No 329 (redaction of 30 April 2013) О Министерстве финансов Российской Федерации [Section 1 of the Decree of the Government of the Russian Federation on the Ministry of Finance of the Russian Federation].

Nadzora), the Federal Tax Service (Федеральная Налоговая Служба; *Federal'naia Nalogovaia Sluzhba*) and the Federal Treasury (Федеральное Казначейство; *Federal'noe Kaznacheistvo*). The Ministry issues legal regulations which the Services and Agencies must implement.

Federal Services are supervision and control agencies in the spheres to which they are assigned.[71] Federal Agencies are subordinate agencies, responsible for the provision of public services, management of public property and some law enforcement functions (for example, border control).[72]

It important to be aware of these government ministries and agencies and their activities because they can be involved in economic relations between legal entities and private individuals; in some situations they can have a major influence on contracts. There are two ways they can do this: first, as supervisory agencies with the power to prosecute companies and individuals for non-compliance with current legal requirements; and secondly, as participants themselves in contractual relations, either directly or through specifically-created state or municipality owned enterprises (унитарные предприятия; *unitarnye predpriiatiia*, see below at p 19 for more details).

Supervisory agencies have the right to impose fines and other penalties if a particular legal entity or individual does not comply with the relevant regulations. Very often the supervisory agency can find non-compliance with legal requirements in contracts used by companies in their everyday business activities. For example, Роспотребнадзор (*Rospotrebnadzor*)[73] supervises compliance with consumer protection regulations; for example, it has used its powers to fine banks for using terms and conditions in consumer credit contracts which are detrimental to consumers' rights.[74]

As another example, the Federal Antimonopoly Service (Федеральная антимонопольная служба; *federal'naia antimonopol'naia sluzhba*) is responsible for protection of competition in various markets. It uses its power to invalidate contractual terms which, in its opinion, are anti-competitive and it can fine companies for using such terms in breach of competition law.

Apart from imposing fines on legal entities and individuals, government agencies also apply to court for invalidation of contracts between individuals. The version of the Civil Code in force before September 2013 allowed 'any person with an interest based on law'[75] to sue for invalidation of a contract and government agencies used that provision widely. The Federal Tax Service

[71] Part 4 of Указ Президента РФ of 9 March 2004 No 314 (redaction of 22 June 2010) О системе и структуре федеральных органов исполнительной власти [Section 4 of the Decree of the President of the Russian Federation of 9 March 2004 No 314 on the System and Structure of Federal Executive Bodies].

[72] Ibid.

[73] Федеральная служба по надзору в сфере защиты прав потребителей и благополучия человека [Federal'naia sluzhba po nadzoru v sfere zashchity prav potrebitelei i blagopoluchiia cheloveka; Federal Service for the Supervision of Consumer Rights and Well-Being].

[74] See, eg the case in Chapter 6 at p 129.

[75] See Chapter 1 at p 41.

has been particularly active. Frequently the tax authorities have viewed certain contracts as being concluded purely to minimise the taxpayer's tax burden. They regard such contracts as invalid and apply for their nullification; see, for example, Chapter 6 at p 129. Unfortunately, due to an historically deep-rooted prejudice against entrepreneurs, in these cases the Russian courts are inclined to support the government agency rather than the legal entity or individual defendant.

As a result of this activity, legal entities and individual entrepreneurs need to pay very close attention to the governmental agencies' practices, because if they fail to do so there is a high risk that they will be fined or their contracts will be invalidated.

The Russian Federation itself, the subjects of the Federation and local government (municipalities) can themselves participate in civil relations. They will make contracts and similar through government agencies authorised to act on their behalf (CC article 125(1)). They are said to be equal with other participants (CC article 124(1)). However, the government agencies acting on behalf of the state have huge administrative resources and have various ways of influencing the counterparty. Courts often seem to be prejudiced in favour of the state in a legal dispute.[76] Therefore, in practice the government agencies can hardly be considered equal participants with private legal entities and individuals.

The Russian Federation, subjects of the Federation and municipalities can also create legal entities of any type, including joint-stock societies (companies with freely traded shares). One particular type of commercial legal entity – the so-called unitary enterprise[77] (унитарное предприятие; *unitarnoe predpriiatie*) – can be only created by the state, either at federal, subject or municipality level, and would be created to fulfil a particular function. The state body which creates a unitary enterprise will provide it with assets necessary to fulfil its function; however, the unitary enterprise does not own those assets. The state remains owner. The assets are held by the unitary enterprise under a limited property right of either economic management (хозяйственное ведение; *khoziaistvennoe vedenie*)[78] or operational administration (оперативное управление; *operativnoe upravlenie*).[79] The first of these gives quite broad rights; the second is more limited. However, a unitary enterprise cannot dispose of its assets without the consent of its owner (the state) and, if it does so, the transaction is invalid. Due to inconsistencies in regulation there is never complete certainty about the validity of transactions concluded by unitary enterprises. These enterprises are fundamentally a relic of the Soviet past, when the State owned the means of production and only the State could create enterprises and give them assets which nevertheless

[76] An empirical study in 2000 reported in T Frye, 'The Two Faces of Russian Courts: Evidence from a Survey of Company Managers' (2002) *East European Constitutional Review* 225 suggested that, at least then, this was more a matter of perception than reality.

[77] See CC arts 113–15.

[78] CC art 294.

[79] CC art 296.

remained in state ownership. In contemporary Russia, unitary enterprises often work not to achieve their statutory goals but rather to enrich their managers who frequently have close connections with the state agency which established the unitary enterprise. This can create legal, political and social problems.

IV THE RUSSIAN COURT SYSTEM

A General Overview

The Russian court system has two main branches; the courts of general jurisdiction (суды общей юрисдикции; *sudy obshchei iurisdiktsii*) headed by the Supreme Court, which hear civil, criminal and administrative cases; and the commercial courts (арбитражные суды; *arbitrazhnye sudy*, sometimes translated as *Arbitrazh* courts) headed by the Supreme Commercial Court, which hear civil and administrative cases. Russia also has a Constitutional Court which is separate and does not belong to either the general jurisdiction or commercial courts.[80]

The jurisdictional division between the courts of general jurisdiction and the commercial courts depends on the litigants. If at least one of the parties is an individual (who is not an individual entrepreneur) then the case will be heard by a court of general jurisdiction. If the dispute is between economic agents (including individual entrepreneurs and public bodies), then litigation is in the commercial courts. In Russia, only individuals can be criminally liable, never legal entities, so criminal cases, as noted above, are only heard in the courts of general jurisdiction.[81]

Procedure in courts of general jurisdiction is regulated either by the Code of Civil Procedure (for civil and administrative cases) or the Code of Criminal Procedure. Procedure in commercial courts is different and is regulated by the Code of Commercial Procedure. In general this allows the parties more initiative. It should be noted that Russia is in the interesting position of having a separate set of commercial courts whilst not having a separate Commercial Code. All courts apply the same legislation apart from the Procedure Codes, which are specific to the particular type of court.

There may possibly be a change to the structure just described. On 21 June 2013 it was reported that President Putin had announced a proposal to unite the Supreme Court and the Supreme Commercial Court. This came as a great surprise. Some commentators saw it as part of a political battle between the (elderly) Chairman of the Supreme Court, Viacheslav Lebedev, and the (comparatively young and friend of Medvedev) Chairman of the Supreme

[80] See Henderson, above n 48, ch 6 at 193 ff.

[81] There are no crimes of strict liability in the 1996 Russian Criminal Code, so the individual perpetrator must be capable of forming the requisite *mens rea* (guilty mind), which a legal entity cannot do.

Commercial Court, Anton Ivanov.[82] There has been deep scepticism over the proposal, with few commentators thinking it would improve the quality of justice. However, on 8 October 2013, President Putin submitted to the State Duma draft constitutional amendments which are the necessary precursors to the creation of a new Supreme Court of the Russian Federation, replacing both the existing Supreme Court and Supreme Commercial Court.[83] It is expected that the amendments will have been adopted by early 2014. The new Supreme Court will have 170 judges, appointed by a special Qualifications Board established for the purpose. There will be a six-month transitional period for the reorganisation, which will require quite extensive amendment to federal law. As reported, the existing separate court hierarchies will be maintained, so the description which follows remains essentially accurate, except for the innovation of a unified top court.

B Structure of the Courts of General Jurisdiction

The structure of the system of general jurisdiction courts is defined by the Federal Constitutional Law on Courts of General Jurisdiction.[84] At the bottom of the pyramid are justice of the peace courts (мировые суды; *mirovye sudy*). They hear minor civil and administrative cases and are not federal courts, but are local to the Federation subject. Civil cases heard by justice of the peace courts include disputes for up to 50,000 roubles (circa £970).[85] Unlike English justices of the peace, judges in these Russian courts are qualified lawyers.

The next level are district courts (районные суды; *raionnye sudy*) which hear civil, criminal and administrative cases and also cases appealed from justice of the peace courts. District courts work as courts of first instance for all civil cases, apart from those heard by justice of the peace courts and cases where a state secret is involved, which are heard at the next higher level.[86]

Above district courts are supreme courts of the subjects of the Federation. For civil cases they are important as appeal courts from cases heard by district courts.

The Supreme Court of the Russian Federation is at the very top of the pyramid. It acts as the court of cassation for the cases heard by district courts and supreme courts of subjects of the Federation. The cassational instance is a form

[82] Eg, 'Moscow Daily senses victory for Supreme Court Chairman over merger with Higher Court of Arbitration', *World News Connection*, 25 June 2013, citing *Nezavisimaia Gazeta*.

[83] Проект No 352924-6 Закон Российской Федерации о поправке к Конституции Российской Федерации и прокуратуре Российской Федерации [*Proekt* No 352924-6 *Zakon Rossiiskoi Federatsii o poprabke k Konstitutsii Rossiiskoi Federatsii O Verkhovnom Sude Rossiiskoi Federatsii i Prokurature Rossiiskoi Federatsii*; Draft No 352924-6 Law of the Russian Federation on the Supreme Court of the Russian Federation and the Procuracy of the Russian Federation].

[84] Federal Constitutional Law of 7 February 2011 No 1-FKZ on Courts of General Jurisdiction; English translation in Butler, above n 64, at 562.

[85] Code of Civil Procedure art 23(1)(5).

[86] Code of Civil Procedure art 24.

of appeal which (unlike in some other 'Romanist' legal systems, where it is merely a review of legal error) involves a review of the entire case. Its decision enters into force as soon as it is given and cannot itself be appealed.[87]

C Structure of the Commercial Courts

Commercial courts are governed by the Federal Constitutional Law of 28 April 1995.[88] The lowest level of commercial courts comprises commercial courts of subjects of the Federation; each subject of the Federation has one commercial court which hears all commercial cases arising there.

The next level comprises 20 commercial courts of appeal. They are named by ordinal numbers, from First to Twentieth. One court of appeal has jurisdiction over courts in several subjects of the Federation.

Above these are 10 federal commercial courts of districts. These are (in Cyrillic alphabetical order):

- Volgo-Viatskii District (Волго-Вятский Округ; *Volgo-Viatskii Okrug*);
- East-Siberian District (Восточно-Сибирский Округ; *Vostochno-Sibirskii Okrug*);
- Far-Eastern District (Дальневосточный Округ; *Dal'nevostochnyi Okrug*);
- West-Siberian District (Западно-Сибирский Округ; *Zapadno-Sibirskii Okrug*);
- Moscow District (Московский Округ; *Moskovskii Okrug*);
- Volga District (Приволжский Округ; *Privolzhskii Okrug*);
- North-Western District (Северо-Западный Округ; *Severo-Zapadnyi Okrug*);
- Ural District (Уральский Округ; *Ural'skii Okrug*); and
- Central District (Центральный Округ; *Tsentralnyi Okrug*).

These courts are cassational courts for the two lower instances.

The Supreme Commercial Court is the highest instance. Among other powers it has the power of supervisory review (пересмотр в порядке надзора; *peresmotr v poriadke nadzora*). This is an exceptional appeal procedure, granted at the discretion of the Court. It can, however, involve reconsideration of not only the legal but also the factual issues. The Presidium of the Supreme Commercial Court can vacate a lower court's judgment and send the case back for fresh consideration, or itself make a final ruling.[89]

D Federal Constitutional Court

The Constitutional Court exercises abstract review of legislation and is the only body in Russia which has the power to declare void laws (or their individual

[87] Butler, above n 1, at 257. See also Burnham and Maggs, above n 1, at 83.
[88] No 1-FKZ; English translation in Butler, above n 64, at 609.
[89] Burnham and Maggs, above n 1, at 88.

provisions) which do not comply with the Constitution.[90] The Constitutional Court has played a very important role in the development of Russian civil law with a number of landmark resolutions.

Unfortunately, in recent years, especially after a number of judges of the Constitutional Court had to retire due to age, there is some fear that the Constitutional Court has been losing its authority and independence.[91]

E Arbitration Tribunals (Третейские Суды; *Treteiskie Sudy*)

For many years (including during the prerevolutionary and Soviet periods) arbitration has been recognised in Russia as an alternative means of dispute resolution. The 'chaotic state'[92] of Russian legislation on arbitration was put in order by the 2002 Federal Law on Arbitration Tribunals, which allows parties to civil disputes to resolve them by arbitration tribunals if they so wish. However, there are several exceptions to this; for instance, disputes over property rights cannot be resolved through arbitration.

The Federal Law allows both permanent and ad hoc arbitration tribunals. The most popular and the most authoritative arbitration tribunal in Russia is the International Commercial Arbitration Court at the Russian Federation Chamber of Commerce (Международный Коммерческий Арбитражный Суд при Торгово-Промышленной Палате РФ; *Mezhdunarodnii Kommercheskii Arbitrazhnyi Sud pri Torgovo-Promyshlennoi Palate RF*).

However, resolution of disputes through mediation is not that popular in Russia. One reason for this is that the normal courts have the right to annul arbitration awards in a number of situations, for example, when an arbitration award 'contradicts the cornerstone principles of Russian law'.[93] This is often a problem when an arbitration tribunal applies foreign law to reach its decision. Russian courts simply regard all foreign law as contradicting the cornerstone principles of Russian law and consequently cancel the arbitration award. Lack of certainty over the durability of the result is a strong disincentive to seeking arbitration.

V SOURCES OF LAW

A Sources of Law

Both historically and now, legislation is the main source of law in Russia. Currently there is a hierarchy of legislative acts, headed by the 1993 Constitution. Below

[90] See Henderson, above n 48, 200–14 and 217–18.

[91] See J Henderson, 'Tenure and Discipline Developments in Russia' (2011) 17(1) *European Public Law* 1; A Trochev, 'Tinkering with Tenure: the Russian Constitutional Court in a Comparative Perspective' in F Feldbrugge (ed), *Russia, Europe, and the Rule of Law* (Leiden, Martinus Nijhoff Publishers, 2007) 47.

[92] Butler, above n 1, at 228.

[93] Code of Commercial Procedure art 233(2)(4).

that, there are federal constitutional laws (федеральные конституционные законы; *federal'nye konstitutsionnye zakony*), federal laws (федеральные законы; *federal'nye zakony*); and an array of 'sub-law' (подзаконные акты; *podzakonnye akty*) including presidential edicts, governmental decrees, and so on (see below).

(i) The Constitution

Article 15(1) of the Constitution declares that the Constitution 'shall have the highest legal force, direct effect, and be applied throughout the entire territory of the Russian Federation'.[94]

Two articles in chapter 1 of the Constitution impact the realm of contract law. Article 8 guarantees unity of economic space, free movement of goods, services and financial assets, competition and freedom of economic activity, and gives equal recognition to private, state, municipal and other forms of ownership. Article 9 includes the provision that 'land and other natural resources may be in private, State, municipal and other forms of ownership'.[95] Three articles in chapter 2 on Rights emphasise the new conditions of Russia's market economy. Article 34 specifies that 'each shall have the right to free use of his abilities and property for entrepreneurial and other economic activity not prohibited by a law' (34(1)), although 'economic activity directed towards monopolisation and unfair competition shall not be permitted' (34(2)).[96] Article 35 protects private ownership and inheritance by anyone, whether or not a citizen. Article 35(3) specifically asserts that 'No one may be deprived of his property other than by decision of the court. The compulsory alienation of property for State needs may be done only on conditions of advance and fair compensation.'[97]

Article 36 gives the right to citizens and their associations to own land privately, and allows 'the possession, use, and disposition of land and other natural resources . . . by their owners freely unless this brings damage to the environment and does not violate the rights and legal interests of other persons'.[98] However, the practicalities of the implementation of private land ownership, particularly of agricultural land, are problematic.[99]

(ii) Federal Constitutional Laws

The Constitution specifies that certain matters are to be regulated by special laws, federal constitutional laws, which require qualified rather than simple majorities (as in case of federal laws) in each of the two legislative chambers, but are not (unlike federal laws) then subject to the possibility of a presidential

[94] Translation in Butler, above n 64, at 6.
[95] Ibid 6.
[96] Ibid 9.
[97] Ibid.
[98] Ibid.
[99] See J Henderson 'The Politics of the Emergence of Private Landholding in Russia' (2012) 7(2) *Journal of Comparative Law* 157.

veto. Relevant to this study of contract law in Russia is that there are federal constitutional laws to regulate the Judicial System, the Constitutional Court, Supreme Court, Supreme Commercial Court and other federal courts.[100] There will no doubt be revisions to these as a consequence of the unification of the Supreme Court and the Supreme Commercial Court into a new Supreme Court of the Russian Federation in process in the first half of 2014.

(iii) Federal Laws

Any topic within federal jurisdiction, other than those specifically relegated to a federal constitutional law, may be the subject of a federal law. The Russian legal system has Codes for the major branches of law. A Code is not a special type of legislation. It is a federal law which is passed under the normal procedure for adoption of a federal law, specified in the 1993 Constitution articles 105–107.[101]

(iv) Other Normative Acts at the Federal Level

Legislation other than federal law may be adopted at federal level. The President has unlimited jurisdiction to issue edicts and regulations (указы и распоряжения; *ukazy i rasporiazheniia*) 'binding for execution throughout the entire territory of the Russian Federation'[102] (Constitution article 90(2)), provided that they are not contrary to the Constitution and federal laws (Constitution article 90(3)).

The Government as a whole, although not the Prime Minister individually, has power under Constitution article 115 to issue decrees and regulations (постановления и распоряжения; *postanovleiia i rasporiazheniia*), although this jurisdiction is more limited. It must be exercised 'on the basis of and in execution of the Constitution of the Russian Federation, federal laws, and normative edicts of the President'[103] (article 115(1)). The President has the unreserved right to repeal any governmental decrees and regulations which he judges to be in breach of that limitation (article 115(3)). Individual federal ministries may also adopt normative acts, adding detail to matters within their jurisdiction. For example, according to CC article 426(4), 'In instances provided for by a law the Government of the Russian Federation may issue rules binding upon the parties when concluding and performing public contracts (standard contracts, statutes, etc)'.[104]

Subjects of the Federation and institutions of local government at different levels may adopt legislation within their area of competence. However, according to Constitution article 71, civil legislation is in the exclusive jurisdiction of

[100] Constitution arts 118(3) (judicial system) and 128 (the other listed topics). English translations in Butler, above n 64, at 27, 29.

[101] For further details see Henderson, above n 48, at 177–81.

[102] Butler, above n 64, at 20–1.

[103] Ibid 26.

[104] WE Butler, *The Civil Code of the Russian Federation Parts 1, 2 and 3: Parallel Russian and English Texts* (Moscow, JurInfoR-Press, 2008) 309.

the Federation. So federal subjects are not allowed to pass any legislation in this field.

(v) Judicial Law-making

In Russia even in Soviet times there was a role for judicial law-making, and more recently it is becoming increasingly accepted that legal precedent has an important function. This is explicit for the Constitutional Court, which has powers under the relevant legislation to create binding legal authority in three different ways.

First, the Constitution empowers the Court to declare void any legislation it deems to be unconstitutional (Constitution article 125; see also Federal Constitutional Law on the Constitutional Court article 79). As Burnham and Maggs point out: 'This "negative" power of the court may be less an exercise in law-making than law-unmaking, but the principle is the same: the shape of the law is forever changed by reason of the Court's decision'.[105]

Secondly, the Constitutional Court has exclusive power to give interpretations of the Constitution (Constitution article 125(5)). The Court's interpretations are authoritative; 'official and binding upon all representative, executive and judicial agencies of state power, local self-government, enterprises, institutions, organisations, officials and citizens and their associations'. (Federal Constitutional Law on the Constitutional Court article 106).[106] They therefore act as a source of law. A limited range of state agencies can request an abstract interpretation, that is, not in relation to specific litigation. These are: the President, the Federation Council, the State Duma, the federal Government, and the legislatures of subjects of the Federation. However, constitutional interpretations are equally authoritative when made in a specific case, either in a court ruling (постановление; *postanovlenie*) following a contested hearing, or in the determination (определение; *opredelenie*) where there was no contested hearing, for example when the Court gives grounds for refusing jurisdiction.[107]

Thirdly, the Court may create a precedent by taking a 'legal position' (правовые позиции; *pravovye pozitsii*) on an issue, which is binding generally though can be overridden by the Court itself.[108] Reforms to the Constitutional Court (in force on 9 February 2011) have strengthened the impact of Constitutional Court precedents. Amendments to the Federal Constitutional Law on the Constitutional Court introduced to the legislature by President

[105] Ibid 18.

[106] As translated in Burnham and Maggs, above n 1, at 19.

[107] On the jurisdiction of the Court, see J Henderson, 'The Constitutional Court of the Russian Federation: the Establishment and Evolution of Constitutional Supervision in Russia' (2008) 3(2) *Journal of Comparative Law* 146; on the types of Court ruling, at 147.

[108] Federal Constitutional Law on the Constitutional Court art 73. See A Fogelklou, 'Interpretation and Accommodation in the Russian Constitutional Court' in FJM Feldbrugge (ed), *Russia, Europe, and the Rule of Law* (Leiden, Martinus Nijhoff, 2007) 34 for examples of change in *pravovye pozitssii*.

Medvedev in September 2010 have simplified the procedure for certain categories of Constitutional Court cases, with expedited consideration if the applicant is challenging legal provisions similar to those previously declared unconstitutional by the Court.[109] 'One can talk about the introduction of certain elements of precedent-based legislation. The Constitutional Court will be able to rely on its earlier decisions.'[110] The new simplified procedure will not apply if there are written objections from the President, the Federation Council, the State Duma, the Government or a regional executive agency.[111] The amendments made other important changes to the Court. They abolished its two-chambered structure, introduced in 1994.[112] Now all hearings are by plenary session with a quorum of at least two-thirds of the 19 Constitutional Court judges; this streamlines the possibility of precedent through a 'legal position', because these can only be made at a plenary session. Now those are the only sessions the Constitutional Court holds.

Apart from these explicit judicial law-making powers, the Constitutional Court has been creating a hierarchy of both written and unwritten constitutional principles through its case law.[113] For example, 'principles of fairness, legal equality, state guarantees of individual rights and just compensation of harm caused by illegal actions of state officials'[114] were identified as early as January 1993 in the *Illegal Dismissals* case:[115]

> 'Generally accepted principles of law', such as fairness, equality, proportionality, legal certainty, judicial independence, 'behavior in good faith', the inviolability of property rights, freedom of contract, and a ban on the abuse of rights are at the top of this judge-made hierarchy . . . Below these are 'constitutional principles', which are specific to the Russian constitutional order and include federalism, separation of powers, *Sozialstaat* and so on. Further down this hierarchy are legal principles, which are specific to various branches of law. For example, freedom of private activity, unity of economic space, free movement of goods and capital, equal protection of property rights and economic competition are the constitutional principles which govern Russia's market economy. [116]

[109] FCL of 3 November 2010 No 7-FKZ on the Introduction of Amendments to the Federal Constitutional Law on the Constitutional Court of the Russian Federation.

[110] L Alexandrova, 'Russian president radically reforms Constitutional Court', *ITAR-TASS World Service*, 30 September 2010.

[111] 'Duma abolishes double-chamber structure of Constitutional Court', *ITAR-TASS World Service*, 22 October 2010.

[112] On the context for the Court's initial establishment see Henderson, above n 48, at 77; A Rahr, 'The Roots of the Power Struggle' (1993) 2 *Radio Free Europe/RadioLiberty Research Report* 9. For the Court under 1991 legislation, see Henderson, above n 47, 203–6.

[113] A Trochev, 'Russia's Constitutional Spirit: Judge-made Principles in Theory and Practice' in G Smith and R Sharlet (eds), *Russia and Its Constitution: Promise and Political Reality* (Leiden, Brill, 2008) 53; S Yakovleva, 'Overview of the Russian Legal System' in *Corporate Counsel's Guide to Doing Business in Russia*, 1st edn (St Paul, MN, Thomson/West, 2009) 45 at 71 ff.

[114] Trochev, above n 113, at 55.

[115] RCC resolution 1-P of 27 January 1993, *VSND i VS RSFSR* (1993) No 14 item 1508, cited ibid 55.

[116] Ibid 55.

Adherence to these generally accepted principles, somewhat akin to the English 'rules of natural justice', is not confined to the Constitutional Court. Yakovleva points out that the general principles should be applied by all branches of state power: the judiciary; legislative and executive branches,[117] although 'the lower courts are more reluctant to apply general principles of law in their everyday practice'.[118]

For the other superior courts in Russia, the Supreme Court and the Supreme Commercial Court, the development of law through cases, although not new, is increasingly acknowledged.

The current Constitution empowers both the Supreme Court and Supreme Commercial Court to 'give explanations [разъяснения; *raz"iasneniia*] regarding questions of judicial practice' (articles 126 and 127, respectively). This wording is repeated in the relevant Federal Constitutional Law governing each court; the Federal Constitutional Law on the Courts of General Jurisdiction of 7 February 2011 article 9(1) and (4)(1), and the Federal Constitutional Law on Commercial Courts in the Russian Federation of 28 April 1995 article 13(1). Explanations are issued by the Plenary Session (Plenum) of each court. These 'explanations are treated as having binding effect and a lower court that ignores a relevant explanation risks being ignominiously reversed'.[119]

As well as explanations based on a review of lower court practice, for both the Supreme Court and the Supreme Commercial Court judicial decisions are having increasing precedential impact, especially in recent years.[120] The two courts did not always see eye-to-eye on the issue of judicial creativity, with the Supreme Court more willing to take a lead.[121] However, the Supreme Commercial Court underwent a generational shift after Anton Aleksandrovich Ivanov (born 1965) took over as Court Chairman in January 2005 from Veniamin Fedorovich Iakovlev (born 1932). Ivanov 'has taken a favourable attitude towards precedent'.[122]

Further, article 13(2) of the Federal Constitutional Law on Commercial Courts provides that on the matters within its competence the Plenum of the Supreme Commercial Court adopts resolutions (постановления; *postanovleniia*) which are binding on all commercial courts. Thus, the explanations of the Plenum of the Supreme Commercial Court, unlike those of the Supreme Court,

[117] Yakovleva, above n 113, at 73.

[118] Ibid 77.

[119] Burnham and Maggs, above n 1, at 23.

[120] See, eg JN Hazard, 'Russian Judicial Precedent Revisited' (1994) 1 *Parker School Journal of East European Law* 471; PB Maggs, 'Judicial Precedent Emerges at the Supreme Court of the Russian Federation' (2002) 9 *Journal of East European Law* 479; A Vereshchagin, *Judicial Lawmaking in Post-Soviet Russia* (Abingdon, Routledge-Cavendish, 2007).

[121] A Vereshchagin, *Judicial Lawmaking in Post-Soviet Russia* (Abingdon, Routledge-Cavendish, 2007) particularly ch 4, Judicial Policies at 131 and the Conclusion at 231.

[122] Burnham and Maggs, above n 1, at 21. See also E Timofeev, 'Russia to apply precedent-based law system', *Moscow Times*, 8 December 2009, available at www.themoscowtimes.com/business/business_for_business/article/russia-to-apply-precedent-based-law-system/391053.html.

are explicitly said to be binding.[123] Article 170(4) of the Code of Commercial Procedure[124] says that the explanatory part of a court decision at first, appellate and cassation instance may contain references to Resolutions of the Plenum and Presidium of the Supreme Commercial Court. Unlike the Plenum which gives generalised explanations of court practice, the Presidium issues resolutions ad hoc, on particular cases. According to the Code of Commercial Procedure article 311(3)(5), a new definition or change of practice of the application of a legal rule given in a Resolution of the Supreme Commercial Court's Plenum or Presidium may be a ground for reopening a case on the basis of the discovery of new facts, provided that the particular resolution explicitly allows that possibility. The commercial courts' obligation to comply with articles 170(4) and 311(3) of the Code of Commercial Procedure does not in any way derogate from article 120(1) of the Constitution, which states that 'Judges shall be independent and subordinate only to the Constitution of the Russian Federation and to a federal law'.[125]

In February 2010, the Constitutional Court in a landmark ruling approved the stance that the Supreme Commercial Court had taken, that not only its explanations but its decisions in concrete cases should bind its lower courts.[126] The question which was before the Constitutional Court was compliance with the Code of Commercial Procedure articles 170(4) and 311(3) (just discussed). This important ruling has generally been seen as confirming that precedents are an important factor in Russian judicial decisions.[127] This expansion away from the 'traditional' approach of codified legal systems has not been uncontroversial, but is unlikely to be reversed.[128]

In its landmark ruling the Constitutional Court explained among other things that the Supreme Commercial Court's interpretation of legal rules in its explanations and decisions ensures their uniform understanding and application in the commercial courts. This, in turn, fosters compliance with the general legal criterion of formal certainty, clarity and unambiguity of a legal rule (formal certainty of law) which is an important part of legal regulation in legal systems based on the principle of supremacy of law and follows from the constitutional principle of equality and the supremacy of the Constitution and federal laws.[129]

[123] Federal Law on the Courts of General Jurisdiction art 14(4)(1) has no equivalent, merely stating that the Supreme Court's Plenum gives explanations. Butler, above n 64, at 566.

[124] Арбитражный Процессуальный Кодекс Российской Федерации; Arbitrazhnii Protsessual'nyi Kodeks Rossiiskoi Federatsii of 24 July 2002 No 95-FZ.

[125] Butler, above n 64, at 27.

[126] Resolution of Constitutional Court of the Russian Federation of 21 January 2010 No 1-P.

[127] See, eg A Vereshchagin, 'Прецедентное право: теперь и в России: Пять мифов о роли судебного прецедента в нашей странс и в мире' ['*Pretsedentnoe pravo: teper' i v Rossii. Piat' mifov o roli sudebnogo pretsedenta v nashei strane i v mire*; Case Law: Now Also in Russia Five Myths about the Role of Judicial Precedent in our Country and the World'] *Forbes.RU*, 5 April 2010, available at www.forbes.ru/column/47477-pretsedentnoe-pravo-teper-i-v-rossii.

[128] Arguments summarised by S Tokmakov, 'Judicial Precedent to Strengthen Russia's Top Courts' 16(12) *The ISCIP Analyst*, 22 April 2010, Institute for the Study of Conflict, Ideology and Policy, Russian Federation, available at www.bu.edu/phpbin/news-cms/news/?dept=732&id=56002.

[129] Resolution of Constitutional Court of 21 January 2010 No 1-P, para 4.

However, despite the Constitutional Court's rousing approval for its actions, in practice unfortunately the Supreme Commercial Court is as yet not very consistent in its interpretations of legal rules. Sometimes within a short time the Court gives inconsistent interpretations of the same legal rule in similar contexts. Given that each of these interpretations is binding, this causes more uncertainty than certainty.

B Sources in relation to Contract Law

(i) Applying the Code

As already noted, Russia's legal system is codified, that is, the main branches of law each have their own thematically-organised code. In concepts and style this fits with other continental European legal systems which trace their heritage from Roman law (categorised by René David as Romano-Germanic legal systems).[130]

As in other similar Romanist legal systems, the law of contract is part of a more general law of obligations, and is dealt with in the Civil Code (CC).

Not all civil law is covered by the Code. There are a number of other pieces of legislation which add important detail, particularly in relation to commercial legal entities and securities regulations. However, the Civil Code specifies that, 'Norms of civil law contained in other laws must conform to the present Code'[131] (CC article 3(2)). The Civil Code therefore acts as a 'grandfather' law, a 'civil constitution' for other legislation in the field. At the same time, the Civil Code is a federal law and according to the Constitution has the same legal force as other federal laws. Like the Civil Code, other Codes contain provisions that legislation within the branch of law regulated by that Code should comply with its provisions.

The Constitutional Court considered the question of the compliance of CC article 3(2) with the Constitution. The problem arose due to the apparent contradiction of CC articles 837 and 839 with article 26 of the Federal Law on Bankruptcy (Insolvency) of Credit Organizations.[132] The Constitutional Court did not consider the case on its merits so issued a determination (определение; *opredelenie*) rather than a ruling (постановление; *postanovlenie*). The Court argued that the Constitution does not and cannot create a hierarchy between different federal laws. Article 76 of the Constitution which defines federal law as having direct effect must mean that no federal law has a higher legal force than any other federal law. The choice of which legal rules are applicable in a particular case and their interpretation is not within the Constitutional Court's juris-

[130] R David, *Les grandes systèms de droit contemporains*, 1st edn (Paris, Dalloz, 1964), first translated into English as R David and JEC Brierley, *Major Legal Systems of the World Today* (London, Stevens and Sons, 1968). The latest edition of this is the 3rd edn, 1985.

[131] Butler, above n 104, at 10.

[132] Federal Law on Bankruptcy (Insolvency) of Credit Organizations of 25 February 1999 No 40-FZ.

diction; these are matters to be dealt with by the courts of general jurisdiction and commercial courts on a case-by-case basis. The Constitutional Court did not say so explicitly, but its determination in fact means that in a particular case courts must rely on the rules of interpretation of laws (discussed below) to decide which federal law's provisions are applicable. Unfortunately, in some cases provisions of two different Codes are contradictory. Then the choice of law to be applied in a case is not always straightforward and, following the Constitutional Court's decision just mentioned, can only be approached as a matter of interpretation of law.

The fact that Russia has a codified legal system leads to three important characteristics. First, the subdivision of law into different branches is taken very seriously. The process of codification entails consideration of a principled basis on which Codes should be drafted. For example, there has been a recurrent debate in Russia about whether there should be a separate Commercial Code (or Code of Entrepreneurial Law) or whether one unified Civil Code is preferable.[133]

Secondly, the order of exposition matters. In general the treatment of topics in a Code moves from the general to the particular. Considering rules impacting contract law, for example, it may be necessary first to look at rules about transactions in general, then at the fundamentals principles of obligations, and the general rules about contracts, before examining the specificities of a particular type of contract.

Thirdly, legal theory in codified legal systems is generally reluctant to accept case law as a source of law. However, in Russia even in Soviet times there was a role for judicial law-making, and, as discussed at p 26, in more recent times it is becoming increasingly accepted that legal precedent has an important function.

The structuring of legal rules according to branches of law in the form of special Codes can lead to problems with their interpretation. The Constitutional Court's determination that there is no hierarchy of federal law does not eliminate the reality that there may be contradictory rules in different laws which have the same legal force, for example, two federal laws, applicable to a particular situation. Alternatively, there may be contradictory rules within the same law, for example, an inconsistency between the Civil Code's General Part on obligations and its provisions on a particular type of contract. To resolve these discrepancies, the following rules rooted in Roman law for interpretation of laws are used.

The first rule is *lex specialis derogat generalis* which means a legal rule regulating a specific subject matter (*lex specialis*) will override a general rule (*lex generalis*). For example, the general Part One of the Civil Code is *lex generalis* in relation to Part Two of the Civil Code regulating particular types of contracts. The provisions of the Civil Code on mutual insurance are *lex generalis* in relation

[133] See, eg VA Dozortsev, 'One Code or Two' (1995) *Parker School Journal of East European Law* 28.

to the provisions of Federal Law on Mutual Insurance.[134] In both cases, the second mentioned will take precedence.

If application of this first rule does not solve the contradiction, then the doctrine *lex posterior derogat legi priori* is applied. It means that the legal rule which was enacted later overrides any earlier provision. In preparing draft legislation, draftsmen are required to prepare a list of normative acts which would need to be amended (and the text of such amendments) or repealed if the draft were to be adopted. Unfortunately in practice these lists are rarely complete, which leads to discrepancies in legislation.

(ii) Application of Civil Legislation by Analogy

One aspect of continental legal systems which Russia shares, which impacts the role of courts in applying law, is the use of analogy to fill gaps in enacted legislation. The Civil Code explicitly allows this in article 6 (analogy is forbidden in criminal law).[135] Two types of analogy are specified, although the contrast is difficult to express in English. In Russian, as with many continental European languages, there are two words for 'law', *pravo* (право) and *zakon* (закон). *Pravo* means law in the general sense of rights, as in the Latin *ius*. *Zakon* means enacted legislation, Latin *lex*. In modern usage *zakon* is the name given to law enacted by the Russian federal legislature or that of a Federation subject. Butler translates CC article 6 using the Latin terms for clarity:

1. In instances where relations provided for by Article 2(1) and (2) of the present Code [ie the range of civil legal relations] have not been expressly regulated by legislation or by agreement of the parties and there is no custom [of business turnover][136] applicable to them, civil legislation regarding similar relations (analogy of lex) shall apply to such relations if this is not contrary to the essence thereof.
2. When it is impossible to use an analogy of lex, the rights and duties of the parties shall be determined by proceeding from the general principles and sense of civil legislation (analogy of ius) and the requirements of good faith, reasonableness, and justness.[137]

Analogy of law in the sense of statute (*lex*) allows the court to apply legislation which regulates similar relations, whereas analogy of law (*ius*) empowers the court to look at 'the general principles and sense of civil legislation'. This may possibly entail application of the general constitutional principles of law discussed at p 27.

CC article 6 on analogy mentions one other source relevant to civil law, that is 'custom'. Before 1 March 2013, when Federal Law amending the Civil Code

[134] Federal Law on Mutual Insurance of 29 November 2007 No 286-FZ.
[135] Criminal Code 1996 art 3(2).
[136] Federal Law amending the Civil Code of 30 December 2012 No 302-FZ (in force on 1 March 2013) changed 'customs of business turnover' to 'customs'.
[137] Butler, above n 104, at 3–4.

of 30 December 2012[138] entered into force, CC article 6 referred to 'customs of business turnover' instead of 'customs'. This change to CC article 6, however, did not lead to overall replacement of the phrase 'customs of business turnover' by 'customs' throughout Part One of the Civil Code. For example, provisions of chapter 22 'Performance of Obligations' still refer to 'customs of business turnover'. Since chapter 22 regulates performance of all types of obligations (not just those arising in entrepreneurial relations) it would be logical to use 'customs' in line with CC article 6. Whether or not the law-makers intentionally refrained from making these substitutions is not yet clear.

Customs are akin to English implied terms arising from custom, trade usage or business practice. CC article 5(1) defines a custom as 'behaviour which has been formed and extensively applied in any domain of entrepreneurial [and other activity] and is not provided for by legislation irrespective of whether it has been fixed in any document'.[139] CC article 5(2) disallows application of custom if it is contrary to legislation or the parties' contract. Butler notes with respect to customs of business turnover (which is also true in relation to customs in general) that:

> They are purely sources of 'civil' law and may exist in any sphere of economic life: they may be regional, local, national, international, or relate to branches of industry or activity or inter-branches. In this sense customs of business turnover relate to the law of obligations, and not the law of things (ownership).[140]

Incorporation of custom law to Russian law after a century of 'exile' is clearly an interesting development and may signify increased maturity and sophistication in the approach to sources of law.

(iii) Economic Analysis of Law

Following the experience of legal scholars in the United States and Europe, Russian scholars are starting to use the tools of law and economics in their interpretation and application of law. At the moment the doctrine of law and economics is at an early stages of development in Russia but its importance has already been recognised by the Chairman of the Supreme Commercial Court, Anton Aleksandrovich Ivanov.

In April 2013 Ivanov, in an interview with the online legal information portal www.pravo.ru, said that one of his recommendations to commercial courts is to 'carry out an economic analysis of law more often in order to assess appropriately the respective legal rules and give them their correct interpretation' in particular cases. Ivanov also noted that this approach is already used by courts in cases on suretyship and pledge, when, for example, creditors try in bad faith to

[138] No 302-FZ.

[139] Butler, above n 104, at 11. In square brackets is the text introduced by Federal Law of 30 December 2012 No 302-FZ (entered into force from 1 March 2013).

[140] Butler, above n 1, at 109.

evade performance of their obligations. The principle also works in consideration of corporate disputes. In Ivanov's opinion 'economic analysis should be the sine qua non, a prerequisite in civil law'.[141]

C Sources of Legal Information

Within the Russian legal system there is a vast number of legislative acts at different levels in the hierarchy of law. It is a characteristic of Russian law that there these acts are frequently changed. For a foreign lawyer whose background is a more mature and stable legal system it may feel almost impossible to keep track of current law within this dynamically changing legal environment. Every lawyer in contemporary Russia manages through the use of one or other of the available legal information systems. The two most widely used are *ConsultantPlus*[142] and *Garant*.[143] These legal information systems contain not only the full range of Russian legislation (both federal and regional) and international law, but also include the court practice of the commercial courts (mostly of the Supreme Commercial Court and Federal District Courts, but also including commercial courts at first and appellate instances) and courts of general jurisdiction (mostly of the Supreme Court, rarely of lower courts) and various additional aids to analysis, such as commentaries to legislation, books, articles, guides, etc. The authors of this book used the *ConsultantPlus* database to access the text of cases and legislation cited.

Both *ConsultantPlus* and *Garant* have free online demonstration versions.[144] The main databases in both *ConsultantPlus* and *Garant* are in Russian. However, Garant also offers a limited database of Russian legislation in English.[145]

D Role of International Law

One other important topic needs to be mentioned in this overview of sources of law in Russia, that is, the impact of international law in the Russian legal system. Article 15(4) of the Constitution states that 'generally recognised principles and norms of international law and the international treaties of the

[141] N Shiniaeva, 'Антон Иванов рекомендовал судьям применять "новый ГК" до его вступления в силу' [*'Anton Ivanov rekomendovan sud'iam primeniat' "novyi GK" do ego vstupleniia v silu*; Anton Ivanov Recommended Judges to Apply "New Civil Code" Before its Entrance into Force'], 25 April 2013, www.pravo.ru/review/view/84682/.

[142] See www.consultant.ru/sys/english/.

[143] See english.garant.ru/.

[144] For *Garant* see ivo.garant.ru/SESSION/PILOT/main.htm; for *ConsultantPlus* see base.consultant.ru/cons/cgi/online.cgi?req=home&utm_csource=online&utm_cmedium=button.

[145] Online demo version of *Garant* database in English at www.en.garant.ru/SESSION/PILOT/main.htm.

Russian Federation shall constitute an integral part of its legal system'.[146] The same article also states 'if an international treaty of the Russian Federation establishes rules other than those stipulated by law, the rules of the international treaty shall apply'.[147] Thus, international law, both treaties and generally recognised principles and norms (international customary law), is directly applicable in Russia, and indeed ousts domestic law if there is a conflict between it and relevant international law. International legal obligations are increasingly being cited in court decisions; in October 2003 the Plenum of the Russian Supreme Court issued an explanation to assist in this.[148]

Russia joined the Council of Europe on 28 February 1996, and on 30 March 1998 ratified the 1950 European Convention on Human Rights and Fundamental Freedoms (ECHR).[149] The ECHR came into force in Russia on 1 November 1998. It has direct application. Article 46 of the Constitution, drafted after Russia had decided to apply for Council of Europe membership in May 1992, specifically gives 'everyone' the right 'to apply to inter-state organs concerned with the protection of human rights and freedoms if all available domestic remedies have been exhausted'.[150] Russians are increasingly petitioning the European Court of Human Rights, and ECHR case law is being referred to in Russia's courts, particularly the Constitutional Court.[151]

Russia is a party to a number of international treaties important for the regulation of contractual relations, one of the most popular and widely applied being the 1980 United Nations Convention for the International Sale of Goods. Provisions of the Convention are directly applied by the Russian Commercial Courts resolving contractual disputes.

E Recognition and Enforcement of Foreign Judgments and Arbitral Awards

Foreign judgments and arbitration awards are recognised and enforced in Russia if provided for in an international treaty to which Russia is a party, and in federal law.[152] For a foreign decision or award to be recognised the party to the dispute has to apply to a Russian court which then decides whether to agree and enforce the decision or award or refuse to recognise it. There are seven grounds for refusal:

[146] Butler, above n 64, at 7.

[147] Ibid.

[148] An English version is posted up on the Supreme Court's website at www.vsrf.ru/catalog.php?c1=English&c2=Documents&c3=&id=6801.

[149] See Henderson, above n 48, at 246–51 for details and further references.

[150] WE Butler, *Russian Public Law* (London, Wildy, Simmonds & Hill Publishers, 2013) 11.

[151] A Trochev, 'All Appeals Lead to Strasbourg? Unpacking the Impact of the European Court of Human Rights on Russia' (2009) 17(2) *Demokratizatsiya* 145.

[152] Code of Commercial Procedure art 241(1).

(1) that the decision/award did not come into force in the territory where it was rendered;
(2) that the defendant was not duly notified of the time and place of the hearing or could not present their explanations to the court for other reasons;
(3) that consideration of that type of case is in the exclusive jurisdiction of the Russian Federation as specified in international treaty or federal law;
(4) that there already is a decision of a Russian court which has come into force involving the same parties and on the same subject matter;
(5) that there is a dispute between the same parties on the same subject-matter initiated in a Russian court before it has been initiated in a foreign court;
(6) that the period for enforcement of the decision/award has expired; or
(7) that enforcement would contradict the public order of the Russian Federation.[153]

These are often used by Russian courts, with the most vague, that of 'contradicting Russian public order', being the most frequent. As a result, obtaining a decision against a Russian party in a foreign jurisdiction can be rather pointless because it is very hard to predict whether a Russian court would be willing or not to enforce it. 'Public order' is a malleable and unpredictable concept which changes every now and then.

VI THE LEGAL PROFESSION

A Legal Education

Academic qualification is the main factor in the creation of a Russian lawyer (юрист; *iurist*). Higher legal education in Russia is quite rigorous, usually involving a four- or five-year course, which must be attested by the Ministry of Higher Education. In recent times a number of private institutions offering law study have been established to rival the existing law institutes, state law academies and university law faculties, and other institutes of higher education.

B *Advokatura* (The 'Bar')

There is a long tradition in Russia of either no representation at trial or representation by a non-lawyer, and it was only in 1864 that a paid Bar (Адвокатура; *Advokatura*) was established. In modern Russia is not necessary to be an *advokat* (адвокат, a member of the *Advokatura*; plural *advokaty*) in order to practise law; in fact anyone can claim to be a 'consultant' without even having a law degree, and can represent a client in almost all proceedings provided the client has retained them. 'The only exception, apart from criminal proceedings, is the proceedings

[153] Code of Commercial Procedure art 244(1).

between [*sic*] the Constitutional Court of the Russian Federation: one has to either be an advocate or have an academic degree in law.'[154]

The number of non-*advokat* unregulated lawyers is not known; the December 2009 American Bar Association *Rule of Law Initiative Newsletter* published an estimate that 'There are currently about 60,000 practicing advocates in Russia, all of whom are licensed and regulated via advocacy laws and ethics codes. In contrast, Russia also has approximately 700,000 non-advocate lawyers (jurists), who are currently unregulated under the Russian legal system'.[155]

The same year, Yuri Lubimov, the Russian Deputy Minister of Justice, reported in a talk to the British Russian Law Association on 24 September 2009 that 'only 6–8 per cent of the Russian legal market is represented by members of the Bar ("advocates") with the other 82 per cent of legal services being provided by companies, auditors, amateur helpers ("lawyers by heart")'.[156] Mr Lubimov identified lack of overall regulation as a problem. Members of the *Advokatura* are subject to disciplinary proceedings; 'lawyers by heart' are not. There is a draft law under consideration by the State Duma which would establish an *advokat*'s monopoly on court representation, but at the time of writing it has not been adopted.

According to the current law regulating the Bar, the Federal Law on Advocate Activity and the *Advokatura* of 31 May 2002,[157] in order to be an *advokat* an applicant must have no criminal record, higher legal education, two years' experience in a legal field or on traineeship, and pass the advocates' examination administered by their regional Qualifications Commission. In return there are some tax advantages, and an *advokat* has the right to demand information related to their clients from relevant agencies, as well as having the dubious privilege of the exclusive right to act in pre-trial criminal process. For many practising lawyers there is clearly little incentive to gain the qualification as an *advokat*.

A number of foreign law firms have established a presence in Russia. Foreign lawyers are permitted to practice provided they are registered with the Federal Registration Service. It is also possible for a foreigner to become an *advokat*. On the whole, foreign law firms are more expensive than Russian firms.[158]

Legal aid and advice to the indigent has been an ongoing problem in recent years. The Federal Law on Advocate Activity and the *Advokatura* imposed on regional Chambers of Advocates (regional Bar Associations) the duty to establish *pro bono* Consultation Offices, called *Konsul'tatsiia* (Консультация), if the number of *advokaty* in a judicial district is less than two per federal judge. This

[154] D Shabelnikov, *The Legal Profession in the Russian Federation* (October 2008) 4, report prepared for the workshop 'Reform of the Legal Profession and Access to Justice', sponsored by OSCE/ODIHR in November 2008, available at www.osce.org/odihr/36312.

[155] Available at www.abanet.org/rol/news/news_russia_advocates_conference_1209.shtml.

[156] Reported in the *British Russian Law Association Newsletter*, Winter 2009 available at thebrla.com/wp-content/uploads/2012/11/BRLA-Winter-2009-Newsletter.pdf.

[157] English translation in Butler, above n 64, at 891. See also WE Butler, *The Russian Legal Practitioner* (The Hague, Eleven International Publishing, 2011).

[158] Butler, above n 1, at 140.

system has not worked well, as the more skilled *advokaty* are unwilling to participate. 'Better-paid attorneys . . . will seek to avoid this responsibility by making a monthly contribution that is used to pay those advocates who take on work for the less fortunate.'[159] There have been recent reforms to bring in law centres on the Finnish model, but there is still unmet legal need.[160]

C The Notariat

One extremely important group of lawyers, whose role is quite familiar to continental European lawyers, is the Notariat (Нотариат; *notariat*).

State notaries existed in Soviet times. They were state-salaried civil servants and as John Hazard commented in 1979: 'The career is said to attract primarily those law graduates who want to avoid the demanding tasks of judges, procurators, and investigators and who prefer routines, standard hours, and a minimum of nervous tension.'[161] During those times, notaries were almost exclusively women.

The transformation to a market economy has revolutionised the context of notarial activity, and put notaries at the centre of finalising business deals. The 1993 Fundamental Principles on the Notariat[162] allowed for the first time the establishment of private notarial offices along with the already existing state notaries. Qualifications for appointment are higher legal education, a year's apprenticeship with a notary and passing the extremely rigorous examination for notaries.[163] State notaries are appointed by the Ministry of Justice which issues the licence to practise; private notaries are nominated to the Ministry of Justice by the Chamber of Notaries.

State notaries are salaried by the state and fees collected for their work go into the state budget. There are currently very few. Private notaries collect and keep the fees, although they are appropriately taxed. If a notarial act is obligatory, the fee is set by the Ministry of Justice and the same will be charged by both state and private notaries. In practice both state and private notaries charge fees for additional services they provide and which a client cannot refuse to accept, such as typing, photocopying and other technicalities. These fees are not regulated and are often higher than the regulated fee for the main service. If a notarial act is not obligatory, there is no limitation on the fee set by the notary.

[159] Eugene Huskey, 'The Bar's Triumph or Shame? The Founding of Chambers of Advocates in Putin's Russia' in FJM Feldbrugge and R Sharlet (eds), *Public Policy and Law in Russia: In Search of a Unified Legal and Political Space: Essays in Honor of Donald D Barry* (Leiden, Brill, 2005) 149 at 161.

[160] M Venalain en, 'Russia Adopts the Model of the Finnish Legal Aid System' (2008) 33(1) *Review of Central and East European Law* 135.

[161] J Hazard, 'Humble Guardians of Routines (Notaries and ZAGS)' in PB Maggs, DD Barry, FJM Feldbrugge and G Ginsburgs (eds), *Soviet Law after Stalin: Soviet Institutions and the Administration of Law, Laws in Eastern Europe* (Alphen aan den Rijn, Sijthoff & Noordhof, 1979) 20(III), 245 at 248.

[162] English translation in Butler, above n 64, at 853.

[163] See law as amended to 2004 in Butler, above n 64, at 747.

Individuals and businesses in Russia have to deal with notaries on a day-to-day basis. As Burnham and Maggs note, 'The services of notaries do not come cheap and it is often observed that notaries are among the better paid of all legal professionals. Where the law requires particular categories of documents to be notarised, fees can be high.'[164]

The notary performs 'notarial actions in the name of the Russian Federation' (Fundamental Principles of Legislation of the Russian Federation on the Notariat article 1).[165] Article 35 of the legislation has an open-ended list of 18 notarial actions. These may be grouped into three main categories.[166]

First, the notary attests the authenticity of copies of documents. Secondly, the notary certifies transactions such as contracts, wills, powers of attorney and others, and acts as a safe repository for copies of the documents. The requirement for notarial certification of contracts is discussed in Chapter 3 (at p 79). A notary can also initiate proceedings to enforce an uncontested contractual debt. Thirdly, a notary oversees inheritance. Wills generally must be notarially certified, and the notary may assist the subsequent dispositions of the deceased's estate. Notaries are required by law to explain the impact of the transaction on those seeking their services, and they must ensure that any document they deal with which would have legal effect conforms to any relevant legislation.

Notarisation of documents and their copies is a legal requirement for many administrative procedures involving businesses and individuals. For example, the application form to register a legal entity of any kind must be notarised before it is presented to the registration authority. Notaries, however, do not accept liability for noncompliance of the form with legal requirements, and if the form is rejected by the registration authority will not issue a refund. In other words, the notary checks the identity of the person signing the form and does nothing else. What the practical impact of this procedure is, apart from making money for the notary, is not clear.

Amendments to the Federal Law on Limited Responsibility Societies which came into effect on 1 July 2009 require that the sale of shares in limited responsibility societies (limited liability companies) is witnessed by a notary. This prompted the following comment:

> Unlike in some other countries, a Russian solicitor can't act as a notary; the number of notaries, being restricted, is comparatively small. Limited liability company is the most popular form of legal entity in Russia, covering, perhaps, 80 per cent of enterprises. The number of transactions now to be notarised is astronomical.
>
> Russian notaries have become the pet of the state. Their job is not rocket science – far from that. In fact, it is quite dull. They just need to be reasonably impartial, moderately accurate, and relatively resistant to corruption.[167]

164 Above n 1, at 170.
165 Butler, above n 64, at 853.
166 Butler, above n 1, at 209.
167 E Istomina, 'God bless notaries!', *Russian Law Online*, 21 April 2009, available at www.russianlawonline.com/Russian-limited-liability-company-amendments-changes-legislation-Russia.

Although not a legal requirement, it is always better to have copies of documents to be used as evidence in court notarised. The imaginative creativity of notaries in inventing new kinds of service and persuading the public that they are necessary is very impressive. One of the latest inventions, related to the development of modern technologies, is notarisation of website pages. For example, if a company or an individual finds a website that breaches their intellectual property rights, the first thing that is recommended they do is to notarise the webpage, that is, have it printed out and stamped by a notary. Otherwise it is very likely that courts will not accept the evidence in any subsequent litigation.

D The Judiciary

The Law of the Russian Federation on the Status of Judges in the Russian Federation[168] sets out the following requirements for judicial candidates:

- a law degree;
- no pending criminal prosecutions;
- not having citizenship or right to reside in other countries;
- not having limited legal capacity;
- not registered with specialist medical institutions in connection with drug/alcohol/toxic substances addiction or chronic psychiatric disorder; and
- not having other illnesses which could prevent them from carrying out the duties of a judge.

There are also requirements of age and work experience which depend on the level of the court:

- to become a judge of a district court of general jurisdiction or commercial court of a subject of the federation the candidate should be a minimum of 25 years old and have at least five years' work experience in a legal field;
- to become a judge of a supreme court of a subject of the Federation or commercial court of appeal the candidate should be at least 30 years old and have seven years' work experience in a legal field;
- to become a judge of the Supreme Court or the Supreme Commercial Court the candidate should be at least 35 and have 10 years' experience in a legal field; and
- to be appointed a judge of the Constitutional Court the candidate should be at least 40 and have 15 years' legal experience (although not necessarily as a judge).

The basic requirements for a judicial candidate seem surprisingly low; apart from the law degree itself, they mainly concern residency or medical issues.

[168] Butler, above n 64, at 417.

However, all eligible candidates must also pass an exam to establish if they have sufficient skills and knowledge to work as a judge in the court to which they are applying. Candidates who have the equivalent (more or less) to a PhD in law (кандидат юридических наук; *kandidat iuridicheskikh nauk*) or a Doctorate of Law (доктор юридических наук; *doktor iuridicheskikh nauk*) do not have to take the exam.

The judge is then selected by a special collegial body of judges of that particular region, the Judicial Qualifications Collegium. For investiture as a judge, the candidate is formally granted judicial power and appointed to their position by the President of the Russian Federation on presentation by the Chairman of the Supreme Court or Supreme Commercial Court, depending in which branch they will work.

Appointment of judges by the President is supposed to guarantee independence of judges from the executive. However, 'Lack of judicial independence, despite the Constitution's recognition of the judiciary as a "self-dependent" branch of state power, seems to be Russia's "Punchinello's secret" [open secret]'.[169] It is hardly a secret that the success and material well-being of an individual judge depends a lot on the chairman (or woman) of the court where the judge works and the chairman is often dependent on the regional and/or federal government.

Lack of independence is not the only problem for the Russian judiciary. A number of judges have retained their positions from Soviet times or got their legal education then. Therefore their approach to resolving cases, and especially cases connected with entrepreneurial activity, tends to be highly prejudiced against entrepreneurs. Private business was not allowed in the USSR until its final few years when commerce was allowed to a limited extent; even then, everyone who was starting a business was treated with suspicion. Even when there is no actual prejudice against entrepreneurs, judges often fail to understand basic business principles and as a result make some rather inexplicable decisions. For example, there are a number of decisions of commercial courts of various levels, including the Supreme Commercial Court, where the use of some financial instruments, such as futures and options, is considered to be purely gambling.

Of course, most Soviet-era judges have retired or will retire soon, but the next generation of judges is not necessarily any better. Very many new judges are former procurators, who in their previous role were known for their loyalty to the state and readiness to follow orders received from executive agencies.

[169] International Commission of Jurists Research Mission on Judicial Reform, *The State of the Judiciary in Russia*, Report to the Russian Federation (Geneva, 20–24 June 2010) 6, available at www.icj.org/dwn/database/Mission_Report_FINAL_ENG.pdf.

VII PRINCIPLES OF CONTRACT LAW

A Duality: Commercial Law versus Civil Law

Traditionally in Russia there is no formal division into commercial and civil law. There is only one single Civil Code and all relations, including all contractual relations, in the economic sphere are regulated by that.

However, there is duality within the Code itself. There are a number of rules which apply only to entrepreneurial relations or activities and other rules which apply only to non-entrepreneurial relations. According to CC article 2(1), entrepreneurial activity is:

> autonomous activity effectuated at one's own risk directed towards the systematic obtaining of profit from the use of property, the sale of goods, the fulfilment of work, or the rendering of services by persons registered in this capacity in the procedure established by law.[170]

The definition is far from perfect and has caused some practical controversies, for example, in relation to the requirement to be registered in accordance with the law, that is, either as a legal entity or an individual entrepreneur. The definition can be construed to mean that only those who are so registered and involved in the activities described carry on entrepreneurial activity. If the definition is interpreted literally, the same activity carried on by a person who is not registered would not be considered entrepreneurial. In fact, such a person would be in breach of the law and criminally liable for illegal entrepreneurship (незаконное предпринимательство; *nezakonnoe predpinimatel'stvo*). The Criminal Code thus regards them as conducting entrepreneurial activity, even if only of an illegal nature.

The Civil Code rules applicable to non-entrepreneurial relations are generally more prescriptive and designed to limit the parties' freedom, in order to prevent one from taking advantage of the other. The rules applicable to entrepreneurial relations assume the parties' professionalism and ability to evaluate their own entrepreneurial risks. They give parties more freedom to decide about their own legal relations. However, the same rules are then applied to companies with multibillion turnovers and individual entrepreneurs involved in micro-businesses.

One of the most significant differences between entrepreneurial and non-entrepreneurial rules relates to liability for contractual breach. No-fault liability is applied to entrepreneurs but liability based on fault is applied to everyone else. This is discussed further in Chapter 10 at p 229.

Some types of contracts described in Part Two of the Code can only be made by entrepreneurs, for example, simple partnership, contract of supply, and others. If a party who is not an entrepreneur concludes a contract of this type, it is void.

[170] Butler, above n 104, at 8–9.

Virtually every chapter in this book discusses the difference between rules applicable to entrepreneurial and non-entrepreneurial relations and activities; the existence of this dualism within the Code is an important point to remember.

B Freedom of Contract

The Civil Code currently in force is the first law in the history of Russia which stipulates that freedom of contract is one of the main principles of Russian civil law (CC articles 1(1), 421). Soviet Civil Codes allowed contractual relations between the parties strictly within the limits set by the Code, and 'everything not permitted was forbidden'.[171]

According to the current Civil Code, freedom of contract means that:

- parties cannot be forced to conclude a contract, apart from cases prescribed by law;
- parties can choose to conclude a contract of a type recognised by law or any other contract (ie not one of the listed types);
- parties can combine elements of different types of contracts; and
- parties are free to choose terms and conditions of the contract, unless the contents of a term is prescribed by law or other legal acts.

Compared to non-codified English law, parties are less free to choose the contractual terms they wish. Merely the existence of the Civil Code is, possibly, the primary reason for that. Civil Codes always contain a number of mandatory norms (**императивные нормы**; *imperativniye normy*), that is, compulsory terms with which the parties must comply, whenever the particular conditions specified in the norm exist. Non-compliance with a mandatory norm is a breach of law. Some mandatory norms apply to all contracts and other mandatory norms apply to some types of contracts. The Civil Code also contains a number of dispositive norms which may be applied in contracts, although they can be excluded by the parties. This is discussed further in Chapter 2 (at p 53).

Classification of contracts into types (such as purchase-sale, bank account, lease, etc) is another substantial limitation imposed by the Civil Code. Even though parties are free to choose a contract of a type which is not described in the Code, courts are always tempted to regard a contract as belonging to one of the types listed in CC Part Two, thus imposing on the contract the application of the corresponding mandatory and dispositive norms, whatever the parties' original intention. Issues related to this are also discussed in Chapter 2 (particularly at p 57).

The division of contracts into types and the use of mandatory norms are two fundamental limitations of freedom of contract which shape Russian contract

[171] The Resolution on Legal Reform adopted at the Nineteenth Conference of the Communist Party of the Soviet Union in 1988 specifically reversed this principle to 'everything not prohibited by law is allowed'.

law. Every chapter of this book refers to such norms and the way courts apply them.

It is also worth remembering the factor mentioned in the beginning of this section. The Russian public in general, including legal professionals of all kinds, are not completely comfortable with the idea of freedom of contract. It is still rather novel to them and strange to those who are not used to it. Only many years of use will allow people to realise the principle's full significance for contractual relations and for the economy of the country as a whole. Meanwhile, it is not uncommon to find court decisions where judges simply ignore freedom of contract. Examples of this unfortunate approach can be found in this book.

C Actual Performance

The principle of actual performance is one of the fundamental principles of Russian contract law. This principle demonstrates Russia's membership of the 'continental Romanist legal family' and, at the same time, recalls Soviet legal traditions. In contemporary contract law the principle of actual performance is based on CC article 396(1):

> The payment of a penalty and compensation of losses in the event of the improper performance of an obligation shall not relieve the debtor from performance of the obligation in kind unless provided otherwise by a law or by contract.[172]

Karapetov gives a very precise explanation of the principle of actual performance as:

> the highest degree of commitment to contractual terms, which allows the creditor [promisee] under the general rule to induce the debtor [promisor] into performance of his [contractual] obligations in kind, depriving him of the right to evade the contract at his own discretion by providing the creditor with the substitute performance – monetary compensation.[173]

Thus, the idea behind the principle of actual performance is that the debtor must perform exactly that obligation which he undertook according to a contract and as a general rule is not allowed to change it unilaterally. As a result, the Russian Civil Code provides the creditor (promisee) with a number of different means to ensure their right to actual performance by encouraging the debtor (promisor) to perform their contractual obligation. Pledge is one of the most commonly used examples of these (further discussion in Chapter 9 at p 212).

[172] Butler, above n 104, at 293.

[173] AG Karapetov 'Соотношение принципа реального исполнения и мер гражданско-правовой ответственности' ['*Sootnoshenie printsipa real'nogo ispolneniia i mer grazhdansko-pravovoi otvetstvennosti*; Correlation Between the Principle of Actual Performance and Measures of Civil Liability'] in Olu Shilokhvost (ed), *Current Problems of Civil Law* (Moscow, NORMA, 2003) vol 6, 313.

The principle of actual performance is also enforced by the possibility of establishing in the contract punitive sanctions (punitive penalty, штрафная неустойка; *shtrafnaia neustoika*) on the debtor (promisor) for non-performance or improper performance of their contractual obligations (discussed in Chapter 10 at p 243).

The principle of actual performance is not absolute. It has limitations which are also discussed in detail in Chapter 10 at p 251.

The principle of actual performance needs to be distinguished from the requirement of proper contractual performance, which, unlike the principle of actual performance, is known to English lawyers as the principle of sanctity of contracts. The requirement of proper performance is also inherent to contract law of Russia and is established in CC article 309, according to which:

> Obligations must be performed duly in accordance with the conditions of the obligation and the requirements of a law and other legal acts, and in the absence of such conditions and requirements, in accordance with the customs of business turnover or other usually presented requirements.[174]

The requirement of proper performance is considered to be met under Russian contract law when an obligation is performed: in accordance with the relevant standard of performance, by and to the right person, by the right method, in the right place and at the right time. Each of these elements is extensively discussed in Chapter 9 (at p 193).

D Compensational Nature and Equivalence

Unlike English law, Russian contract law generally recognises as legally binding contracts without compensation, although only in non-entrepreneurial relations. However, the same CC article 423(3) confirms a presumption that contracts will involve compensation, 'unless otherwise follows from law, other legal acts, or the content or essence of the contract'.[175]

The Civil Code does not set any requirements about the value of compensation which would be sufficient to allow a contract to be categorised as a contract for compensation. As under English law, if one party offers the other party a peppercorn in return for performance, from the strictly legal perspective this should be sufficient for the contract to have a compensational nature. CC Article 424(1) stipulates that 'The performance of a contract shall be paid for at the price established by agreement of the parties'.[176] The parties' right to set their own price is one manifestation of the principle of freedom of contract; in particular, the parties' freedom to determine at their own discretion the terms of their contract (CC article 421(4)).

[174] Butler, above n 104, at 243.
[175] Ibid 307.
[176] Ibid.

When they discuss the principle of compensation for performance, legal scholars often mention the principle of equivalence of performance as one of the principles lying at the heart of contracts.[177] So do Russian courts.

For example, the Supreme Commercial Court and the Supreme Court have developed a presumption of equality of parties' mutual obligations. In one of their joint resolutions[178] the courts held that, in relation to the consequences of invalidity of a contract which has been performed by both parties, where one party received money and the other goods, work or services, the court should consider the parties' mutual obligations equal unless it is proved otherwise.

It is not uncommon for commercial courts to assess the equality of what parties exchange under commercial contracts. The issue arises when a commercial court thinks that the performance of one party is clearly disproportionate to the performance of the other. If after consideration of this issue the court decides that the performance of one party was obviously not equivalent, it will deem the contract to be a sham contract concealing a contract of gift. Since contracts of gifts are prohibited between commercial legal entities and/or individual entrepreneurs, the contract will be deemed void.

Examples of how principles of compensational nature of contract and equality are applied in practice are found in Chapter 5. The consequences of deeming a contract void are discussed in Chapter 6 (at p 126).

E Good Faith

A significant step in the official recognition of the utility of judicial law-making as a source of Russian civil law in general, and contract law in particular, was the explicit inclusion at the end of 2012 of the principle of good faith into the Civil Code. For the first time in the history of Russian civil law the principle of good faith was enshrined in a Code. This was done by the Federal Law of 30 December 2012, in force on 1 March 2013.[179] Among other things, the law amended CC articles 1 and 10. While the draft law was being prepared, the Russian professional and academic community extensively discussed whether the principle of good faith should be provided for in the Civil Code at all, and, if so, should its application cover only contract law or civil law in general. In the end the decision was made in favour of recognising the principle of good faith in the Civil Code and expanding its application to civil law as a whole.

The principle of good faith is now formulated as 'an obligation of participants of civil law relations to act in good faith while establishing, effectuating

[177] MI Braginskii and VV Vitrianskii, Договорное Право. Книга первая: Общая Часть [*Dogovornoe Pravo. Kniga pervaia: Obshchaia Chast'*; *Contract Law: Book One: General Part*] (Moscow, Statut, 2001) 327–8.

[178] Resolution of Plenum of the Supreme Court No 13 and Plenum of the Supreme Commercial Court No 14 of 8 October 1998 'On the practice of application of provisions of the Civil Code of the Russian Federation concerning the interest for the use of another's monetary means' para 27.

[179] No 302-FZ.

and protecting their civil law rights and performing civil law obligations' (article 1(3)). Article 1(4) adds that nobody has a right to gain an advantage from their unlawful or bad faith behaviour. The principle of good faith has been formulated as an 'open rule' as in other continental legal systems (Germany, France, Netherlands, etc). This strongly suggests that it is meant to serve as a legal mechanism for judicial law-making, as the principle of good faith does in other continental legal systems.

Together with the introduction of a positive obligation to act in good faith into CC article 1, CC article 10 was amended explicitly to enshrine a negative prohibition against bad faith behaviour. According to CC article 10(1), 'Limits of Effectuation of Civil Rights':

> The effectuation of rights exclusively with the intention to cause harm to another person, actions aiming with unlawful purpose at the evasion of law, as well as *other knowingly bad faith effectuation of rights (abuse of right)* is not allowed. (emphasis added)

Thus the converse of good faith behaviour – that is, bad faith behaviour – has been equated with the concept of abuse of rights already widely accepted in Russian civil law. It could be argued that this is not necessarily correct from a theoretical perspective, but the approach fully complies with established court practice.[180]

Treating bad faith behaviour as equal to abuse of rights, CC article 10 (in its new version) suggests the following remedies available to courts, depending on circumstances, when they discover bad faith behaviour: refusing to protect the rights of a person who behaves in bad faith in full or in part, or applying other remedies provided by a law or the Civil Code.

So far the Civil Code only explicitly provides consequences of bad faith behaviour in CC article 302 dealing with the protection of rights of a good faith purchaser of property in circumstances when it had been purchased from a person with no right to dispose of it. This rule already existed and was also applied extensively in the absence of a general principle of good faith. So far no other federal laws regulating civil law relations have stipulated any specific consequences for bad faith behaviour.

The new version of article 10(4) also provides the right of a participant in civil law relations (of which contractual relations form a part) to claim damages for the violation of rights through bad faith behaviour.

The most recent amendments have kept in CC article 10(5) the presumption of good faith which already existed from the time of adoption of Part One of the Civil Code (then in CC article 10(3)). This presumption shifts the burden of proof of bad faith behaviour to the person who is alleging it, or to the court, if

[180] This court practice is discussed by S Yakovleva, 'Принцип добросовестности и запрет злоупотребления правом в договорном праве' ['*Printsip dobrosovestnosti i zapret zloupotrebliniia pravom v dogovornom prave*; The Principle of Good Faith and Prohibition of Abuse of Right in Contract Law'] (2010) 11 Хозяйство и Право [*Khoziaistvo i Pravo*] 60.

it is applying the consequences of bad faith behaviour on its own initiative. The 2012 amendments have broadened the scope of its application. Previously, the presumption was applicable only 'in instances when a law makes defence of civil rights dependent upon whether these rights have been effectuated reasonably and in good faith'.[181] The current version of the presumption no longer has that limitation. According to CC article 10(5) 'good faith of the participants of civil law relations and reasonableness of their actions is presupposed'. So the new amendments have extended the scope of application of the presumption to all civil law relations.

Despite the law-makers' attempt to limit judicial discretion in the application of the principle of good faith by providing (even if only through referring to other laws and Civil Code provisions) particular remedies which the courts may apply to punish bad faith behaviour, it seems unlikely that any limitations will be strictly applied in practice.

The fact that the Civil Code did not explicitly mention the principle of good faith before 2012 did not stop the courts from applying it. Through analysis of court practice, Yakovleva demonstrates that at least for the last 15 years the courts have implied a principle of good faith in Russian contract law and have decided cases as if the principle was in the Civil Code. The courts inferred it from various Civil Code articles (6, 10, 309, 431) and, at times, even declared it to be one of the fundamental principles of Russian contract law.[182]

In spite of the principle of freedom of contract, courts have applied the principle of good faith contrary to the express terms in contracts and, at times, even contrary to the law, to correct the incompleteness of contracts, balance asymmetry of expertise and protect the reasonable expectations of the contractual parties.[183] Of course, on occasion the courts have also applied the implicit principle of good faith for no particularly obvious reason.

In order to correct the adverse consequences of bad faith behaviour of one party the courts have ignored or changed explicit contractual terms. Referring to the principle of good faith, they have obliged one party in the course of performance of its obligations to take into account the interests of the other, and imposed additional obligations on the parties over and above those the contract provided, including an obligation to compensate for losses caused by bad faith performance, even though based on the actual contractual terms the performance could be considered as proper.[184] All in all, the courts have not felt constrained in choosing the remedy they regarded as appropriate in the particular circumstances, in the absence of any relevant legal provisions.

[181] Butler, above n 104 at 15.

[182] S Yakovleva 'Принцип добросовестности в договорном праве: российское законодательство и судебная практика' ['*Printsip dobrosovestnosti v dogovornom prave: rossiiskoe zakonodatelstvo i sudebnaia praktika*; Principle of Good Faith in Contract Law: Russian Legislation and Court Practice'] (2009) 1 *Хозяйство и Право* [Khoziaistvo i Pravo] 105.

[183] Ibid 111–20.

[184] Yakovleva, above n 180, at 60–1.

This is why it seems unlikely that, with the explicit provision in the Civil Code of the principle of good faith, the courts will be any more accurate now in applying the consequences of bad faith behaviour. Moreover, shortly after the respective amendments to CC articles 1 and 10 entered into force, the Head of Administration of the Supreme Commercial Court, Andrei Egorov, in an interview published in the online legal information portal www.pravo.ru, acknowledged that the new principle of good faith does give broader possibilities for judicial discretion. The law-makers cannot foresee everything in the law, hence, the court should have a chance to take care of any gaps on a temporary basis, and then the law-makers may agree or not with the courts by correcting the problem through legislation. Egorov also admitted that the courts may apply the principle of good faith to justify *contra legem* (against the letter of the law) interpretation.[185] This approach might in earlier times have been regarded as quite heretical.

VIII CONCLUSION

This chapter has covered a lot of ground in order to create for the reader a picture of the legal world in Russia within which the contract law described in the succeeding chapters operates. Clearly it is not comprehensive, but we have tried to select relevant information. We also highlight some of the main principles of contract law, an understanding of which will complement the more detailed exposition to follow.

[185] N Shiniaeva, Роль бабушки в судейском усмотрении [*Rol' babushki v sudeiskom usmotrenii;* The Role of Grandmother [Babushka] in Judicial Discretion] (20 May 2013), available at pravo.ru/review/view/85224/.

2

The Terms of a Contract

I INTRODUCTION

Terms lie at the heart of contract law. They define for each of the contractual parties their rights and obligations under the contract. In Russian law, there is a tension between freedom of contract – one of the fundamental principles of modern Russian contract law[1] – and the convenience of particular types of contract having their terms set by the Civil Code (CC). Thus, on the one hand, parties are free to choose contractual terms at their own discretion (CC article 421(4)), and on the other, a court may decide that the nature of their contract makes it a particular type, and therefore by default includes any mandatory terms the Code specifies. Furthermore, the court may find that certain terms of the contract do not comply with the Civil Code rules for that type of contract and, therefore, are invalid and are not considered part of the contract even though the parties agreed to them. That consequence is discussed in more detail in Chapter 6 at p 128. Basically in Russian contract law the will of the legislator predominates over the will of the contracting parties, which may seem a rather incongruous legislative solution, considering that the main goal of contract law is to enforce agreements between parties on the terms they choose.

This chapter deals with the framework and rules for deciding what are the terms of a contract, their impact and interpretation. This chapter also deals with the classification of contracts into types in Russian contract law and explains the implications of that classification.

II TERMS VERSUS REPRESENTATIONS

Although, as we see below, in Russian contract law there are different classifications of contractual terms, there is currently no equivalent of representations as found in English law, that is, precontractual statements which, if false, make the contract voidable. In Russian law, when parties conclude a contract in due form, they are bound by its terms, and in general all other statements made before the contract was concluded have no legal effect.

[1] Made explicit in CC arts 1(1) and 421(1).

However, in some situations the courts take a different approach and treat statements made before the contract was concluded similarly to representations in English law. The following case is a good example of the courts deciding that a contract had no legal effect because statements made by one party before the contract was made misled the other.

> Pensioner P concluded a contract of maintenance of a dependant for life (договор пожизненного содержания; *dogovor pozhiznennogo soderzhaniia*) with company A. Under the contract P transferred her flat to A in return for A paying P an immediate lump sum followed by monthly stipends, and also A covering the cost of P's utility bills. The contract was signed by both parties in the presence of a notary and was duly notarised as required by law.
>
> However, the Civil Code also requires state registration of contracts of maintenance of a dependant for life (CC article 584) and such a contract will only take effect after state registration. Both parties need to apply for registration. In this case P refused to apply and A sued to enforce her application for the required state registration. During the hearing P claimed that she was an old woman and A had exploited her legal illiteracy to persuade her to sign the contract. She said that A led her to believe that if she signed, she would also get nursing care; as a disabled and elderly person that belief was a material inducement.
>
> The Supreme Court stated that when parties sign a contract they are supposed to be expressing a mutual will to establish their contractual relationship; they exercise free will to bind themselves to an agreement. However in the opinion of the Court in this case P was misled about the nature of the contract and circumstances which had material significance, and as a result signed a contract which put her in a worse position. The Court held that P had not exercised her free will in entering into the contractual relationship on the terms provided and the contract should therefore not be enforced.[2]

Here the Supreme Court took an approach similar to an English court dealing with a false representation, refusing, in circumstances for which the Civil Code does not directly provide, to enforce an apparently valid contract.

The Supreme Court's approach clearly epitomises the courts' aspiration to protect weaker members of society. This protective approach is more common in the courts of general jurisdiction, in contrast to the commercial courts, because the general jurisdiction courts hear cases involving individuals. The commercial courts hear business disputes and work on the principle that businesses act at their own risk, as explicitly stated in CC article 2(1).[3] In some situations the

[2] Ruling of Supreme Court of the Russian Federation of 23 June 2009 No 5-V09-51.

[3] WE Butler, *The Civil Code of the Russian Federation Parts 1, 2 and 3: Parallel Russian and English Texts* (Moscow, JurInfoR-Press, 2008) 8: 'Article 2(1)(3) Civil legislation shall regulate

commercial courts will also protect weaker contractual parties, but in a much more limited range of situations. These are considered below in relation to interpretation of contracts.

In the case of P, the Court did not refer to the Civil Code provisions on either delusion or fraud. However, the Code does provide remedies for these in CC articles 178 and 179, respectively. As well as fraud, CC article 179 also deals with the effect of 'coercion, threat, or ill-intentioned agreement of a representative of one party with the other party'[4] and undue influence.

CC article 179(1) states that a transaction concluded under the influence of fraud (or another of the vitiating circumstances) may be deemed invalid by a court following an application by the victim. As claimant, they must prove *the presence of fraud in a positive action* by the defendant. Analyses of cases where CC article 179 has been applied shows the fraud to be some action preceding the contract's conclusion.

As the Federal Commercial Court of the North Caucasus District explained in one of its Resolutions,[5] CC article 179 presupposes that *fraud is a deliberate misrepresentation with the purpose of inducing the other party to enter a transaction.* The inducing party intentionally portrays the transaction in a way which does not correspond with its actual character, its terms, the characteristics of the participants and other circumstances which affect the other party's decision.

CC article 178(1) allows a victim to apply for a declaration of invalidity of a transaction concluded under the influence of *delusion* (заблуждение; *zabluzhdenie*). The Code explains that:

> delusion is relative to the nature of the transaction, the identity of such qualities of its subject which significantly reduce the possibility of using it for its purpose shall have material significance. Delusion relative to the motives for the transaction shall not have material significance.[6]

In applying CC articles 178 and 179, the courts analyse statements made before the contract is concluded. Thus they have created a concept of representations even though currently the text of the Civil Code neither recognises nor regulates them.

The consequences of deceit and misrepresentation are discussed in more detail in Chapter 6 at p 153.

It should be pointed out that soon representations may become a part of the Civil Code. Draft Amendments to the Civil Code under preparation suggest

relations between persons effectuating entrepreneurial activity or with the participation thereof, proceeding from the fact that autonomous activity effectuated at one's own risk directed towards the systematic obtaining of profit from the use of property, the sale of goods, the fulfilment of work, or the rendering of services by persons registered in this capacity in the procedure established by law shall be entrepreneurial'.

[4] Butler, above n 3, at 157.

[5] Resolution of 9 December 2008 No F08-6849/2008, case No 63-4852/07-S1.

[6] Butler, above n 3, at 156–7.

that article 431.2 'Representations' (заверения об обстоятельствах; *zavereniia ob obstoiatel'stvakh*) may be introduced. According to this article, representations are defined as 'statements regarding the circumstances which are important for the conclusion of the contract or its performance'.[7] However, false representations will not make a contract voidable, as such. Instead the party who relied on a false representation which had material significance is given the right unilaterally to refuse to perform the contract and, thus, terminate it. The party would also have a right to claim damages caused by reliance on the false representations.[8]

III TERMS: EXPRESS AND IMPLIED

A Distinction between Express and Implied Terms

In neither Russian legislation nor commentary by contract law scholars is the distinction between express terms and implied terms discussed. However, it does exist.

The situation is clear for express terms: the contractual parties are bound by contract terms to which they agreed in the form provided for by law. Once bound, there is the possibility of release by the contract being avoided on various grounds, discussed further in Chapter 6 at p 126.

(i) Mandatory and Dispositive Norms

Russian law takes the approach that it is impossible for the parties to regulate by express terms all possible contract-related situations. To make contractual interactions easier and more predictable, codified systems of law, such as Russia, regulate contractual relations by means of mandatory and dispositive norms (legal rules). Mandatory norms (also known as imperative norms, or imperative rules) are compulsory prescriptions which the parties must comply with, whenever the conditions specified in the norm are met. Non-compliance with a mandatory norm is a breach of law. A mandatory norm regulating contractual relations of a certain type applies to all contracts of that type. The parties to a contract cannot choose not to apply a mandatory norm. For example, CC article 859(1) stipulates that a contract of bank account may be terminated upon application of the client at any time. This is a mandatory norm and so applies to any contract of bank account. If the parties to a contract of a bank account agree that the contract cannot be terminated by the client's application, that term would not be valid as it contradicts a mandatory norm of the Civil Code.

[7] Draft Federal Law on Amendments to Parts One, Two, Three and Four of the Civil Code of the Russian Federation, and certain other legal acts of the Russian Federation No 47538-6 approved by the State Duma at first reading on 27 April 2012 art 1 para 222.

[8] Ibid.

The client would have the right to apply to court to have the contract deemed void for illegality (for more on this, see Chapter 6 at p 136).

By contrast, dispositive norms set out a rule but also allow the parties to regulate that aspect of their contractual relationship differently. The dispositive norms would apply when the parties have not specifically included in their contract their own terms to deal with the particular situation. For instance, CC article 711(1) provides that:

> unless preliminary payment for work fulfilled or individual stages thereof has been provided for by the contract of independent-work, the customer shall be obliged to pay the independent-work contractor the stipulated price after the final handing over of the results of the work.[9]

This is a dispositive norm which allows the parties to provide for pre-payment or staged payment for the work. If the parties do not bother to do so, the default rule in the dispositive norm will apply and payment will be due on completion.

Some dispositive norms give the parties more freedom. For example, CC article 957(1) stipulates that: 'A contract of insurance, unless provided otherwise therein, shall enter into force from the moment of payment of the insurance premium or first contribution thereof'.[10] Here the law gives the parties an opportunity to agree whatever term they like defining when the insurance contract enters into force; they do not have to choose between limited alternatives.

In other words, mandatory norms predominate over the will of the parties, while dispositive norms substitute for the expression of the will of the parties when they have decided not to express it.

These Civil Code norms constitute a part of a contract, that is, they can be treated as *terms implied by statute*. Applicable mandatory norms are always a part of a contract and applicable dispositive norms are a part of a contract when the parties have not expressly provided alternative terms.

A dispositive norm offers a 'template' contractual term but parties are free to alter it or include their own term relating to that issue. As an example of a dispositive norm for a particular issue, CC article 456(2) stipulates that:

> Unless provided otherwise by the contract of purchase-sale, the seller shall be obliged simultaneously with the transfer of the thing to transfer to the purchaser the appurtenances thereto (technical passport, certificate of quality, instructions relating to operation and so forth) provided for by a law, other legal acts, or the contract.[11]

Thus, if the parties do not expressly include a term dealing with the transference of such 'appurtenances', a term requiring simultaneous transfer as specified in CC article 456(2) will be implied. If the parties expressly agree a different arrangement, their express term applies.

[9] Butler, above n 3, at 498.
[10] Ibid 663.
[11] Ibid 331.

Furthermore, CC article 421(5) provides that 'If the condition of a contract has not been determined by the parties or by a dispositive norm, the respective conditions shall be determined by the customs of business turnover applicable to the relations of the parties'.[12] The Civil Code defines a custom of business turnover as 'a rule of behaviour which has been formed and extensively applied in any domain of entrepreneurial activity and is not provided for by legislation irrespective of whether it has been fixed in any document'.[13] (CC article 5(1)). It is analogous to a term implied by 'custom or trade usage' in English law.[14]

The Civil Code contains both general norms (general rules) on contracts and norms which regulate particular types of contracts. General norms are terms implied into all contracts. For example, there is a general norm that a promisee has a right to claim damages for a breach of contract (CC article 393(1)); this is implied in any contract regulated by Russian law.

B Types of Contract

(i) Classification of Contracts in the Civil Code

As in other codified legal systems, Russian law uses the concept of *types of contract*. The Civil Code provides an open-ended list of types of contract, recognising that others may exist. Those listed are regulated in Part Two of the Code, and are the following types of contracts (in the order they are dealt with there):

- contract of purchase-sale;
- contract of barter;
- contract of gift;
- contract of rent and contract of maintenance of dependant for life;
- contract of lease;
- contract of rental of dwelling premises;
- contract of uncompensated use;
- contract of independent work;
- contract for fulfilment of scientific research, experimental-construction design and technological work;
- contract of compensated rendering of services;
- contract of carriage;
- contract of transport expediting;
- contract of loan and contract of credit;
- contract of financing under assignment of monetary demand;
- contract of bank deposit;
- contract of bank account;

[12] Ibid 306.

[13] Ibid 11.

[14] As, eg, in *Hutton v Warren* (1836) 1 M&W 466; *British Crane Hire Corporation Ltd v Ipswich Plant Hire Ltd* [1975] QB 303.

- settlement of accounts;
- contract of keeping;
- contract of insurance;
- contract of mandate;
- contract of commission;
- contract of commission agency;
- contract of trust management of property;
- contract of commercial concession;
- contract of simple partnership.

These types of contracts sometimes have specific subtypes. For example, the contract of lease has the following subtypes: contract of rental; contract of lease of means of transport; contract of lease of buildings and installations; contract of lease of enterprises; and contract of finance lease.

(ii) Distinguishing Types of Contract by Subject Matter

Types of contract are distinguished by the *subject matter of the contract* (предмет договора; *predmet dogovora*). The subject matter of a contract is supposed to be the core of the contractual relationship, the substance of a contract, the attribute that distinguishes that contract from any other. However, it would be wrong to say that a contract has one single subject matter. Under CC article 307(2), contract is one of the 'grounds for an obligation' (other grounds include the consequence of causing harm – the Russian equivalent of common law tortuous liability). In general, the subject matter of an obligation is the action which one party, the promisor, is obliged to perform to the benefit of the other, the promisee. In a bilateral contract, the parties will each have an obligation, but the subject matters will differ. For example, a contract of purchase-sale is the ground for two main obligations: the seller's obligation to transfer property in the goods to the buyer and the buyer's obligation to pay the purchase price to the seller. Thus, the subject matter of a contract is the combination of the subject matters of the different obligations under that contract.

In creating their list of types of contract, those drafting the Civil Code used the most common combinations of subject matters to create a useful set of 'templates'. For all other contracts there is freedom of contract: parties are free to enter into any contract not listed in the Civil Code, provided only that it will 'correspond to rules established by a law and other legal acts (imperative [mandatory] norms) which are binding on the parties and prevailing at the moment of its conclusion' (CC article 422(1)).[15]

The Civil Code regulates each particular type of contract by: providing a definition of contracts of that type; specifying the mandatory norms which apply to them; and setting out any dispositive norms for that contract type. (See above

[15] Butler, above n 3, at 306.

at p 53 for discussion of mandatory and dispositive norms.) As noted, mandatory norms will apply to all contracts of the particular type without the need for express incorporation; the Civil Code will always imply them into those types of contracts.

(iii) Qualification of a Contract

In theory freedom of contract Russian style looks simple: if parties do not want to use a template offered by the authors of the Code, they are free to use any contractual structure they like. In practice however this freedom is tempered by the concept 'qualification of a contract'.

Qualification of a contract is an analytical process used by courts to establish what type a particular contract is. It is one of the first things a court does in resolving any contract dispute. To 'qualify a contract' the court considers the subject matter of the contract, leading to the following possible outcomes.

Situation 1: the court qualifies the contract as being of a type provided for in the Civil Code. The court then applies the parties' contractual terms, provided that there are no relevant mandatory norms in the Civil Code. If there are mandatory norms, the court determines whether or not the parties' contract terms are consistent with them, and if not, has the power to declare any inconsistent terms invalid. This is a discretionary power, based on CC article 167 (for more detail see Chapter 6 at p 136). If the contract does not have terms expressly regulating a particular issue, the court will apply the relevant provisions of the Code for that particular type of contract to fill in the gap. The court's finding as to 'type' overrides any views of the parties, although there could be grounds for an appeal.

Situation 2: the court qualifies a contract as 'mixed', that is, as combining elements of two or more of the different types provided for in legislation. CC article 421(3) explicitly allows that 'The parties may conclude a contract which contains elements of various contracts provided for by a law or other legal acts (mixed contracts)'.[16] In a mixed contract, the relevant elements of the different types of contracts are applicable. For example, if a contract provides that party A will deliver elevators to a construction site and then install them, the contract will be qualified as a mixed contract, containing elements of a contract of purchase-sale and a contract of independent work. The court will apply all the parties' agreed contractual terms so long as there are no relevant mandatory norms applicable to either of these types of contract. If there are mandatory norms for the types of constituent contracts, they will be applied but only to the part of the mixed contract which belongs to that particular type of contract.

In a mixed contract, application of norms relevant to different types of contract can lead to interesting results. The Supreme Commercial Court resolved a dispute between the parties to a contract of financial lease of manufacturing

[16] Ibid 305.

equipment. The Court's decision gives a good example of how rules provided in legislation for different types of contracts may be applied to one particular contract.

> Under a contract of financial lease, one party, leasing company A, agreed to buy manufacturing equipment and provide it to the other party, company B, the lessee, in return for a periodic payment. The contractual lease period was 29 months, after which the equipment would become B's property.
>
> A had purchased the equipment and provided it to B. B initially made payments as stipulated in the contract but after some time stopped. The contract of financial lease was discharged for breach at the behest of A, and the equipment returned to them. B claimed for the return of the payments already made, since there was no longer a lease agreement and the equipment was back in A's possession. The lower courts held that the inclusion in the contract of a term providing for the transfer from A to B of property rights to the equipment constituted an element of purchase-sale. Thus the contract was classified as mixed, combining elements of financial lease and purchase-sale.
>
> Applying the rules relevant to contracts of purchase-sale, the lower courts classified the payments made in accordance with the contract of financial lease as a purchase price, with the equipment being the subject of the sale. Since the agreement was discharged and the parties' obligations terminated, A had no legal ground to keep the money paid under the contract.
>
> The Supreme Commercial Court held that the lower courts had applied the law incorrectly. Both the Civil Code provisions and other specific legislation on leasing include the possibility of transferring property rights over the leased items at the end of the lease term. During the lease, periodic payments are not made as a part of a purchase price but as payment for use of the property which belongs to the leasing company. Here B was using the equipment and paying A for its use, so there was no legal basis for the money already paid to be returned, and no need to apply any purchase-sale provisions.
>
> The Supreme Commercial Court agreed that the contract was mixed, but held that the payments stipulated in the contract were rent for the lease not a purchase price for the equipment.[17]

As with contracts of a single type (situation 1 above), if a court finds that contract terms in a mixed-type contract contradict Civil Code norms, it has the power to declare those terms invalid. If a particular issue is not expressly regulated by the contract, the court will apply the Code provisions for the relevant type of contract, to fill the gap.

[17] Resolution of Supreme Commercial Court of 18 May 2010 No 1729/10.

Difficult situations can arise when the court cannot separate one subject matter from another. That can result in the application of irrelevant Civil Code norms, or failure to apply relevant ones, as in the first instance decision in the leasing case above.

Situation 3: the final alternative is that the court may qualify a contract as 'non-classified' (непоименованный; *nepoimenovannyi*) in the Civil Code or other legislation. Usually courts prefer to qualify a contract as a type regulated by legislation because it saves them a lot of effort. However, sometimes they have to qualify a contract as non-classified in legislation. When it happens, only the general rules in the Civil Code on transactions, obligations and contracts will apply, as in this example.

> Under a contract between company A and commercial telephone network company B, A allowed B to install a telecom cable in a cable duct belonging to A. B failed to pay for use of the cable duct and A sued for payment.
>
> At first instance the commercial court classified the contract between the parties as rent of real property. In the court's opinion, the cable duct was a piece of real property and under the contract A allowed B possession and use of it. Transfer of the right to possess and use real property is the subject matter of a contract of rent of real estate. CC article 608 provides that a lessor should be the owner (or other person empowered by the owner) so the party to a contract of rent must prove that they have the relevant property right in order to receive rent; A failed to prove this and the contract was held void as contradicting the law.
>
> The Court of Appeal disagreed. Its decision to annul the first instance ruling was supported by both the Court of Cassation and the Supreme Commercial Court. The higher courts explained that the subject matter of this contract was not equivalent to the subject matter in a contract of rent of real estate. Here, the cable duct was used for cables belonging to different providers, including both A and B. Thus it could not be said that B had possession and use as in a contract of rent of real estate.
>
> The higher courts held that the contract here was *sui generis*; no relevant equivalent contract form was defined anywhere in the Civil Code or other legislation. Consequently, the rules on rent were not applicable and the contract was a valid non-classified contract. It was enforced by reference to the Civil Code general provisions on due performance.[18]

It is possible that in the course of the qualification process the court will state that the contract belongs to one of the types of contracts provided for in the Code but that the necessary *material terms of the contract* have not been agreed by the parties and thus *there is no contract* (the contract is considered to be not concluded). This situation seems perverse especially when we bear in mind that

[18] Ruling of Supreme Commercial Court of 3 March 2011 No VAS-2032/11.

it can happen even when the parties have already performed the contract (this is thoroughly discussed in Chapter 6 at p 156).

Draft Amendments to the Civil Code introduce a new provision which stipulates that norms for particular types of contract shall not be applicable to contracts which are not contracts of that type or mixed contracts.[19] It can be argued that anyway this follows logically from the current text of the Code. We can only hope that if this is brought into force the innovation will indeed make courts more considerate in relation to the parties' freedom to regulate their own contractual relations in the most convenient and reasonable way.

IV MATERIAL TERMS

A Definition of Material Terms

The concept of the material terms of a contract is one of the cornerstones of Russian contract law. CC article 432(1) provides that 'A contract shall be considered to be concluded when agreement regarding all the material conditions [terms] of the contract has been reached in the form required in appropriate instances'.[20] Thus the contract cannot exist unless the parties have agreed on its material terms; it will be deemed to be not concluded (see Chapter 6 at p 156 for more on the consequences of this).

This raises the issue: if there is an apparent contract, which the parties are in the process of carrying out, how can it be considered not to be concluded? To answer that question first we need to consider in more detail what are the material terms of a contract.

There are three kinds of material terms: terms setting out the subject matter; terms stipulated in legislation as being material for the particular type of contract; and any terms defined as material by one of the parties to the contract.

B Subject Matter as a Material Term

As noted above (at p 56), the subject matter is the core of a contract; the characteristic which distinguishes one contract from another. Since the principle of freedom of contract means that parties have the right to conclude any contract, whether or not it is of a type provided for in legislation, it follows that every contract could be regarded as unique, with its own subject matter. However, in practice courts often declare contracts 'not concluded' because the parties have not agreed expressly on the subject matter. A good example of this is the Supreme Commercial Court decision in 2011, upholding the lower courts' decisions.

[19] Draft Federal Law on Amendments, above n 7, art 1 para 214 amending CC art 421(2).
[20] Butler, above n 3, at 313.

Under a contract between companies A and B, B undertook to provide the services of pre-sales preparation, introduction into operation, and guaranteed technical support for A's tram carriages.

B sent an invoice which A paid. Later, A claimed that the contract was not concluded and sued for return of the payment. The courts held that the subject matter of the contract had not been agreed by the parties; in a contract where the subject matter is services, the contract should contain an agreed list of the services which the service provider is obliged to perform. Here, the contract between A and B did not contain any such list and thus was considered not concluded. The money paid was therefore to be considered unfounded enrichment of B and A was able to recover it on that basis.[21]

Another example of the Supreme Commercial Court agreeing with the lower courts that a contract was not concluded involved a contract for postal services.

The courts noted that one party's copy of the contract contained a list of 24 delivery destination points, while the other party's had 37. As a result, the courts concluded that the parties had not agreed about the subject matter of the contract and so the contract was not concluded.[22]

As noted above at p 56 on distinguishing types of contract by subject matter, the subject matter of a contract is the core of the contractual relationship; that is, those actions which the contractual parties oblige themselves to perform under the contract. However, there is another possible meaning of the phrase 'subject matter of contract'.

When the parties' actions relate to an *individually-defined thing* (индивидуально-определенная вещь; *individual'no-opredelennaia veshch'*), the thing itself is often called the subject matter of the contract. For example, in a contract for a sale of a house, the house itself may be called the subject matter of the contract. Technically, this is incorrect. The actual subject matter of this contract is the parties' actions of, on the one hand, transferring ownership of the house and, on the other, paying the purchase price. However, the terminology frequently (and confusingly) may be used incorrectly as described.

To conclude a contract involving an individually-defined thing, it is necessary to provide a description of it which is sufficient to distinguish it from other similar items. If, in the opinion of the court, the thing is not sufficiently identified, the court can decide that the parties have not agreed on the subject matter of the contract and thus the contract is not concluded. This is a particular issue in transactions involving real property, because that is always regarded as an individually-defined thing. The consequences of a failure to describe such a thing sufficiently can be seen in the following example.

[21] Ruling of Supreme Commercial Court of 15 March 2011 No VAS-907/11.

[22] Ruling of Supreme Commercial Court of 29 July 2010 No VAS-10329/10.

> The Russian Ministry of Defence signed an investment contract with construction company D, under which the Ministry would provide a plot of land on which D would construct a block of flats. In return, once the block was completed, D would transfer ownership of eight of the flats to the Ministry.
>
> The block of flats was built, however in breach of the contract D registered rights to all the flats to third parties and failed to transfer any to the Ministry. The Ministry claimed damages for breach. The courts held that the land plot which the Ministry had provided was not sufficiently identified in the contract. The only characteristic mentioned was the size of the plot and its address. No plan was provided, and the plot was not included in the official State Cadastre of Land. Thus, in accordance with CC article 432, the subject matter of the contract was not agreed upon, so the contract was not concluded; consequently the Ministry had no right to damages for breach. The court held that the registration number and a plan of the plot are de facto necessary to define a land plot. Without registration with the State Cadastre of Land it was also impossible to obtain a cadastre plan of the plot, individually identifying it.[23]

The court did not pay any attention to the fact that the address and dimensions could be sufficient to define the plot. The parties had clearly expressed their will to transfer the land plot and knew which plot it was. In declaring the contract not concluded the court was following a norm of the Code formally and keeping literally to the text but failing to respect the parties' will as expressed in the contract.

C Terms Mentioned in the Code or Other Legislation as Material for the Particular Type of Contract

There are a number of different ways in which the legislator can indicate that a certain term is material for a particular type of contract. This variety results from imperfections of legal technique and can lead to unfortunate controversies about what is, and what is not, a material term.

Some articles of the Civil Code and other legislation directly state that certain terms are material for particular types of contracts. This excludes any misunderstanding and uncertainty. For example, CC article 942, entitled 'Material Conditions of Contract of Insurance', provides an exhaustive list of the material terms for a contract of insurance.[24]

Alternatively, the Code may not specify that a particular term is material but will stipulate that if such a term is not agreed for inclusion in the contract, the contract will be considered not concluded.

[23] Ruling of Supreme Commercial Court of 30 December 2010 No VAS-17142/10.

[24] Butler, above n 3, at 653–4. Briefly, these are (1) the thing or person insured; (2) the event insured against; (3) the insured amount; and (4) the period of operation of the contract.

A third way to indicate that a particular term is material is by indicating that the parties should agree such a term, although not explicitly specifying it to be material. A good example of this is in the contract of independent work. CC article 708(1) states that 'The beginning and the ending periods of fulfilment of the work shall be specified in the contract of independent work'.[25] The fact that the Code does not explicitly say that the beginning and ending periods are material terms led to litigation and some very controversial court practice. Finally, in 2000, the Supreme Commercial Court directly ruled that a contract of independent work is not concluded if it does not establish the relevant times.[26]

A number of legal scholars believe (and for some time this view was also reflected in court decisions) that *price* is a material condition of any contract for which the Civil Code, when defining the subject matter of the contract, mentions that one party pays the contract price or other remuneration. Very often a court will consider price to be a material term when the parties agreed in the contract that they would stipulate the price in an addendum to the contract but then failed to do so,[27] or fail to be sufficiently precise in the contract. The following is an example.

> In 2009 the Supreme Commercial Court declared a contract for a transfer of trademarks void because the price for the transferred trademarks had not been explicitly stated. The Court held that the contract stipulated that it was concluded on a 'reimbursable basis' (in a contract for compensation) but did not state the sum to be paid. The Court held that the parties clearly considered the price to be a material term but failed to stipulate it in the contract. Thus, in the Court's opinion, the whole contract should be considered not concluded.[28]

However, it is submitted that it is wrong for a court to deny the existence of a contract merely because the price is not explicit. This approach contradicts both the Civil Code's wording and logic. Price is a contract term specifically regulated in the Civil Code's 'General Provisions on Contract'.[29] Within that subsection, the first paragraph of article 424(1) states 'The performance of a contract shall be paid for at the price, established by agreement of the parties'.[30] CC article 424(3) adds:

[25] Ibid 495.

[26] Informational Circular of Presidium of the Supreme Commercial Court of 24 January 2000 No 51 Part 4 'Review of Court Practice on Resolution of Disputes Arising out of Contracts of Independent Work'; Informational Circular of Plenum of Supreme Commercial Court of 25 November 2008 No 127 Part 6 'Review of Court Practice on the Application of Article 10 of the Civil Code'.

[27] Resolution of Federal Commercial Court of Moscow District of 31 July 2009 No KG-A41/5653-09, case No A41-26955/08; Resolution of Federal Commercial Court of Moscow District of 6 December 2004 No KG-A41/11213-04.

[28] In Ruling of 17 September 2009 No VAS-11880/09.

[29] Butler, above n 3, at 304.

[30] Ibid 307.

> In instances when in a contract for compensation the price has not been provided for and may not be determined by proceeding from the conditions of the contract, the performance of the contract must be paid for at the price which under comparable circumstances usually is recovered for analogous goods, work or services.[31]

This clearly provides a solution for the exact situation described above,[32] contrary to the view of those courts which have given lack of explicit price as grounds to declare a contract not concluded.

Applying CC article 424(3) necessitates determining 'the price which under comparable circumstances usually is recovered for analogous goods, work or services'. Courts have applied different techniques for this. For example, in a case in 2010, the Supreme Commercial Court agreed with the lower courts' logic in the following case.

> A state-owned enterprise (seller, S) signed a contract for the delivery of coal to a municipal company (buyer, B). S delivered the agreed amount of coal to B, who accepted delivery. B failed to pay for the coal so S sued. The courts found that the contract did not stipulate the price of the coal and applied CC article 424 to define the price to be paid by B. The courts examined other contracts S had made with other buyers of coal and calculated an average price for one tonne of coal based on these. They then compared the price S was claiming from B with this average price and found that S was actually claiming below the average. The court was happy to enforce S's claim against B and treat it as 'the price which under comparable circumstances usually is recovered for analogous goods, work or services' despite the fact that it was actually lower than in other comparable contracts.[33]

The approach illustrated by the case above is popular with the courts even though it does not literally follow the rule in CC article 424(3). It is more of an 'accept whatever price the promisee asks so long as the judges deem it reasonable' approach. The following is another example of similarly pragmatic logic.

> The courts declared invalid the terms of a contract for legal services which stipulated a 10 per cent contingency fee for winning a court case. However, legal services had been provided and the courts had to apply CC article 424(3) to determine a price. They concluded that a payment of 10 per cent of the sum awarded was reasonable and so accepted it to be 'the price which under comparable circumstances usually is recovered for analogous goods, work or services', thus in fact applying a term which the courts had earlier invalidated.[34]

[31] Ibid.
[32] See above, text to n 28.
[33] Ruling of Supreme Commercial Court of 9 July 2010 No VAS-8530/10.
[34] Ruling of Supreme Commercial Court of 4 March 2009 No 17483/08.

D Terms Defined as Material by the Parties to the Contract

The third type of material terms are terms defined as material by the parties themselves. Unfortunately, it is not clear what steps a party conducting precontractual negotiations should take to ensure that a particular term will be considered material. The courts have developed two inconsistent approaches.

In the first, the court may consider all terms, which one party asked to be included in the contract, to be material. However, this can easily result in the contract being deemed not concluded.

Contracts are concluded by offer and acceptance (see Chapter 4 for details). Unfortunately, during precontractual negotiations it is not uncommon for an offeror to send the offeree a draft contract which the offeree duly returns signed but at the same time sends to the offeror a signed discrepancy report (протокол разногласий; *protocol raznoglasii*) proposing the removal of particular terms or use of different terminology. This results in uncertainty over which terms are actually in the contract.

If the dispute comes to court, the result frequently is that the court holds the contract to be not concluded. It reasons that the discrepancy report is a new offer, in which its author, the initial offeree, specifies terms which they consider material; if the discrepancy report is then not signed by the initial offeror the parties have not agreed upon all material terms and hence the contract is not concluded.[35]

In the second approach, the court may ignore claims by one party that certain terms should be considered material because that party had insisted that they should be included into the contract. This has the advantage that it tends to preserve the apparent contract rather than declare it not concluded, but of course leaves the party without the material term they had hoped to include.

To add further complication, in many cases the attempt by one party to prove that the contract was not concluded may be considered by the court to be an abuse of right (злоупотребление правом; *zloupotreblenie pravom*). The Supreme Commercial Court took this position in a case in 2011. The example deals with the type of material terms discussed in the previous section but it illustrates the point about an abuse of right.

> A dispute arose over a contract for construction works. For this type of contract, CC articles 702 and 708 define the beginning and end dates to be material terms. However, in the disputed contract these dates had not been specified. After the construction was complete, one party, the client, claimed that the contract was not concluded, as it lacked material terms.
>
> In its rejection of this, the Supreme Commercial Court explained that the purpose of the Civil Code rules about the mandatory inclusion of the

[35] Resolution of Federal Commercial Court of East-Siberian District of 10 April 2006, case No A78-11270/05-C1-1/331-F02-1491/06-C2.

> beginning and end dates in construction contracts was to provide legal certainty for the contracting parties. However, once construction is completed by the contractor and accepted by the client, there can be no such uncertainty. Thus the actual dates should be considered as part of the contract and the contract therefore considered concluded.[36]

The Court also highlighted one very crucial point: when resolving disputes over the conclusion of a contract, courts should evaluate as a whole all the circumstances, and, if possible, preserve an apparent contract rather than annulling it. The Supreme Commercial Court emphasised that lower courts should bear in mind the provisions of CC article 10(5), that 'the reasonableness of the actions and the good faith of the participants of civil law relations shall be presupposed'.[37] The first paragraph of the same article stipulates that 'The actions of citizens and juridical persons [legal entities] effectuated exclusively with the intention to cause harm to another person, and also abuse of right in other forms, shall not be permitted'.[38] 'In the event of the failure to comply with the requirements'[39] of that paragraph, CC article 10(2) gives a court the right to 'refuse to defend the right belonging to the person'.[40]

Draft Amendments to the Civil Code[41] mention a new category of material terms: terms essential for contracts of that type. The necessity for introducing this is not obvious. Neither is it clear how it will be understood which terms are essential, and if they are essential, why they are not mentioned in the Civil Code as material. It may be that the legislators share these doubts and will not adopt this particular proposed amendment.

V INCORPORATION OF TERMS

For a term to be considered as incorporated, it needs to be clear that the parties agreed in due form to incorporate it. Since most contracts are concluded in a signed written form (as required), most terms are incorporated by signature. If a contractual party does not sign a document stating that certain terms are in the contract, a court will not apply those terms; bold print, red ink – nothing will avail to incorporate them, as in this example.

> The Supreme Commercial Court refused to apply prices in a price list. A legal services agreement contained a term saying that the price for the provided services was defined in a price list made known to the client.

[36] Resolution of 8 February 2011 No 13970/10.
[37] Butler, above n 3, at 15.
[38] Ibid 14.
[39] Ibid 15.
[40] Ibid.
[41] Draft Federal Law on Amendments, above n 7 art 1 para 223 amending para 2 of CC art 432(1).

> However, as the price list was not signed by the client, the court considered that prices listed on it did not constitute contract terms.[42]

It should be borne in mind that under Russian law it is not possible to have incorporation of terms by notice. The parties need to agree the contract terms in due form; for contracts in written form, agreement means that the contract is signed by both parties (or sometimes that certain actions to perform the contract have been taken; see Chapter 4 at p 97), as in this example.

> The Terms and Conditions for the provision of mobile telephone services contained a term which allowed the mobile operator to change certain terms in the Terms and Conditions (including tariffs, billing pattern, etc), provided the mobile operator published in the public media a notification of the change 10 days before it would come into effect. The Federal Service for the Supervision of Consumer Rights and Well-Being (Федеральная Служба по Надзору в Сфере Защиты Прав Потребителей и Благополучия Человека; *Federalnaia Sluzhba po Nadzoru v Sfere Zashchity Prav Potrebitelei i Blagopoluchiia Cheloveka*) found that this term infringed consumer rights and issued an order to prohibit it.
>
> The mobile operator challenged this in court. The courts referred to CC article 310 which disallows 'unilateral refusal to perform an obligation and a unilateral change of its conditions'.[43] Furthermore, under CC article 450(1) 'A change and dissolution of a contract shall be possible by agreement of the parties unless provided otherwise by the present Code, by other laws, or by contract'.[44]
>
> Provision of mobile telephone services is a public contract[45] between the service provider (acting in the course of business) and private individuals. Its Terms and Conditions must comply with the Terms and Conditions for the Provision of Communication Services approved by a Government Regulation.[46] This Regulation, in compliance with provisions of the Civil Code, stipulates that variation of a contract shall be made by an agreement in written form.
>
> In this case, the court held that unilateral alteration of the Terms and Conditions by the services provider contradicted the applicable law, including the binding Government Regulation, and was therefore not allowed.[47]

[42] Ruling of 15 October 2010 No VAS-13379/10.
[43] Butler, above n 3, at 243.
[44] Ibid 324.
[45] The concept of a public contract is explained below at p 74.
[46] Regulation of the Government of the Russian Federation of 25 May 2005 No 328.
[47] Resolution of Federal Commercial Court of Volgo-Viatskii District of 9 February 2011 No A28-7796/2010.

Incorporation by consistent course of dealing is somewhat more controversial. There is no rule in the Civil Code or other legislation which stipulates that a term can be incorporated in this way. However, CC article 431 setting out the rules for interpretation of contracts (discussed below) indicates that one factor which should be taken into account by courts trying to define the terms of a contract is 'practice being established in the mutual relations of the parties'.[48]

In many fields standard forms of contract are adopted by authorised governmental authorities in a binding regulation. These standard forms are thus mandatory. Contractual terms stipulated in this way in a binding regulation are considered incorporated in relevant contracts. One such document, the Terms and Conditions for the Provision of Communication Services, is mentioned in the case discussed above. Another example is the Rules for the Provision of Transportation of Passengers by Rail Services, as well as Transportation of Luggage and Freight for Personal, Family, Household and Other Needs not Connected with Business Activity.[49] This sets a standard contract for rail transportation. Neither service providers nor passengers can opt out of it. As soon as a passenger buys a train ticket, the Rules become applicable. No express agreement with the Rules is needed. Neither is there any necessity for notice of the contractual terms imposed by the Rules. Because they are established by legislation, incorporation is unconditional.

VI INTERPRETATION OF CONTRACT TERMS

CC article 431 sets out the rules for interpretation of contractual terms. These may be summarised as follows.

A Rule 1: Literal Meaning

The *literal meaning* of words and expressions in the contract should be used. If the literal meaning of a contractual term is ambiguous, the court should interpret it by comparing it to the other contractual terms and 'with the sense of the contract as a whole'.[50] The application of this rule by the commercial courts is illustrated here.

> A contract of lease between a lessee, company A, and lessor, company B, allowed B to increase the rent once a year by up to 20 per cent, provided A was notified one month in advance. B notified A of an increase but A paid the old price, which was stipulated in an addendum to the lease contract

[48] Butler, above n 3, at 313.

[49] Approved by the Regulation of the Government of the Russian Federation of 2 March 2005 No 111.

[50] Butler, above n 3, at 313.

as a fixed price in USD per square metre. B sued for the difference between the old and the new prices.

The court applied an explanation of the Supreme Commercial Court[51] that parties to a lease contract can stipulate rent *either* as a fixed price *or* through a suitable mechanism to define the price. In this case the court found that in this contract the rent was stipulated as a fixed price per square metre per year. Another term stated that any changes to the lease should be made by signing an addendum to it.

In assessing the validity of the term allowing B to increase the rent annually, the court took into account the Supreme Commercial Court's approach to establishing the value of rent (here, a set amount per square metre per year), and applying CC article 431 considered the contract as a whole. As a result it held that B had no right to change the price unilaterally; it was fixed and another term in the contract required signed agreement for any variation.[52]

B Rule 2: Parties' Intention

If a literal interpretation under Rule 1 does not allow the contract's content to be determined, 'the true common will of the parties must be elicited by taking into account the purpose of the contract'.[53] All relevant circumstances shall be taken into account, including, 'negotiations preceding the contract and correspondence, practice being established in the mutual relations of the parties, the customs of business turnover, and the subsequent conduct of the parties'.[54] The following gives an example of Rule No 2 being used by the courts.

Company B rented storage facilities at an airport from company A. Because access to the airport was restricted on some days because of an annual air show, the lease contained a term that A was obliged to provide B with alternative storage space during those periods.

In May 2009 A informed B that the air show would take place from 18 to 23 August. A also assisted B to rent storage space from a third party for that period. B had a rental contract with the third party, paying them rent for those days' storage.

After the air show B claimed that A had failed to provide alternative premises, as their original contract stipulated, and thus A was in breach. B claimed as damages the amount of rent paid to the third party.

[51] Informational Circular of Supreme Commercial Court of 11 January 2002 No 66 'Overview of the Practice of the Resolution of Disputes, connected with Lease Agreements' para 11.

[52] Resolution of Federal Commercial Court of Moscow Region of 30 March 2011 No KG-A40/1095-11.

[53] CC art 431; Butler, above n 3, at 313.

[54] Ibid.

> The lower courts stated that A had not breached the contract, since it assisted B in arranging to rent from the third party. On appeal, the Court of Cassation held that the term obliging A to assist B with renting temporary storage should be interpreted taking into account the practice established between the parties in their course of dealing. The Court found out that in the previous two years A had themselves provided temporary storage facilities for B. Thus the court concluded that that was what the contract provided for. In these circumstances, assistance with renting from a third party could not be considered due performance and thus B was entitled to recover damages for breach.[55]

C Rules from Court Practice

As well as the two rules above, which stem from CC article 431, there are some rules of contractual interpretation which developed purely through court practice, for example, the *contra proferentem*[56] rule to protect a weaker contractual party. In most cases where the *contra proferentem* rule is applied there is a considerable difference in the professionalism and bargaining power of the two parties, so most frequently for example in insurance contracts and contracts for the provision of other professional financial services.

A Resolution of the Federal Commercial Court of the North Caucasus District gives a very good example of the application of the *contra proferentem* rule.

> An entrepreneur E insured goods (mobile phones) which he had as stock to sell in his shop. The application form E filled in before the insurance contract was signed gave one address where the goods were kept but the insurance contract had another. The insured goods were stolen from E's shop which was at the address stated in the application form.
>
> The insurer refused to pay compensation, claiming that the goods were insured at a different address, that is, the address in the insurance contract. The first instance court referred to explanations given by the Supreme Commercial Court and proposed to take into account both the application form and the insurance contract to establish the actual will of the parties. The Court of Cassation explained that the insurer is a provider of professional services in the insurance market with extensive knowledge in identifying risk factors for an insurance contract. They had every opportunity to discover before the insured goods were stolen that the address in the application form was different from the address in the

[55] Resolution of Federal Commercial Court of Moscow District of 2 February 2011 No KG-A41/16933-10.

[56] The principle that any restrictive contractual term will be interpreted 'against [the interests of] the person putting forward [that term]'.

insurance contract. Thus, since it was clear that E had the intention to insure his goods at a certain address, that address should be considered a term of the contract. Consequently, the insurer had no grounds to refuse to pay the indemnity for the insured goods stolen from that address.[57]

In another case the Supreme Commercial Court upheld the position of the lower courts which determined that a bank should not be allowed to impose on the other party contractual terms which were one-sided and impractical.

Bank B and company C signed a credit line (loan) contract. The contract stipulated 11.25 per cent interest on the loan with an increased interest of 22.5 per cent if the loan was not repaid on time. The contract also contained a term giving B a right to claim increased interest if conditions in the monetary market changed, including a change in the refinancing rate set by the Central Bank. Any change in the interest rate was supposed to be fixed in an addendum signed by both parties to the credit line agreement. The parties signed three such addenda increasing the interest rate.

The courts ignored the fact that the addenda were signed by both parties. They declared that the contract term allowing B to increase the interest rate was invalid, so the part of the addenda increasing the interest rate was also invalid. The courts explained that the interest rate is a material term of a loan contract. However, in this case the parties had not stipulated in the contract the exact correlation between the change of the interest rate and the change of the refinance rate set by the Central Bank; they only mentioned it as an example of changing market conditions. To interpret the term otherwise would have given too much power to B.[58]

In a situation of inequality between contractual parties, the courts will often interpret the contract with the reference to the *principle of good faith*, which was introduced into the Civil Code in the process of the reform of civil legislation in the early 1990s but previously was popular with judges who applied it for a number of different purposes, one of which was interpretation of contract terms. In the following case the principle of good faith was used to overcome a lacuna in the contract.

The parties signed a contract for the service maintenance of some heat metering units. Neither the contract nor any legislation specified the period within which inspection of the units should be completed.

The claimant C handed over the meter units to the defendant D for inspection but did not get them back for one and a half months. The absence of the meter units for more than 15 days caused C considerable

[57] Resolution of Federal Commercial Court of North Caucasian District of 31 December 2008 No F08-7779/2008, case No A32-4690/2008-65/99.

[58] Ruling of Supreme Commercial Court of 24 November 2010 No VAS-15748/10.

> extra expense, and C claimed that this was caused by the inspection taking an unreasonably long time, in breach of the contract. C sued D for damages.
>
> The court found that D had completed the inspection within the first 14 days, then did nothing. The court held that D should have been acting in good faith which meant that they should have taken all necessary steps to complete inspection of the meter units within 14 days, and return them. By failing to do so, D breached CC article 309 which establishes that[59] 'Obligations must be performed duly'.[60]

In this case, the combination of the court requiring good faith backed by CC article 309 filled in a lacuna with reasoning similar to that of an English court implying a term as a matter of fact.[61]

VII UNFAIR CONTRACT TERMS

The Civil Code neither defines nor regulates unfair contract terms in any way. However, there is a problem of unfair contract terms in Russia and, even though the concept of unfair contract terms does not exist, there are other ways to protect the weaker party in a contractual relationship.

A Controls on Contracts of Adhesion

One way to protect weaker parties is through the rules about contracts of adhesion (often referred to in English law as standard form contacts). Under Russian law, a contract of any type can be a contract of adhesion. It is not one of the types of contracts listed in Civil Code Part Two; it is a way to conclude a contract.

CC article 428(1) defines a contract of adhesion as:

> a contract whose conditions [terms] have been determined by one of the parties in records or other standard forms and which can be accepted by the other party not other than by means of adhering to the contract as a whole being offered.[62]

If such a contract contains certain terms which although not contrary to legislation are regarded as 'dangerous',[63] the adhering party is given the right to demand dissolution or variation of the contract. A 'dangerous' term is listed in article 428(2) as one which:

[59] Butler, above n 3, at 243.
[60] Resolution of Federal Commercial Court of North-Western District of 6 November 2007, caseNo A56-51888/2006.
[61] As, eg, in *The Moorcock* (1889) 14 PD 64.
[62] Butler, above n 3, at 310.
[63] The term 'dangerous' is not used in the Code, but included here for clarity.

> deprives [the adhering] party of rights usually granted under contracts of that type; excludes or limits the responsibility of the other party for variation of obligations; or contains other conditions [terms] clearly burdensome for the adhering party which it, proceeding from its own reasonably understandable interests, would not accept if it had the opportunity to participate in determining the conditions of the contract.[64]

This vague set of criteria are somewhat reminiscent of factors specified in English law for the 'reasonableness test' for certain classes of exclusion clauses under the Unfair Contract Terms Act (UCTA) 1977 [65] and considerations for whether a term is 'fair' for the Unfair Terms in Consumer Contract Regulations (UTCCR) 1999.[66] In the Russian Civil Code the list of 'dangerous' terms which give rise to a remedy is rather underdeveloped and in practice courts are reluctant to apply CC article 428(2).

What remedies does CC article 428(2) give to a party who realises that they have adhered to a contract containing a 'dangerous' term? They have a right to sue for the contract to be terminated or varied. This affords little protection to the interests of a weaker party and, as noted, the courts are rather reluctant to apply the vague and ambiguous provisions to contracts of adhesion.

The remedies are also limited in application; they do not apply if the adhering party entered into the contract in the course of their business and knew or should have known what the actual contract terms were. In practice this means that CC article 428(2) is never applied to any commercial contract.

B Protection of Consumer Rights

There are provisions aimed at protecting a weaker party in the Law of the Russian Federation on the Protection of Consumer Rights.[67] Article 16(1) of this Law declares invalid any contract terms which affect consumer rights adversely when compared to provisions in laws or other legal acts. The consumer also has a right to claim damages caused by contractual performance which adversely affects his or her rights. The problem with this is that court procedure is time-consuming and costly and very often the outcome is disappointing for the consumer because damages awarded by the court are very limited (the difficulty of recovering damages is discussed in more detail in Chapter 10 at p 224).

However, there is an alternative process. The provisions in article 16 of the Law on the Protection of Consumer Rights are very often enforced by state authorities responsible for health and safety regulation and consumer rights,

[64] Butler, above n 3, at 310.
[65] See UCTA 1977 s 11 and Sch 2.
[66] See UTCCR 1999 reg 5 and Sch 2.
[67] No 2300-1 of 7 February 1992. See also JP Nehf, 'Empowering the Russian Consumer in a Market Economy' (1992–93) 14 *Michigan Journal of International Law* 739 and P Jordan, 'Russian Lawyers as Consumer Protection Advocates, 1992–1995' (1996) 4–5 *Parker School Journal of East European Law* 486.

such as the Federal Service for the Supervision of Consumer Rights and Well-Being.[68] For example, a contractual term allowing a mobile telephone service provider to change the terms and conditions of a service contract unilaterally was considered by the Federal Service for the Supervision of Consumer Rights and Well-Being to be 'a term adversely affecting the rights of consumers compared to the rules stipulated in laws or other acts' as proscribed in the Law on the Protection of Consumer Rights. The courts agreed with the position of the Federal Service for the reasons discussed above.[69]

C **Public Contract** (Публичный договор; ***publichnyi dogovor***)

One further provision in Russian contract law specifically designed with consumer fairness in mind is the public contract. This is defined in CC article 426(1) as:

> A contract concluded by a commercial organisation and establishing its duties relating to the sale of goods, fulfilment of work, or rendering of services which this organisation by the character of its activity must effectuate with respect to everyone who has recourse to it (retail trade, carriage by common-use transport, communications services, electric power supply, medical, hotel servicing, and so forth) shall be deemed to be a public contract.
>
> A commercial organisation shall not have the right to prefer one person to others with respect to the conclusion of a public contract except for the instances provided by law or other legal acts.[70]

In a public contract, the price and other terms 'shall be established identically for all consumers except for instances when the granting of privileges for individual categories of consumers is permitted by law and other legal acts'.[71] If a public contract fails to conform to the rules relating to it, it is void.

The institution of a public contract is thus a comparatively simple way to ensure basic fairness at least between different individual consumers dealing with the same contractor, whilst allowing special deals for particular groups, for example, pensioners, at particular times, provided that there is equal application for all qualifying customers.[72]

[68] For Russian name, see above, text to n 47.

[69] See above, text to n 47 based on the Resolution of Federal Commercial Court of Volgo-Viatskii District of 9 February 2011 No A28-7796/2010.

[70] Butler, above n 3, at 308.

[71] CC art 426(2); ibid 309.

[72] Dutch law has a similar provision; see J Henderson, 'Entrepreneurs and Consumers as Subjects of Civil Law' in WB Simons (ed), *Private and Civil Law in the Russian Federation* (Leiden, Brill, 2008) n 14 at 56.

VIII CONCLUSION

Any codification of contract law limits freedom of contract to some extent. Courts applying the rules on contracts have a choice: to apply the Code provisions literally as a limitation means or to use legal mechanisms to broaden the freedom of the parties to choose contractual terms which suit their situation. Russian courts have tended to treat freedom of contract with suspicion and, as can be seen from this chapter, use every available method to limit freedom of contract as much as possible and often even go beyond the limits set out in the Civil Code itself. It may be hoped that in due course, as the legal culture in Russian modulates, that courts will tend to take a less restrictive and formalistic approach. There are already encouraging signs, including some (although not all) of the recent reforms to the Civil Code, which will be discussed as appropriate in the following chapters.

3

Requirements of Form

I INTRODUCTION

Russian law takes a predominantly different approach to English law in setting the form a contract must take. While English law imposes requirements of form for some types of contract (although comparatively few), in most instances under English law it is not its form which makes a contract binding, but the agreement, with consideration and intent to be legally bound; in English law, form tends to impact enforceability not validity. By contrast, despite the fundamental principle of freedom of contract, in Russian law almost every contract which is regulated by the Civil Code (CC) must comply with particular requirements of form. Compliance with form is in many cases a prerequisite for the contract's existence.

The requirement of a specific form for a Russian contract may be established not only by the Civil Code or some other law, but also by the parties themselves. In that case non-compliance entails the same general consequences as failure to observe any requirements of form prescribed by law.

This chapter sets out the types of contractual form specified in the Civil Code and the consequences of failure to comply with the set requirements.

II TYPES OF FORMS OF CONTRACT

According to CC article 158, 'transactions shall be concluded orally or in written form'.[1] The Civil Code distinguishes the following types of written form: simple; notarial; or subject to state registration. The difference between these forms is discussed below.

A Oral Contracts

Under Russian legal theory, the possibility of concluding a contract orally is based on the so-called 'residual' principle. If written form is not required, there may be an oral contract. In the words of CC article 159(1): 'A transaction for

[1] WE Butler, *The Civil Code of the Russian Federation Parts 1, 2 and 3: Parallel Russian and English Texts* (Moscow, JurInfoR-Press, 2008) 144.

which the written (simple or notarial) form has not been established by a law or by agreement of the parties may be concluded orally'.[2] Compulsory written form is not required, for example, for contracts of purchase-sale, gift or 'compensated rendering of services'. Most oral contracts are concluded between individuals (in legal terminology, 'natural persons') because, as seen below, written form is required for contracts by legal entities ('legal persons') between themselves and with individuals. Even though non-compliance with the simple written form does not always lead to invalidity of a contract, the problems of enforceability explain why legal entities nevertheless try to avoid concluding oral contracts.

Parties can conclude an oral contract if it is an instantaneous contract, that is, the process of conclusion and performance cannot be separated, unless, as stated in CC article 159(2), the parties have agreed otherwise, notarial form has been established for this type of contract, or it is one of the types of contracts which is invalid if there is failure to comply with the simple written form. Words do not need to be spoken, as any contract which may be concluded orally can be 'considered to be concluded also when from the behaviour of the person his [or her] will to conclude the contract is manifest'[3] (CC article 158(2)).

B Written Contracts

A contract in written form may be concluded as a document signed by both parties and also by 'exchange of documents by means of postal, telegraph, teletype, telephone, electronic, or other communications, enabling it to be reliably established that the document emanates from a party under the contract' (CC article 434(2)),[4] or by acceptance by performance (конклюдентные действия; *konkliudentniie deistviia*) of a written offer (CC article 434(3)).

CC article 160(2) allows the use:

> when concluding a transaction of a facsimile reproduction of a signature with the assistance of mechanical or other means of copying, electronic-cipher signature, or other analogue of a signature in one's own hand . . . in the instances and procedure provided for by a law, other legal acts, or by agreement of the parties.[5]

In the absence of these conditions, use of an analogue signature instead of a handwritten one will be regarded as non-compliance with written form and lead to the consequences discussed below.

As noted already, acceptance of a written offer by performance is considered to comply with the requirement for written form. The performance would need to be made within the period established in the contract for acceptance by conduct

[2] Butler, above n 1, at 145.
[3] Ibid.
[4] Ibid 315.
[5] Ibid 146.

in the form of, for example, 'shipment of goods, provision of services, fulfilment of work, or payment of respective amount [of money]' as specified in CC article 438(3).[6] However, the Supreme Court and the Supreme Commercial Court have made clear that to consider the offeree's actions as acceptance by performance, the Code does not require that they perform in full all the terms of the offer.[7] It is enough if the person who has received a written offer (including a draft contract) begins to perform according to the offer terms and within the time set for acceptance.

This provision in CC article 438(3) is extremely important in situations when the parties have negotiated a written contract, which is then not signed or signed only by one party but nevertheless has been performed to a certain extent by one or both parties, as in the following example.

> In a case resolved by the Federal Commercial Court of Moscow District a purchaser brought a claim against the seller to render their purchase-sale contract void, on the basis that the seller had signed it using a cliché (mechanically) and not by hand, in violation of CC article 160(1). The claimant contested the seller's intention to conclude the contract and asserted that the requirement of written form had not been met.
>
> At all instances the courts rejected the claim. They held that even though the seller's signature was not made by hand, the parties had partially performed the contract. The courts applied CC article 438(3), taking the written contract as an offer and the partial performance as acceptance. In this way the requirement of the written form of the contract was sufficiently met.[8]

It must be noted, however, that the Civil Code requires that some types of contract are concluded in the form of one written document. For example, under CC article 550, a contract of sale of immovable property is concluded in written form by drawing up one document signed by both parties. Failure to comply makes the contract invalid. So the rule in CC article 434(3) only works for those written contracts which are not specifically required to be in the form of one written document. Draft Amendments to the Civil Code introduce an additional paragraph 4 to CC article 434 which would explicitly enact this conclusion. According to the proposed amendment in instances provided for by law or the contract a written contract may be concluded only by drawing up one document signed by both parties.[9] Effectively this formalises and clarifies the existing situation.

[6] Ibid 317.

[7] Resolution of Plenum of the Supreme Court and Plenum of the Supreme Commercial Court No 6/8 of 1 July 1996 'On particular questions connected with the application of Part One of the Civil Code' para 58.

[8] Resolution of Federal Commercial Court of Moscow District of 16 April 2010 No KG-A41/3313-10.

[9] Draft Federal Law on Amendments to Parts One, Two, Three and Four of the Civil Code of the Russian Federation, and certain other legal acts of the Russian Federation No 47538-6 approved by the State Duma in first reading on 27 April 2012 art 1 para 224(b).

The Civil Code provides the requirement of a written form of contract in two ways; first by general rules specifying which contracts must be concluded in the written form, and secondly, by specifying in the individual chapters of Part Two of the Civil Code requirements of form for particular types of contract. These specific requirements will prevail over any general rule. As noted above, the parties themselves may also agree to require written form.

(i) Simple Written Form

'Simple' written form means a contract concluded in the written form described above, in contrast to a written contract which requires in addition notarial certification or state registration.

Under the general rule of CC article 161(1), the following contracts should be concluded in simple written form (unless because of their type they also require notarial certification or are subject to state registration):

- contracts between legal entities;
- contracts between legal entities and individuals;
- contracts of individuals between themselves for an amount not less than 10,000 roubles (approximately £200); and
- other specific instances provided by law, irrespective of the contract value.

An example of a specific instance requiring writing is CC article 574(2), under which a contract of gift of moveable property containing a promise to give the gift at a future date must be concluded in written form. If concluded orally, it is void.

However, as seen below, failure to use written form does not automatically preclude the existence of a contract. This only occurs if it is one of these instances where a law or the contract explicitly establishes invalidity to be the consequence of non-compliance with form.

(ii) Contracts Subject to Notarial Certification

Notarial certification is made to a written contract by an endorsement of certification by a notary or other official having the right to perform such a notarial action. According to a recently introduced new version of CC article 163(1),[10] notarial certification of a contract means verification of its lawfulness, including the verification of the right of each party to enter into it. At the time of writing notaries are not personally liable for certification of contracts which are subsequently deemed to be invalid. However, it is possible that such personal liability will be introduced at some point. The new version of CC article 163(1) explicitly defining the meaning of notarial certification may indicate the likelihood of this in the near future.

Notarial certification of a contract is required either when it is specified by law or the parties have agreed that their contract should be notarised. The Civil

[10] Federal Law of 7 May 2013 No 100-FZ.

Code itself requires notarial certification under CC article 584 for only one type of contract: the contract of 'rent and maintenance of a dependant for life' (рента и пожизненное содержание с иждивением; *renta i pozhiznennoe soderzhanie s izhdiveniem*), dealt with in chapter 33 of the Civil Code. Under this contract the recipient of rent transfers ownership of property to the rent-payer, and in return the rent-payer periodically pays a defined sum of money or other assets for the payee's maintenance (CC article 583). It is possible to set this arrangement up on a permanent basis (so that the right is inherited after the death of the original beneficiary); alternatively it can be maintenance for life of a dependant. An example of the requirement of notarial certification provided in another federal law is a contract to transfer ownership in a share in the charter capital (доля в уставном капитале; *dolia v ustavnom kapitale*) of a limited responsibility society.[11]

(iii) Contracts Subject to State Registration

Registration of a contract is required in instances provided for in the law (CC article 164(1)). These are mostly contracts for land and other immovable property. Thus, for example, state registration is required under the Civil Code for a contract of sale of a dwelling house, apartment, or a part of either (article 558(2)); the contract of sale of an enterprise[12] (article 560(3)); contract of gift of immovable property (article 574(3)); contract of lease of a building or installation concluded for a period of not less than one year (article 651(2)); or contract of lease of an enterprise (article 658(2)), and similar.

In certain instances the law establishes compulsory state registration of some contracts for movable property as well. An example of this is compulsory state registration of contracts for cultural items or collections of such items listed in the Museum Fund of the Russian Federation. Such contracts must be registered with the State Catalogue of the Museum Fund of the Russian Federation (Государственный каталог Музейного фонда Российской Федерации; *Gosudarstvennyi Katalog Muzeinogo Fonda Rossiiskoi Federatsii*).[13]

As well as state registration of contracts for the sale of immovables, there is also a separate system of state registration of the rights to immovable property and their transfer. The right to immovable property irrespective of how it was acquired only vests on registration with a competent state authority (CC articles 219, 223(2)). Information about the rights to immovable property and their encumbrances is recorded in the Unified State Register of Rights to Immovable Property and Transactions with It (Единый государственный реестр прав на

[11] Federal Law on the Limited Responsibility Society of 8 February 1998 No 14-FZ art 21(11).

[12] An enterprise is a property complex used to effectuate entrepreneurial activity. An enterprise is deemed to be an immovable by the Civil Code. An enterprise as a property complex may include all types of property designated for its activity, including land plots, buildings, installations, equipment, tools, raw material, etc (CC art 132).

[13] Federal Law on the Museum Fund of the Russian Federation and Museums in the Russian Federation of 26 May 1996 No 54-FZ.

недвижимое имущество и сделок с ним; *Edinyi Gosudarstvennyi Reestr Prav na Nedvizhimoe Imushchestvo i Sdelok s Nim*).

It is important to distinguish between state registration of a contract and state registration of the rights to immovable property and its transfer. Unlike state registration of contracts, which is required only for some contracts for immovable property, state registration of the rights to immovable property and its transfer is compulsory, even if the contract itself is not subject to state registration. It should be borne in mind that if a contract for immovable property is subject to state registration, that registration does not replace state registration of the rights to the immovable property transferred under the contract. In such a situation both the contract itself and the rights to immovable property must be registered.

State registration of contracts for immovable property, and for rights to immovable property and its transfer, is carried out by a special public authority. As of May 2013, the relevant authority is the Department of Federal Service for State Registration, Cadastre and Cartography (Федеральная Служба Государственной Регистрации, Кадастра и Картографии; *Federal'naia Sluzhba Gosudarstvennoi Registratsii, Kadastra i Kartografii*). Information about both the contracts and rights to immovable property is held on the Unified State Registry of Rights to Immovable Property. Anyone can obtain from the Registry information held there about a particular immovable for a small fee (as of May 2013, 250 roubles for individual and 500 roubles for legal entities; around £5 and £10, respectively).

III CONSEQUENCES OF NON-COMPLIANCE WITH THE REQUIRED FORM OF CONTRACT

The Civil Code provides three consequences of non-compliance with the form of a contract: a prohibition against referring to witness testimony to confirm the transaction or its terms; non-conclusion of the contract; or invalidity of the contract.

The difference between non-conclusion and invalidity of contracts will be discussed in more detail in Chapter 6 at p 126. The result of both is that a contract is considered to have never existed, that is, to be void.

A Prohibition against Witness Testimony

Under CC article 162(1):

> The failure to comply with the simple written form of a transaction shall deprive the parties of the right in the event of a dispute to refer in confirmation of the transaction and its conditions to witness testimony, but shall not deprive them of the right also to cite written and other evidence.[14]

[14] Butler, above n 1, at 147.

This provision shows that non-compliance with the simple written form does not always adversely impact the fact that the contract exists, but limits the types of evidence a party can bring to prove the contract's existence, and/or its individual terms. If a party nevertheless manages to adduce proof, the contract will be considered as concluded, as in the following example.

> In one case, although there was no written purchase-sale contract, a supplier (company S) delivered 1,488,380 kg of grain to a poultry farm (company K). K failed to pay anything so S sued them. The Supreme Commercial Court upheld the lower courts' findings that the parties' actions showed the existence of a purchase-sale contract. Their contractual relations originated from an oral contract which did not require written form. The Court also held that the contract's main terms were established in the consignment notes signed by the parties. Although the price of the grain has not been specified, it could be determined on the basis of the price for that quality grain provided by the Chamber of Commerce of the region where the poultry farm was located.[15]

In fact, as noted above, a contract between two legal entities ought to be concluded in simple written form, which did not happen in this case. But the law does not lay down any requirement that purchase-sale contracts must be in a written form, and here the supplier managed to prove the existence of the contract by providing written proof – consignment notes signed by the poultry farm (purchaser) – and the Commercial Court accepted that as sufficient to support the contract's existence.

B Non-conclusion of the Contract

Compliance with the due form requirement is often considered to be one of the prerequisites for the conclusion, and hence, the existence of a contract (more details in Chapter 4 on 'Formation of Contracts'). It should follow logically that if the parties to a contract fail to comply with the due form requirement, the contract should be considered not concluded. However, as discussed above, that is not necessarily the consequence of non-compliance with the requirement of a simple written form.

According to CC article 433(3), 'A contract subject to state registration shall be considered to be concluded from the moment of the state registration thereof, unless established otherwise by a law'.[16] It means that the contract is not considered concluded until its state registration. According to article 164(1), in instances when the law requires state registration of a contract, the legal conse-

[15] Ruling of 8 October 2010 No VAS-13109/10.
[16] Butler, above n 1, at 314.

quences arise at registration. However, some contractual terms are nevertheless considered to be both existent and valid before registration. For example, if the contract provides an obligation for one party to submit the documents for state registration, the other party has a right to claim for the fulfilment of that obligation. Under CC article 165(2)[17] (before 1 September 2013, Article 165(3)):

> If a transaction requiring state registration has been concluded in the proper form but one of the parties evades the registration thereof, a court shall have the right at the demand of the other party to render a decision concerning registration of the transaction. In this event the transaction shall be registered in accordance with the decision of the court.[18]

In this case the contract was registered in accordance with the court decision. It should be mentioned that article 165(4), which was introduced into the Civil Code by Federal Law of 7 May 2013,[19] establishes a shortened period of limitation, of one year (as opposed to the general limitation period of three years) with respect to claims for state registration of a contract under this provision. An example of court involvement in registration is the following.

> An individual entrepreneur, E, was a lessee in a contract of lease for ten years. However, the contract was never registered. E tried to use the right granted to him by this provision of the Civil Code, taking a case against both the lessor (company L) and the registration authority. In the course of the hearing L claimed that, according to CC articles 651 and 433, a contract of lease of a building for more than one year is subject to state registration and is considered to be not concluded without such registration. L therefore asserted that E was in fact suing to compel conclusion of the contract. However, CC article 445(4), which deals with the circumstances under which a party can apply to court to compel conclusion of a contact, would not give the lessee in the circumstances any right to bring such a claim. Nevertheless, the court ordered registration of E's contract.[20]

From the Supreme Commercial Court's reasoning here follows that the Civil Code provision entitling a party to go to court to demand state registration of a contract is applicable despite the fact that, under the law, the contract should be considered as not concluded without state registration. Thus the claimant has gained a right to enforce an otherwise 'non-existent' contract.

The same rule that a contract is not concluded without compliance with the due form is applicable to situations where the parties themselves have agreed on

[17] The changes to this article were introduced by Federal Law of 7 May 2013 No 100-FZ. The respective changes took effect on 1 September 2013.

[18] Butler, above n 1, at 149.

[19] No 100-FZ.

[20] Informational Circular of Presidium of Supreme Commercial Court of 16 February 2001 No 59 'Overview of Practice of Resolution of Disputes connected with the Application of the Federal Law on State Registration of Rights to Immovable Property and Transactions with It' para 7.

a specific form for their contract. In such cases under CC article 434(1) the contract will only be considered concluded once it is in the agreed form, even though no law requires that particular form for that type of contract.

Thus, generally, the consequence of non-compliance with the form of contract prescribed by law is that the contract is treated as not concluded. However, in practice this general rule (*lex generalis*) is often overridden by a special rule (*lex specialis*), with the result that a contract will only be considered to be not concluded because of failure to comply with the required form in two situations:

(1) when the parties themselves have agreed on a particular form of contract and then fail to comply;
(2) the requirement of state registration of a contract has not been met, but only provided that the law does not entail such contract being invalid (see below).

C Invalidity of the Contract

Invalidity of contract as a result of non-compliance with the form of a contract only arises when specifically provided by law or by agreement of the parties, provided that such agreement is allowed by law, as described below.

According to CC article 162(2), 'In the instances expressly specified in a law or in the agreement of the parties the failure to comply with the simple written form of a transaction shall entail its invalidity'.[21]

In the chapters in Part Two of the Civil Code regulating particular types of contracts, the Code explicitly specifies that certain types of contracts are void as a result of non-compliance with the written form of contract. Examples include the contract of gift (article 574(2)); credit contract (article 820); contract of bank deposit (article 836(2)); and contract of commercial concession (article 1028(2)).

Failure to comply with notarial form when required always leads to the invalidity of the contract (CC article 163(3);[22] before 1 September 2013, article 165(1)): 'such a transaction shall be considered to be void'.[23] Under the same paragraph non-compliance with the requirement of state registration also leads to invalidity of contract if such registration is explicitly required by law for that particular type of contract.

Since, under the general rule, non-compliance with the requirement of state registration of a contract means that the contract is regarded as being not concluded, the law needs to indicate explicitly the instances when such contracts would be void. As one example, under CC article 339(3) and (4), a contract of

[21] Butler, above n 1, at 147–8.

[22] The changes to this article were introduced by Federal Law of 7 May 2013 No 100-FZ. The respective changes took effect on 1 September 2013.

[23] Butler, above n 1, at 149.

mortgage is subject to state registration, and failure to register entails its invalidity (it is deemed to be void).

However, the invalidity of a contract because it is non-compliant with the requirement for notarial certification or state registration is not absolute. If one party has wholly or partially performed a contract of a type requiring notarial certification, and the other party has evaded getting the requisite certification, the party who had performed the contract may apply to a court for a declaration that the contract is valid. Then consequential notarial certification of a contract is not required (CC article 165(1); before 1 September 2013, article 165(2)).

Similarly, as already seen above, if a contract requiring state registration has been concluded in the proper form but one of the parties has evaded registration, a court may, on the application of the other party, take the decision that the transaction should be registered. It will then be registered in accordance with the court decision (CC article 165(2); before 1 September 2013, article 165(3)). This rule is also applicable to instances where failure to comply with the requirement of state registration would lead to a contract's invalidity. Then the contract will be considered valid, concluded from the moment of its state registration.

As already noted, CC article 165(4) provides a reduced limitation period of one year (in contrast to the general limitation period of three years) for claims for state registration of a contract under article 165(2) as well as for claims to deem a contract, otherwise void as non-compliant with the requirement of notarial certification, as valid under article 165(1).

IV CONCLUSION

Russian contract law provides for extensive requirements with respect to the form of contract, as compared to English contract law. Their variety and number indicate that for Russian contract law not only agreement itself but also the form of agreement is important for the existence of a contract. In many cases, as demonstrated above, compliance with the form of contract is not merely a matter of enforceability of contract, but also a matter of its existence – being concluded and valid. It is not unusual in a codified legal system that form is regarded as important. However, the extent to which this applies – and also the possibility that in some instances there can be court rectification – could be a trap for the unwary or ill-advised.

4

Formation of Contracts

I INTRODUCTION

This chapter considers different methods of concluding a contract and the conditions which have to be met for a contract to be considered as concluded and therefore entered into force. This is an important topic, as being not concluded is a frequent ground for vitiation of a contract (see Chapter 6 at p 156).

Civil Code (CC) article 420(1) defines a contract as 'an agreement of two or several persons concerning the establishment, change, or termination of civil rights and duties'.[1] This demonstrates that the central pillar of an enforceable contract in Russian law as in English law is an agreement between two or several parties. (The agreement will contain actionable promise(s), each promise involving at least two parties, a promisor and a promisee.) However, there is a crucial difference between English and Russian law in the understanding of what the agreement should be like. While English law is more concerned whether there has been an offer and corresponding acceptance, Russian law generally provides some other requirements with respect to the content of the offer and form of the agreement. Also, in contrast toEnglish law, neither intention to be legally bound nor consideration have any legal significance for the conclusion of a contract in Russia, although as we will see below, equivalent concepts may impact the subsequent validity of a contract.

II REQUIREMENTS FOR CONCLUSION OF A CONTRACT

Formation of contracts under Russian law is regulated primarily by Part One of the Civil Code, Section III (General Part of the Law of Obligations), Subsection 2 (General Provisions of Contract), chapter 28 'Conclusion of a Contract'. Under the general rule in CC article 432(1), 'A contract shall be considered to be concluded when agreement regarding all the *material conditions [terms]* of the contract has been reached in *the form* required in appropriate instances'[2] (emphasis added). (The concept of 'material terms' is explained in Chapter 2 at p 60.)

[1] WE Butler, *The Civil Code of the Russian Federation Parts 1, 2 and 3: Parallel Russian and English Texts* (Moscow, JurInfoR-Press, 2008) 304.

[2] Ibid 313.

The Civil Code's approach both to conclusion of a contract and the requirements for conclusion is clearly rather formal. The Code does not require courts to ascertain any intention by the parties to conclude and perform the contract. Unlike English law, the Civil Code indicates that the issue of whether or not a contract is formed is solely resolved by taking into account formal criteria. However, a lack of intention to contract (отсутствие воли на заключение договора; *otsutstvie voli na zakliuchenie dogovora*) can lead to invalidation of a contract (see Chapter 6). Also, there are legal provisions in Russian law with functions somewhat analogous to that of consideration in English law, but these do not have any legal significance at the stage of conclusion of a contract (see Chapter 5 for further details).

CC article 432 cited above defines as the requirements for conclusion of a contract that the material terms should be agreed in due form.[3] This provides the majority of Russian legal scholars with grounds to assert that due form is one of the two requirements for conclusion of a contract (the other being agreement on all the material terms).

However, as discussed in the previous chapter, non-compliance with the form of a contract does not always lead to a contract not being concluded. For many cases, the Civil Code provides other consequences (see Chapter 3 at p 81). Because failure to conform to a particular form can lead to different outcomes, despite its clear importance contractual form cannot be considered as a requirement for the conclusion of a contract. Nevertheless, failure to comply with form will usually give rise to legal consequences, just not necessarily complete nullity of the contract.

III FORMATION OF A CONTRACT: OFFER AND ACCEPTANCE

As in many other legal systems as a general rule offer and acceptance is the method by which a contract is concluded in Russia. The Civil Code regulates this in detail. In fact, in relation to the time of conclusion of a contract, CC article 433(1) refers only to this method: 'A contract shall be deemed to be concluded at the moment of receipt by the person who has sent an offer of its acceptance'.[4]

However, in reality, simple agreement – acceptance of an offer – is not the only method under Russian law to conclude a contract. The Civil Code rules on contracting through offer and acceptance apply generally to the process of making a contract, but at times they are specifically overridden by special provisions for particular types of contract in the Code or other legislation. For some contracts the Civil Code explicitly provides a specific method of conclusion. This might be, for example, in the form of a single written document, conclusion of a

[3] See above, text to n 2.
[4] Butler, above n 1, at 314.

contract at a public sale, and conclusion of a contract by adhesion to a standard form contract. Both the Civil Code and other laws mandate specific methods for some types of contract, for example, contracts of insurance. Although it could be argued that in all these particular situations there clearly is some sort of agreement between the parties, so it would be possible to identify an offer and acceptance, Russian law does not base the validity of the contract's creation on that agreement, but only on whether the prescribed method has been correctly executed.

A Offer

CC article 435(1) defines an offer quite straightforwardly:

> A proposal addressed to one or several specific persons which is sufficiently definite and expresses the intention of the person who has made the proposal to consider himself to have concluded a contract with the addressee who will accept the proposal shall be deemed an offer.
>
> An offer must contain the material conditions [terms] of the contract.[5]

Although oral contracts are possible, particularly between individuals, most offers (apart from those in public contracts discussed in Chapter 2 at p 74) will be in writing.

(i) Requirements for an Offer: Material Terms of a Contract

One very important characteristic of an offer in Russian contract law is the requirement that it contains all the material terms of the contract to be concluded (see CC article 435(1) cited above).[6] The concept of material terms is explained in Chapter 2 at p 60. When a Russian court has to decide if a particular invitation to make a contract was actually an offer, the first, and often the only thing the court will take into account is whether the document which is the purported offer includes all the material terms. Material terms can never be implied by a court. The court can, however, look at the available evidence, even if it is not labelled as 'offer' or 'agreement'. The working of the 'material terms' rule can be seen in the following two contrasting cases. In the first, the court found a contract because the material terms were clearly expressed.

> Company S sent an invoice to company M for goods to be delivered by S to M. S failed to deliver the goods so M brought a claim for unfounded enrichment. M claimed that S should return the payment because of the absence of any contract concluded between the parties. However, evidence was presented at court that M had paid the invoice.

[5] Ibid 315.

[6] See above, text to n 5.

> The courts of all instances rejected M's claim. They reasoned that for conclusion of a contract of purchase-sale of goods (movable property) the law does not require there to be a single written document signed by both parties. The issued invoices contained in writing all the material terms necessary for a purchase-sale contract (such as the designation and quantity of goods and the price), so such a contract had actually been concluded between the parties. Therefore M's payment had been made under a contract and there were no grounds for a claim against S for unfounded enrichment.[7]

In another case:

> Company K also brought an action for unfounded enrichment, in this case against company V. V had issued a pre-payment invoice (счет на предварительную оплату; *shchet na predvaritel'nyiu oplatu*, otherwise known as advance payment invoice счет на уплату аванса; *schet na uplaty avansa*) to K for the services of an excavator and crane. The pre-payment invoice specified the services to be provided as 'provision of works with automotive equipment' and stated the price. K paid the amount stipulated in the pre-payment invoice and, in the box for 'purpose of payment' in the accompanying paperwork, referred to the services listed in the pre-payment invoice and included the invoice number.
>
> Afterwards K sent V a letter demanding that V either prove the services had been performed or return the payment. K claimed that the contract between K and V was not concluded and thus the prepayment constituted unfounded enrichment for V. In court V claimed that it had actually provided the services (provision of works with automotive equipment) to K but that K had evaded signing the confirmatory documentation, the 'acts of rendered services' (акты об оказанных услугах; *akty ob okazannykh uslugakh*), despite being sent the relevant documents twice. V claimed that the pre-payment invoice had been an offer, and the payment was acceptance, therefore there were contractual relations between the parties, so the money paid could not be unfounded enrichment.
>
> Courts of all instances sustained K's claim. They held that for conclusion of a contract, it is required that there is a general consensus of the wills of the parties. A pre-payment invoice can only be an offer if it contains all the material terms for the particular type of contract. The subject matter of the contract is a material term necessary for any contract (CC article 432(1)). The courts emphasised that the prepayment invoice issued by V could not be considered to be an offer because it did not sufficiently define the subject matter for a contract of compensated rendering of services, namely the information which would allow the parties to determine definitively the

[7] Resolution of Federal Commercial Court of Moscow District of 30 August 2010 No KG-A40/9227-10.

> content and quantity of services to be provided. Evidence presented by V that the services had been actually performed was not accepted by the court.[8]

In the second case, even though the parties behaved as though there were actually contractual relations between them, the courts preferred to be concerned about the formal requirements of an offer. However, this rather harsh approach is not universally taken by courts; see Chapter 3 at p 82 for further discussion.

(ii) Offer or Invitation to Make Offers

CC article 437 draws the line between an offer and an invitation to make offers (приглашение делать оферты; *priglashenie delat' oferty*). As a general rule, an advertisement or other proposal addressed to an indefinite group of people is regarded as an invitation to make offers 'unless expressly specified otherwise in the proposal'.[9]

However, if a proposal addressed to an indefinite group sets out all the material terms for a particular type of contract, 'from which the will of the person making the proposal is seen to conclude a contract on the conditions specified in the proposal with anyone who responds' (CC article 427(2)),[10] then it is regarded as a public offer, that is, the equivalent of an 'offer to all the world' in English law.[11] The contract would be concluded when that offer is accepted by any person who knows about it and responds in the required manner.

Thus, the key distinguishing feature between a public offer and an invitation to make offers is the presence of all the material terms in the public offer and their absence in an invitation to make offers. Here again we see the importance of the concept of material terms in Russian contract law.

(iii) Advertisement as a Public Offer

As in English law, an advertisement is usually regarded as an invitation to make offers, so those who respond would each make an offer, which the person advertising can accept or reject. However, in Russian law in certain situations an advertisement is considered to be a public offer, which then results in obligations on the offeree. A public offer is defined in CC article 437(2):

> A proposal containing all the material conditions of the contract from which the will of the person making the proposal is seen to conclude a contract on the conditions [terms] specified in the proposal with anyone who responds shall be deemed to be an offer (public offer).[12]

[8] Resolution of Third Commercial Appellate Court of 5 July 2010 No A33-21875/2009.
[9] Butler, above n 1, at 316.
[10] Ibid.
[11] Per Bowen LJ in *Carlill v Carbolic Smoke Ball Co* [1893] 1 QB 256 at 267.
[12] Butler, above n 1, at 316.

An advertisement would therefore be a public offer when it contains all the material terms of the particular type of contract and clearly expresses the offeror's will to enter into that contract. Russian law also sets a default time limit; unless otherwise provided by the advertisement, a public offer in an advertisement will be valid for two months from the date of publication.[13]

This can be compared to the situation in English law where there can be an offer for a unilateral contract to consider all tenders (offers) received by a deadline specified in the advertisement calling for tenders, as, for example, in *Blackpool and Fylde Aeroclub v Blackpool County Council.*[14] However, under English law, if in these circumstances the tender is not considered, the party who made it is compensated for the fact that their tender was ignored, but they cannot force the person who advertised to contract with them. By contrast, under Russian law, if an advertisement promises that any person may buy in a certain place certain goods at a certain price, then within a two-month period anyone can claim the promised goods at that price. The advertiser may be forced to enter into a contract (CC articles 426 and 445) or will be held liable for damages. Furthermore, for refusal to fulfil a promise made in a advertisement, an advertiser can be held liable for the administrative offence of inaccurate advertising (недостоверная реклама; *nedostovernaia reklama*).[15]

(iv) Proposal of Goods as a Public Offer

Unlike English law, in relation to the retail sale of goods (CC art 494(1)):

> The proposal of a good in its advertisement, catalogues, and descriptions of the goods addressed to an indefinite group of persons shall be deemed to be a public offer (article 437(2)) if it contains all the material conditions [terms] for a contract of retail purchase-sale.[16]

The material terms for such a contract are its subject matter, that is, the name, quantity, quality, description and price of goods. Moreover, CC article 494(2) states:

> Exhibition at the place of sale (on counters, in showcases, and so forth) of goods, the demonstration of models thereof, or the granting of information concerning goods to be sold (descriptions, catalogues, photographs, and so forth) at the place of sale shall be deemed to be a public offer irrespective of whether the price and other material conditions [terms] of the contract of retail purchase-sale have been specified, except for an instance when the seller visibly determined that the respective goods are not intended for sale.

[13] Federal Law on Advertisement of 13 March 2006 No 38-FZ art 11.

[14] [1990] EWCA Civ 13.

[15] Code of Administrative Offences of the Russian Federation of 30 December 2001 No 195-FZ art 14.3.

[16] Butler, above n 1, at 360.

These important provisions effectively guaranteeing Russian consumers the opportunity to enter into advantageous purchase-sale contracts is an example of the way in which Russian contract law is generally supportive of individual consumers.

(v) Ways to Make an Offer

An offer can be made by word of mouth, or in writing. If there is no requirement of a written form of contract, an offer is considered to be made when the will to make an offer is manifest from the behaviour of the offeror. This is relevant primarily for instantaneous contracts, when it is not necessary to prove that the offer has been made and when it was made; it is immediately accepted. Contracts requiring a written form are discussed in more detail in Chapter 3 on 'Requirements of Form' at p 77.

(vi) Written Offer

In general, apart from instantaneous contracts, which are in most cases concluded by way of oral offer and acceptance, parties, especially in business relations, try whenever possible to conclude contracts in the form of a single written document signed by them both. If a party to a contract is a legal entity then, as well as the signature of an authorised individual, a stamp is required, that is, endorsement from an inked rubber stamp. However, this requirement to stamp a business contract is not provided anywhere in the law. It is merely a custom of business turnover with which legal entities conventionally comply. Such contracts normally also indicate the date and the place of their conclusion. Alternatively, the date on which a contract is made will be the date of the second party's signature.

However, exchange of offer and acceptance is frequently used in relation to purchase-sale. In this case the most typical form of the written offer is a prepayment invoice, as in the case between K and V above.[17] The written offer can be made by sending a document by 'postal, telegraph, teletype, telephone, electronic, or other communications, enabling it to be reliably established that the document emanates from a party under the contract' (CC article 434(2)).[18] It has been held by a court that terms proposed and discussed in the body of an email (as well as sending a document by email as an attachment) may also be considered to be an offer. In this case the way to prove that the email emanated from the particular person would be to prove that they are the owner of the domain from which the email or emails were sent.[19]

[17] See above, text to n 8.

[18] Butler, above n 1, at 315.

[19] Resolution of Federal Commercial Court of Volgo-Viatskii District of 9 August 2010 No A43-39816/2009.

In response to developments in the use of electronic documents and other electronic commerce, Draft Amendments to the Civil Code propose changes to the provisions of CC article 434(2) just cited.[20] Under the proposed changes the definition of a written offer in the article would also include 'an electronic document transmitted through communication channels' and the draft Civil Code amendments would introduce a definition of this, as 'information which is prepared, sent, received or stored with the use of electronic, magnetic, optical or similar means, including electronic exchange of data and electronic mail'.[21] It seems likely that these amendments are aimed at eliminating any uncertainty over the legal status of an electronic document and to create the possibility of construing the term 'document' in the legislation to include an electronic document on a par with a traditional document. If these amendments are adopted, it will eliminate any question about the validity of sending an offer in the body of an email, putting this on a statutory footing rather than as a matter of court practice, as now.

(vii) Binding Power and Revocation of an Offer

CC article 435(2) specifies that:

> An offer shall bind the person who sent it from the moment of its receipt by the addressee.
>
> If notice of the revocation of an offer has been received earlier than or simultaneously with the offer itself, the offer will be considered not to be received.[22]

An offer may include as one of its terms the period within which acceptance can be made. In that case, an offer received by an offeree may not be revoked within that period, unless the offer itself says differently, or unless it arises 'from the essence of the proposal or situation in which it was made'[23] (CC article 436).

One example of circumstances arising 'from the essence of the proposal or situation' under which an offer to sell an immovable could lawfully be revoked would be in relation to market conditions for municipal real property with a subsequent increase of the value of the property being sold, as in the following example.

> A municipal administration ('the Administration') announced a public auction[24] for the sale of shop premises which it owned. Applications to

[20] See above, text to n 18.

[21] Draft Federal Law on Amendments to Parts One, Two, Three and Four of the Civil Code approved by the State Duma at first reading on 27 April 2012 No 47538-6 art 1 para 224(a).

[22] Butler, above n 1, at 315.

[23] Ibid 316.

[24] The procedure of holding a public auction for sale of state or municipal property is regulated by Federal Law of 21 December 2001 No 178-FZ on Privatisation of State and Municipal Property. The procedure is initiated by an announcement of sale which, among other things, contains the initial price of the property, the period for filing applications to participate in the auction and the amount of deposit to be paid by the applicants. Then within the specified period potential buyers

participate were filed by both Ms K and Mr K, but no one else. Since Mr K subsequently refused to participate, it was held to be void because of too few participants.

Sometime later, the Administration issued a decree on privatisation of the premises through a 'public offering' (публичное предложение; *publichnoe predlozhenie*) ie without an auction, at a price equal to the initial auction price. The decree also specified the date after which applications to purchase the premises could be submitted. However, before then the Administration cancelled its earlier privatisation decree because the value of the premises had increased and there was now demand in the municipal real property market. Ms K went to court claiming that the Administration's second decree cancelling its earlier privatisation decree relating to the premises was unlawful and violated her rights.

The court of first instance rejected the claim. In its decision, which was upheld by both the appellate and cassation courts, the first instance court held that the presence of a demand for municipal premises at a price higher than the price of the public offering had been proved by letters to the Administration from individual entrepreneurs A and T, as well as by the Administration's own written statement. The court also noted that, given the presence of a market demand for the premises, its sale by a public offering would contradict the principle of equality of buyers of state and municipal property, as well as the principle of using rational processes and conditions for privatisation, which means that municipal property should be sold at the highest possible price. As a result Ms K could not hold the Administration to the promise in its earlier privatisation decree of a public offering at the original price.[25]

However, a change of circumstances does not always allow an offer to be revoked, as seen in another case.

The Fourth Appellate Commercial Court held that a change of legislation regulating the parties' contractual relations after the offer had been made but before it was accepted was not a basis for revocation of the offer on the grounds of 'the essence of the proposal or situation in which it was made'.

On 21 April 2010 the Committee for Management of Public Property (Комитет по управлению имуществом; *Komitet po upravleniu imush-*

file applications for participation in the auction and pay a deposit. If only one application is filed within the required time the auction is called off as having failed. When the term for filing applications expires the seller decides which applicants comply with the legal requirements and can be admitted to the auction. At the auction participants make bids exceeding the initial price of the property. The one who makes the highest bid is the winner, and they must conclude the contract of purchase-sale for the property. If they refuse they lose their deposit.

[25] Resolution of Federal Commercial Court of North-Western District of 28 June 2007 No A66-8327/2006.

> *chestvom*) made a public offer of sale of a particular property. On 15 June 2010 new amendments to the law regulating the procedure for the sale of public property entered into force. On 29 June 2010 the April public offer was accepted by someone who wished to buy the property, but on the same day that person was informed that the offer was revoked by the change in the legislation applicable to the parties' relations.
>
> However, the court held that the new law would only be applicable to legal relations which arose after it had entered into force. Here, the legal relation leading to the purchase-sale of the property had arisen before the entry into force of the new law, in fact on 21 April 2010, when an irrevocable public offer had been made. Therefore the Committee for Management of Public Property had no legal grounds to refuse to make a contract with the person who accepted that offer.[26]

It is clear that this is a difficult area of law, quite unfamiliar to a lawyer trained under the English legal system. Both the concept of a contract coming into existence on a basis other than offer and acceptance, and the consequential limitation on revocation of offer, may strike an English lawyer as strange. Under Russian law, someone who makes an offer needs to be prepared to be held to its terms, and will only be able to change their mind, even before acceptance is made, in very limited circumstances.

B Acceptance

(i) Requirements for Acceptance

An acceptance is the reply to the offer made by the person to whom the offer was addressed (the offeree). Acceptance must be full and unconditional (CC article 438(1)), and comply with the so-called 'mirror image rule' meaning it must fully correspond to the terms of the offer. A response indicating agreement to conclude the contract on different terms is not an acceptance. It is regarded as a refusal to accept and, at the same time, a new offer (CC article 443). As in English law refusal to accept destroys the original offer.

(ii) Period for Acceptance

When a time period for acceptance is included in the offer, a contract is concluded if acceptance is received by the offeror within that time limit (CC article 440).

When a written offer does not specify an acceptance period, the contract will be concluded if acceptance is received by the offeror before the end of any time

[26] In Resolution of Fourth Commercial Appellate Court of 17 September 2010 No A78-5002/2010.

period established by legislation, and if there is none, within the time normally required for acceptance (CC article 441(1)).

If the offer is made orally without specifying a period for acceptance, the contract is concluded if the offeree declares their acceptance immediately (CC article 441(2)).

If notification of acceptance is sent in good time but received after the relevant period, the acceptance will not be considered late unless the offeror immediately informs the offeree of its late arrival. Conversely, if the offeror immediately communicates to the offeree that they accept the acceptance despite its lateness, the contract is considered to be concluded (CC article 442). However, it should be noted that there is absolutely no equivalent of the default English 'postal acceptance rule' where an acceptance is deemed to be made when put in the post box.

As mentioned above, as a rule a pre-payment invoice containing all the material terms, and subsequent payment, will be considered by the courts to constitute an offer and acceptance.[27] A pre-payment invoice normally indicates the time period for payment. This raises the question whether this time period should also be considered as the acceptance period, hence what should the consequences be of not paying within that period? The following case is one example.

> The seller (company M) issued to the buyer (company R) a pre-payment invoice for payment for cable products. The pre-payment invoice specified the designation and quantity of the products, price per kilometre, total price of the products to be delivered, terms of purchase, obligations of buyer and seller, and terms of delivery. According to the invoice R had to make a pre-payment within five days of receipt of the invoice. R partially paid, but after the five-day period. Subsequently R sued M, claiming back the amount paid on the basis of unfounded enrichment.[28]
>
> The courts of first and appellate instances upheld R's claim, reasoning that since the payment was made outside the time period specified in the pre-payment invoice (the offer), that payment could not be considered to be full and unconditional acceptance, so no contract was ever concluded.
>
> However, the court at cassational instance and the Supreme Commercial Court overturned the lower courts' decisions and considered the contract of purchase-sale to be concluded on the following basis.
>
> The pre-payment invoice met all the requirements specified in the Civil Code for an offer and, therefore, should be considered to be an offer. According to CC article 438(3), performance by an offeree 'within the period established for its acceptance of actions relating to the fulfilment'[29] of the contractual terms in the offer will be considered to be an acceptance, unless the contrary is established in legislation, or specified in the offer.

[27] See above, text to n 18.

[28] The case report is silent as to whether any cable was delivered; presumably not.

[29] Butler, above n 1, at 316.

> The five-day time period in the pre-payment invoice should not be considered as the time period for reply by the offeree. Rather, it is the period within which the buyer must pay. Therefore, the pre-payment invoice (offer) did not specify a time period for acceptance and so, in accordance with CC article 441,[30] the contract would be concluded if the acceptance has been received by offeror during the time normally required for this, as indeed it had been. [31]

Here the Supreme Commercial Court established an apparent contract by construction. The offeree's action in making a part payment, although late, was within the 'normal time' for acceptance. The court's role in concluding otherwise incomplete contracts is also discussed in Chapter 6 at p 158–9.

(iii) Revocation of Acceptance

In Russian law, it is possible to revoke acceptance. Under CC article 439, if notice of such revocation is received by the offeror earlier than or simultaneously with the acceptance itself, the acceptance is considered not to have been received.

(iv) Acceptance by Performance

Besides a written or oral reply acceptance can be made by:

(1) performance of actions relating to fulfilment of the terms of the contract (конклюдентные действия; *konkludentnie deistvia*); or
(2) silence.

The first of these is covered by CC article 438(3). It states that:

> Performance by a person who has received an offer within the period established for its acceptance of actions relating to the fulfilment of the conditions of the contract specified therein (shipment of goods, provision of services, fulfilment of work, payment of respective amount, etc) shall be considered to be an acceptance unless provided otherwise by a law, other legal acts, or specified in the offer.[32]

As noted in Chapter 3 at p 77, if a written offer to conclude a contract has been accepted by performance, the written form of the contract is considered to have been complied with. It should be noted, however, that the Civil Code requires some particular types of contracts to be concluded in the form of one written document, in which case acceptance cannot be made by performance; see Chapter 3 at p 79 for further details.

[30] Paraphrased at the beginning of this section.
[31] Ruling of Supreme Commercial Court of 11 January 2008 No 17536/07.
[32] Butler, above n 1, at 316–17.

If the offeree chooses to accept an offer by performance and begins to perform their obligations, it is essential that the offeror is informed. As discussed later, if a contract is concluded by means of offer and acceptance, it is considered to be concluded 'at the moment of receipt by the person who has sent an offer of its acceptance' (CC article 433 (1)).[33] So if acceptance is made by performance, this is only effective from the moment the offeror is informed about it. This can be problematic, as in the following example.

> Company V (a seller) and company T (a buyer) were in dispute over a contract for the purchase-sale of coal. On 12 December 2008 T had sent a letter to V requesting that V organise a delivery to T in January 2009 of a specified quantity of coal of a particular type, and asking V to issue an appropriate pre-payment invoice. V received T's letter on 18 December 2008. V neither replied nor issued any pre-payment invoice. However, on 19 December 2008 V submitted an order to the Russian Railways to transport coal in January 2009 in the quantity T had requested in their letter. Then, on learning that the price of coal would increase on 30 December 2008, T sent a further letter to V, informing V that it did not want the coal delivered as requested in its first letter.
>
> In January 2009 the Russian Railways fined V for not using the transportation services it had earlier ordered. V sued T to recover this amount. V asserted that T's letter requesting delivery of the coal was an offer, and its performance of the action of arranging for transportation was acceptance. V claimed the value of the fine imposed on it by the Russian Railways as its damages for T's non-performance (refusal to perform) of its contractual obligation to buy the coal it had requested.
>
> The courts of all instances rejected V's claim. They held that V's actions could not be considered to be acceptance because T was not informed about them, and under the general rule silence is not acceptance. Therefore, V's actions were not considered by the courts to have been performed in fulfilment any of contractual obligations to T.[34]

(v) Silence as Acceptance

There is a presumption in Russian civil legislation that silence cannot be a legal fact. It follows that there cannot be acceptance by silence (as the case just discussed between V and T illustrates). However, CC articles 158 and 438 provide for exceptional circumstances when silence can have legal consequences.

Under CC article 158(3) 'Silence shall be deemed to be an expression of will to conclude a transaction in the instances provided for by a law or by agreement

[33] Ibid 314.

[34] Resolution of Federal Commercial Court of East-Siberian District of 24 February 2010 No A19-15655/09.

of the parties'.[35] Under article 438(2), 'Silence shall not be an acceptance unless it arises otherwise from a law, custom of business turnover, or former business relations of the parties'.[36]

As a result the Russian Civil Code does allow acceptance by silence in particular cases. However, it should be noted that courts rarely recognise silence as acceptance when parties claim it arises from the customs of business turnover, or former business relations between the parties, because in most cases parties are unable to provide any evidence of silence as acceptance in an existing trade custom or in prior dealings.

In some contracts of adhesion (standard form contracts) it is often supposed that a customer's silence and continued use of services might be recognised as acceptance of the service provider's offer to change the terms of an existing contract. However, in these cases the courts declare the changed terms void and refuse to recognise acceptance by silence. One example is a court decision on contracts for the provision of mobile phone and telecommunication services.

> The Federal Service for the Supervision of Consumer Rights and Well-Being [Федеральная служба по надзору в сфере защиты прав потребителей и благополучия человека; *Federal'naia sluzhba po nadzoru v sfere zashchity prav potrebitelei i blagopoluchiia cheloveka*] ('the Federal Service') issued an order to a mobile services provider pointing out a violation of the relevant legislation and fining the provider for that violation. The mobile services provider brought a case to get the order revoked. The Federal Service claimed, in particular, that the terms of the mobile services provider's standard contract in relation to a change of contractual terms were not compliant with legislation.
>
> Contractual terms for provision of mobile communication services must be compliant with Rules approved by the Russian Government. According to these, any change in the contract should be made either by a written addendum agreed by both parties or, alternatively, can be accepted by performance of actions relating to fulfilment of the terms of the contract (конклюдентные действия; *konkludentnie deistvia*) following a procedure previously set out by the mobile communications provider. Neither pertained here and therefore the court held that any unilateral change by the mobile communication provider of the contractual terms was not allowed.
>
> The provider's standard contract included a term which gave them the right to propose changes in the contractual terms by sending the customer an offer of new terms (by an SMS or publication on the Internet or in other mass media or otherwise). If, within 15 days of receipt of this information, the provider did not receive from the customer a written refusal

[35] Butler, above n 1, at 145.
[36] Ibid 316.

> to accept the changes (in full or in part), the customer would be considered to have agreed with the proposed changes if they continued to use the service.
>
> The court rejected the provider's argument that the contract set out a procedure for a customer to exercise actions indicating their acceptance of the change to contractual terms. The court gave the following reasons. According to CC article 438(2), silence shall not be acceptance 'unless it arises otherwise from a law, custom of business turnover, or former business relations of the parties'.[37] However, under the provider's standard contract, a customer's consent was to be indicated by the provider failing to receive the customer's refusal to accept proposed changes within a specified period, along with the customer failing unilaterally to exercise their right to terminate the contract. In other words, the standard form contract imposed acceptance by the customer's silence, which contradicts the law.[38]

Draft Amendments to the Civil Code propose to include in CC article 438(2) a provision that silence as acceptance may also be provided for in a contract between the parties.[39] This change is clearly meant to make lawful the terms of the mobile services provider's contract discussed above. This possibility is very important because for services providers whose customers number in the millions, this may be the only practicable way to change the terms of their contracts.

The court decision above also illustrates an important distinction between acceptance by performance of actions relating to fulfilment of the contractual terms (*konkludentnie deistviya*) and by silence. The first implies not only performance of certain actions by the offeree, but also communication of that to the offeror. It would successfully accept an offer. Silence means no action at all and no communication from the offeree; no acceptance is made.

IV FORMATION OF A CONTRACT: SINGLE WRITTEN DOCUMENT SIGNED BY BOTH PARTIES

As noted in above at p 97 (and in Chapter 3 at p 79), one way to conclude a contract in written form under CC article 434(2) is by drawing up one document signed by both parties. Since conclusion of the contract is then based on the creation of that document rather than on any agreement between the parties, the rules of offer and acceptance are not applicable. However, these rules are often applied by courts if there is a dispute over the contract's terms.

[37] See above, text to n 35.

[38] Resolution of Federal Commercial Court of Volgo-Viatskii District of 8 February 2011 No A28-14037/2009.

[39] Draft Federal Law No 47538-6, above n 21 art 1 para 226(a).

Very often the parties negotiate a contract to be drawn up in one document by exchanging different versions. This process of exchange when each party adds something new could be analysed as numerous offers and counter-offers. The contract is considered to be concluded, though, from the moment when it is signed by both parties, and not from the moment when one party finally accepts the other party's version.

The courts apply the logic of offer and acceptance in cases when the parties exchange multiple versions of a contract but, without signing the contract, start performing it. Here the question arises whether the terms of the contract which was not signed should be applicable to the relations between the parties.

It is important to keep in mind that in Russia the fact that the parties have signed a document called 'contract' (договор, *dogovor*; контракт, *kontrakt*) or 'agreement' (соглашение; *soglashenie*) does not necessarily imply that a contract is concluded. As pointed out above, a contract is considered to be concluded only when all the material terms have been agreed by the parties. So if the signed 'contract' or 'agreement' does not include all the material terms, the contract may be considered to be not concluded. Sometimes a court will consider a contract which has been performed either partially or fully as concluded, despite a lack of agreement on some material terms, but there is a serious risk that in the circumstances the court will declare the contract not concluded (for more on this issue, see Chapter 6 at p 156). At the same time if the parties did make an agreement on the material terms but failed to negotiate some other terms, those will merely not be considered to be a part of the concluded contract, as in the following example.

> Company Z and company A signed a contract of delivery of automotive parts. Z (the seller) delivered the automotive parts to A (the buyer) in accordance with its terms. However, within the guarantee period A found that some parts were defective, and returned them to Z. Subsequently, A claimed from Z both the price of the defective parts and the cost of returning them. Z refused to pay, so A sued. The courts at all instances upheld the claim only in part, holding that A should only be compensated for the price of the defective goods and not the cost of returning them. The reasoning was as follows.
>
> The courts held that the parties had agreed on all the material terms of a contract of delivery, set out in a written document signed by both parties, but had disputed the method for calculating the cost of returning any defective parts. However, the courts held that the disputed terms were not material terms of a contract of delivery, hence the contract was held to be concluded.
>
> Z's actions on receipt of A's draft contract of delivery showed that it did not intend to accept that offer. This was also substantiated by the fact that Z drafted a protocol of disagreements, which it sent to A. Having received it, A (as offeror) did not take any measures to settle the disagreements but

> considered the contract to be concluded on its own terms. Thus A violated CC article 507(1), which requires: 'when in concluding a contract of delivery, disagreements arise between the parties with regard to individual conditions of the contract the party proposing to conclude the contract and receiving a proposal from the other party to agree these conditions must within thirty days from the date of receipt of this proposal . . . take measures relating to agreeing the respective conditions of the contract or inform the other party in writing of his refusal to conclude it'.[40]
>
> In these circumstances the courts held that the contract of delivery was concluded in A's version except for the terms in Z's protocol of disagreements, to which A had not agreed. Since the provision on compensation for A's costs of returning the defective goods was in that protocol, the courts did not apply it so rejected that part of A's claim.[41]

Unlike the situation in a 'battle of the forms' in English law, where the existence of a contract is not in doubt and the terms are taken to be those in the 'last shot',[42] in a contract under Russia law, such as this contract of delivery, active steps need to be taken to clarify exactly which terms have been included beyond the material terms necessary for the contract's existence.

V FORMATION OF A CONTRACT: SPECIAL CASES

For certain types of contract regulated in Part Two of the Civil Code and other federal laws, specific methods for their conclusion, other than the general offer and acceptance method, are stipulated. The general 'offer and acceptance' method is thus excluded. Three obvious examples are contracts of retail purchase-sale, contracts of carriage and insurance contracts. For the first two, it is the receipt of documentation which concludes the contract.

A contract of retail purchase-sale is concluded in the moment when the receipt is given to the customer (CC article 493).[43] The general offer-acceptance rule is not applicable. Under that, the contract would be concluded when the buyer indicates acceptance, because demonstration of goods for sale is a public offer, but instead the Code specifies an unequivocal event – handing over a receipt – to define the time of conclusion.

Under CC article 785(2):

> The conclusion of a contract of carriage of goods shall be confirmed by drawing up and issuing to the consignor of the goods a transport waybill (bill of lading or other document for goods provided for by the respective transport or code).[44]

[40] Butler, above n 1, at 371.

[41] Ruling of Supreme Commercial Court of 4 February 2011 No VAS-597/11.

[42] *Butler Machine Tool Co Ltd v Ex-cello Corp (England) Ltd* [1979] 1 WLR 401.

[43] See below, text to n 50.

[44] Butler, above n 1, at 550.

CC article 786(2) goes on to say that: 'The conclusion of a contract of carriage of a passenger shall be certified by a ticket, and the handing over of baggage by the passenger, by a baggage receipt'.[45] Thus, as with retail purchase-sale, a clear action sets the time the contract is concluded.

A contract of insurance must be concluded in written form (CC article 940(1)) but this may be done 'by means of drawing up one document ([as under] article 434(2)) or handing over by the insurer to the insurant [insured] on the basis of his written or oral application the insurance policy (or certificate, receipt) signed by the insurer'[46] (article 940(2)).

Here it can be seen that the application of the insured and issuance of the insurance policy cannot be analysed from the perspective of offer and acceptance, not least because the application must not and cannot contain all the material terms of the insurance contract. Thus the offer and acceptance rules do not apply to the procedure for concluding an insurance contract by issuing a policy on the basis of the insured's application. It is the written form which 'makes' the contract, in either of the two ways set out in article 940(2).

VI MOMENT OF CONCLUSION OF THE CONTRACT

In addition to asking, 'Is the contract concluded?', in the light of the Russian Civil Code it is also essential to pose the question, 'At what point in time is the contract concluded?'. If that is not clear, even if the parties have agreed on all the material terms, the contract might nevertheless be considered to be not concluded.

In relation to the time of their conclusion, the Civil Code divides all contracts into two categories: 'real' contracts and 'consensual' contracts. The time at which a contract is considered to be concluded thus depends on, first, whether it is classified as a 'real' or 'consensual' contract, and secondly, the form of contract prescribed by law or agreed by the parties.

A Real Contracts

A real contract is a contract which according to the law is considered to be concluded only on the transfer of property (CC article 433(2)). Consequently, to conclude a real contract, not only must the material terms be agreed in the required form, but also the property that is the subject matter of the contract must be transferred. The basic concept behind a real contract is that the contractual party confirms their will to enter into contractual relations by the transfer of property of some sort.

[45] Ibid 551.
[46] Ibid 652.

One example is the contract of loan (заем; *zaem*). CC article 807(1) specifies that a contract of loan 'shall be considered to be concluded from the moment of transfer of the money or other things'.[47] CC article 808(1) also requires that a contract of loan between individuals:

> must be concluded in written form if the amount thereof is not less than ten times the minimum amount of payment for labour established by a law,[48] and in an instance when the lender is a legal person, irrespective of the amount.[49]

The effect of CC article 807(1) is that for a contract of loan, even if there is a written document signed by both parties which includes all the material terms, the contract will not be concluded until the lender actually transfers the loan to the borrower. One important effect of this is that under a contract of loan the borrower may have in hand the written loan agreement but cannot demand that the lender transfers the loan to them, because as yet the contract is not concluded. Fortunately, as we will see shortly, this is not the only form of contract under which borrowing may be undertaken.

B Consensual Contracts

A consensual contract is a contract which is considered to be concluded when all the material terms have been agreed by the parties in the correct form. The point at which that occurs will depend on which method the parties have chosen to conclude their contract (provided that they have choice – that the form is not fixed by legislation). Generally, a contract is deemed to be concluded at the moment of receipt of acceptance by the offeror (CC article 433(1)).

In contrast to the contract of loan (заем; *zaem*) just discussed, an example of a consensual contract is the credit contract (кредитный договор; *kreditniy dogovor*). By CC article 819(1):

> Under a credit contract a bank or other credit organisation (creditor) *shall be obliged* to grant monetary means (credit) to the borrower in the amount and on the conditions provided by the contract, and the borrower shall be obliged to return the monetary amount received and to pay interest on it.[50] (emphasis added)

The phrase 'shall be obliged' (обязуются; *obiazuiutsia*) here demonstrates that the contract is a consensual one, because unlike the contract of loan it creates an obligation on the creditor to transfer the credit to the borrower once the contract is completed, that is, as soon as the parties have agreed all the material terms in written form. At that stage the borrower may enforce the transfer. In

[47] Ibid 563.

[48] At the time of writing the minimum amount of payment for labour for this calculation is 100 roubles which is approximately £2, so 10 times this is approximately £20. There is a more realistic value of the minimum amount of payment for labour used for other purposes of 5,250 roubles.

[49] Butler, above n 1, at 564.

[50] Ibid 570.

contrast to loan, property does not need to be transferred in order for the contract to come into existence.

C Special Cases

Classification of a contract as real or consensual is not always obvious and is not always necessary. A vivid example is the contract of retail purchase-sale. From the definition of a retail purchase-sale contract it is not entirely clear whether it would be real or consensual. Fortunately, as seen above, the Civil Code explicitly defines the time when a retail purchase-sale contract is considered to be concluded. CC article 493 states that:

> Unless provided otherwise by a law or a contract of retail purchase-sale, including the conditions of standard contracts or other standard forms to which the purchaser adheres (article 428), a contract of retail purchase-sale shall be considered to be concluded in proper form from the moment of the issuance by the seller to the purchaser of a cashier or goods cheque or other document confirming payment for the good.[51]

Thus any necessity to qualify a retail purchase-sale contract as real or consensual is bypassed by a special provision of the Civil Code defining the moment of its conclusion, that is, when a receipt is handed over.

D Preliminary Contract: Binding 'Agreement to Agree'

Russian law specifically allows parties to create a binding 'preliminary contract' (предварительный договор; *predvaritel'nyi dogovor*) under which, 'the parties shall be obliged to conclude in future a contract concerning the transfer of property, fulfilment of work, or rendering of services (principal contract) on the conditions provided for by the preliminary contract'[52] (CC article 429(1)). The preliminary contract must be in written form, unless the principal contract is required to be in a particular form, in which case the preliminary contract must match that. It has to contain sufficient terms to allow the subject matter and other material terms of the principal contract to be established. It should also set the time within which the parties must conclude their principal contract; if it is silent, then the second paragraph of CC article 429(4) sets a time limit of one year from the conclusion of the preliminary contract.

The point of a preliminary contract is to give a potential party to a complex business deal some security that the potential counterparty will not walk away during the negotiation process. If the counterparty 'evades the conclusion of the principal contract'[53] (CC article 429(5)), then the other party can apply to a

[51] Ibid 360.
[52] Ibid 311.
[53] Ibid 312.

court under CC article 432(4) to compel its conclusion, and also seek damages for losses caused by an unjustifiable evasion of the principle contract's conclusion. If necessary, the court will hear a precontractual dispute (CC article 446) to determine the exact terms of the contract.

These provisions may appear to undermine freedom of contract. However, the intention is more to enhance commercial transactions by allowing parties to agree to the main features of a contract and accept mutual obligations, the details of which can be elaborated later. Any court resolution of the dispute over the formation of the principal contract should be based on the parties' agreement in the preliminary contract.

E Conclusion of a Contract Compared to Entry into Force of a Contract

As well as the expression 'conclusion of a contract' (заключение договора; *zakliuchenie dogovora*) the Civil Code uses the expression 'the contract enters into force' (договор вступает в силу; *dogovor vstupaet v silu*).

CC article 425(1) provides that 'A contract shall enter into force and become binding for the parties from the moment of its conclusion'.[54] The fact that the Code distinguishes between these two expressions means that they may not coincide and in particular instances could be separated in time. Otherwise, why would the Code employ two separate expressions?

Indeed, under CC article 425(2), the parties have the right to establish that the terms of a contract they have concluded 'shall apply to their relations which arose before the conclusion of the contract'.[55] Here the terms of the contract enter into force despite the contract itself not being formally concluded.

A contract may also have been concluded but not yet entered into force, meaning neither party can claim anything from the other under it. This issue is of particular interest in relation to the contract of insurance (страхование; *strakhovanie*). According to CC article 957(1), 'A contract of insurance, unless provided otherwise therein, shall enter into force from the moment of payment of the insurance premium or first contribution thereof'.[56] In practice, the parties very seldom provide otherwise, so in most cases this general provision applies.

Insurance protection provided by a contract of insurance only covers insured events which occur after the insurance contract enters into force, unless the contract provides a different start time (CC article 957(2)). Again, the parties very seldom do that.

A contract of insurance, concluded but not yet entered into force, does not give insurance protection to the insured. However, it is still a 'legal fact' which creates the grounds for paying the insurance premium. This does not make contract of insurance a real contract. In a real contract property must be transferred by the

[54] Ibid 307.
[55] Ibid 308.
[56] Ibid 663.

person entering into contractual relations; it is a means to prove their will to make the contract. By contrast, an insurance premium under CC articles 939(1) and 954(1) can be paid not only by the insured, but also by a beneficiary, who is not a party to the contract and is therefore not confirming their will to be contractually bound.

Careful analysis of the exact type of contract is therefore necessary in order to be clear when the rights and obligations created by the contract actually come into being, as seen from the above. The moment of conclusion of the contract thus may not be as obvious as the contracting parties might expect.

VII CONCLUSION

Formation of a contract under Russian law is not necessarily a straightforward process. A requirement of agreement (offer and acceptance) is necessary but in some cases not sufficient; some requirement of form is needed. Also, it is possible with written contracts that the signature and sometimes the stamp of both parties on a single contractual document will establish the contract, irrespective of any actual exchange of offer and acceptance. Moreover, real contracts add a further criterion for enforcement. Until property has been handed over, the contract is not concluded, despite agreement. Overall, then, successful formation of a contract under the rules of Russian civil law can be rather problematic, and absolute clarity is needed as to the particular type of contract and any associated specific requirements it might have.

5

Consideration

I INTRODUCTION

Consideration is one of the compulsory requirements in English contract law for a binding informal contract,[1] along with agreement (offer and acceptance) and intention to be legally bound. Consideration, in English law, is what party B gives to party A to support a promise by A which B wishes to enforce. This applies for both bilateral and unilateral contracts.[2]

Russian contract law does not have an exact equivalent of consideration. Consideration is not required for a contract to be considered concluded. However, there are two legal mechanisms in Russian contract law which are to a large extent analogous to executed consideration in English law and perform a similar function. These are:

- counter-performance (встречное исполнение; *vstrechnoe ispolnenie*) of obligations; and
- counter-giving for performance (встречное предоставление; *vstrechnoe predostavlenie*).

These expressions sound rather awkward in English, but the role each concept plays matches its literal translation, as will be seen in this chapter.

II COUNTER-PERFORMANCE

A Definition of Counter-Performance

Counter-performance is defined in Civil Code (CC) article 328(1): 'The performance of an obligation by one of the parties which in accordance with a contract *is conditioned* by the performance by the other party of its obligations shall be deemed to be counter-performance'[3] (emphasis added).

[1] Informal in the sense that it is not binding as a result of being in a special form, ie a deed under seal.

[2] Bilateral contracts are contracts where both sides have obligations. Unilateral contracts are contracts where only one side is under an obligation, eg, to pay the promised reward in return for the successful retrieval of a lost dog.

[3] WE Butler, *The Civil Code of the Russian Federation Parts 1, 2 and 3: Parallel Russian and English Texts* (Moscow, JurInfoR-Press, 2008) 252–3.

Thus to qualify as counter-performance, it must be performance in circumstances where the two parties A and B do not perform their contractual obligations simultaneously, and have the following two characteristics: first, it is performed by B after A has already performed their contractual obligation. Performance by A, the party who performs first, can never be regarded as counter-performance. Secondly, to qualify as counter-performance, B's actions must be *conditioned* (that is, conditional on) performance by A.

The practical application of these is illustrated by examples from court practice below.

Bearing these characteristics in mind, it is be apparent that counter-performance, unlike English consideration, only occurs in bilateral contracts. However, as noted, it is not a requirement, unlike English consideration, and its absence does not adversely impact the formation or binding force of any contract. Rather, it affects what B may do if A fails to perform as promised.

B Function of Counter-Performance

If the conditions outlined above are fulfilled so that B's performance qualifies as a counter-performance, and the other party, A, fails to perform at all or on time, B is given specific rights under CC article 328. It is important to emphasise that in these circumstances B does not have any other alternatives except for those provided in CC article 328 and discussed below.

According to CC article 328(2), if the other party, A, fails to perform, or it is clear that A's performance will not be made in due time, B 'shall have the right to suspend the performance of his obligation'.[4] Alternatively, B may 'waive the performance of this obligation and demand compensation of losses'.[5] The difference between suspending performance and waiving performance is that suspending performance means merely postponing the contractual obligation to perform; waiving performance terminates that obligation.

Under this provision, if B elects to suspend its counter-performance, B will have no right to sue A for either required performance[6] or compensation for losses. However, if B elects to waive performance of its own counter-obligation and sue A for its losses, B is entitled to compensation from A. But, as in the first alternative, B will have no right to sue A for required performance.

CC article 328(3) gives a third alternative. If B provides the counter-performance, then B has a right to sue A for both compensation and also required performance, and A is obliged to provide them.

[4] Ibid 253.

[5] Ibid.

[6] See Chapter 9 at p 193 and Chapter 10 at p 251 for details of required performance as a remedy (in instances when it is other than payment of an agreed sum).

If A only performs in part, B has the right either to suspend performance of its own obligation, or to waive its performance, in proportion to the performance A has failed to provide.

It is worth stressing that if B has not provided any counter-performance, B has absolutely no right to demand that A performs its obligation. In return, A cannot demand that B performs B's obligation before A has itself provided performance. Therefore, in a bilateral contract which is not performed simultaneously, the Russian concept of counter-performance has a similar effect to the English doctrine of consideration, in supporting the right to enforce the other party's duty to perform.

This can be illustrated by cases of claims for pre-payment, when the delivery of goods, provision of work or services is conditional on such payment. In Russia it is very common to include a contractual term requiring partial or full pre-payment. Most purchase-sale contracts, for example, would include such a term.[7] Then the delivery of goods by seller B is conditional on the pre-payment by buyer A. The delivery is B's counter-performance, in return for A's pre-payment. In many instances when a buyer fails to make pre-payment the seller will sue for non-performance, demanding both the pre-payment and compensation for losses; such claims are normally rejected by courts on the grounds that the option to sue for the pre-payment is only available to the seller after they have performed their contractual obligation to deliver the goods.

The Supreme Commercial Court has held in multiple Resolutions[8] that the provisions of CC article 328 which sets out the exhaustive list of rights that the party who would provide the counter-performance (in our example, B) has if A fails to perform, are imperative. This means that the parties cannot agree on any other options. For example, A and B cannot include a term in the contract that B may, without providing any counter-performance, sue A for required performance.

Thus, in a contract containing a pre-payment clause, seller B can demand that buyer A provides pre-payment and compensates B's losses arising from late payment of pre-payment only once B has delivered the goods to A, ie has made its counter-performance. The Supreme Commercial Court has also underlined that the Civil Code does not contain any provisions which would allow a seller B to sue A for pre-payment for the goods before the goods have actually been delivered.[9] The idea behind this approach is rather simple. From CC article 487 it follows that a pre-payment is payment *for the goods* to be delivered under a

[7] For discussion about the lack of institutional trust in business contracts, see K Hendley, 'Coping with Uncertainty: The Role of Contracts in Russian Industry During the Transition to the Market' (2010) 30(2) *Northwestern Journal of International Law and Business* 417.

[8] See, eg Ruling of Supreme Commercial Court of 16 November 2010 No VAS-15009/10; Ruling of Supreme Commercial Court of 27 December 2010 No VAS-17344/10; Resolution of Presidium of the Supreme Commercial Court of 30 November 2010 No 921, case No 56-47705/2008.

[9] See also Resolution of Federal Commercial Court of Volgo-Viatskii District of 9 February 2011 No A79-4622/2010; Ruling of Supreme Commercial Court of 1 July 2011 No VAS-8289/11; Resolution of Federal Commercial Court of Moscow District of 17 January 2012 No 40-25631/11.

purchase-sale contract which is paid before the actual delivery. The courts deduce that no one can be *coerced* to pay for something they have not yet received. The same approach is applied in courts dealing with claims for pre-payments in other types of contracts.

It should be mentioned that according to CC article 328(4), the rules in article 328 outlined at the beginning of this section apply 'unless provided otherwise by the contract or by a law'.[10] In line with the Supreme Commercial Court's established position on this, this provision is narrowly interpreted by courts to the extent that parties may provide in a contract that some or all of the CC article 328 rules do not apply. In other words, A and B may agree to deprive B, the party who must counter-perform, of one or all the rights granted by CC article 328, limit those rights or agree on the losses which could be claimed. Thus, this provision allows the parties to alter some aspects of their contractual relationship but does not override the imperative rule, that a party who would be providing counter-performance (in our example, B) cannot sue the other party (A) for required performance before providing their own counter-performance.

Draft Amendments to the Civil Code propose a new paragraph to CC article 328, which explicitly states that:

> neither of the parties to an obligation, which provides for counter-performance, has a right to claim in court the performance of the other party if it has not provided the other party with the performance due from it under the obligation.[11]

This rule is clearly aimed at formalising the Supreme Commercial Court's established position, noted above.

C Main Characteristics of Counter-Performance

The main characteristics of counter-performance were outlined above. Here each of them is discussed in greater detail.

(i) Counter-Performance is Performance by the Second Party, B

We have seen above that the Civil Code provides certain rights to B if A does not perform its contractual obligation, including B's right to suspend or waive counter-performance. The following Supreme Commercial Court case illustrates the fact that that counter-performance is always the performance of the second party B and, hence, only B may exercise these rights.

> Company A and company B concluded a contract of barter, under which A was obliged to deliver sunflower oil to B by 1 May 2000, and B was obliged

[10] Butler, above n 3, at 253.

[11] Draft Federal Law on Amendments to Parts One, Two, Three and Four of the Civil Code approved by the State Duma at first reading on 27 April 2012 No 47538-6 art 1 para 165.

> to deliver diesel fuel to A by 15 May 2000. Although this was a contract of exchange, not purchase-sale, under its terms A had to make delivery first. A did not deliver the sunflower oil by the due date, which led B to exercise its right under CC article 328 to suspend its own performance.
>
> Afterwards B sued A for the penalty set in the contract for non-performance by A. A objected that the penalty should only be paid for the period between 1 and 15 May 2000, claiming that, as B had not performed its obligation by 15 May, A had the right under CC article 328 to suspend its own performance.
>
> The Supreme Commercial Court declared that A had no right to do this, because performance by the first party, here A, can never qualify as counter-performance. It followed that A could not exercise the rights in CC article 328.[12]

(ii) Counter-Performance is Always Conditional on Performance by the First Party

Qualification of a performance as counter-performance is important because it directly affects the rights of the second party, B, when the first party, A, has failed to perform.

The issue of whether or not B may use the rights granted to it by CC article 328 is a frequent ground for litigation in the Russian commercial courts. Interpreting the notion of counter-performance as defined in CC article 328(1), most courts reasonably conclude that, to be counter-performance, B's performance must be conditional on A's performance, as in the following example.

> In a case reviewed by the Fifteenth Commercial Appellate Court, S, a service provider and C, a client, concluded a contract for the provision of services. The contract specified that payment was to be made in two instalments; the first as a pre-payment and the second by 4 September 2009. The contract also provided that the provision of services was to start on 8 July 2009. No services had been provided by the end of 2009 so C sued S, claiming for reimbursement of the pre-payment. S counterclaimed and demanded payment of the second instalment. S asserted that, in accordance with CC article 328, he had suspended performance of his obligation to provide the services because C had not paid the second instalment.
>
> The court noted that under CC article 328(1) counter-performance is performance which is conditional on performance by the other party. Therefore, counter-performance has to be something provided *only after* the other party has performed their obligation. The court emphasised that a necessary prerequisite to qualify as counter-performance is that the

[12] Informational Circular of Supreme Commercial Court of 24 September 2002 No 69 'Overview of Practice on Resolution of Disputes connected with the Contract of Barter' para 16.

contract explicitly provides this. The exact wording can vary. It can specify precisely that performance is only to be provided after the first party has performed; or it can set a sequence for the two parties' performances which makes this clear, for example, by a term under which a contractor will commence work no later than one month after receiving prepayment.

Following this reasoning, the court rejected S's counterclaim and upheld C's claim. It held that the contract between the parties did not include a term under which S's performance of its obligation was conditional on C's payment of the full fee for the services (including the second instalment). Rather, the dates in the contract showed that S should provide services two months before the second payment, so clearly not consequential on it. Here clearly S was not providing a counter-performance.[13]

Another case shows court reasoning based on the requirement for conditionality.

Leasing company L and airline E contracted for E to lease an aircraft engine from L. According to the contract L was also obliged to extend the engine's lifetime beyond 3,000 hours at its own expense.

After a certain time E requested that L extended the engine's lifetime up to 4,800 hours. L refused. It held that its obligation to extend the engine's lifetime was a counter-performance conditional on E's payment of rent; since E had not paid the rent for leasing the engine, L claimed the right to suspend its performance on the basis of CC article 328(2).

L sued E for the rent for E's use of the aircraft engine. Among other claims, L demanded the payment of the minimal rent specified by the contract for the period when E could not use the engine because L had failed to extend its lifetime.

The court found for L in respect of the rent of the aircraft engine but rejected L's claim for the minimal rental fee for the period when E could not use the aircraft engine. The court held that E only had to pay the rent for the period when the engine functioned.

The court rejected L's argument that it had a right to suspend its obligation to extend the engine's lifetime. It held that CC article 328 only applied to counter-performance, and here the engine rental contract did not specify that L's obligation to extend the engine's lifetime was conditional on E paying rent for its actual use of the engine. Therefore, L's obligation to prolong the engine's lifetime could not be counter-performance; hence L could not rely on CC article 328 as grounds for refusing to carry out its contractual duty to prolong the engine's lifetime.[14]

[13] Resolution of Fifteenth Commercial Appellate Court of 23 June 2011 No 15AP-5186/2011/.

[14] Resolution of Federal Commercial Court of Moscow District of 23 August 2007 No KG-40/7679-07.

The Federal District Commercial Court of Far-Eastern District in one of its decisions used a different approach to decide whether a performance was counter-performance.

> In 2000 landlord L contracted to let premises to tenant T for 10 years for T to use for his sewing business. Unfortunately, T stopped paying rent to L from 1 February 2004. As a result, on 20 April 2004 L instructed the security guards at the entrance to the premises not to let in T's workers. At the end of 2004 L sued T for the unpaid rent for the period from 1 February until 1 December 2004.
>
> The court upheld L's claim but only in part. It held that a landlord's obligation to a tenant is to provide premises for possession and use. The tenant's obligation is to pay for that possession and use. Therefore, payment of rent is counter-performance. So if L did not fully perform his side of the contract, T, who was due to provide counter-performance, might accordingly suspend or waive his obligation to pay, exercising his rights under CC article 328. The court therefore concluded that T did not have to pay rent for the period when L had denied access to the premises for T's workers. [15]

In this case the court construed CC article 328 by applying a notion of fairness rather than the literal wording of the article as commonly understood in court practice. Even though the outcome of this decision is reasonable from a legal standpoint, the Civil Code provides other legal instruments which might have been more appropriate in this situation to achieve the same result. For example, after T failed to pay the rent on time twice in a row, L could have used the right to demand early discharge of the contract under CC article 619(3) and claim in court the amount of rent due from T. According to this article, a rental contract may be dissolved before time by a court at the demand of the landlord if the tenant does not pay rent 'more than two times in succession upon the expiry of the period established by the court'.[16] However, this case is particularly interesting in the way the court based its reasoning on reciprocity, analogous to the English concept of consideration, instead of applying the provisions of CC article 619(3) on early discharge.

(iii) No Counter-Performance if Obligations are Performed Simultaneously

Performance by the party which actually performs second can never be counter-performance, if the wording of the contract requires both parties to perform their obligations simultaneously or within the same short timeframe, for example, within one week of the contract being concluded. If the contract does not

[15] Resolution of Federal Commercial Court of Far-Eastern District of 19 May 2006 No A51-18938/04-2-307/23.

[16] Butler, above n 3, at 447.

explicitly specify that one performance must be earlier in time, it does not define which party would be counter-performing, therefore there can be no counter-performance.

The contrast between a contract with counter-performance and one without can be demonstrated using the example of a contract of barter. CC article 569 specifies in relation to barter:

> if the periods for delivery of the goods to be exchanged do not coincide, the rules concerning counter-performance of obligations (article 328) apply to the performance of the obligation to transfer the good by the party which must transfer the good after the transfer of the good by the other party.[17]

Thus, if A and B conclude a barter contract under which B has to deliver to A 100 kg of chicken meat within five days from the date when A delivers to B a ton of sawdust, B's performance will be qualified as counter-performance. By contrast, if B and A specify in their barter contract that they will exchange 100 kg of chicken meat for a ton of sawdust within seven days after formation (conclusion) of the contract, performance of neither party can be considered as counter-performance, as the contract does not determine which party must perform first. The following case is an example.

> Cooperative W and company C agreed to exchange three wagon-loads of construction materials for a certain number of personal computers (PCs) within one week from the conclusion of the barter contract between them. On the last day of the exchange period W had only delivered to C one wagon-load instead of three. C could not reasonably expect delivery of the two remaining wagon-loads. C considered its performance to be counter-performance, so, on the basis of CC article 328, suspended performance of its obligation.
>
> In this situation, on one hand both parties had to deliver within the same period. On the other hand, by the last day of that period it was clear that W would not fully perform its obligation, but C was ready to deliver the required number of PCs when it decided to suspend its performance.
>
> Both the Court of Cassation and the Supreme Commercial Court held that C's readiness to perform could not be considered as counter-performance, because both parties had to perform within the same period, and not necessarily sequentially. Moreover, C's performance was not conditional on W's performance. Therefore C could not apply CC article 328.[18]

From the discussion above we can deduce the following differences between the English doctrine of consideration and the Russian concept of counter-performance:

[17] Ibid 419.

[18] Informational Circular of Supreme Commercial Court of 24 September 2002 No 69 'Overview of Practice on Resolution of Disputes connected with the Contract of Barter' para 10.

(1) While consideration is any performance (or promise of performance) by one party to the other, counter-performance is always the performance by the second party (whom we have called B above) which is conditional on performance by the first party, A, provided that the contract specifies different time limits for the performance of each party's obligations, such that A performs before B.
(2) While there must be consideration from the party seeking to enforce a promise in unilateral, as well as bilateral contracts, by definition counter-performance can only be present in bilateral contracts.
(3) While the absence of consideration negates the existence of a contract, the presence or absence of counter-performance does not affect the validity of the contract.

Thus Russian counter-performance is a narrower concept than the English doctrine of consideration.

What makes counter-performance similar to consideration is the function it performs in bilateral contracts. When the performance by B is qualified as counter-performance, B cannot sue A for non-performance unless B has provided the counter-performance (under English analysis, has provided executed consideration). B does have an option to claim damages, but cannot obtain required performance if the reciprocity of B's performance is lacking.

III COUNTER-GIVING FOR PERFORMANCE

The second concept in Russian law which has an analogous function to English consideration is 'counter-giving for performance' (встречное предоставление; *vstrechnoe predostavlenie*), which is particularly important in relation to contracts in Russian law which may be binding despite there being no payment or other compensation by one party in return for something they receive from the other party, such as a contact of gift.

A Understanding the Concept of Counter-Giving for Performance

As noted in the introduction to this chapter, in English law consideration is an indispensable requirement for all legally binding informal contracts. It thus works as a mechanism to exclude promises for which nothing is given in return (so *nudum pactum* – a bare promise) from being binding in law as part of an English contract.[19] In Russian contract law, as well as 'counter-performance' discussed above, there is also the concept of 'counter-giving for performance'. This is used to distinguish between contracts for compensation and contracts without compensation which are nevertheless binding.

[19] Some promises may be enforced under the equitable doctrine of estoppel (promissory or otherwise) but they are arguably outside the ambit of contractual promises.

(i) Contracts for Compensation and Contracts without Compensation

Contracts for compensation and without compensation are defined in CC article 423. 'A contract under which a party must receive payment or other *counter-giving* for the performance of his duties shall be *for compensation*'[20] (emphasis added). A contract without compensation is 'a contract under which one party is obliged to grant something to the other party without receiving payment from him or other counter-giving' (article 423(2)).[21]

The reciprocity of counter-giving in a contact for compensation makes it similar to English consideration. However, the fact that there is no counter-giving in a contract without compensation does not necessarily render that contract not legally binding and unenforceable.

Some types of contracts regulated by Part Two of the Civil Code are by definition contracts for compensation, eg a contract of rent (lease) (dealt with in chapter 34) or a contract of sub-rent of dwelling premises (article 685). Others are by definition contracts without compensation, eg a contract of uncompensated use (chapter 36) or contract of gift (chapter 32). Note that as in English law the promise to give a gift in the future is only legally binding on the donor if it is made in a specific form (in English law, a deed); CC article 574(2) requires written form for a promise of a gift in the future.

Some types of contracts are not *a priori* defined as either contracts for compensation or contracts without compensation and hence can be either, depending on their particular terms. For instance, a contract of commission (CC chapter 49) is a contract for compensation only 'if this is provided by a law, other legal acts, or the contract of commission'[22] (article 972(1)).

Where the Civil Code defines a type of contract as a contract for compensation but the terms of a particular contract of this type do not actually provide any counter-giving (so in fact it is a contract without compensation), that contract may be considered as a sham contract under CC article 170(2).[23] The same applies to a contract which is defined by the Civil Code to be a contract without compensation but its terms provide for some counter-giving (compensation); it also may also be a sham contract under article 170(2). This approach is explicit in CC article 572(1) with respect to a contract of gift:

> When there exists a counter transfer of a thing or a right or a counter obligation the contract shall not be deemed to be a gift. The rules provided for by article 170(2) of the present Code shall apply to such contract.[24]

[20] CC art 423(1). Butler, above n 3, at 306.

[21] Ibid 307.

[22] Ibid 674–5.

[23] Ibid 152 gives the wording before May 2013. Amendments of 7 May 2013 to this article added a clarification that a contract concluded to conceal another contract on other terms also falls under the definition of a sham contract and is void.

[24] Butler, above n 3, at 419.

According to CC article 170(2) in its revised wording:

> A sham transaction, that is, a transaction which is concluded for the purpose of concealing another transaction, including a transaction on other terms, shall be void. To the transaction which the parties actually had in view, taking into account the essence and the content of the transaction, shall apply the rules relevant thereto.

Deeming a contract sham may therefore simply lead to its transformation from one type of contract to another, for example if the parties purportedly conclude a contract of purchase-sale but do not provide for any counter-giving, their contract becomes a contract of gift. Thus, even here, the mere absence of counter-giving of itself does not automatically deprive the contract of legal force. Sham contracts and their consequences are discussed in greater detail in Chapter 6 (at p 138).

(ii) Invalidity of Contracts without Compensation between Commercial Legal Entities

In some cases the absence of compensation does make a contract invalid, and problems arise when qualification of a contract without compensation as a contract of gift does affect its validity. CC article 575 specifies that 'A gift shall not be permitted, except for ordinary presents the value of which does not exceed five minimum amounts of payment for labour established by law'[25] (500 roubles; approximately £10) in four instances. These are:

(1) giving by the legal representatives of those who are under-age or lack dispositive capacity;
(2) by spouses or relations of patients in residential care;
(3) to state employees in connection with their official position or in relation to their duties; and
(4) between commercial organisations.

Any contract made contrary to CC article 575 is void.

It is the fourth category which causes the most problems in commercial practice. Its effect is that any contract concluded between two or more commercial organisations which does not provide for any (or any adequate) counter-giving may be considered by a court to be a sham contract, further qualified as a contract of gift and then, based on the rules prohibiting such gifts, declared void (the consequences of a contract being void are discussed in Chapter 6). Thus counter-giving in contracts between commercial organisations is as important to the validity of such contracts as consideration is in any English contract.

It should, however, be stressed that the presence or absence of counter-giving does not affect validity of contracts which are not between commercial organisations, but are instead, for example, between two individuals (unless both are

[25] Ibid 421.

registered individual entrepreneurs contracting in the course of business); or between a commercial organisation and a non-governmental organisation (NGO); or between a commercial organisation and an individual (unless acting as an individual entrepreneur). Therefore, unlike English law, where the requirement of consideration is the same for all informal contracts, the Russian concept of counter-giving only affects commercial contracts, that is, contracts between two commercial legal entities; a commercial legal entity and an individual who is an individual entrepreneur carrying out their business activity; or between two such individual entrepreneurs.

Helpfully, CC article 423(3) states that 'A contract shall be presumed to be for compensation unless it arises otherwise from a law, other legal acts, or the content or essence of the contract'.[26] Counter-giving is thus presumed and in court its absence must be proved by the party making that assertion. The Supreme Commercial Court has made clear that an agreement between two commercial legal entities to assign a right may only be qualified as a gift if it is proved there was clear intention to transfer the right without compensation. Mere absence of a contract term stipulating the price is not sufficient to render the agreement void as a contract of gift between commercial legal entities.[27]

B Counter-Giving for Performance Compared to Consideration: Requirements of Sufficiency and Adequacy

In English law there is an important maxim that 'consideration must be sufficient but need not be adequate'. To be sufficient consideration should be 'something of value in the eyes of the law'.[28] 'Consideration need not be adequate'[29] means that a court will not, except in relation to repayment of debt, verify whether the value of what is given by each party is financially equivalent. If one party is happy to rent out a cottage in return for 'a peppercorn rent', that is entirely up to the parties; but there must at least be the peppercorn, as agreed.

The approach of Russian courts to sufficiency and adequacy of counter-giving is rather different and, at times, controversial.

It is generally accepted by Russian academic authorities that at the heart of civil law relationships, and in particular contracts, lies the principal of equivalence.[30] As noted above, in order to be legally binding, a commercial contract

[26] Ibid 307.

[27] 'Review of practice of application by commercial courts of the provisions of Chapter 24 of the Russian Civil Code' approved by Informational Circular of Presidium of the Supreme Commercial Court of 30 October 2007 No 120 para 9.

[28] *Thomas v Thomas* [1842] 2 QB 851 at 859, as cited in E Peel, *Treitel: the Law of Contract*, 13th edn (London, Sweet and Maxwell, 2011) 71.

[29] Peel, above n 28, at 77.

[30] MI Braginskii, VV Vitrianskii, *Договорное Право. Книга первая: Общая Часть* [Dogovornoe Pravo. Kniga pervaia: Obshchaia Chast'; *Contract Law: Book One: General Part*] (Moscow, Statut, 2001) 327–8.

must provide for some counter-giving. However, the Civil Code gives absolutely no indication that the counter-giving must be adequate or have equivalent financial value. CC article 424(1) stipulates that 'The performance of a contract shall be paid for at the price established by agreement of the parties'.[31] This right of the parties to set their own price is regarded as an important expression of freedom of contract, in particular, the parties' freedom to determine at their own discretion the conditions of their contract (CC article 421(4)).

The Supreme Court and the Supreme Commercial Court in one of their joint Resolutions[32] held that, in relation to the consequences of invalidity of a contract which has been performed by both parties, where one party received money and the other goods, work or services, the court should consider the parties' mutual obligations equal unless it is proved otherwise.

Thus, at least in this context, the courts have developed a *presumption of equality of counter-giving*. Courts are not required to assess the actual value of goods, work or services and compare it to the price paid, unless the actual value of such goods, work or services is proved to be clearly disproportionate to the price paid for them. From this it can be seen that that Russian courts in some circumstances will consider the *equality* of counter-giving for performance, that is, its adequacy, and not just its sufficiency.

C Adequacy of Counter-Giving as an Issue in Russian Commercial Courts

The commercial courts explicitly assess whether the counter-giving in a commercial contract is financially equivalent to the other party's performance. If the court decides that the counter-giving was *obviously not equivalent*, it will deem the contract to be a sham contract concealing a contract of gift and hence void. Until recently the court could do this even if neither party raised the issue of equivalence or claimed that the contract was void.

The Supreme Commercial Court confirmed that a commercial court is obliged to evaluate the formation and validity of a contract, even if the parties did not request it to do so.[33] Assessing the equivalency of counter-giving despite it not being challenged by either party is justified by the commercial courts as an aspect of verification of the validity of the particular contract, which they are directed to do by the Supreme Commercial Court's Resolution. However, this practice may change in the very near future. Recent amendments to the Civil Code which took effect from 1 September 2013[34] considerably limit the right of

[31] Butler, above n 3, at 307.

[32] Resolution of Plenum of the Supreme Court No 13 and Plenum of the Supreme Commercial Court No 14 of 8 October 1998 'On the Practice of application of provisions of the Civil Code of the Russian Federation concerning the interest for the use of another's monetary means' para 27.

[33] Resolution of Plenum of the Supreme Commercial Court of 23 July 2009 No 57 'On particular procedural issues of practice of consideration of cases connected with non-performance or undue performance of contractual obligations' para 2.

[34] Federal Law of 7 May 2013 No 100-FZ on Amending Subsections 4 and 5 of Chapter I of Part One and Article 1153 of Part Three of the Civil Code of the Russian Federation.

a court to interfere at its own discretion in contractual relations by declaring a contract void. While it is not yet clear how the courts will apply the new provisions, we believe that this amendment will have a positive effect on contractual relations by adding more certainty and predictability to them. The previous unlimited right of a court to deem counter-giving for performance as not equivalent and therefore make a contract void had always left a risk of any contract being declared void. The amendment to article 166(4) should help reduce that risk.

The following case illustrates the danger of a contract being rendered void because of inadequacy of counter-giving.

> Two commercial entities, the seller, company S, and the buyer, company P, concluded a contract of purchase-sale of immovable property. One of S's shareholders sought a court declaration that the contract was void because S sold the property for a price many times lower than its market value, thus causing loss to S.
>
> The court agreed. The market value of the property was estimated as 55,434,000 roubles, and the contract price was only 278,000 roubles, a fraction of the market value. The court held that the manifest and deliberate under-pricing in the contract concealed a contract of gift of the difference in value. It was impossible to identify which particular parts of the property had not been paid for and hence transferred without compensation. In the circumstances the whole contract was deemed a sham and qualified as a contract of gift, which is prohibited between commercial legal entities, therefore the contract was void.[35]

However, a different approach was taken in another case.

> The Supreme Commercial Court held that, in a contract of assignment of rights between commercial legal entities, inequality between the values of the counter-giving and the assigned rights was not of itself sufficient grounds to render the contract void. The Court referred to CC article 1(2): 'Citizens (natural persons [individuals]) and juridical persons [legal entities] shall acquire and effectuate their civil rights by their own will and in their own interest. They shall be free in establishing their rights and duties on the basis of contract and in determining any conditions of a contract which are not contrary to legislation'.[36]
>
> Taking this into account, the Court noted that, in determining the equivalence in value of the transferred rights and the counter-giving, it is necessary to consider the exact circumstances of each case. In particular, courts should consider the financial situation of the promisor, whether the

[35] Resolution of Federal Commercial Court of the West-Siberian District of 1 March 2011 No 75-4776/2007.

[36] Butler, above n 3, at 7.

transferred rights might be disputed, the nature of the relative liabilities of the contractual parties, and other conditions which would influence the rights' actual value.[37]

Application of the Supreme Commercial Court's proposition that the equivalence should be evaluated in the light of the circumstances of each particular case is illustrated in the following case, where the court decided that an obviously small payment of US$1 for a ship could in the particular circumstances be a sufficient and adequate counter-giving.

> A shipping corporation, N, bought two ships for US$1 each from two foreign companies. The tax authority carrying out a tax inspection took this sum to be the purchase price of each ship and resolved that N should therefore use the cost of US$1 when calculating its profit for tax purposes. N had used the actual value of the ships so, in the opinion of the tax authority, had paid markedly less profit tax than it should have. The tax authority calculated the shortfall on N's profit tax and fined N for not paying their full tax in due time. N appealed this to court.
>
> The court annulled the tax authority's decision. It held that in the particular case the contract price of US$1 each for the ships should be considered in the light of N's previous contractual relationships with the two foreign companies and their prior commercial relations. The court found that N had previously made a long-term capital investment in the two foreign companies, in the form of the two ships which were to be returned to N after a certain time. The sale of each ship for US$1 was the legal mechanism for its return to N.
>
> Taking this into account, the court concluded that the US$1 price of the ships did not comply with the principles for determining the price for taxation purposes, and should not be classified as payment and have its adequacy considered. Moreover, the contracts could not be treated as normal purchase-sale contracts concluded in the course of normal commercial dealings. They were exclusively concluded to allow the legal transfer of ownership to the ships back to N and ensure compliance with currency control requirements, and not for the purpose of selling ships for profit.
>
> Thus neither contract presupposed payment of a real market price for each ship. The parties had just used the nominal price of US$1 as a symbolic counter-giving to comply with CC article 575, which prohibits uncompensated property transfer between two commercial legal entities.

[37] 'Review of Practice of Application by Commercial Courts of the Provisions of Chapter 24 of the Russian Civil Code', approved by Informational Circular of Presidium of the Supreme Commercial Court of 30 October 2007 No 120 para 10.

> The US$1 paid was not intended to be, and was not, an actual purchase price, but in the overall circumstances was sufficient and adequate.[38]

These examples illustrate that the courts do verify the adequacy of counter-giving, but their decision about adequacy or inadequacy is not simplistic and will take into account the particular circumstances, the parties' true intentions and the real purpose of the contract.

D Counter-Giving in Forgiveness of Debt (Прощение Долга; *Proshchenie Dolga*)

CC chapter 26 specifies the requirements in Russian contract law for the termination of contractual obligations. Among other grounds, such as by performance, subsequent impossibility, set-off, etc, the Civil Code includes forgiveness of debt (прощение долга; *proshchenie dolga*). This is the voluntary discharge of the other party's obligation, where the 'debt' in this context is whatever is due under the contract, not just a sum of money, as is made clear from the definition in CC article 415: 'An obligation shall be terminated by the release of the debtor [promisor] by the creditor [promisee] from the duties on him unless this violates the rights of other persons with respect to the property of the creditor'.[39]

A promisee may thus at their own discretion make a legally binding promise to release the promisor from a contractual obligation to the promisee. That promise will be binding irrespective of the nature of the obligation, monetary or non-monetary. The forgiven 'debt' ceases to exist and the promisee can no longer claim it.

A debt can be forgiven in full or in part. Thus, a promisee's voluntary promise to accept less money than is owed, or even no money at all, is legally binding under Russian contract law. There is no issue of 'inadequacy of consideration' as in the English part-payment of debt cases.[40] This is quite surprising in the light of the fact that Russian contract law does pay close attention not just to the sufficiency, but also to the adequacy of counter-giving for performance. Nevertheless, it recognises forgiveness of debt as a binding contract.

To be fair, recognition in Russian law of forgiveness of debt is not absolute. If the forgiveness is between two commercial legal entities, counter-giving is required, because of the prohibition of gifts between such entities, discussed above. Then the adequacy of the counter-giving will be considered by the courts, although, as also discussed, in the light of the parties' actual commercial relationship.

[38] Resolution of Federal Commercial Court of Moscow Region of 21 March 2011 No KA-A40/1302-11-P.

[39] Butler, above n 3, at 302.

[40] *Pinnel's Case* (1602) 5 Co Rep 117a; *Foakes v Beer* (1884) 9 App Cas 605.

CC article 572(1) includes, as one of the forms of gift, a donee being relieved by a donor of a duty to provide contractual performance, by either (1) the donor transferring to the donee the donor's right to demand the donee's performance; or (2) relief of the donee of his obligation to provide performance to the donor or a third person. This is effectively the same as forgiveness of debt in CC article 415. Bearing in mind the prohibition against gifts between commercial legal entities, it would be natural to conclude that forgiveness of debt is also similarly prohibited. However, that is not entirely correct.

The Supreme Commercial Court held that forgiveness of debt will only be regarded as a contract of gift if the court determines that it was the promisee's intention. Then forgiveness of debt must comply with the prohibition against gifts between commercial legal entities in CC article 575(4). If the intention was not to waive the debt as a gift, then a contract between commercial entities of forgiveness of debt is not rendered void by article 575(4). The Supreme Commercial Court gave the following example.

> Company L concluded a contract of loan with company B, by which B received money from L and undertook to repay to L both the loan and interest on it.
>
> B paid neither so L sent a letter to B asking for immediate repayment of the loan and saying that, if B complied, L would relieve B of both the duty to pay the interest and also the penalty for late payment.
>
> B paid up as asked. Nevertheless L sued B for the interest and late payment penalty and won at first instance. The court held that forgiveness of a debt is relief by a promisee of a promisor's property duty (имущественная обязанность; *imushchestvennaia obiazannost'*),[41] hence a form of a gift (CC article 572), which is prohibited between commercial legal entities. As a result, L's letter setting out forgiveness of B's interest and penalty debt was void and had no legal consequences. Having paid back the loan, B was still obliged to pay the interest and late-payment penalty.
>
> This was overturned on cassational appeal. The higher court rejected L's claim, with the following reasoning. Under CC article 572(1) the main characteristic of a gift is that it is gratuitous. Furthermore, CC article 423(3) presumes that a contract will be for compensation unless 'it arises otherwise from a law, other legal acts, or the content or essence of the contract'.[42] So forgiveness of debt should only be deemed to be a gift if the court found that the promisee had the intention to relieve by way of gift the promisor's obligation to pay. The absence of such intention could be shown by the forgiveness of debt being linked to the promisee's receipt of some pecuniary benefit from another contract between the same parties.

[41] This Russian expression indicates that aspect of a bilateral contract which is the relevant party's binding duty to perform (as contrasted to the other party's right to demand performance).

[42] Butler, above n 3, at 307.

In the case of B and L, the Cassational Court held that the purpose of L's offer of forgiveness of debt was to get B to repay the loan to L without L having to go to court. Therefore, L did not have any intention for this to be a gift to B, so the contract of forgiveness of debt as set out in L's letter to B was legally binding; B did not have to pay the interest or late-payment penalty. This approach was upheld on appeal to the Supreme Commercial Court.[43]

IV CONCLUSION

Although the bases of counter-performance and counter-giving for performance as described above are different to consideration in English law, as they are not a requirement for the validity of an informal contract, nevertheless it is apparent that there are some situations in Russian law where reciprocity is required. Whether the value of that reciprocal contractual undertaking is policed by the Russian courts will depend on the exact circumstances, and in particular, there are special rules relating to contracts between commercial entities.

It has also been seen that in the case of forgiveness of debt, in Russian law relating to legal relations between commercial legal entities, there is a tension between upholding a promisee's promise to forgive the debt and holding the promisor nevertheless responsible for their full obligation. In English law this is analogous to the contrast between the common law rule that part payment of (monetary) debt does not discharge the debt[44] and the support in equity though promissory estoppel for a promise to accept the lesser sum.[45] The context is rather different, but the necessity of balancing competing interests in a principled and consistent manner is common to both the Russian and English legal systems.

[43] 'Review of court practice regarding the application of some norms of the Russian Civil Code setting out the grounds for termination of obligations', approved by Informational Circular of Supreme Commercial Court of 21 December at 2005 No 104 para 3.

[44] See above n 40.

[45] *Central London Property Trust v High Trees House Ltd* [1947] KB 130; and see Arden LJ in *Collier v P & MJ Wright (Holdings) Ltd* [2007] EWCA Civ 1329 at para 42.

6

Factors Tending to Defeat Contractual Liability

I INTRODUCTION

This chapter explores the circumstances under which vitiation of a contract can occur, that is, the contract is undone. This is an area where there have been recent reforms in Russian law. It also has serious significance beyond the interests of the parties immediately affected. One of the main functions of contract law in any jurisdiction is to guarantee the stability of civil transactions. Parties to a contract need to be confident that, unless something extraordinary happens, they will be able to enjoy any agreed lawful benefits gained through their contract. Unfortunately, under Russian law, the parties' will may be overridden. Contractual parties may think that they have concluded a contract in due form and may even have performed their part, but the contract might still be vitiated by a court, with all the relevant consequences. This happens much more frequently under Russian law than under English law and represents a serious threat to the reliability of legal transactions. It is one reason why many businesses based in Russia choose English law to govern their commercial dealings.

Under Russian law there are two different circumstances under which contractual obligations can be vitiated. These are, first, when a contract is regarded as invalid (недействительный; *nedeistvilelniy*) or, secondly, when a contract is deemed to be 'not concluded' (незаключенный; *nezaklyuchenniy*).

In both situations the contract is generally regarded as never having existed, similar to being void under English law. However, there are a number of important differences between the effects in Russian and English law. For example, under Russian law the validity of a contract can in certain cases be 'restored', which would be impossible for a void contract in English law. Also, under Russian law, one of the parties to a void contract may have a right to claim damages suffered as a result of the contract's invalidity.

In this chapter we explore the two situations under which contracts may be vitiated, starting with invalidity, then followed by discussion of the situations when contracts are considered 'not concluded' (in relation to the latter, see also Chapter 4 at p 86).

II INVALIDITY OF CONTRACTS

A Invalidity of Contracts under Russian Contract Law

There are two types of invalid contracts in Russian contract law: 'void contracts' (ничтожные договоры; *nichtozhniye dogovori*) and 'contested contracts' (оспоримые договоры; *osporimiye dogovori*). Either of these types of invalidity can also apply to individual terms within a contract, as well as to a contract as a whole (Civil Code (CC) article 180). The general rule is that neither type of invalid contract gives rise to any legal consequences except for those flowing from its invalidity, and it is regarded as invalid from the moment of its apparent conclusion. However, as we will see below, there are exceptions to this general rule.

The important difference between a void contract and a contested contract (or, for example, contested terms within a contract) is that a void contract is invalid irrespective of any court action but a contested contract only becomes invalid when declared so by a court (CC article 166(1)).

The situation with regard to void contracts is slightly complex. A contract is void when particular circumstances specified in law are present, irrespective of whether it has been deemed void by a court. The types of circumstances which render a contract void are discussed in detail below; they are such things as illegality, immoral purpose, lack of capacity, and similar. However, a party must apply to court and prove that the relevant legal grounds for invalidity are indeed present which make the contract void, otherwise they are unable to enforce the consequences of the contract's invalidity.

The concept of a contested contract has some similarity to the English concept of a voidable contract; that is, that the contract exists until it is 'avoided', although in Russia, unlike in England, that step must be taken by a court. Thus if a contract under Russian law has been concluded and has not been contested by a party or other person with standing to contest it (discussed below), the contract remains in force. Property passes under the contract and can be passed to a third party, unless and until the contract is successfully contested. Again in contrast to English law, the right to contest such a contract is not extinguished when the property is passed to a third party but when the limitation period stipulated by law expires.

In practice the difference between a contested and a void contract is as follows. If a party to a contract considers a contract or particular term within it void, they can refuse to perform, referring to CC article 167(1) which provides that invalid contracts do not entail any legal consequences. However, the party doing this must accept the risk that the other party might sue them for breach, and the court might consider the questionable term valid, not void, in which case they will be liable. By contrast, a party has no legal right to refuse to fulfil a contract, or particular term within it, on the ground that the contract (or term) is contested. They would first have to prove in court that the contract or term is contested and thus no obligations arise.

(i) Applying for Application of Consequences of Invalidity of a Contract

(a) Applying in relation to Void Contracts

If one contractual party considers that the whole contract is void, on one of the grounds provided in the legislation (see below), they may offer the other party the possibility of resolving the problem amicably in some way, for example, by signing a contract on different terms which comply with the relevant law, or agreeing to restitution of anything transferred under the invalid contract.

Alternatively, they may go directly to court and apply for the application of the consequences of invalidity of the contract, or any terms in it which they claim are void. Application to court for a declaration that a contract or any of its terms is void can not only be made by a party to the contract, but also by other people, to whom the law directly awards such a right. The definition of who is in this group has recently changed.

For contracts concluded before 1 September 2013, the second paragraph of the original version of CC article 166(2) applies. It said that, 'A demand concerning the application of the consequences of the invalidity of a void transaction may be presented by *any interested person*. The court shall have the right to apply such consequences at its own initiative' (emphasis added).[1] The first sentence here was interpreted to mean that anyone who was in any way affected by a contract could apply for the application of the consequences of invalidity; as the Supreme Commercial Court stated, disputes connected with void contracts are resolved upon application from any *interested* person.[2]

The courts' role has been very important in deciding who was considered to be an interested person (apart from the parties to the contract, who are always considered to have an interest). In one case, someone who had unsuccessfully submitted a tender was held to have a right to claim for the invalidation of the contract concluded between the organiser of the tender and party whose tender was accepted.[3] Another case was as follows.

> Participants (shareholders) of a limited responsibility society (общество с ограниченной ответственностью; *obshchestvo s ogranichennoi otvetstvennost'iu* (OOO))[4] were considered to have a right to claim for the

[1] WE Butler, *The Civil Code of the Russian Federation Parts 1, 2 and 3: Parallel Russian and English Texts* (Moscow, JurInfoR-Press, 2008) 150.

[2] Resolution of Plenum of the Supreme Court No 6, Plenum of the Supreme Commercial Court No 8 of 1 July 1996 'On Certain Questions of Application of Part I of the Civil Code of the Russian Federation' para 32.

[3] Resolution of Federal Commercial Court of Volgo-Viatskii District of 24 December 2010, case No A11-3657/2010.

[4] An OOO is type of Russian legal entity where a participant/shareholder will own a participatory share (доля; *dolia*) (see CC arts 87–94). This contrasts, for example, with a joint stock society

application of the consequences of invalidity of a contract the OOO had concluded which contradicted the law. In the particular case the OOO had concluded a contract for the sale of a building it owned. The contract did not conform to law. The OOO's shareholders therefore considered it invalid and brought a claim for the application of the consequences of invalidity.

The lower courts decided that the shareholders were not interested persons because they could not prove that the contract affected their rights and duties nor that the conclusion of the contract caused them any negative consequences.

The Supreme Commercial Court held that the lower courts' decisions were incorrect. Under CC article 166(2) in the version in force at the time, any interested person was entitled to go to court claiming invalidity of a transaction. The Code did not oblige them to prove that they suffered any negative consequences as a result of the contract.

Shareholders of an OOO have rights arising from their ownership of a share in it, one of these being a right to receive the value of their share in the OOO if they withdraw from it. Thus they would have an interest in the success of the OOO's activities and so were considered interested persons for the purposes of an application of the consequences of invalidity of a contract concluded by the OOO.[5]

It has also been common for government agencies to claim that contracts or certain terms within contracts were invalid and apply the corresponding consequences. For example, the tax authority could claim that a contract was invalid and as a result apply penalties for the incorrect calculation of taxes by the taxpayer.[6] Government agencies such as the tax authority have been especially privileged in that they have not had to go to court to apply the consequences of invalidity of a contract. They could act on their own initiative and at their own discretion. If the contractual parties disagreed they might challenge in court the government agency's decision about the invalidity of their contract, and prove either that the contract is valid or that the government agency should not be considered to be an interested person.

This question of who is an interested person with regard to the invalidity of a contract is still extremely important. First, the, old rules just outlined are applicable to all contracts concluded before 1 September 2013 which means that the courts will be applying those rules for some time. Secondly, the new version of CC article 166(3) stipulates that a person 'who has an interest protected by law'[7] to deem the contract invalid can apply for invalidation of the contract 'if such

(акционерное общество; *aktsionernoe obshchestvo* (AO)) (see CC arts 96–104) where shareholders hold stock (акция; *aktsiia*) which is freely transferable through a stock exchange.

[5] Resolution of Supreme Commercial Court of 22 December 2009 No 9503/09.

[6] Resolution of Supreme Commercial Court of 1 June 2010 No 16064/09.

[7] Federal Law of 7 May 2013 No 100-FZ, amending the Civil Code.

application is not connected with the application of consequences of contractual invalidity'.[8]

It follows that a government body, such as tax or competition authority, would potentially still be able to invalidate contracts between companies and individuals.

Also, unfortunately, use of the vague criterion of 'a person who *has an interest protected by law*' offsets the positive effect of the new rules regarding the application of consequences of invalidity of a contract. It is for the courts to apply the new rules and choose whether to follow the old pattern of creating uncertainty for the contracting parties about the legal validity of their contract, or to follow the new rules in new spirit and try to enhance the stability of civil relations.

The court has retained the right to apply the consequences of invalidity of a contract on its own initiative, including restitution, but only when 'it is necessary to protect public interests and in other cases stipulated by law'[9] (new version of CC article 166(4)). Again, the old rules in CC article 166(2)[10] apply to all contracts concluded before 1 September 2013. These allow courts to apply the consequences of invalidity at their own discretion. It has not been easy to define when the courts might decide to exercise this right. The Supreme Commercial Court accepted in one case that a lower court had correctly refrained from doing this 'considering the circumstances of the case, inter alia, that the parties did not refer to the possible application of restitution and the case materials did not contain enough evidence to make conclusions on the order for restitution'.[11] The case was as follows.

> A state-owned unitary enterprise (унитарное предприятие; *unitarnoe predpriiatie*), E, had rented equipment to company C. C did not pay for the use of the equipment and E sued, demanding payment of the unpaid rent. C counterclaimed that the contract was void. The commercial court hearing the case rejected E's claim on the grounds that the lease agreement was invalid because E did not have the right to rent out the equipment.[12]

It should be pointed out that the payment could still be recovered in the form of unfounded enrichment. However, in the particular case the claim was based on contract and under procedural rules the basis of the claim could not be changed. In order to recover the debt as unfounded enrichment, E would have to bring a new claim based on unfounded enrichment (for more on this, see below at p 134).

[8] Ibid.
[9] Ibid.
[10] See above, text to n 1.
[11] Informational Circular of Supreme Commercial Court of 13 November 2008 No 126 'Overview of the Court Practice on Certain Questions connected with the Vindication of Property from Unlawful Possession by Other Persons' Part 1.
[12] Ibid Part 3.

Under the original version of CC article 166(2), if none of the parties has applied for the application of the consequences of invalidity, the court had a right rather than a duty to make a ruling on its own initiative. Thus to be sure that a ruling on consequences of invalidity would be considered, a disputing party needed to apply for that; it would be unwise to rely on the court's own discretion.

The version of CC article 166(4) applicable to contracts concluded after 1 September 2013, quoted above,[13] limits the right of a court to apply the consequences of invalidity on its own initiative to situations where 'it is necessary to protect public interests and in other cases stipulated by law'. This approach should make contractual disputes more predictable. However, it is not obvious what 'public interest' will mean with respect to contractual relations. There is always a risk that the new rule will be applied selectively and thus will not fulfil the purpose of contributing to the stability of civil law transactions.

One interesting novelty has been introduced to the Civil Code for contracts concluded after 1 September 2013. A new rule incorporated into the Code (article 166(5), as amended by Federal Law of 7 May 2013) states that:

> A claim of invalidity of a contract does not have any legal effect if the person making the claim is acting in bad faith and in particular if that person's behaviour after the conclusion of the transaction induced other persons to rely on the validity of the contract.[14]

This not only raises the issue of motivation but also creates protection somewhat analogous to estoppel in, for example, Australian law, where reliance by another induced by deliberate behaviour gives rise to an enforceable right.[15]

Further, the revised version of CC article 167(1) has an added paragraph which stipulates that 'A person who knew or should have known of the grounds for invalidity of a contested transaction after the transaction has been deemed invalid shall not be considered as having acted in good faith'.

These provisions are a complete novelty and there has been nothing similar in any previous version of the Code. It may therefore take several years before it can be seen how the courts are going to use these new rules and in what situations they will be applied.

(b) Applying in relation to Contested Contracts

A contested contract can only be challenged by a person whose rights and lawful interests it violates, although they do not necessarily have to be a party to the contract. The definition of who can challenge a contested contract is one of the recent reforms to the Civil Code, as will be discussed shortly.

For contracts concluded before 1 September 2013, CC article 166(2) in its original form said rather simply, 'A demand to deem a contested transaction to

[13] See above, text to n 9.
[14] See above n 7.
[15] As in *Waltons Stores (Interstate) Ltd v Maher* (1988) 164 CLR 387.

be invalid may be brought by the person specified in the present Code'.[16] Only those specifically identified in the law for each kind of contested contract were allowed to challenge the contested contract.

The amended provision in CC article 166(2) broadens the range of potential claimants to include those whose rights and lawful interests have been breached. Further, it connects such breach with 'unfavourable consequences suffered by such person'.[17] The new version of the Article creates a presumption that if a person suffered unfavourable consequences as a result of a contract, even if they are not a party to it, they have a legitimate interest which allows them to challenge the contract.

It is clear that the amendment has widened the circle of potential applicants for invalidity of contested contracts. At the time of writing it is too early to predict the practical implication of this. However, we fear that the new version is potentially dangerous as creating uncertainty for many contracts.

(ii) Consequences of Invalidity of a Contract

CC article 167(2) sets out the general consequences of invalidity of contracts, and applies to contracts invalid both as a result of being void and being 'contested'. It provides that:

> In the event of the invalidity of a transaction [contract], each of the parties shall be obliged to return to the other everything received according to the transaction, and if it is impossible to return that received in kind [restitution] . . . to compensate its value in money, unless the consequences of the invalidity of the transaction have been provided for by a law.[18]

This means that, for example, if both parties to an invalid purchase-sale contract have already executed the contract, the seller will get their goods back and will return the purchase price to the buyer.

However, this remedy for invalidity is complicated by the fact that there is a conflict between the Civil Code provisions on restitution and its provisions on vindication and the protection of a *bona fidei* purchaser.

In respect of the latter, CC article 301 (in chapter 20 'Defence of Right of Ownership and Other Rights to Things') gives a right of vindication, based on the right of ownership: 'The owner shall have the right to demand and obtain his property from another's illegal possession'.[19] CC article 302 then deals with the situation where a third party has obtained property in good faith from someone who had unlawful possession. In slightly tortuous language it says:

> If property has been acquired for compensation from a person who did not have the right to alienate it, of which the acquirer did not know and could not have known (good

[16] Butler, above n 1, at 150.
[17] Federal Law of 7 May 2013 No 100-FZ, amending the Civil Code.
[18] Butler, above n 1, at 150. The wording has not been amended.
[19] Ibid 239.

> faith [*bona fidei*] purchaser), then the owner shall have the right to demand and obtain this property from the acquirer when the property has been lost by the owner or person to whom the property was transferred by the owner in possession, or stolen from one of the other, or left the possession thereof by means other than the will thereof.[20]

The effect of this can be illustrated in the following example. A sells a flat to B and then B sells the flat to C. If, after the contract between B and C has been signed, the contract between A and B is deemed void, B would not have gained ownership of the flat, therefore does not have any right to sell it to C. Does this mean that C, who did not know about the problems with the contract between A and B, should return the flat to A? Application of the simple restitution rules would mean that C would keep the flat (the B-C contract is unaffected); B therefore cannot give A restitution in kind, so pays A damages instead, as suggested in CC article 167(2) . Application of the rules on vindication would suggest that A could reclaim the flat from C, despite C's claim that they bought the flat in good faith, because A would be able to say that the property left them 'by means other than the will thereof' (CC article 302) as a result of the invalidity of their contract with B.

CC article 9 gives individuals and legal entities the freedom to choose whatever procedure they prefer to defend their infringed civil rights.[21] So, theoretically, a party who transferred property under an invalid contract could base their claim for the return of the property on the invalidity of the contract (claiming for restitution) or on their property right (claiming for vindication). In the former case a *bona fidei* third party purchaser would be protected, in the latter, they would not be.

The Russian Constitutional Court ruled that the courts of general jurisdiction and the commercial courts should decide for each case which civil law provisions are applicable, as there was no inherent unconstitutionality in CC article 167.[22]

The Supreme Commercial Court has taken the position 'since the law specifically regulates the consequences of invalidity of transactions, rules on demanding and obtaining property from another's unlawful possession [vindication] shall not be applicable [in such cases]'.[23] Thus, according to the Supreme Commercial Court, a party to an invalid contract whose property was transferred under the contract has only one remedy, restitution, that is, a claim based on the invalidity of the contract to get the property back, and does not have a vindicatory claim based on their ownership. Application of this to the example with two consecutive transactions would mean that C would keep the flat, and B pay A compensation.

[20] Ibid.

[21] Resolution of Constitutional Court of the Russian Federation of 21 April 2003 No 6-P para 3. See also M Lomovsteva and J Henderson, 'Constitutional Justice in Russia' (2009) 34 *Review of Central and East European Law* 37 at 48.

[22] Ibid.

[23] Informational Circular of Supreme Commercial Court, above n 11, Part 1.

As we saw at the beginning of this section,[24] CC article 167(2) says that if it is impossible to return in kind everything received under the invalid contract, compensation shall instead by made in money to the value of the received goods. The Supreme Commercial Court and the Supreme Court have jointly made clear that when one party to an invalid contract received money and the other received goods, works or services, the obligations of both parties should be regarded as having equal value.[25] This reflects the principle of presuming each contract is mutually beneficial; both parties have acted in their own best interest, so set the values to be equivalent. However, the courts also point out that if the money received by one party clearly exceeds to a considerable extent the value of the goods, services or work received by the other, the rules on unfounded enrichment are applicable. It means that if a party to an invalid contract proves that the performance they received is worth considerably less than the performance they made, they have the right to claim the difference.[26]

A good example of the application of this approach is given by the Supreme Commercial Court in one of its important decisions.[27]

> A lease agreement was deemed invalid following an application by the tenant, T. T also claimed for the return of all sums paid to the landlord L as rent under the invalid agreement. The Supreme Commercial Court explained that T had been using the premises and L could not recover such use in kind. Instead, the value of the use should be paid to L as a consequence of the invalidity of the contract. Since T had already paid for the use of the premises, he did not have to pay a second time, and neither did L have to return to T the money received as rent under the invalid contract. The court hinted, however, that if the rent had been higher than the normal rent for similar premises in that region, T would have the right to receive the difference between the normal rent and the higher rent he had paid.

In fact, through its interpretation of the Civil Code the Supreme Commercial Court has invented this extra consequence of contractual invalidity in addition to the consequences directly stipulated in the Code. The Court specifically stated that the right of a party to an invalid contract to claim unfounded enrichment for the difference in value between their performance and the other party's constitutes an additional consequence of the invalidity.[28] This concept is widely applied in the commercial courts.

[24] See above, text to n 16.

[25] Resolution of Plenum of the Supreme Court No 13, Plenum of the Supreme Commercial Court No 14 of 8 October 1998 'On the Practice of Application of the Provisions of the Civil Code of the Russian Federation on the Interest for the Unlawful Use of Monetary Funds' Part 27.

[26] Ibid.

[27] Informational Circular of Presidium of the Supreme Commercial Court of 11 January 2000 No 49 'Overview of the Practice of Resolution of Disputes connected with the Application of Norms on Unfounded Enrichment' Part 7.

[28] Ruling of Supreme Commercial Court of 22 February 2011 No VAS-1312/11.

Previously, it was very common for a party in breach of contract to try to avoid their contractual obligations by claiming that the contract was invalid. If the grounds for invalidity of the contract existed, the courts had no choice but to deem the contract invalid. At the same time they tried to protect the interests of the party who had performed in good faith. The following case is an example.

> Contractor C performed their obligations under a contract for independent work, carrying out all the work stipulated. Customer P did not pay and brought a claim to deem the contract invalid. Since there were grounds for invalidity, the court declared the contract invalid. However, the court also noted the impossibility of returning the work in kind and ruled that P should therefore pay a fair price for it, as determined by an independent surveyor.[29]

Thus, even though technically invalidity is a factor which would defeat contractual liability, in practice it can act as a ground for an obligation of a different type, such as restitution or an obligation to compensate for services received under the invalid contract, to avoid unfounded enrichment. This works fairly well with respect to payment for a service already performed on the basis of an invalid contract. However, when the performance due under an invalid contract is non-monetary, the approach taken by the Russian Civil Code can be rather punitive to one of the parties, as seen in the following example.

> A construction company, C, entered into an investment contract with the Moscow Local Government, M. The investment project included the demolition of a hotel belonging to M and the construction of a new hotel on the same site. Under the contract C was obliged to prepare and obtain the necessary administrative approval, and also obtain permits for the demolition and construction work. The contract provided that on the completion of the new hotel, C and M would each acquire a specified share of it. C's share in the finished hotel was its remuneration for the services and works C provided.
>
> The investment contract was deemed invalid and C applied for the application of the consequences of invalidity. By that time C had prepared the project documentation, and hired a number of subcontractors to fulfil its contractual obligations. In C's opinion, M was obliged to compensate for C's expenses incurred in connection with performance of the invalid contract. However, the Supreme Commercial Court held that there was no unfounded enrichment by M and thus C was not entitled to any compensation.[30]

[29] Ruling of Supreme Commercial Court of 27 December 2010 No VAS-17039/10.

[30] Ruling of Supreme Commercial Court of 10 December 2010 No VAS-16663/10.

So far we have been discussing the general consequences of invalidity. However, for some vitiating factors the law provides special consequences of invalidity. They will be discussed in detail below in relation to those particular vitiating factors.

B Grounds of Invalidity: Void Contracts

The Civil Code provides for a number of factors which may lead to a contract being void and a number of factors which may lead to a contract being contested. In this section we deal with the first: factors which make a contract void. Below in the next section we examine contested contracts.

(i) Non-Conformity of a Contract with a Law or Other Legal Act

As discussed in Chapter 2 (at p 53), contracts must comply with mandatory norms of law and other legal acts (mandatory legal norms). Logically enough, if a contract or any term within it does not comply, it is void.

Before amendments to the Civil Code which came into force on 1 September 2013,[31] non-conformity with legislation was the most common ground for contractual invalidity; such contracts would be void.

Now, following the amendments, they are considered to be contested and can become invalid if they are invalidated by a court. (For the difference between void and contested contracts, see above.) The amendments to the Civil Code have changed the rules on invalidity of contract which do not comply with mandatory legal norms. In this section we focus on the circumstances under which a contract (or a term within it) will be considered to contradict such norms. We refer to court decisions prior to September 2013 because they illustrate the way courts substantiated their positions on non-compliance of contracts with legislation. It is unlikely that their approach will change under the amended rules.

Predicting whether or not a contractual term complies with mandatory legal norms is not straightforward. Courts have to interpret both the contract term and the legislation, to decide about the validity of the challenged contractual terms.

In practice, the issue of non-conformity with mandatory legal norms mainly arises in relation to a particular term of a contract. It is relatively uncommon for a whole contract to be declared void for non-conformity with legislation. However, such cases do exist. They are mainly concerned with special legislative requirements for certain contracts as a whole, for example, if the law sets out special requirements for one contractual party and they do not comply, the whole contract is void. For instance, the Civil Code stipulates that all parties in

[31] Federal Law of 7 May 2013 No 100-FZ on Amending Subsections 4 and 5 of Chapter I of Part One and Article 1153 of Part Three of the Civil Code of the Russian Federation.

a contract of partnership must be registered as private entrepreneurs. If one of the parties is not registered as such, the contract is void.

The amendments mentioned above to the Civil Code have incorporated a very interesting change the Code. Now, all contracts which contradict mandatory legal norms are divided into three categories (CC article 168, as amended):

(1) contracts which break the law or other legal acts are void if the law or the legal act stipulates that such contracts are void;
(2) contracts which break the law or other legal acts and the public interests or rights and lawful interests of third persons are void if it does not follow from the law that such a contract is contested; and
(3) all other contracts which contradict the law are voidable if it does not follow from the law that other consequences, not connected with invalidity of contract, should be applicable.[32]

As noted in relation to the impact of the recent amendments on the courts' judgments on the adequacy of counter-giving (see Chapter 5 at p 116), it is as yet unclear how the rules on public interest will be applied. There is a danger that legal certainty and stability in commercial relations will be undermined, although it is hoped that this will not be the outcome.

(ii) Conclusion of a Contract for a Purpose Contrary to Fundamental Principles of Legal Order or Morality

Under CC article 169, any transaction, such as a contract, will be void if it is 'knowingly contrary to the fundamental principles of legal order or morality [заведомо противной основам правопорядка или нравственности; *zavedomo protivnoi osnovam pravoporiadka ili nravstvennosti*]'.[33] However, legislation does not define these fundamental principles. Thus, it is purely at the discretion of the judge to decide what they are and if a particular contract contradicts them.

The Supreme Commercial Court has made clear that courts applying CC article 169 should take into account that contracts 'contrary to the fundamental principles of legal order or morality' do not simply contradict the law or other legal acts. They must be in breach of the basic principles of the Russian legal order, the principles of the social, political and economical organisation of society and their moral bases. As an example of this type of contract, the Supreme Commercial Court cites contracts for the production and distribution of prohibited objects (weapons, drugs, etc); contracts for the production and distribution of literature and other goods advocating war or national, racial and/or religious conflict; or contracts for the production and distribution of counterfeit documents. The Court explained that for the application of CC article 169 it therefore needs to be established that:

[32] Ibid.
[33] Butler, above n 1, at 151.

- the purpose which the parties intended to achieve; or
- the rights and obligations which the parties intended to establish; or
- the intended alteration of rights and obligations

contradict the fundamental principles of legal order or morality.[34]

In practice, CC article 169 is mainly used by the tax authorities challenging contracts which seem (to them) to be concluded for the purpose of tax evasion. An analysis of court practice shows that in most of these cases the tax authorities fail to prove their allegation.

Invalidity on the basis of CC article 169 needs to be distinguished from other grounds of invalidity, especially non-conformity with the requirements of law and other legal acts, discussed above. When a contract is considered to be concluded for a purpose contrary to the fundamental principles of legal order or morality there is no direct contradiction of any law or other legal acts. The contract will comply with all formal legal requirements. This will clearly not be true for contracts invalid on the basis of non-conformity with the requirements of law.

The Supreme Commercial Court notes that a contract 'contrary to the fundamental principles of legal order or morality' could be camouflaged by another contract which does not contradict any legal formalities. In such cases the contract which the parties were ostensibly making would be invalid as a sham contract (see below) while the contract which the parties were trying to conceal considered 'contrary to the fundamental principles of legal order or morality' if there is evidence of that.[35]

CC article 169 provides special consequences for invalidity based on it: if both parties to such transaction acted intentionally the court may apply the sanction that everything received by them under the transaction will be recovered to the revenue of the Russian Federation, or apply other consequences stipulated by law. It is obvious from these provisions why the tax authorities might seek to use CC article 169, since if successful the consequences are likely to be a gain for the Russian treasury.

(iii) Contracts Void as Being Fictitious or Sham

A fictitious contract is defined as 'a contract concluded only for form, without the intention to create legal consequences corresponding to it'[36] (CC article 170(1)). It is void.

Qualification of a contract as fictitious is rather difficult. It can be argued that if the parties have concluded a contract, they must have had certain conse-

[34] Resolution of Supreme Commercial Court 'On Certain Questions Connected with the Practice of Application of Article 169 of the Civil Code of the Russian Federation' of 10 April 2008 No 22 Part 1.

[35] Ibid Part 2.

[36] Butler, above n 1 at 152.

quences in mind. It is rather hard to imagine no intention by the parties when there is objective proof that they acted in a way which creates legal consequences: a contract concluded in due form and formally complying with all the legal requirements for a contract of that kind.

It could be argued that if parties conclude an apparent contract but do not provide any performance, that contract could count as being fictitious. But the Supreme Commercial Court has a clear position on this: 'mere non-performance of the terms of a contract does not by itself stand as a ground for invalidity of the contract as fictitious'.[37] This is understandable since non-performance of a contract normally constitutes a breach of contract, not its invalidity.

So the question arises: what would establish that the parties had no intention to create legal consequences? Court practice gives us the following examples.

> A football agent, A, and a football club, C, signed a contract under which A would provide services connected with the transfer to C of a footballer named in the contract. Later C and A signed a formal document (акт; *akt*) stating that all services in accordance with the contract had been provided. A assigned to Mr Z the right to claim payment for the services A provided to C (see Chapter 8 for assignment). The club refused to pay Z, so Z sued. The court found that a contract between C and the footballer had been signed before the contract between C and A. Furthermore, by the time the latter contract was signed, the former contract had been terminated. On that basis, the court held that the contract between C and A was fictitious.[38]

Unfortunately there is no information in the text of the decision which allows us to understand why the club and the agent made their fictitious contract. Another case was the following.

> Company A and company B signed a contract for the transfer of several buildings from one company to the other. A procurator[39] challenged the contract in court claiming it was fictitious. The court found that the buildings to be transferred under the contract had already been demolished by the time the contract was signed, and both parties were aware of this. The court held that the aim of the contract was actually to transfer from A to B the plots of land on which the buildings had stood. Legal limitations prevented the parties from doing this directly, so the contract to transfer the buildings had been signed to circumvent these. In the court's opinion, the transfer of non-existent buildings could not be the subject matter of a contract; thus the parties did not have, and could not have had, any

[37] Ruling of Supreme Commercial Court of 13 July 2010 No VAS-8661/10.

[38] Ruling of Supreme Commercial Court of 2 February 2010 No VAS-526/10.

[39] Member of the Procuracy, an important agency in Russia tasked, amongst other things, with overseeing legality.

> intention to create legal consequences in relation to the buildings. The contract was therefore fictitious.[40]

In the opinion of the Supreme Commercial Court what matters is 'the reality of the contract and its reasonable business purpose'. These circumstances should be identified in relation to a contract for it not to be considered a fictitious transaction.[41]

A *sham contract* is a contract which is concluded for the purpose of concealing another contract (CC article 170(2)). When parties conclude a sham contract, they do not intend to perform it; their intentions are directed at creating the legal consequences of a contract which is being concealed.[42]

It is also a very important part of the definition of a sham contract that it must be the intention of both parties to make it in order to conceal another contract. Intention of only one party is not enough.[43] Both parties must have the aim of concealing one contract behind another and agree on all the essential terms of the concealed contract.[44] This could be achieved by signing one contract or several contracts. The main evidence that a contract is sham is the non-conformity between the expressed will of the parties when making it and their real will.[45]

The necessity to prove an inconsistency between the parties' real will and their expressed will makes it very difficult to establish that a contract is sham. Frequently, one contractual party, or a third party, tries to prove a contract to be a sham but the court holds there is insufficient evidence. The problem is that in many cases a third party's interests may be detrimentally affected by a contract but they do not have any appropriate legal method to protect their interests so they try, usually unsuccessfully, to invalidate the contract as a sham.

Also, courts are reluctant to hold a contract void as a sham following a claim by one contractual party. They see it as an attempt to act in bad faith and avoid liability, and often this is true, as in the following example.

> Entrepreneur E sued for invalidity of a contract between company A (the seller) and company B (the buyer) for the sale of real property. A owed E money and, in E's opinion, had sold its property to avoid court-imposed seizure of it to satisfy a debt to E. Thus E claimed the contract for the sale of the real property was a sham, concealing a contract of gift between the two companies, A and B. This concealed contract of gift would be invalid since gifts are not allowed between commercial legal entities (see Chapter

[40] Ruling of Supreme Commercial Court of 23 July 2008 No 9205/08, case No 56-12086/07.

[41] Ruling of Supreme Commercial Court of 25 December 2008 No VAS-16667/08.

[42] Ruling of Supreme Commercial Court of 25 February 2011 No VAS-1792/11.

[43] Ruling of Supreme Commercial Court of 2 August 2005 No 2601/05.

[44] Resolution of Federal Commercial Court of North-Caucasian District of 24 November 2010, case No A32-8665/2010.

[45] Resolution of Federal Commercial Court of North-Caucasian District of 14 February 2011, case No A32-3596/2010.

> 5 at p 121). E's position was based on the fact that B did not pay an actual purchase price; instead the price was set off against a previously existing debt A owed B.
>
> The Commercial Court of Cassation held that the contract between A and B was a contract of sale of real property. The companies provided documents to prove that the contract had been performed by both sides, including documents showing the set-off. The Court thus held that the contract was valid.[46]

Unfortunately, situations like this are common. Most probably E was right and the real purpose for the sale was to avoid seizure of the property to recover the debt owed by A to him and, possibly, to other creditors. However, in this particular situation invalidation of the contract as a sham was not appropriate, as the contract appeared genuine and had been performed.

The Civil Code also provides under article 170(2) that, having declared a sham contract void, the court would apply the rules relevant to the underlying contract which the parties actually had in mind.

(iv) Contracts Concluded by Citizens Deemed to Lack Dispositive Legal Capacity

Dispositive legal capacity of a citizen is defined in CC article 21(1) as:

> the capacity of a citizen by his own actions to acquire and effectuate civil rights, to create civil duties for himself [or herself] and to perform them (civil dispositive legal capacity) shall arise in full . . . upon attaining 18 years of age.[47]

Dispositive legal capacity is limited for anyone under 18 unless that person has been declared to have full dispositive legal capacity; legal capacity of minors is discussed in more detail below (at p 142).

In certain situations a person over 18 years of age can be deemed to be incapable or have only limited capacity, for example, lack capacity if 'as a consequence of mental disturbance [that person] cannot understand the significance of his [or her] actions or direct them' (CC article 29(1)).[48] Only a court may decide; inability to understand the significance of actions and inability to direct them must be proved in a special judicial procedure. A trusteeship (опека; *opeka*) is then established over the person deemed to lack dispositive legal capacity. The trustee will conclude all transactions in the name of the incapable person.

Any contracts concluded personally by an incapable person are void under CC article 171(1). The justification for this is simple: when a contract is understood as

[46] Resolution of Federal Commercial Court of North-Caucasian District of 26 November 2010, case No A63-17014/2009.

[47] Butler, above n 1, at 20–1.

[48] Ibid 27.

the meeting of the minds of the contracting parties, there can be no contract if one of the parties is incapable of understanding the meaning of their actions.

CC article 171 is only applicable if, at the time the contract was concluded, one party has already been deemed to lack dispositive legal capacity. If the person was deemed incapable after the contract has been concluded (however short the time), CC article 171 is not applicable.[49] However, the contract may be invalid on other grounds.

CC article 171(2) goes on to provide that a contract concluded by a person deemed to lack dispositive legal capacity 'may, at the demand of his [or her] trustee, be deemed by a court valid if it was concluded to the advantage of this citizen'.[50] Legal commentators advise that a contract may be considered to be concluded to the advantage of an incapable person if the court finds that their trustee, acting in good faith under the same circumstances, would have concluded that contract on behalf of them.[51]

Thus, the validity of a void contract can be 'restored', even though this rather contradicts the principle that there can be no contract when there is no *will* to conclude it. The law is trying to protect people deemed to lack dispositive legal capacity, so it provides a special consequence of invalidity of a contract concluded by such a person. Special consequences are applicable if the other party who makes a contract with an incapable person has themselves full legal capacity and either knew or should have known about the counterparty's lack of legal capacity. In that case the party with full legal capacity is also obliged *to compensate the other party for any actual losses* incurred by them as a result of the void contract. These provisions have been set up as a matter of policy rather than logic.

(v) Contracts Concluded by Minors Who have Not Attained 14 Years of Age

Minors who have not yet attained 14 years of age have very limited dispositive legal capacity. Minors aged from six to 14 years are allowed to conclude contracts described in CC article 28(2); any other contracts need to be concluded on their behalf by their parents or trustees. All contracts on behalf of minors below six years of age have to be concluded by their parents or trustees (опекуны; *opekuny*).

Minors from age six to 14 have the right under CC article 28(2) to conclude autonomously:

(1) petty domestic transactions;
(2) transactions directed towards receiving advantages without compensation which do not require notarial certification or State registration;

[49] Resolution of Presidium of St Petersburg City Court of 28 March 2007 No 44G-214/07.
[50] Butler, above n 1, at 153.
[51] VP Mozolin and MN Malein (eds), *Научно-практический комментарий к Гражданскому кодексу РФ, Части* 1 [Nauchno-prakticheskii kommentarii k Grazhdanskomu Kodeksu RF, Chasti 1; *Research and Practice Commentary to the Civil Code of the Russian Federation, Part One*] (Moscow, NORMA, 2004) 260.

(3) transactions relating to the disposition of assets granted by a legal representative or with the consent of the last by a third person for a specified person or free disposition.[52]

Under CC article 28(3), the parents and trustees 'bear property responsibility for the transactions'[53] of a minor unless it is proved that the obligation was not violated through their fault.

The law treats contracts concluded by minors aged under 14 similarly to contracts concluded by persons who lack dispositive legal capacity; if such contracts were concluded to the minor's advantage, they may be deemed to be valid by a court on application by the minor's parents or trustees.

The same special consequence of invalidity also applies;: if the other party to a contract with a minor had full legal capacity and knew or should have known about the lack of legal capacity of the minor, the party having full legal capacity is obliged also *to compensate to the minor for any actual losses* incurred. These consequences do not apply to those contracts listed above which minors are allowed to conclude autonomously.

We now move on to the grounds under which a court might declare a contract invalid as a result of it being a 'contested contract'.

C Grounds for Invalidity: Contested Contracts

There are a number of grounds listed in the Civil Code on which a court may deem a contract invalid on the basis of it being 'contested'. The following sections give details of them all.

(i) Contracts by a Legal Entity Exceeding the Limits of Its Legal Capacity

CC article 173 stipulates that:

> A transaction concluded by a juridical person [legal entity] which is contrary to the purposes of the activity specifically limited in its constitutive documents, or by a juridical person not having a licence to engage in the respective activity, may be deemed by a court to be invalid.[54]

In Russian law, all legal entities are divided into legal entities with general legal capacity and legal entities with limited legal capacity.

As a general rule, under CC article 49(1), commercial organisations, except unitary enterprises and certain others, possess general legal capacity. It means that they have civil rights and bear civil duties 'necessary for the effectuation of

[52] Butler, above n 1, at 27.
[53] Ibid.
[54] Ibid 153–4.

any activity not prohibited by law'[55] (although sometimes special authorization or a licence is required; see below).

All other organisations (that is, non-commercial organisations) have limited legal capacity. It means that they only have civil rights to suit the purposes of the particular activities allowed in their constitutive documents.

It was mentioned that a contract may be invalidated if it is concluded by a legal entity which does not have a licence to engage in certain types of activity. The Federal Law on Licensing of Certain Types of Activity[56] lists many of these types of activity; others, such as banking and insurance, are regulated in separate federal laws. If a law provides that a certain type of activity requires a licence, and a company does not have the relevant one, all contracts concluded by the company to conduct such activity are invalid.

A claim to court to establish contractual invalidity on the basis of exceeding the limits of legal capacity may be brought by:

- the legal entity itself;
- the founder of the legal entity or a participant in the legal entity;[57] or
- the state agency which effectuates control or supervision over the particular activity.

Note that the contractual parties as such do not have the right to claim for invalidity on the basis of CC article 173.[58]

Importantly, a contract with a legal entity will only be deemed invalid for lack of legal capacity if it is proved that the other party knew or should have known about that lack.

(ii) Contracts Concluded by a Person Whose Powers to Conclude a Contract have been Limited

CC article 174 gives a court the power to deem a contract invalid if:

> the powers of a person to conclude a transaction [contract] have been *limited by a contract*; or
>
> the powers of the organ [agency] of a juridical person [legal entity] have been *limited by its constitutive documents*, in comparison with those as determined in a power of attorney or in a law, or which may be considered to be obvious from the situation in which the transaction was concluded, and, when concluding it such person or organ exceeded the limits of these limitations.[59] (emphasis added)

Note that this article only applies to limitations in the entity's constitutive documents; it is not applicable to situations where a legal entity exceeds limitations

[55] Ibid 43.
[56] Federal Law of 4 May 2011 No 99-FZ.
[57] See above n 4 for an explanation of participants in one particular type of legal entity, the OOO.
[58] Resolution of Supreme Commercial Court of 17 July 2007 No 3386/07.
[59] Butler, above n 1, at 154.

imposed by legislation. Such contracts would be void because of non-conformity with the law (see p 136 above).[60]

A claim to a court for a declaration that a contract is invalid under CC article 174 can only be brought by *a person in whose interest the limitation of powers was established.* Thus, before deciding whether or not the contract is invalid under CC article 174, the court has to decide whether or not the claimant had a right to bring the claim.

The Supreme Commercial Court in the process of interpreting CC article 174 has explained that the legal entity itself is always considered to be an interested person, if the limitation of powers was established in its statutory constitutive documents.[61] According to the Supreme Commercial Court in a guiding interpretation, other persons only have the right to claim for a contract to be invalid as concluded by a person whose powers have been limited in cases provided for by law.[62] Arguably, in interpreting CC article 174 in that way, the Court has limited the potential application of the provision in contradiction to its actual text.

However, the Supreme Commercial Court has not been consistent in following its own guiding interpretation. For instance, in a number of cases the owner of a unitary enterprise has been considered to be an interested person for the purposes of application of the Civil Code rules on invalidity. A unitary enterprise is a 'commercial organisation not endowed with the right of ownership to property consolidated to it by the owner'.[63] A unitary enterprise does not have a right to dispose of the property it holds.[64] If a unitary enterprise concludes a contract to dispose of that property, the contract can be deemed invalid *upon request of the owner of the unitary enterprise who is considered to be an interested person.*[65]

Contracts may only be deemed invalid under CC article 174 if it is proved that the other party to the transaction knew or should have known about the relevant limitations. According to the Supreme Commercial Court, it follows that the law allows for the possibility that the other contractual party did not know and should not have known about the limitations established in the legal entity's statutory constitutive documents. Mere reference in a contract that an agency of a legal entity, concluding a contract on behalf of it, is acting in

[60] Resolution of Plenum of Supreme Commercial Court 14 May 1998 No 9 'On Certain Questions of Application of Article 174 of the Civil Code of the Russian Federation when the Organs of Judicial Persons Execute their Powers to Enter into Transactions' Part 1.

[61] Resolution of Plenum of Supreme Commercial Court 14 May 1998 No 9 'On Certain Questions of Application of Article 174 of the Civil Code of the Russian Federation when the Organs of Judicial Persons Execute their Powers to Enter into Transactions' Part 4.

[62] Ibid.

[63] CC art 113(1); Butler, above n 1, at 111. See also above n 4.

[64] CC art 295(2); Federal Law on State and Municipal Unitary Enterprises art 18(2). See also above at 19.

[65] Resolution of Plenum of Supreme Court No 10, Supreme Commercial Court No 22 of 29 April 2010 'On Certain Questions Arising in the Court Practice when the Disputes connected with Protection of Property Rights and Other Ownership Rights are Resolved' Part 9.

accordance with its constitutive documents, cannot be taken automatically to mean that the other contractual party knew about any limitations.[66]

According to Russian company law, in most cases the director of a company has authority to sign contracts on behalf of the company; the director's powers are based on the company's constitutive documents. When a contract is concluded in Russia it is common practice to refer in the introductory part of the contract to the documents on which the signatories' powers are based. This reference does not mean that the parties to the contract have read or should have read each others' constitutive documents. Other specific evidence is necessary to prove that a contractual party knew or should have known of the limitations.[67]

The Civil Code does not mention any possibility of subsequent approval of a contract concluded by a person whose powers to conclude a contract have been limited. However, the Supreme Commercial Court ruled that the person, in whose interest the limitation of powers was established, does have the right to approve such a contract retrospectively. The Court explained in an opinion that the principle of analogy of law makes CC article 183(2), on subsequent approval of agents, applicable to regulate the consequences of subsequent approval of these contracts (for analogy of law see p 32).[68] Applying CC article 183 by analogy means that a contract concluded by a person in excess of their limited powers can be 'healed' by the person in whose interests the limitations of powers are established and thereby become valid. The interested party does not have to go to court for the contract to be 'healed'.

(iii) Contracts Concluded by Minors from 14 to 18 Years of Age

As discussed in above, minors are limited in their dispositive legal capacity. From the age of 14 dispositive legal capacity becomes broader although remains limited until the point in time when full dispositive legal capacity is attained; as a general rule this is when a person reaches the age of 18 (CC article 21(1)).

In some circumstances dispositive legal capacity is gained earlier:

(1) When a person under the age of 18 marries, he or she immediately acquires full dispositive legal capacity (CC article 21(2)). This is not lost if they subsequently divorce before becoming 18. The marriage is possible from the age of 16 with consent of the local governmental authorities when there is a justifiable reason;

[66] Resolution of Plenum of Supreme Commercial Court 14 May 1998 No 9 'On Certain Questions of Application of Article 174 of the Civil Code of the Russian Federation when the Organs of Judicial Persons Execute their Powers to Enter into Transactions' Part 5.

[67] Resolution of Supreme Commercial Court of 21 May 2010 No KG-A40/4680-10, case No A40-106901/09-25-433.

[68] Resolution of Plenum of Supreme Commercial Court 14 May 1998 No 9 'On Certain Questions of Application of Article 174 of the Civil Code of the Russian Federation when the Organs of Judicial Persons Execute their Powers to Enter into Transactions' Part 7.

(2) When a person who has attained 16 years of age works under a labour contract, or, with the consent of their parents or guardian, engages in entrepreneurial activity (CC article 27(1)), he or she may be declared to have full dispositive legal capacity. Such a person is declared to have full dispositive legal capacity by decision of an agency of trusteeship and guardianship together with the consent of both parents or their guardian, or, in the absence of such consent, by decision of a court.

CC article 26(2) makes clear that, for minors between 14 and 18 years of age, their dispositive legal capacity allows them autonomously and without the need for anyone's consent to:

(a) dispose of their earnings, stipends and other revenues;
(b) effectuate the rights of an author of a work of science, literature, art or other results of his (or her) intellectual activity protected by a law;
(c) in accordance with the law, make deposits in credit institutions and dispose of them;
(d) conclude petty domestic transactions and other transactions provided for by CC article 28(2) (that is, contracts which minors aged six to 14 are allowed to be concluded autonomously).[69]

Any other contracts need to be concluded with the written consent of the legal representatives of the minor, that is, their parents, adoptive parents or guardian (CC article 26(1)). Written approval can be given retrospectively. Failing that, the parents or guardian can apply to a court for a declaration that the transaction for which their written approval was required but withheld is invalid.

The law imposes special circumstances of invalidity if the other party to the contract with a person from 14 to 18 years of age themselves had full legal capacity and knew or should have known about the young person's lack of full legal capacity. Then they are obliged to compensate the young person for any actual losses incurred as a result of making the invalid contract (CC article 175(1) paragraph 2, referring also to article 171(1) paragraphs 2 and 3). Here is another example of legal consequences – damages being paid – as result of an otherwise invalid contract. As earlier, it seems likely that this is based on policy considerations.

(iv) Contracts Concluded by Citizens Whose Dispositive Legal Capacity is Limited by a Court

> A citizen who as a consequence of abusing alcoholic beverages or narcotic means places his family in a grave material position may be limited in dispositive legal capacity by a court in the procedure established by civil procedure legislation. A guardianship [попечительство; *popechitel'stvo*] shall be established over him.[70] (CC article 30)

[69] Butler, above n 1, at 25.
[70] Ibid 28.

Such a person retains the right to conclude petty domestic transactions autonomously. Any other transactions, and receipt and disposal of their earnings, may only be made with the consent of the guardian. A contract concluded without consent may be deemed invalid by a court following an application by the guardian. If the alcoholic or drug addict subsequently recovers, a court can restore them to full legal capacity.

(v) Contracts Concluded by Citizen Not Capable of Understanding the Significance of his Actions or Guiding Them

A contract concluded by a person who normally has full legal capacity but who, at the time they made the contract, was in such a state that they were 'not capable of understanding the significance of [their] actions or directing them'[71] may be deemed by a court to be invalid under CC article 177.

The rationale for such contracts being deemed void is the lack of correlation between the party's actual will and their expressed will.[72] The logic is that if the person is not able to understand the significance of their actions or direct them, they cannot form any actual intention to make a contract.

As one of the courts explained, situations where such circumstances might arise are various but include illness, alcoholic or drug intoxication (on a comparatively temporary rather than chronic basis, for which CC article 30 is more appropriate) or an emotional disturbance caused by specific events or actions.[73]

Understandably, for a contract to be deemed invalid on this basis the most difficult component is to prove that the party was, indeed, unable to understand the significance of their actions or direct them. The most common way to prove this is through psychiatric examination. The Supreme Court took the legal position that psychiatric examination is mandatory for a claim is brought under CC article 177.[74] However, it can be carried out several years after the contract has been concluded, as in the following case.

> The Supreme Court confirmed the position of the lower courts and deemed a contract of purchase-sale of a flat invalid because the seller had been unable to understand what he was doing when he signed the contract. The contract was signed in 2003 but the psychiatric examination which evidenced his condition was held in 2008.[75]

[71] Ibid 156.

[72] Resolution of Federal Commercial Court of East-Siberian District of 26 January 2009, case No A79-2594/2007; Resolution of Second Court of Appeal of 15 April 2009, case No A31-4660/2008-14.

[73] Summary of Practice by Kemerovo Region Court, 15 February 2011, No 01-07-/26-113 para 2.

[74] Resolution of Plenum of the Supreme Court 'On the Preparation of Civil Cases for Court Hearings' of 24 June 2008 No 11 para 13.

[75] Ruling of Supreme Court of the Russian Federation of 6 August 2009 No 5-V09-78.

In another case the expert evaluation was even allowed after the death of the contractual party.[76] The court decided that there were no reasons why a report of *post mortem* psychiatric evaluation should not be accepted.

Unsurprisingly, a court is much more reluctant to deem a notarised contract void under CC article 177. The court explains this by reference to the notary's obligations to ensure that the parties to a transaction possess full dispositive legal capacity and to explain the substance of the transaction to them.[77] However, the law does not currently oblige a notary to ascertain whether the parties to a contract are able to understand the significance of their actions.

Under CC article 177(1) a contract may be deemed by a court to be invalid on application by:

- the person who concluded a contract and was not capable of understanding the significance of his/her actions or directing them; or
- 'other persons whose rights or interests protected by law have been violated as a result of the conclusion thereof'.[78]

For example, after a testator's death, an heir has a right to challenge a contract to which the testator had been a party.[79]

One interesting question is whether or not a legal entity has a right to challenge contracts concluded by their executive agencies on behalf of the company, if there is evidence that the executive office-holder (for example, the director) was not capable of understanding the significance of his or her actions. There are cases where companies have brought claims on that basis and no court has ever stated that a company cannot bring a claim under CC article 177. The following is an example.

> A director-general of a company signed a contract on behalf of the company for the sale of real property belonging to it. The transfer of property title was duly registered. Later the company brought a claim to court saying that the director was not able to understand the significance of his actions. The court did not deem the contract void because that was not proven. However, no doubts were expressed about the right of the company to bring the claim.[80]

CC article 177 does not give rise to any special consequences of invalidity, as have the articles discussed earlier.

[76] Cassational Ruling of St Petersburg City Court of 15 February 2011 No 33-2038.

[77] Fundamental Principles of Legislation on the Notariat of 11 February 1993 No 4462-1 arts 43 and 54. English translation in WE Butler, *Russian Public Law*, 3rd edn (London, Wildy Simmonds & Hill Publishers, 2013) 853 at 872, 874.

[78] Butler, above n 1, at 157.

[79] Ruling of Supreme Court of 16 May 2006 No 5-V06-25.

[80] Resolution of Federal Commercial Court of the Central District of 12 January 2011 No A68-12669/09.

*(vi) Contracts Concluded under the Influence of Delusion (*заблуждение*; zabluzhdenie)*

CC article 178(1) provides that contracts 'concluded under the influence of delusion having material significance may be deemed invalid by a court upon the suit of the party who acted under the influence of delusion'.[81]

The main question which arises is what is considered to be a 'delusion having material significance'. The only clarification in the article is that:

> Delusion relative to the nature of the transaction, the identity or such qualities of its subject which significantly reduce the possibility of using it for its purpose shall have material significance. Delusion relative to the motives for the transaction shall not have material significance.[82]

Court practice gives some explanations and clarifications of this. The list of situations in CC article 178 when the delusion has material significance is exhaustive. Any other misunderstanding, based on circumstances not listed in article 178, will not be considered to be delusion having material significance and cannot be a ground of invalidity of a contract.[83]

Delusion can be described as a disparity between a person's subjective understanding about certain circumstances and events and objective reality (taken to be the commonly accepted understanding of those circumstances and events). In other words, the expression of the party's will did not correspond with their actual will; the contractual party did not receive what they intended to receive.[84]

A good example of the application of CC article 178 is given by the Supreme Commercial Court in one of its declarations.

> A municipality, M, organised a tender for the sale of a house. The house was advertised as having a certain floor area. Company C won the tender and concluded a purchase-sale contract with M. In fact the actual floor area of the house was not as M had stated in the advertisement. C claimed that the contract was invalid as concluded under the influence of delusion and the court upheld C's claim.[85]

There was a similar result in another case.

> A City Administration, A, leased a plot of land to company B for the construction of a residential estate. However, after the contract was concluded it turned out that the plot was located within the protective zone surrounding an airport where residential construction was not allowed.

[81] Butler, above n 1, at 156.
[82] Ibid 156–7.
[83] Resolution of Federal Commercial Court of North-Western District of 17 January 2011 case No A13-2968/2010.
[84] Ibid.
[85] Ruling of Supreme Commercial Court of 6 December 2010 No VAS-16117/10.

> This limitation was in place before the contract was concluded. B claimed that A failed to inform it about the situation so the contract was concluded under the influence of delusion. The court noted that the circumstances prevented B from using the plot for the purpose stipulated in the contract and thus B was deluded about the commercial prospects of the use of the plot. As a result the contract was deemed invalid.[86]

In the latter case, it can be seen that the courts hearing the case accepted that there was a duty of the City Administration to inform the company of all the circumstances connected with the plot of land. They did not refer to provisions of the Civil Code which stipulate that entrepreneurial activity is carried on at the person's own risk who thus should act with due reasonableness and diligence. However, in a number of cases courts do apply those provisions, as in the following example.

> Mr S bought a share in a limited responsibility society (OOO).[87] S considered the OOO to be financially sound and profitable. However, it turned out that it was suffering losses. S sued to invalidate the contract for the sale of the share claiming that it had been concluded under the influence of delusion. The courts held that S had examined the OOO's documentation before the contract was signed and so was in a position to make himself aware of the true situation. Acting with *due reasonableness and diligence* he could have refused to acquire the share. It was his own fault that he purchased the share and the contract was valid.[88]

Unfortunately, court practice is insufficiently consistent to be able to draw the line between the one party's duty to reveal information relevant to the contract and the other party's duty to act reasonably and with due care.

One thing is clear: CC article 178 specifically says that delusion about the motives for the contract does not have material significance. This was applied in the following case.

> A company, C, a Municipal Unitary Enterprise [муниципальное унитарное предприятие; *munitsipal'noe unitarnoe predpriiatie*],[89] U, and a Municipality (local town administration), M, signed a contract under which C was obliged to deliver fuel oil to U. U was obliged to pay for the fuel oil, and M provided a guarantee for that payment.
>
> C fully performed its part of the contract but U failed to pay. C sued M to enforce the guarantee. It turned out, however, that the guarantee was

[86] Ruling of Supreme Commercial Court of 25 November 2010 No VAS-15498/10.

[87] See above n 4 for an explanation about this type of legal entity.

[88] Ruling of Supreme Commercial Court of 31 March 2011 No VAS-3597/11.

[89] This is a type of state-owned enterprise, with limited ownership rights; see CC arts 113–15. It has similar limitations to the state unitary enterprise in the case above, text to n 11.

> invalid (as contradicting the law) because M had not followed the proper procedure established under budgetary law. C claimed that the main contract was invalid as concluded under the influence of delusion, because the only reason it had contracted with U was because of M's guarantee of payment.
>
> The court found that M knew from the very outset that the guarantee was invalid. However, the court also held that the main contract itself was valid. In the court's opinion, there was no delusion about 'the nature of the contract', since by that expression the law means the type of contract and C knew it was entering into the contract of sale; there was also no delusion regarding the identity or any qualities of the subject matter which would significantly reduce the possibility of using it for its contractual purpose and thus have material significance, because the parties knew the contract was for the sale of fuel oil.[90] C's motivation in making the contract was immaterial.

If one contractual party proves that the delusion arose through the fault of the other, not only is the contract void, but the party at fault is obliged to compensate the other party for any actual losses incurred as a result. If fault is not proved, the party who brought the claim of delusion which rendered the contract invalid (the deluded party) is obliged to compensate the other party if they counterclaim for any actual losses caused to them, even if the delusion arose through circumstances which were not dependent on the deluded party. In practice this latter (rather unfair) rule is rarely applied.

The Civil Code treats deliberate behaviour by one contractual party to delude the other as a breach of contract. That can be seen from the duty stipulated by law to compensate the other party for any actual losses caused by the breach. However, the liability for breach by delusion is limited compared to the general rules on contractual liability (see Chapter 10 at p 222). It is not clear why the authors of the Code decided to limit liability for this particular type of breach. It could be argued that this limitation does not create the right incentives for contracting parties to reveal all pertinent information about the subject matter of a contract. The following is an example.

> Company C rented a plot of land for residential construction from City Administration A. It turned out that there was a cattle mortuary (скотомогильник; *skotomogil'hik*, ie a place where dead cows which cannot be used for meat are deposited) on the plot and for that reason residential construction was not allowed. C brought a claim to deem the contract invalid as concluded under the influence of delusion. The court held that A was aware of the mortuary but failed to inform C about it. The court confirmed that the delusion was caused by A's actions, therefore

[90] Ruling of Supreme Commercial Court of 22 October 2010 No VAS-14081/10.

A should compensate C for its losses. However, these losses were limited to the pre-payment C made, so the only practical consequence of the contract's invalidity was restitution to C of its pre-payment.[91]

Amendments to the Civil Code in force on 1 September 2013 aim to clarify the concept of 'delusion having material significance'. Under the new version of CC article 178(2), delusion has material significance when:

- the party misspoke, miswrote or misprinted, etc;
- the party is deluded about the subject matter of the contract or its qualities which are considered to be important;
- the party is deluded about the nature of the contract;
- the party is deluded about the person with whom the contract is made; or
- the party is deluded regarding a circumstance which they have mentioned or on which they relied when they made the contract.

The list is exhaustive and no other circumstances can be considered as leading to delusion having material significance.

Delusion relating to motivation is still said not to have 'material significance' (CC article 178(3)). Hopefully, this clearer specification in the revised law of the range of circumstances which will be regarded as delusion will assist in the development of a consistent approach to this vitiating factor.

(vii) Contracts Concluded under the Influence of Fraud, Coercion, Threat, or Ill-intentioned Agreement of Representative of One Party with Other Party or Confluence of Grave Circumstances

CC article 179(1) provides that:

> A transaction concluded under the influence of fraud, coercion, threat or ill-intentioned agreement of a representative of one party with the other party, and also a transaction which a person was forced to conclude as a consequence of the confluence of grave circumstances on conditions extremely disadvantageous for himself [or herself] which the other party took advantage of . . . may be deemed by a court to be invalid by the court upon the suit of the victim.[92]

As with most of the other vitiating factors discussed so far, evidently the principle behind CC article 179 is inconsistency between the expressed will of the party, who was forced into the contract, and their actual will. There is no mutual consent, so no contract. No doubt the idea behind CC article 179 is correct; however, practical implementation could be improved.

Essentially, the Civil Code draws no clear line between delusion as a ground of invalidity under CC article 178 and fraud as a ground of invalidity under CC

[91] Resolution of Federal Commercial Court of North-Caucasian District of 2 March 2010, case No A53-7576/2009.

[92] Butler, above n 1, at 157–8.

article 179. According to one of the commercial courts, fraud in civil law is defined as 'intentional delusion of one party to the contract by the other party to the contract or a third party in the interests of whom the contract is concluded'.[93] Thus confusion exists in court practice between delusion and fraud, and very often if there was any misunderstanding caused by the other party's actions a claimant will bring a claim in which they refer to both CC articles 178 and 179. A good example of the approach where both articles were used to try to substantiate the claimant's position is the case of S discussed above at p 151.[94] The essence of S's claim was that he became deluded by the actions of the other contractual party, the OOO. However, as discussed, the courts did not consider S's delusion sufficient to deem the contract invalid as he had the opportunity to check the information himself.

Even though the courts themselves often fail to do so, it is very important to distinguish between invalidity based on delusion under CC article 178 and invalidity based on fraud under CC article 179, since the consequences are different, and in particular, article 179 is more punitive.

As courts have explained, fraud presupposes deliberate faulty behaviour by one party trying to persuade the other to make a contract. The fraudster knows that the qualities and consequences the victim expects from the contract cannot happen. Thus the victim has the will to conclude a contract, and has expressed that will, but the formation of their will is not free; it has been affected by the other party's fraud.[95]

The main difference between delusion under CC article 178 and fraud under CC article 179 lies in the way the guilty party acts. For their actions to constitute fraud, they must act intentionally to create for the victim (the other contractual party) a wrong impression about the contract. For CC article 178, negligent or even innocent misleading might still cause delusion.

A major problem is the difficulty, within the procedures used in the domestic courts and in the commercial courts, of proving the presence of fraud, coercion or threat. As a result courts often interpret CC article 179 narrowly and say that since, for example, coercion and fraud are illegal actions, their presence should be established with due evidence such as, *primarily*, a sentence imposed by a criminal court.[96]

In fact, the Russian Criminal Code provides (coincidently in its article 179) punishment for the crime of coercion to conclude a contract or coercion to refrain from concluding a contract. However, it does not mean that a criminal conviction is a necessary prerequisite for a contract to be invalid under CC arti-

[93] Resolution of Federal Commercial Court of Volgo-Viatskii District of 26 January 2009, case No A79-2594/2007.

[94] Ruling of Supreme Commercial Court of 31 March 2011 No VAS-3597/11; see above, text to n 88.

[95] Cassational Ruling of St Petersburg City Court of 28 March 2011 No 4176; also Ruling of Supreme Commercial Court of 7 June 2010 No VAS-7140/10.

[96] Resolution of Federal Commercial Court of Moscow District of 19 January 2006, case No KG-A40/13646-05.

cle 179. The commercial courts and the courts of general jurisdiction hearing civil cases are distinct from criminal process and hear cases independently. When hearing a civil case, the court should consider all evidence independently and not require a criminal conviction as the primary evidence of coercion to conclude a contract under civil law.

The Supreme Commercial Court defined coercion to conclude a contract as influencing the victim so as to induce them to act in accordance with the will of the influencing party. Their actions could influence the victim psychologically, through a threat, or physically, through violence. To render a contract invalid, the threat or violence must be the direct reason the contract was concluded. It must also be serious, credible and unlawful.[97]

'Ill-intentioned agreement of a representative of one party with the other party' is another ground of invalidity provided by CC article 179. When deciding cases on this basis, courts have to grapple with the question of the formation of the will of a legal entity, since, as is seen in court practice, when a contract is concluded by a representative of a legal entity as a result of their 'ill-intentioned agreement with the other party', the actual will of the legal entity may be held not to correspond with the will expressed by its representative,[98] As in the following example.

> Z, as a director of company C, concluded a contract for the sale of one of C's building to Mr Y. Afterwards, Y leased the building back to C for rent. C never received any payment for the sale of the building because the sale price was set off against the rent.
>
> C brought a claim to deem the contract of sale invalid as concluded as a result of ill-intentioned agreement of Z with Y. The court held the contract invalid and explained that although Y had benefited from the contract, the contract concluded by Z ostensibly on behalf of C was against C's interests and its conclusion led to C's insolvency. Thus, stated the court, the will of the represented company C was replaced with the will of its representative, Z.[99]

However, in the same ruling, the Supreme Commercial Court stated in relation to another case that 'mere sale of an asset for a low price does not prove invalidity of a contract'.[100]

As seen above, CC article 179 also lists 'a transaction which a person was forced to conclude as a confluence of grave circumstances on conditions extremely disadvantageous for himself' as a ground for invalidity. The interesting question then arises as to what is considered to be 'a confluence of grave circumstances' in this context. As the Supreme Court explains, it is necessary to prove that one party has entered into a contract under the influence of grave

97 Ruling of Supreme Commercial Court of 4 February 2011 No VAS-185/11.
98 Ruling of Supreme Commercial Court of 7 September 2010 No VAS-11494/10.
99 Ibid.
100 Ruling of Supreme Commercial Court of 29 June 2010 No VAS-9890/10.

circumstances, the conditions of the contract are extremely disadvantageous for that party and there is evidence that the other party took advantage of these grave circumstances.[101] Thus, it must be proved that the other party knew about the grave circumstances and knowingly exploited them. It must also be proved that there is a causal link between the grave circumstances and the conclusion of the contract on very unfavourable terms to the disadvantaged party.[102] It is important that the terms of the contract are not just unfavourable to the party but extremely disadvantageous. The following is an example.

> S and O concluded a contract of loan in accordance with which S gave O a certain sum of money and O would repay the capital sum plus 14.5 per cent annual interest. S tried to challenge the contract as concluded as a result of confluence of grave circumstances. The court did not uphold S's claim. It held that the annual rate of 14.5 per cent could not be considered to be an extremely disadvantageous contractual term when at that time the Russian Central Bank's refinance rate was 13 per cent.[103]

If the transaction is deemed invalid on one of the grounds in CC article 179, the wrongdoing party returns to the victim everything received in kind. If that is impossible, they instead pay its value as monetary compensation. In addition, they compensate the victim for any consequential losses. However, any property received by the victim from the wrongdoing party, and also anything due to that party, is forfeited to the revenue of the Russian Federation.

III CONTRACTS BEING NOT CONCLUDED

As discussed in Chapter 4 at p 86, a contract is considered to be concluded when there is agreement in the required form on all the material terms. If one or several material terms have not been agreed and set down in the contract, the contract is considered to be 'not concluded', that is, it will be treated as if it had never existed.

Even though a 'not-concluded contract' is an independent legal expression, distinct from 'void contract', the consequences are basically the same: nullification of all rights and obligations under the (non-existent) contract.

It might be supposed that a not-concluded contract would have little practical value, since, if there is no contract, there are no rights and obligations and there is nothing to perform. If the parties have in fact provided and accepted performance it would seem logical that some sort of contract must have existed between them. However, the logic of Russian law is different. All the obligations under an apparent contract could have been duly performed but the con-

[101] Ruling of Supreme Court of 12 October 2010 case No 41-B10-13.
[102] Ruling of Supreme Commercial Court of 18 May 2010 No VAS-5949/10.
[103] Ruling of St Petersburg City Court of 20 December 2010 No 33-17164/2010

tract might still be considered to be 'not concluded'. There may, however, be consequences.

A Performance of a 'Not Concluded' Contract as Unfounded Enrichment

As just noted, if a contract is considered to be not concluded it means that the contract never existed and hence could not give rise to any contractual rights or obligations. Anything acquired by the would-be parties to a not-concluded contract is therefore considered to be unfounded enrichment. According to CC article 1102(1):

> A person who without grounds established by a law, other legal acts, or transaction acquired or saved property (acquirer) at the expense of another person (victim) shall be obliged to return to the last property unfoundedly acquired or saved (unjustified enrichment), except for instances provide for by Article 1109 of the present Code.[104]

Therefore, if one would-be party has performed an apparent contract which in fact was 'not concluded', they have the right to claim the performance or its monetary value from the other would-be party, on the basis of unfounded enrichment.

It should be noted that, in Russian procedural law, there is no joinder of actions and alternative claims are not allowed. When a claimant sues a person with whom they appeared to have a contract and the claim is based on that contract, the claimant can only bring an action under the contract. If the court finds that the contract was not concluded, it has to dismiss the claim; an action based on a contract cannot be upheld if there was, in fact, no contract. Under the procedural rules, the court is not allowed to change the basis of a claim. To enforce his or her rights, the claimant would have to bring a new claim based on unfounded enrichment.

Unfortunately, the Code's formal approach to the conclusion of a contract and the application of strictly formal grounds for rendering a contract 'not concluded' have frequently been used in bad faith as a way to postpone or avoid contractual performance. This usually occurs in the situation when one party wants to opt out of a contract for one reason or another but there are no valid grounds for termination. This is illustrated by the following case.

> State enterprise E sued company C claiming debt arising from C's failure to pay for services of transporting heat through a heating network belonging to E. The service was provided by E to C under a contract of 'compensated rendering of services', with interest for late payment of the debt. The court acknowledged that E had proved that C was using E's heating network to transport heat. At the same time the court pointed out that E had not provided any evidence to prove that they had a contract with

[104] Butler, above n 1, at 769.

C. There was no written contract and therefore the court would not acknowledge that there was in fact any contractual relationship between the parties.

The court held that under the general procedural rules it could only consider the case within the bounds of the asserted claim. The basis of the claim was recovery of debt resulting from improper performance of a contract. Therefore, the court rejected E's claim but held that E might then bring an action in unfounded enrichment in order to recover the debt.[105]

The following is a further example.

Construction company C brought a claim against an entrepreneur, E, to recover outstanding payment for work provided in accordance with three independent construction work contracts. E counterclaimed to render all three contracts 'not concluded' and recover unfounded enrichment from C. E claimed that the unfounded enrichment should be calculated as the pre-payment made less the value of the work actually performed. The parties also disagreed about the value and amount of the completed construction work. C claimed that it had completed work worth almost twice the pre-payment, while E claimed that it was only worth one-third of the pre-payment.

Even though C had partially performed the independent construction work contracts and performance had been accepted by E, the courts of all instances rendered all three contracts 'not concluded'. Their reasoning was as follows: in two of the contracts the subject matter, that is, the work to be performed, was not clearly defined and none of the contracts stipulated the time periods within which the work should have been performed. Since there were no contractual obligations, the courts acknowledged E's right to recover unfounded enrichment (his pre-payment less the cost of the work already performed). C was considered to have received due payment for the work performed and so had no right to any further payment.[106]

It is important to note that there is inconsistency. Some courts ignore the formal Civil Code requirements about conclusion of contracts and uphold claims on a contract even though there might be formal grounds to consider it to be 'not concluded', as in the following example.

[105] Resolution of Federal Commercial Court of Volgo-Viatskii District of 16 August 2010 No A79-237/2010.

[106] Ruling of Supreme Commercial Court of 18 May 2007 No 5353/07; Resolution of Federal Commercial Court of Moscow District of 22 January 2007; Resolution of Ninth Commercial Appellate Court No 09P-15797/2006-GK.

> Entrepreneur E was receiving and sending goods by rail. When E's carriages arrived at the station, company A brought them to the branch-line leading to E's premises. A sued E to recover a debt for the services it had rendered doing this between March and June 2007.
>
> The court pointed out that even though a written contract had not been concluded, A did provide the respective services during that period. The services were accepted by E, but not fully paid for. This gave the court the basis to conclude that the actual relationship of 'compensated rendering of services' regulated by CC chapter 39 was established between the parties. Therefore, E, who had accepted the services, had to pay for them.[107]

Even though here the court would have had a legitimate right to reject A's claim and suggest instead that A brought a new case based on unfounded enrichment, contrary to the formal requirements of the law the court decided to protect the interests of a party to an apparent contract which it had performed in good faith.

In 2011 the Supreme Commercial Court formulated a general rule to be used by lower courts in handling situations when one party is trying to avoid a contract or the fulfilment of their obligations under a contract by claiming that it was 'not concluded on formal grounds'.[108] The Court held that when a claim to render a contract 'not concluded' is brought by a party who has accepted the other party's performance but has not fulfilled their own obligation to pay for it, that claim should be qualified as an abuse of right under CC article 10. If there is a dispute about whether a contract is concluded or not, the court must assess the circumstances and evidence as a whole in favour of preservation and not invalidation of an apparent contract. When doing so, the court should take into account the presumption of reasonableness and good faith of the participants of civil relationships envisaged in CC article 10.

Draft Amendments to the Civil Code would introduce a new article 446.1.[109] Inter alia, this article is meant to eliminate the use in bad faith of a contract being deemed 'not concluded'. In particular, according to part 3 of the new article, a party who has accepted in full or in part the performance under an apparent contract, or has otherwise confirmed its existence, has no right to claim that the contract is not concluded, unless otherwise is provided by law.

This sensible provision should enhance contractual certainty and go a long way towards supporting apparent contracts. At the time of writing, this particular amendment has not yet been adopted but there is a reasonable expectation that it will be.

[107] Resolution of Federal Commercial Court of North-Western District of 4 May 2009 No A05-6686/2008.

[108] Resolution of Supreme Commercial Court of 8 February 2011 No 13970/10.

[109] Draft Federal Law on Amendments to Parts One, Two, Three and Four of the Civil Code No 47538-6 approved by the State Duma at first reading 27 April 2012 art 1 para 229.

IV CONCLUSION

There is a complex array of provisions in the Civil Code, under which an apparent contract may be vitiated. However, even when a contract is deemed invalid, there may be consequences beyond the simple restitution of goods or money. In some circumstances, for example, when one party defrauded the other party, compensation for consequential losses may be claimed by the victim. In others, for example, when the contract contradicts morality, the state confiscates the fruits of the wrongful activity. One unfortunate side-effect of the complexity of this area of Russian contract law is that the courts are not always consistent in their application of the rules, and indeed may be misled by parties using vitiating provisions in bad faith to evade contractual responsibility. However, both the Supreme Commercial Court and those drafting revisions to the Civil Code are aware of these issues and moves are being made to reduce some opportunities for illegitimate application of the rules detailed in this chapter.

7

Third Parties to the Contract

I INTRODUCTION

Contracts for the benefit of third parties is an institution which vividly demonstrates the difference in the way Russian and English contract law operates. There is nothing analogous to the doctrine of privity in Russian contract law. Even though a contract is understood as an agreement between parties who have expressed their consent to be bound by it, for a long time contracts for the benefit of a third party have been recognised in Russian law as enforceable by the third party.

The Civil Code (CC) currently in force, as well as the three previous codifications (the 1922 and 1964 RSFSR Civil Codes and the 1991 USSR Fundamental Principles of Civil Law which was brought into operation in Russia in 1992),[1] recognise the right of a person who is not a party to a contract to bring a claim based on it, provided certain conditions stipulated in legislation are met.

In English law traditionally the doctrine of consideration has been another obstacle to the enforcement of promises by third parties. In Russian law there is no concept fully equivalent to English consideration. The rules in Russian law which perform functions analogous to it (discussed in detail in Chapter 5) do not require that a third party need provide any equivalent to consideration to have a right to claim under a contract concluded for their benefit. The result is that Russian law takes a similar position to English law since the Law Reform (Rights of Third Parties) Act 1999.

However, despite the absence of any requirement of privity of contract or consideration, contracts for the benefit of third parties can hardly be called a well-developed concept in Russian law. The understanding of the concept is very limited, both compared to English law and to other continental legal systems.

[1] The USSR Fundamental Principles of Civil Law were adopted on 31 May 1991, to enter into force on 1 January 1992. In the interim, the USSR dissolved so they did not enter into force as ordained. Pending the passage of a new Russian Civil Code, they were generally brought into force in Russia by a decree of 14 July 1992.

II BURDENING THE THIRD PARTY

Russian law does not allow a burden to be imposed on a person who is not a party to a contract (CC article 308(3)). Any such contractual term would be invalid as contradicting the law (see Chapter 6 at p 136 on that form of invalidity), as shown in one example.

> Company A signed a contract with company B for B to provide A with security services. At the time the contract was signed, A was in administration and did not have the financial resources to pay for the services provided. A asked company C to pay for the services B was providing under the contract between A and B. C duly paid for some time and then stopped. B then sued C to recover the money still owed. By the time the claim was brought A had been liquidated and ceased to exist.
>
> The courts held that the contract for the provision of security services was only between A and B; there were no obligations between B and C. A was the recipient of the services and was obliged to pay for them. C was a third party to that contract and could not be obligated without prior consent to pay B for services provided to someone else (here, A). Payments had been made by C to B to discharge part of A's obligation, but the provision by C of some payments did not mean that C had also agreed to pay for all the services provided to A under a contract to which C was not a party.[2]

Another case concerned a contract.

> Company A sued company B for the price of construction materials delivered by A to company C. C was a contractor in a construction project for B. A delivered construction materials to C in accordance with a purchase-sale agreement between A and C. C failed to pay A for the delivered materials, maintaining that the delay in its payment was due to B's failure to perform its obligations under the construction contract between B and C.
>
> The courts held that B was not a party to the purchase-sale contract between A and C and thus was not obliged to pay for the goods A had delivered to C. On the other hand, A was not a party to the construction contract between B and C. The fact that B owed money to C did not allow A to sue B, either under the contract between B and C, or under the contract between A and C.[3]

[2] Ruling of Supreme Commercial Court of 21 October 2009, case No VAS-13467/09.

[3] Resolution of Federal Commercial Court of Ural District of 13 September 2010, case No F09-7357/10-C3, case No A07-2543/2010.

This rule that a burden may not be imposed also applies to a contract for the benefit of a third party. Contractual parties are not allowed to restrict a third party's right to enforce a contract themselves by making it conditional that they perform certain actions, or provide some performance. If the contract is for their benefit, the third party has a right to enforce that benefit, as discussed below.

III DEFINING A CONTRACT FOR THE BENEFIT OF A THIRD PARTY

CC article 430(1) defines a contract for the benefit of a third party as a contract in which:

> the parties have established that a debtor [promisor] is obliged to make performance not to the creditor [promisee] but to a third person specified or not specified in the contract and having the right to demand performance of the obligation to his benefit from the debtor.[4]

It follows from this that the main characteristic of a contract for the benefit of a third party is that the third party is given an independent right to enforce the contract. However, unfortunately, the law does not give any clues as to when that right exists.

The simplest situation for courts is when parties directly stipulate in their contract that a third party has an independent right to sue for performance of the contractual obligation that is for their benefit. The following case illustrates a situation when the courts had no doubt that the third party had such a right.

> A state-owned unitary enterprise (унитарное предприятие; *unitarnoe predpriiatie*), E, leased premises to Golden Star Limited Responsibility Society (общество с ограниченной ответственностью; *obshchestvo s ogranichennoi otvetstvennost'iu* (OOO)).[5] The premises were state-owned. The contract stipulated that all payments under the contract should be made to the state budget. It also stipulated that if the OOO failed to pay the rent, the Committee for the Management of State Property (GKI)[6], as a representative of the Russian state, had the right to demand payment.
>
> The OOO did not pay the rent and the third party, GKI, brought a claim against them. Courts at all instances agreed that the contract was

[4] WE Butler, *Civil Code of the Russian Federation, Parts 1, 2 and 3* (Moscow, JurInfoR-Press, 2008) 312.

[5] An OOO is type of Russian legal entity where a participant/shareholder will own a participatory share (доля; *dolia*) (see CC arts 87–94). This contrasts, for example, with a joint stock society (акционерное общество; *aktsionernoe obshchestvo* (AO)) (see CC arts 96–104) where shareholders hold stock (акция; *aktsiia*) which is freely transferable through a stock exchange.

[6] GKI is the standard abbreviation in Russian for this committee whose acronym is Госкомимущество; *Goskomimushchestvo*.

> concluded for the benefit of the state in the form of GKI, which could therefore sue under the contract.[7]

The decision was primarily based on the fact that the contractual parties specifically stated that the third party should have a right of enforcement.

Another situation when it is clear that the third party has a right to demand performance of an obligation is when the Civil Code directly states this for a particular type or subtype of contract. The Civil Code stipulates that certain contracts are *always* concluded for a third party's benefit, whether or not this is stated in the contract. For example, all liability insurance contracts are for the benefit of a third party. When the law stipulates that a particular type of contract is for the benefit of a third party, the contractual parties do not have any power to exclude the third party beneficiary's right to sue. Also, when the law says that a certain type of contract is always concluded for a third party's benefit, it also stipulates particular rules for those contracts, not applicable to other contracts for the benefit of a third party.

A good example of such special provisions relates to liability insurance in CC article 931. CC article 931(3) states:

> The contract of insurance of the risk of responsibility for causing harm shall be considered to be concluded to the benefit of the persons to whom harm may be caused (beneficiary) even if the contract was concluded to the benefit of the insurant or other person responsible for causing harm or it is not said in the contract to whose benefit it was concluded.[8]

The contract for trust management of property (CC article 1012) is another example of a contract for the benefit of a third party by virtue of law.

When neither the law nor the text of the contract expressly stipulate that the third party has a right to sue for performance of a contractual obligation but, at the same time, the contract confers a benefit on the third party, courts face a difficult situation. The wording of CC article 430(1) is such that it remains unclear if the third party, to whom performance is made under a contract between two other parties, has the right automatically to 'demand performance of the obligation"[9] when the contract does not specifically mention them, but the contract clearly confers a benefit on them as a third party.

Unlike the English Contracts (Rights of Third Parties Act) 1999,[10] the Russian Civil Code does not create any presumptions, such as, if a benefit is conferred on a third party, the third party should have a right to enforce the contract unless the contractual parties expressly state that they did not have an intention to provide the third party with such right.[11]

[7] Resolution of Federal Commercial Court of Far-Eastern District of 5 May 2003, case No F03-37/03-1/878.
[8] Butler, above n 4, at 646.
[9] Ibid 312.
[10] In s 1(1)(b).
[11] As in Contracts (Rights of Third Parties) Act 1999, s 1(2).

Unfortunately, with the absence of any clues in the law, the courts have tended to decide whether or not a third party has a right to sue on a case-by-case basis. The following is one example.

> Under a contract for services between company A (the client) and company B (a contractor), B undertook to provide the technical connection between A's network and B's electricity network. A was obliged to pay 40 per cent of the price to B and the remaining 60 per cent to company C, a third party. C was a partner of B and participated in the provision of services to A.
>
> A failed to pay the 60 per cent owed to C, and C sued. The courts held that the contract between A and B was made for the benefit of a third party, C, and that C had an independent right to sue for payment. The contract did not directly stipulate that the third party should have such a right to sue. The courts' position was based on the Civil Code provisions on freedom of contract (CC article 421) as well as the provisions on contracts for the benefit of third parties.[12]

In another, rather similar case, the courts took the opposite position.

> Company A was delivering heating and hot water to company B. The contract stipulated that all payments for the consumed heating and hot water were to be made by B to company C, a third party, in accordance with invoices provided by A. C was the provider of heating and hot water to A.
>
> The court held that the contract between A and B was not a contract for the benefit of a third party. Neither was A acting as an agent for C. In the court's opinion, the parties did not intend to provide a third party with a right to demand performance on its own behalf. Rather, the parties had agreed that payments under the contract were to be made to C for convenience and simplicity.[13]

The following is yet another example.

> Company A and company B signed a contract under which A would sell 49,580 kg of oil to B. A was also responsible for transporting the oil to B. A hired a transport company, T, to transport the oil by rail. When it arrived, the purchaser B found that the amount of oil was less than stipulated in its contract with A. There was sufficient evidence that the correct amount of oil had originally been dispatched. Thus the missing oil had disappeared during transportation.

[12] Resolution of Federal Commercial Court of West-Siberian District of 3 March 2011, case No 03-8060/2010.

[13] Resolution of Federal Commercial Court of West-Siberian District of 20 December 2006, case No F04-8315/2006 (29307- 03-22).

> B brought a claim for breach of contract against T. The court held that under the contract between A and T, T was obliged to compensate A for any losses which occurred during transportation. The court concluded from this that the transportation contract had not been concluded for the benefit of the third party, B, the recipient under the transportation contract. The fact that B accepted contractual delivery did not imply B had a right to sue as a third party.[14]

The examples so far have been from the commercial courts. The following is an example from a court of general jurisdiction, which has a different attitude.

> Company B, a contractor for the renovation of a flat, concluded a contract with company D, a door manufacturer. The contract provided for the manufacture of doors and their delivery to the flat belonging to Ms M. The doors were made and delivered but were of lower quality than specified in the contract between B and D. The court held that M, as the owner of the flat, was a third party beneficiary of that contract and had a right to claim against D for poor performance.[15]

Even more controversial are situations where the parties do not provide anything under the contract to the third party but the third party for various reasons clearly benefits from it. We might call these contracts which have a 'protective effect' for the third party, as in the following example.

> Private entrepreneurs A and B signed a contract under which A rented a market stand in B's market. B in turn was to manage the market, providing cleaning, security, and other necessary services. Accordingly, B signed a contract with company C to provide security services to all those renting premises at B's market.
>
> A was charged for the security services in proportion to the size of her market stand. She paid the security service fee to B in accordance with an invoice for services provided by B; the security service fee was always shown separately from the other fees.
>
> A's market stand was robbed. A sued C for damages caused by their breach of the security contract between C and B, which A considered to be for her benefit as a third party.
>
> The Court of Cassation, however, held that A had no rights under the contract between B and C. The parties had not directly stated in the contract that A should have rights under it; as a result the contract could not be considered to be for the benefit of third party A, even though as a

[14] Resolution of Presidium of the Supreme Commercial Court of 1 December 2009, case No 11320/09.

[15] Cassational Ruling of St Petersburg City Court of 4 October 2011, case No 14951.

> matter of fact she did benefit from the contract and suffered loss as a result of its breach.[16]

An analysis of case law indicates that there is a general tendency for the courts to be cautious and not give a third party any right to sue when the contract does not provide for direct contractual performance to the third party. Even when there is such performance, the courts are also quite restrained and tend not to allow the third party a right to sue unless there is a clear indication in the contract that the parties agreed to it. In court practice the problem is dealt with in the simplest way: when there are any doubts whether the contract is concluded for the benefit of a third party and that party is not clearly defined, the court will conclude that the third party has no rights under the contract.

IV VARIATION AND CANCELLATION OF CONTRACTS FOR THE BENEFIT OF THIRD PARTIES

If a contract is for the benefit of a third party, unless special provisions are made by legislation or under the contract itself, the law disallows variation without the third party's consent. This is clearly specified (CC article 430(2)):

> Unless provided otherwise by a law, other legal acts, or a contract, from the moment of the expression by the third party to the debtor [promisor] of an intention to take advantage of the right under the contract, the parties may not dissolve or change the contract concluded by them without the consent of the third person.[17]

We can see an example of this protection operating in a case brought before the commercial courts:

> Company T and a charity organisation C signed a contract under which T was obliged to transfer 1,000,000 roubles to C and C was obliged to use the money exclusively to buy particular goods for a Community of indigenous people.
>
> T transferred 350,000 roubles to C. C proved that it used part of this sum in accordance with the contract but it could not provide evidence of appropriate use of the rest of the money. T sued C, demanding the discharge of the contract and return of the sum which, in the opinion of T, had not been used in accordance with the contract.
>
> The courts considered the contract between the parties to be for the benefit of the Community of indigenous people which, so the courts held, therefore had its own right to demand performance in accordance with the contract. The third party had clearly expressed an intention to take

[16] Resolution of Federal Commercial Court of Volgo-Viatskii District of 19 September 2007, case No 82-9414/2006-11.

[17] Butler, above n 4, at 312.

> advantage of the contract, so T had no right to dissolve the contract with C without the consent of the third party, the Community of indigenous people. The court also mentioned that the Community of indigenous people had a right to demand payment of the missing sum from C.[18]

However, the courts do not consistently pay attention to the fact that, to prevent variation or termination of a contract, it has to be proved that the third party expressed in some way their intention to take advantage of their right under the contract. This is illustrated in the following case.

> Company B concluded a contract with an insurer to provide medical insurance to its employees. The contract had been in force for some time when the parties signed an addendum decreasing the range of medical services available for the employees. The court declared the addendum void as contradicting CC article 430(2). The court explained that the employees were third party beneficiaries to the contract and so it could not be changed without their consent.[19]

The court did not address the issue of the intention of the third parties to take advantage of their medical insurance. According to the text of the decision, the third parties' consent was required purely because the contract was concluded for their benefit; no overt expression of intention was adduced.

V RIGHTS OF THE PROMISEE

Unlike English law, Russian law does not stipulate that the promisee in a contract for the benefit of a third party retains their usual promisee's rights.[20] However, if performance is due to a third party who has a right to claim under the contract, Russian courts deny the promisee any right to claim performance.

In Russia, there are also procedural obstacles to such a claim. Under the rules of court procedure, a claimant is only allowed to sue when his or her rights or lawful interests are breached or challenged.[21] Demanding contractual performance for the benefit of a third party is not seen as falling under that rule, as the following case illustrates.

[18] Resolution of Federal Commercial Court of Far-Eastern District of 23 March 2004, case No F03- 37/04-1/489.

[19] Resolution of Federal Commercial Court of Ural District of 25 January 2007, case No F09-12299/06- 5.

[20] Contracts (Rights of Third Parties) Act 1999 s 4. Of course, under English law, the promisee would only be able to sue for their own losses, not those of the third party; see E Peel, *Treitel: the Law of Contract*, 13th edn (London, Sweet and Maxwell, 2011) 625.

[21] Code of Arbitration Procedure art 4(1), Code of Civil Procedure art 3(1).

> Company C insured some real property with insurance company I for the benefit of a Bank, B. A claimable event occurred but I did not pay the insurance indemnity. C sued I, demanding they pay the indemnity to B.
>
> At all instances the courts held that C had no right to make such a claim. Their conclusions were based on CC article 430(1), defining contracts for the benefit of third parties as contracts where the third party rather than the promisee has the rights to contractual performance. The courts also referred to articles 3 and 4 of the Commercial Courts' Code of Procedure as disallowing a litigant to sue for the benefit of a third person.[22]

However, in certain circumstances the promisee may receive performance under a contract for the benefit of a third party. When a third party has waived their right granted under the contract, the Civil Code allows the promisee 'to take advantage of this right unless this is contrary to a law, other legal acts, and the contract' (CC article 430(4)).[23] The following example illustrates this.

> An insurance company, I, insured a building belonging to company A. The building was under a mortgage with bank B, which was identified as a beneficiary in the insurance contract. The building was destroyed by fire. B notified I that it was waving its right to receive the insurance indemnity.
>
> I refused to pay the insurance indemnity so A sued for it. B also brought a claim demanding the insurance indemnity for its benefit to be paid. B claimed that the waiver of its right was invalid as contradicting the Commercial Court Code of Procedure which stipulates that a waiver of a right of action is invalid.
>
> The Supreme Commercial Court held that waiver under CC article 430 should be distinguished from the waiver of the right of action. In this case the court decided that B had waived its right under CC article 430 and thus A as the promisee had a right to claim for the insurance indemnity.[24]

In another apparently similar case, the Supreme Commercial Court ruled differently:

> Company C concluded a contract of car insurance. Bank B, which had given C a loan to buy the car, was named as beneficiary in the insurance contract. The car was damaged in a crash, an event covered by the insurance. C evaluated the damage as US$34,000 to be paid in roubles. However, the insurance company did not accept the valuation and only paid C US$18,000. C sued the insurance company to recover the balance.

[22] Resolution of Federal Commercial Court of Moscow District of 21 June 2006, case No KG-A40/5245-06.

[23] Butler, above n 4, at 312–13.

[24] Ruling of Supreme Commercial Court of 2 March 2011, case No VAS-1874/11.

> The Supreme Commercial Court held that, since C was not named as a beneficiary in the insurance contract, it had no right to receive performance under the contract, and therefore did not have a right to sue the insurer. The Court ignored a letter from B stating that it did not mind if the insurance indemnity was paid to C. The Court also considered the fact that the insurance company has already paid part of the insurance indemnity to C irrelevant. In the Court's opinion, the latter two circumstances meant only that C received the money *at the order of the beneficiary*, ie B, and not in its own right.[25]

The main difference between this case and the previous one is that here the court did not regard the letter from the beneficiary B, stating that it 'did not mind' if performance was provided to the promisee, to be a waiver of contractual rights. The position of the Supreme Commercial Court in such a situation is clear: if a third party has not clearly waived its rights under a contract for its benefit, the promisee has no right sue for performance.

At the same time the courts agree that when a third party has waived its rights, the promisee can even assign its rights under a contract for the benefit of the third party, as illustrated by the following case.

> Company A insured cars belonging to it with an insurance company, I. The insurance contract was concluded for the benefit of bank B. Following an insured event, A assigned the right to claim the insurance indemnity to company C.
>
> I refused to pay C, and sued to declare the assignment contract between A and C to be void, as contradicting the law. I claimed that only B, the beneficiary, had the right to claim the insurance indemnity and thus only B could assign that right. The court explained that beneficiary B had expressed in a letter its consent for the assignment by the promisor A of the right under the contract for B's benefit. The court held that in expressing that consent the beneficiary had waived its right, so the A could take advantage of it, and therefore, for example, could assign it.[26]

VI DEFENCES AVAILABLE TO THE PROMISOR

We saw above that a promisee in a contract to the benefit of the third party may be treated differently to a promisee in a normal contract. However, the promisor is not similarly handicapped. CC article 430(3) provides:

[25] Ruling of Supreme Commercial Court of 30 April 2008, case No 5620/08.

[26] Resolution of Thirteenth Commercial Court of Appeal of 21 July 2005, case No 56-3210/2005. Also Resolution of Federal Commercial Court of Moscow District of 16 April 2012, case No A40-65232/11-117-440; Resolution of Federal Commercial Court of Moscow District of 16 February 2012, case No 40-138052/10-151-1175.

> The debtor [promisor] in the contract shall have the right to advance against the demand of the third person objections which he could have advanced against the creditor [promisee].[27]

Such objections can be based, for instance, on the promisee's breach of contract, as in the following case.

> Company C concluded a contract with an insurance company, I, for insurance of goods. Bank B, C's creditor, was named as the third party beneficiary in the insurance contract. The goods were destroyed by fire. B claimed the insurance indemnity for the destroyed goods. I agreed that the fire was an insured event. However, it also referred to CC article 430(3) and claimed that C was in breach of contract because it had not provided I's representatives with any opportunity to examine the remains of the goods, as the contract stipulated. The court agreed with I, declaring that B, as third party beneficiary, did not have a right to claim the insurance indemnity since there was a breach of contract by C, the party to the insurance contract.[28]

In another case the court held that if a promisee does not comply with procedures prescribed under the contract for settlement by mediation and, as a result, the interests of the promisor are affected, the third party beneficiary also loses its rights.[29]

VII LIABILITY IN CONTRACTS FOR THE BENEFIT OF THIRD PARTIES

There are no specific rules in the Civil Code or other laws regulating liability in contracts for the benefit of third parties. The courts just apply the general provisions.

Usually the courts do not accord to the third party any right to receive damages for breach of contract. This position is based on a very literal interpretation of CC article 430(1) which stipulates that the third party has 'the right to demand performance of the obligation to his benefit'[30] under the contract; the case discussed already mentioned above[31] illustrates the restrictive approach.

> The court held that the contract between the parties (E and the OOO) was concluded for the benefit of the third party, GKI, since it was directly stated in the contract that GKI as representative of the Russian state had a

[27] Butler, above n 4, at 312.

[28] Resolution of Federal Commercial Court of North-Western District of 23 January 2012, case No A56-47368/2010.

[29] Resolution of Federal Commercial Court of North-Western District of 13 July 2007, case No A56-55408/2005.

[30] Butler, above n 4, at 312.

[31] See above, text to n 7.

> right to sue for performance of the contractual obligation. The contract also provided a penalty for delay in performance, ie if the OOO paid its rent late. The court held that the third party GKI did not have any right to claim the penalty for late payment because this was not mentioned in the contract. In the court's opinion in that situation only the promisee E had the right to sue for that, not the third party.[32]

The definition in CC article 430(1) of a contract for the benefit of a third party taken literally does not include 'contracts with protective effects' for third parties (discussed above).[33] Thus, third parties to contracts which may have protective effects for them, but where they are not specified to gain a benefit as third parties, are given no rights to sue. One of the main reasons why contracts having a protective effect for third parties are neglected is that third parties in such contracts cannot claim for performance but suffer damages if the contract is not performed properly. The following example illustrates the point.

> Company A sold goods to company B. The parties agreed that the seller A would be responsible for their transportation. A arranged transportation and, among other things, concluded a contract with company C to provide security services while the goods were in transit. The goods were stolen during transportation. B, the buyer, sued C for damages caused by C's faulty performance of its contractual obligations under its contract with A. B considered itself a beneficiary under the contract between A and C.
>
> The courts held otherwise; that B had no right to sue for damages because it was not a party to the contract and neither had the contract been concluded for B's benefit as a third party. The courts explained that even though the contract conferred certain benefits on B it did not name B as a third party beneficiary nor did it stipulate that B had a right to demand contractual performance.

If the case had been considered under English law the result could have been very different. In accordance with section 1(2)(b) of Contracts (Rights of Third Parties) Act 1999 a person who is not a party to a contract 'may in his own right enforce a term of the contract'[34] if the term purports to confer a benefit on him unless the parties to the contract prove that they did not have an intention to give such right to the third party. In the case just discussed it is clear that the parties to the security services contract (A and C) intended to confer benefit on the third party B – the recipient of goods. Thus, under English law the third party would have been given a right to enforce the contract.

[32] Resolution of Federal Commercial Court of Far-Eastern District of 5 May 2003, case No F03-A37/03-1/878.

[33] See above, text following n 15, case example above, text to n 16.

[34] Available at www.legislation.gov.uk/ukpga/1999/31/section/1.

When a third party to a contract sues for payment of the interest made by unlawful use of a sum of money, the courts apply the same logic as they use for damages and penalties for breach of contract. The courts do not allow such claims, but often without any explanation. For instance, in one case where property was insured for the benefit of a bank, the bank received the insurance indemnity but not the interest; the court gave no explanation of this omission.[35]

It does not follow, however, that the promisee in a contract for the benefit of a third party is automatically entitled to receive damages for a breach of the contract. The situation is clear in circumstances where CC article 430(4) is applied and the courts acknowledge the promisee's right to sue because the third party has waived its right under the contract. In such cases the promisee can recover any recompense which is provided under the contract or by law.[36] However, as discussed above, the promisee has no right to claim for the performance of the obligation to the third party. Thus, the promisee is not able to receive any penalties, interest or other 'extras' payable as a result of breach through failure to perform.

VIII CONCLUSION

Compared to English law, Russian contract law was early to recognise that a contract concluded between two persons can create an independent right for a third party who had not participated in the conclusion of the contract and did not themselves have to provide any performance under the contract. However, the manner in which the concept has been implemented in Russian law is far from perfect.

First of all, Russian law does not give judges sufficient tools to define whether or not a third party has a right under a contract to which they are not a party. Secondly, due to lack of clarity in the law, too often courts fail to recognise the right of a promisee to enforce a contract for the benefit of a third party, and by doing so make it impossible for the promisee, a party to the contract, to receive the benefit they contracted to receive. And, finally, contracts having protective effect for third parties are not covered by the definition of this type of contract given in the Civil Code and this omission often leads to results which are unfair both to the contractual parties and to the third party who is potentially benefiting from such a contract.

[35] Resolution of Federal Commercial Court of Moscow District of 26 August 2010, case No KG-A40/9273-10.

[36] See, eg Resolution of Federal Commercial Court of Povolzhskii District of 30 September 2008, case No A72-8086/06.

8

Assignment

I INTRODUCTION

The contractual right to demand performance from another party can be considered a valuable object of commerce and therefore it is desirable to have procedures to make it possible to transfer that value. One of the goals of contract law is to facilitate such transfer. On the other hand, some contractual rights have a personal character and should not be transferrable; another task of contract law is to define these rights clearly, without detriment to the procedures to transfer the value of the commercial rights just mentioned.

Russian contract law, like modern English contract law, allows contractual rights to be transferred (assigned). The Civil Code specifically deals with 'Transfer of Rights of Creditor to Another Person'[1] and allows that:

> The right (or demand) belonging to a creditor on the basis of an obligation may be transferred by him to another person with regard to the transaction (assignment of demand) or pass to another person on the basis of law.[2]

However, assignment in Russian law has a wider application than in English law. In English law the effect of assignment is merely to transfer the assignor's contractual rights to the assignee, who is then entitled to sue the contractual promisor. English law, for instance, does not consider change of a party to court proceedings as assignment. In Russian law there is no limit to when assignment can occur. A right may be assigned before the performance is due, after its delay, after the original creditor started suing the debtor and even after the original creditor succeeded in getting a court order of execution against the debtor.[3] When the right is assigned at the trial stage the court is obliged to change the claimant from the assignor to the assignee, if, at execution stage, the name of

[1] CC chapter 24.

[2] CC art 382(1); WE Butler, *The Civil Code of the Russian Federation Parts 1, 2 and 3: Parallel Russian and English Texts* (Moscow, JurInfoR-Press, 2008) 286.

[3] In Russian legal terminology, the word 'creditor' is used generally to describe the party to whom a contractual duty is owed, and 'debtor' the party who is obliged to perform. In most chapters in this book we have substituted the more general terms 'promisee' and 'promisor', as most English-language readers associate 'creditor' and 'debtor' only with financial obligations. As assignment is almost invariably of the right to claim a sum of money, we have generally retained the terms 'creditor' and 'debtor' in this chapter, although technically assignment could also be of a non-monetary performance.

the recipient in the court order is changed. This very expansive approach to assignment allows participants in the commercial market to use more efficiently rights belonging to them on the basis of an obligation. It could be argued that, when assignment is relatively simple, rights based on obligations can be transferred to those individuals or legal entities which can enforce them in the most cost-effective manner, ie spending less resources to do so than the original rightholders, an efficient assignment process therefore creating economic efficiency.

II EFFECT OF ASSIGNMENT

On assignment, the initial creditor's contractual right passes to the new creditor at the same value and under the same conditions as existed at the time of transfer. In particular, the new creditor gains any rights to secure the obligation's performance, and also other associated rights, including the right to unpaid interest.[4]

Contractual rights which can be transferred include not only the right to performance and any ancillary rights to secure it, but also the rights to penalties or contractual damages for breach (the availability of penalties is discussed in Chapter 10 at p 243). Court practice has even shown that, if under the original contract the right was secured by a pledge, that will also pass to the new creditor, together with the main right, as in the following example.

> Company A assigned to company B the right to receive performance under a contract A had with company C. The right was secured with a pledge of assets belonging to C, the debtor. B brought a claim against C to receive the due sum through sale of the pledged assets. C objected, saying that the pledge securing the original obligation could not pass to the new creditor and should have been arranged separately.
>
> The courts, however, ruled that the pledge set up to secure the obligation's performance was part of the original contract's terms, so would pass to B together with the main assigned right.[5]

The courts also interpret the law to allow assignment of rights to secure performance separately from the main contractual right, as in the following example.

> Company A assigned to company B the right to damages for breach of A's contract with company C. As the new creditor, B sued C for damages. The Supreme Commercial Court confirmed that such assignment was valid

[4] CC art 384; Butler, above n 2, at 287.

[5] Informational Circular of Presidium of the Supreme Commercial Court of 30 October 2007 No 120 'An Overview of the Practice of the Application of Chapter 24 of the Civil Code by Commercial Courts' para 19.

> since the right to contractual damages is a monetary right and thus can be transferred to another person.[6]

It should be remembered, however, that as in English law, the assignee's position in relation to the debtor cannot be any better than that of the assignor.

III ASSIGNMENT AS A CONTRACT

A Making a Valid Assignment

The definition in CC article 382(1)[7] allows the transfer of rights (1) as a result of a transaction between the assignor and assignee (assignment); or (2) by operation of law. The first of these understands assignment to be a contract between the assignor and the assignee, so the general rules on contracts will apply. One important feature of any contract, as discussed in Chapter 4 (at p 60), is its subject matter (material terms). If the subject matter is not properly described in the contract there is a risk that it may be deemed not concluded and thus have no legal effect, as in the following example.

> Company A, electricity supplier, assigned to company B a right to payment from company C for electricity. B sued A, claiming that the contract of assignment was void. The courts found that the contract did not define the obligation which gave rise to the assigned right. It was clear that A did not transfer the right to receive for all time all payments for electricity supplied under the contract. Rather, the subject matter of the assignment was the right to receive payment for the electricity supplied to a particular customer during a certain period. However, the parties had failed to define the period so the courts upheld B's claim that the contract was not concluded because its subject matter was not sufficiently defined.[8]

The normal practice to avoid the risk that the assignment contract will be deemed not concluded is for it to refer explicitly to the original contract on which the right being assigned is based. It is not uncommon to read in court decisions that the assignment contract is not concluded because it does not contain that explicit reference.[9]

However, this is not always necessary as sometimes the courts may decide that the subject matter of the contract can be clearly defined from the circumstances, as in the following example.

[6] Ibid para 17.

[7] See above, text to n 2.

[8] Informational Circular of Presidium of the Supreme Commercial Court of 30 October 2007, above n 5, para 13.

[9] Resolution of Federal Commercial Court of West-Siberian District of 21 December 2006, case No F04-8333/2006 (29304- A46-10).

> Bank B assigned to collector C the rights under loan agreements with a number of its clients. The assignment contract contained a list of debtors and the sum due from each, but no reference to their loan agreements. When C brought a claim against A, one of the listed debtors, A refused to pay; A claimed the assignment contract was not concluded because it was not stated from which specific loan agreement the right had been assigned. However, the courts found that there was only one loan agreement between A and B and held that the right assigned could only have been from that. Thus, the subject matter of the assignment was clear and the assignment contract was concluded.[10]

Apart from the general rules on contractual relations, the courts may also apply to assignment transactions the rules for particular types of contracts, such as purchase-sale, gift, pledge or others, depending on the circumstances. The following is an example.

> Company A brought a claim against entrepreneur E. The claim was based on a right assigned to A by company B. E claimed that the assignment was invalid because it constituted a gift between two legal entities and thus contradicted the law.
>
> The courts found that even though the contract of assignment did not mention any remuneration, the transfer was made as release-money (отступное; *otstupnoe*),[11] since B owed A a debt. Thus, the intentions of the parties were to provide partial pay-off of B's debt. The contract was a contract of indemnity and so the rules on indemnity should be applied, not those relating to gifts.[12]

As with any contract, assignment can be disputed by the parties or some other persons. The rules on invalidity of contracts, as discussed in Chapter 6, are applicable.

The validity of an assignment does not depend on whether the transferred right is incontestable. It also does not depend on the assignor's performance of their obligations to the contractual promisor. The following case, discussed by the Supreme Commercial Court, is an example.

> Company A was assigned by company B the right to receive payment from D under a construction contract. At the time of assignment the

[10] Informational Circular of Presidium of the Supreme Commercial Court of 30 October 2007, above n 5, para 12.

[11] As in CC art 409: by agreement of the parties an obligation may be terminated by granting release-money in place of performance (payment of money, transfer of property, etc). The amount, periods, the procedure for granting release-money will be established by the parties.

[12] Informational Circular of Presidium of the Supreme Commercial Court of 30 October 2007, above n 5, para 9.

construction work had not yet been carried out. Payment was due only if and when construction was duly completed.

A sued D claiming payment. D objected that the works had not been properly carried out and thus payment was not due. The higher courts, including the Supreme Commercial Court, held that the payment was not due until the defects were eliminated. Nonetheless, in the courts' opinion, the assignment was valid and, as soon as all the conditions were met, A could receive the payment.[13]

Assignment does not alter who is a party to the contract. It is important to mention here that Russian law distinguishes between assignment, which is a change of a party to an obligation, and change of a party to the contract. When a right is assigned the original creditor remains a party, liable for his or her own contractual obligations. When a party to the contract changes, the new party obtains the rights and accepts the obligations of its predecessor. Technically, to change a party to the contract not only rights should be assigned by the previous creditor to the new creditor but also obligations should also be transferred to the new party. Furthermore, consent of the other contractual party is required for the transfer of an obligation to be valid. The following case, similar to that discussed above, of assignment by A to B of the right to receive payment from C for electricity,[14] illustrates the difference between the two situations.

Following the assignment by company A to company B of the right to claim payment from company C, B sued C for payment. However, C claimed the assignment was invalid because A was still a contractual party responsible for supplying electricity to C. C asserted that B should have also acquired A's obligation to supply in order to receive the right. The court of first instance accepted this but was overturned by the Court of Cassation, later supported by the Supreme Commercial Court.

The higher courts explained that there is no need for the assignee to accept the assignor's obligations under the ongoing contract. The right to receive payment for electricity already supplied exists independently of any contractual obligations and thus can be assigned to a third party, in this case, B.[15]

As we can see from the example, A remained a party to the contract even though A had assigned the right to obtain payments under the contract to B, which did not become a party to the contract. For B to become a contractual party, A would also have had to transfer to B its obligation to supply electricity; B would

[13] Ibid para 8.

[14] See above, text to n 8.

[15] Informational Circular of Presidium of the Supreme Commercial Court of 30 October 2007, above n 5, para 6.

have had to accept it and C, the other contractual party, would have had to agree to the change.

Unlike English law, Russian law allows assignment of rights which have not yet arisen, as in the following example.

> Company A and company B contracted that A would assign to B the right to receive the payments for goods which A would sell in the future. The parties agreed that the right to receive payments would pass from A to B as soon as they fell due to A.
>
> A brought a claim that the assignment was invalid. This was supported at first instance but overturned on appeal and that decision confirmed by the Supreme Commercial Court. The latter explained that in substance the contract between A and B was a purchase-sale contract. The rules on purchase-sale contracts allow for the sale of goods which the seller acquires in the future. Thus, the right to a sale which will take place in the future complies with the law and can be validly assigned.[16]

B Notification of the Debtor

Russian law does not require the debtor to be notified of an assignment in order for it to be valid. However, the new creditor bears the risk of any adverse consequences caused to the debtor by non-notification. Also, any performance of the obligation to the original creditor is still deemed to be performance.[17] This is illustrated in the following example.

> In March 2003 company A concluded a purchase-sale agreement with company B and made a pre-payment for the goods B would supply. On 1 October 2009 A assigned to C its right under the contract with B. The assignment contract stipulated that C must notify B of the assignment within 30 days. C sent notification to B on 21 November 2009.
>
> C sued B claiming that, having received full pre-payment, B failed to deliver all the goods under its contract with A and so was obliged to return part of A's pre-payment to C as the assignee. The court found that in October 2009, after A's rights had been assigned to C, B had delivered a certain number of goods to A, which A had accepted without any objection.
>
> The court held that, since B had not yet been notified of the assignment, B's performance to A was considered to be performance to the proper creditor. C had to bear the negative consequences of its own failure to notify B in time of the assignment.[18]

16 Ibid para 4.

17 CC art 382(3).

18 Ruling of Supreme Commercial Court of 28 April 2011 No VAS-4918/11.

An assignee's claim based on the assignment will be valid even if the debtor has not been notified of the assignment. The assignee only bears negative consequences of the assignment if the debtor performs their obligation to the original creditor, the assignor.[19]

The Civil Code does not directly regulate relations between the assignor and the assignee in situations where a debtor, who has not been notified of the assignment, performs their obligation to the assignor. This question was resolved by the Supreme Commercial Court. The Court explained that in such a case the assignee has a right to demand that the assignor transfer to him (as assignee) everything received from the debtor. According to the Court, the debtor's performance constitutes unfounded enrichment for the assignor and thus can be claimed as such by the assignee.[20]

CC article 385(1) states that, 'The debtor shall have the right not to perform the obligation to a new creditor until the submission to him of evidence of the transfer of the demand to this person'.[21] As substantial evidence of the assignment, the Supreme Commercial Court refers to notification from the assignor or a document (акт; *act*) signed by both assignor and assignee, formalising the transfer.[22]

Notification from the assignee (rather than the assignor) could also constitute evidence of the assignment but may cause some problems. For example, if the debtor is only notified by the assignee and there is no signed document formalising the transfer and the assignor then challenges it, the notification is not considered to be sufficiently substantial evidence, so the debtor will bear any risks connected with performance to the wrong party, in this case, the assignee.[23] In other words, the Supreme Commercial Court has made it clear that is it a duty of the debtor to make sure that he or she is performing the obligation to the correct creditor. They bear the negative consequences if they fail to do so.

C Consent of the Debtor

As noted above (at p 176), as a general rule assignment is between the assignor and assignee and, as with statutory assignment in English law, does not require the debtor's consent. However, the law establishes an exception to this general rule. CC article 388(2) provides that, 'The assignment of the demand regarding an obligation in which the person of the creditor has material significance for

[19] Resolution of Supreme Commercial Court of 29 June 2010 No 15842/09.

[20] Informational Circular of Supreme Commercial Court 'An Overview of the Practice of Resolution of Disputes connected with the Application of the Norms on Unfounded Enrichment' of 11 January 2000 No 49 para 10.

[21] Butler, above n 2, at 287.

[22] Informational Circular of Presidium of the Supreme Commercial Court of 30 October 2007, above n 5, para 14.

[23] Resolution of Presidium of the Supreme Commercial Court of 6 March 2012 No 14548/11.

the debtor without the consent of the debtor shall not be permitted'.[24] Without such consent the assignment is void as contradicting the law in accordance with CC article 167 (see more details in Chapter 6 at p 132ff).

If the debtor seeks to claim that the assignment is void on this basis, they are obliged to prove that the person of the creditor has material significance for them.[25]

Unfortunately, the law does not give any indication how to identify obligations in which 'the person of the creditor has material significance for the debtor'. Court practice gives some guidance although does not lay down any easily recognisable characteristics of such obligations. The following is an example.

> State enterprise E and company A concluded a joint-operation contract to produce furniture. A bought equipment to be used in this joint production. Under the contract, expenses for any equipment were to be shared equally between the parties. A did not receive any contribution from E and assigned the right to claim it to company C. C sued E.
>
> The Supreme Commercial Court, however, supported the position of lower courts that 'the person of the creditor had material significance' so the debtor (State enterprise E) should have given consent to any assignment. Without that consent the assignment was deemed invalid. The court explained that under a joint-operation contract all revenues and produced goods are jointly owned by the parties. Also, any party to a joint-operation contract has a right to contract on behalf of all parties. For these reasons the personality of the creditor in a joint-operation contract has material significance, so no rights under such a contract could be assigned without the consent of the other party or parties.[26]

Another common situation when the courts will not allow assignment without the debtor's consent is with motor liability insurance contracts. Under Russian law such contracts are *always* considered to be for the benefit of the victim who has rights based on the contract. According to court practice, the beneficiary has no right to assign the right to receive the insurance indemnity because the person of the creditor has material significance for the insurer.[27]

[24] Butler, above n 2, at 289.

[25] See, eg Ruling of Supreme Commercial Court of 23 August 2010 No VAS-259/10.

[26] Paragraph 4 of Informational Circular of Presidium of the Supreme Commercial Court of 25 July 2000 No 56 'Overview of the Practice of Dispute Resolution connected with the Contracts for the Participation in Shared Construction', also Ruling of Supreme Commercial Court of 24 February 2009 No 1478/09, Resolution of Federal Commercial Court of Western Siberian District of 17 December 2008 No 19-14273/07-7-F02-6345/08.

[27] Resolution of Federal Commercial Court of Western Siberian District of 10 April 2007, case No F04-1803/2007(32874- 03-12); Appeal Ruling of St Petersburg City Court of 4 April 2012 No 33-4256; the opposite opinion also appears occasionally: Resolution of Federal Commercial Court of Moscow District of 11 August 2011 No KG- 40/8863-11, case No 40-105897/10-112-553.

Court practice in many cases gives a negative indication, that is, explains when the person of the creditor *does not* have material significance. This is so, for instance, when:

(1) there are long-term ongoing relations between the debtor and the creditor based on mutual trust;[28]
(2) the creditor is a supplier of electricity and continues to supply the debtor;[29]
(3) the creditor remains responsible to the debtor under the same contract, for example, by providing guarantee services;[30]
(4) the creditor is a bank assigning a right under a consumer contract to a collector;[31]
(5) the creditor is an organisation appointed by an authorised governmental agency and which provides state services following a request by that agency and the debtor is the state budget.[32]

Although it is helpful to have some guidance as to when the debtor's consent is not required, this does not give sufficient clarity on the criteria for a positive requirement.

D Rights which are Not Assignable

Continuing the theme of the impact of the 'person of the creditor', CC article 383 forbids assignment of certain rights to another person because they are 'inextricably connected with the person of the creditor, in particular, demands concerning alimony and compensation of harm caused to life or health'.[33]

Unfortunately, there are no objective criteria to define whether or not rights in this category are 'inextricably connected with the person of the creditor'. Also, there is no clear way to distinguish between cases where assignment is not valid unless the debtor gives consent (see above) and cases where the rights are not assignable. The application of one or the other rule seems to be on a case-by-case basis with no obvious guiding principles. For example, in the following cases the courts found no inextricable connection with the person of the creditor and did not apply CC article 383; as a result the assignment contract stood, despite the debtor not having agreed to it:

[28] Ruling of Presidium of the Supreme Commercial Court of 7 December 2009 No VAS-15421/09.

[29] Ruling of Presidium of the Supreme Commercial Court of 15 September 2011 No VAS-11428/11.

[30] Ruling of Presidium of the Supreme Commercial Court of 28 February 2011 No VAS-1632/11.

[31] Informational Circular of Supreme Commercial Court 'Overview of the Court Practice on Certain Issues connected with the Application to Banks of Administrative Liability for a Breach of Consumer Protection Legislation when Concluding Credit Contracts' of 13 September 2011 No 146 para 16.

[32] Ruling of Presidium of the Supreme Commercial Court of 17 April 2009 No VAS-7052/06.

[33] Butler, above n 2, at 287.

(1) assignment by a bank of rights from a consumer credit contract to a company which did not have a banking licence;[34]
(2) assignment of a right received through subrogation by an insurance company to a company which did not have an insurance licence;[35]
(3) assignment by the insured after the occurrence of an insured event of the right to receive the insurance indemnity;[36]
(4) assignment after the occurrence of an insured event of the right to receive the insurance indemnity by the beneficiary, in whose favour the contract was concluded;[37]
(5) assignment by the depositor of goods to a third party of the right to receive goods stored in a warehouse;[38] and
(6) assignment of a right to receive compensation from the state budget of expenses, connected with the provision of public services.[39]

By contrast, in the following cases, the courts found that assignment was not possible due to an inextricable connection of the rights with the person of the creditor:

(a) assignment, by the winner of a tender for the conclusion of the contract, of the right to conclude a contract of lease of a plot of land for residential construction;[40]
(b) assignment of the right to use a lake by the person who won the right under a contract concluded as a result of a tender;[41]
(c) assignment by a beneficiary of a motor liability insurance contract of the right to receive the insurance indemnity, when the beneficiary had taken action to receive the indemnity.[42]

As can be seen from the lists, one type of case falls into both categories: rights of beneficiaries under liability insurance contracts. The same type of case was mentioned as one where the assignment is only possible with the debtor's consent. The only rational explanation for the discrepancy is that court practice in this type of case is not yet fully developed and thus inconsistencies occur. Furthermore, for Russian courts, contracts for the benefit of third parties represent a difficult category of cases to deal with and for that reason it is,

[34] Informational Circular of Presidium of the Supreme Commercial Court of 30 October 2007, above n 5, para 2.

[35] Ibid para 3.

[36] Ruling of Presidium of Supreme Commercial Court of 28 December 2007 No 16719/07.

[37] Resolution of Federal Commercial Court of Moscow District of 3 February 2012, case No A40-68422/11-30-574.

[38] Ruling of Presidium of the Supreme Commercial Court of 20 September 2007 No 10998/07.

[39] Resolution of Federal Commercial Court of Far-Eastern District of 27 August 2007, case No F03-A51/07-1/3728.

[40] Ruling of Presidium of the Supreme Commercial Court of 18 April 2008 No 3351/08.

[41] Resolution of Federal Commercial Court of Eastern-Siberian District of 25 April 2012 No A33-6755/2011.

[42] Resolution of Federal Commercial Court of Western-Siberian District of 2 September 2008 No F04-4878/2008 (9549-A46-8).

perhaps, not very surprising that the way the courts approach these cases varies so widely.

As with any other contract, assignment should comply with legislation, otherwise it could be deemed invalid. There is also a requirement that the assignment must comply with the original contract. This requirement could be interpreted to allow the parties to prohibit in the original contract any assignment of rights.

E Form of Assignment

The Civil Code requires that the form of an assignment contract is the same as the contract which gave rise to the assigned right. This is the effect of CC article 389(1). So if the original contract was concluded in simple written form, the assignment must also be in simple written form. CC article 389(1) specifies that the assignment of a right in a transaction requiring state registration must also be registered in the same procedure 'unless established otherwise by a law'.[43]

The situation becomes more complicated when the original contract is secured. For example, if performance of a contractual obligation is secured by a mortgage and a right in the main contract is assigned, the assignee will also acquire the mortgage rights. Russian legislation requires state registration of mortgages; a mortgage comes into effect from the moment of its state registration. So an assignee of an obligation secured by a mortgage has a right to apply for state registration of the mortgage in his name.[44] However, in this particular case, assignment of the main right itself is not subject to state registration; it should be executed in the same form as the original contract. For example, if there is a loan agreement concluded in simple written form but secured with a properly registered mortgage, the assignment of rights from the loan agreement should be in simple written form and the mortgage registered to the assignee in order to have effect.[45] Although these arrangements seem complex, they follow the procedures associated with the initial establishment of the relevant right and so are relatively clear.

F Documents Certifying the Assigned Rights

CC article 385(2) states that 'The creditor who has assigned a demand to another person is obliged to transfer to him the documents certifying the right of demand and to communicate information having significance for the effectuation of the

[43] Butler, above n 2, at 289.

[44] Informational Circular of Presidium of the Supreme Commercial Court of 28 January 2005 No 90 'Overview of Practice of Dispute Resolution connected with Contract of Mortgage' para 14.

[45] Informational Circular of Presidium of the Supreme Commercial Court of 28 January 2005 No 90 'Overview of Practice of Dispute Resolution connected with Contract of Mortgage' para 13.

demand'.[46] Transfer of any documents confirming the right should take place in conjunction with a valid assignment.[47] However, if the assignor fails to transfer the documents it does not automatically invalidate the assignment.

The consequences of a breach of the duty to transfer documents and communicate information connected with the transferred right are the following. Such a breach could be considered to be a material breach of the assignment contract and therefore the basis for termination of the contract by a court decision. If this happens the assignee also has a right to claim back as unfounded enrichment anything transferred under the assignment contract. This is possible, of course, only if unfounded enrichment actually occurred.[48] (For further explanation about termination for material breach, see Chapter 11 at p 269.)

If the failure to transfer the documents is not regarded as a material breach, the assignment will stand.

G Objections to the Demand of the New Creditor

CC article 386 declares that:

> The debtor shall have the right to advance against the demand of a new creditor objections which he had against the initial creditor at the moment of receipt of notification concerning the transfer of the rights regarding the obligation to the new creditor.[49]

As the Supreme Commercial Court has explained, the Civil Code envisages the possibility of a dispute over the right that was assigned; that possibility does not automatically vitiate the assignment, although may affect the new creditor's claim as in the following example.

> Company A hired company B to carry out construction work. After the work was completed the parties signed a formal document confirming completion and that A was satisfied with the quality of the construction. After that B assigned to C the right to payment under the contract and notified A of the assignment.
>
> A then found hidden defects in the construction for which B was responsible. When C, the new creditor, sued A for payment, A defended the claim on the basis that payment was not due until the defects were fixed. The Supreme Commercial Court supported the position of the court of first instance and ruled in A's favour. The Court explained that the defects existed before the assignment. Therefore A's right to object to making

[46] Butler, above n 2, at 288.

[47] Informational Circular of Presidium of the Supreme Commercial Court of 28 January 2005 No 90 'Overview of Practice of Dispute Resolution connected with Contract of Mortgage' para 11.

[48] Resolution of Presidium of the Supreme Commercial Court of 5 April 2011 No 16002/10; Informational Circular of Presidium of the Supreme Commercial Court of 11 January 2000 No 49 'Overview of Practice of Dispute Resolution connected with the Application of the Rules on Unfounded Enrichment' para 1.

[49] Butler, above n 2, at 288.

> immediate payment arose before the assignment and before A was notified about it. As a result the Court held that A had the right to advance against the new creditor C any objections which he had against the original creditor B, so C's claim for immediate payment was dismissed.[50]

However, it was noted that the assignee C had a right to sue the debtor A again once the defects were removed.[51] The next example illustrates the reverse situation, where the debtor was held to have no right to advance objections on the basis of CC article 386.

> Company A and company B signed a contract for the sale of alcohol. A delivered the alcohol but B only made partial payment. The right to the remaining payment was assigned to company C; B was duly notified.
>
> B failed to pay voluntarily so C sued. B's defence was that the quality of the alcohol delivered was not compliant with the contract and so B had no obligation to pay for it. The court found that the assignment had taken place in July. B was notified shortly after. However, documents complaining about the alcohol's substandard quality were only sent by B to the new creditor C in September. The court held that at the time of the assignment, B would have had no objections to a claim by the original creditor A and, as a result, could not advance any objections to the claim of C, the new creditor.[52]

The contrast with the first case is that here B had every opportunity to check the quality of the delivery as soon as it was made, and should have done so, which would have given grounds to a defence against the original creditor A and hence against his assignee C; in the construction case the defects were latent and did not come to light until after the assignment, so gave a valid defence against a claim for immediate full payment.

H Liability of the Original Creditor

Under CC article 390, 'The original creditor who has assigned a demand shall be liable to the new creditor for the invalidity of the demand transferred to him but shall not be liable for the failure to perform this demand by the debtor'.[53] In other words, if the right which has been assigned is invalid the assignor will have failed to perform the contract of assignment and so is liable for breach, as in the following case.

[50] Informational Circular of Presidium of the Supreme Commercial Court of 30 October 2007, above n 5, para 7.

[51] Ibid para 8.

[52] Ruling of Presidium of the Supreme Commercial Court of 4 December 2009 No VAS-14514/09.

[53] Butler, above n 2, at 289.

> Individual entrepreneur E brought a claim against company A for payment for sale of some real property. The right to the payment had been assigned to E by company B, the original seller. A raised a defence based on the invalidity of the original contract and the assignment. A claimed that the original contract was void as contradicting the law so no rights had arisen under it and the assignment of non-existent rights was impossible.
>
> The Court of Cassation, supported by the Supreme Commercial Court, agreed that the original contract was void. However, it further explained that even though rights under the original contract were void, the assignment contract was valid, so that the assignor who had failed to perform it was liable for breach.[54]

Inter alia, an assignee can claim damages caused by breach of the assignment contract.[55] Liability for breach is discussed more generally in Chapter 10 at p 222.

The wording of CC article 390 quoted above is unfortunate. It has been interpreted widely and as a result the 'invalidity' in it has been held to include not only standard invalidity as discussed in Chapter 6, but also any other situation where the assigned right does not exist, for example, because due payment has already been made to the original creditor.[56]

In some situations the existence of a party's contractual right depends on their own counter-performance of certain obligations, as for example when payment for construction work is due only after the work is completed and conforms to all the applicable quality requirements. As discussed above (at p 179), the right to payment from such a contract can be assigned before the payment is due. However, if the assignor fails to take all the actions necessary to give rise to the right which is being assigned, they are liable for breach of the assignment contract.[57] For example, if a construction company assigns its right to demand payment from the client for a finished building and then fails to build it, they will be liable for the breach of the assignment contract.

There is one situation in which, according to CC article 390, the original creditor will not be liable for the debtor's failure to perform. This is only possible 'when the initial creditor has assumed a suretyship for the debtor to the new creditor'.[58] Then the initial creditor will carry liability if the debtor fails to perform. Such suretyship does not have to be assumed simultaneously with the

[54] Informational Circular of Presidium of the Supreme Commercial Court of 30 October 2007, above n 5, para 1.

[55] Resolution of Federal Commercial Court of 19 January 2010 No 13834/09.

[56] Ruling of Presidium of Supreme Commercial Court of 20 July 2011 No VAS-9277/11.

[57] Informational Circular of Presidium of the Supreme Commercial Court of 30 October 2007, above n 5, paras 7 and 8; the details are discussed in the paragraph on the Objections against the Demand of the New Creditor.

[58] Butler, above n 2, at 290.

assignment. A contract establishing suretyship can be concluded by the assignor and the assignee later, if they wish.[59]

IV ASSIGNMENT BY OPERATION OF LAW

CC article 382(1) includes the possibility that 'The right (or demand) belonging to a creditor on the basis of an obligation may pass to another person . . . on the basis of law'.[60] Further details are given in CC article 387:

> The rights of a creditor relating to an obligation shall pass to another person on the basis of a law and ensuing the circumstances specified therein:
>
> - as a result of universal legal succession to the rights of the creditor;
> - by decision of a court concerning the transfer of the rights of the creditor to another person when the possibility of such transfer has been provided for by a law;
> - as a consequence of the performance of the obligation of the debtor by his surety, or by a pledgor who is not the debtor with regard to this obligation;
> - in the event of the subrogation to an insurer of the rights of the creditor against the debtor who is responsible for the ensuing of the insured event;
> - in the other instances provided for by a law.[61]

Note that the general rules on assignment apply fully to assignment by operation of law. For example, it is important to be aware that subrogation, as with any other transfer of a right, is not possible when the claim is closely connected with the person of the creditor.[62]

We will now examine in more detail the specific instances of assignment by operation of law, listed in CC article 387.

A Universal Legal Succession

Universal legal succession may arise from the following.

(i) Reorganisation of a Legal Entity

This could be by merger, accession, division or separation.[63] Universal legal succession means that the rights and obligations of the legal entity remain valid after reorganisation and either pass to the newly formed legal entity or remain with the original entity if it was preserved during the process of reorganisation.

[59] Resolution of Federal Commercial Court of Moscow District of 6 July 2010 No KG-A40/5521-10, case No A40-135981/09-40-1036.

[60] Butler, above n 2, at 286.

[61] Ibid 288.

[62] Resolution of Federal Commercial Court of Far-Eastern District of 21 January 2008 No F03-A59/07-1/5809.

[63] See CC art 58.

In the event of merger of legal entities, the rights and duties of each pass to the newly created legal entity 'in accordance with the act of transfer'.[64] In the event of the accession of one legal entity to another, the rights and duties of the acceding legal entity also pass to the other 'in accordance with the act of transfer'.[65] If there is division or separation, the rights and duties pass to the new legal entities in accordance with the division or separation balance sheet, as appropriate.[66]

(ii) Death of a Person

When a person dies all his or her assets, including obligations, pass to their heirs apart from those rights and obligations:

> which are inextricably connected with the person of the deceased, in particular, the right to alimony, the right to compensation of harm caused to the life or health of a citizen, and also rights and duties whose transfer by way of inheriting is not permitted by the present Code or by other laws.[67]

The general rule is thus the same as for assignment based on a transaction, as described above.

The Supreme Court has set out the following rights and obligations which on its view do not pass on death: rights and duties which arose from contracts for uncompensated use of property, commission, commission agency and agency.[68] The following case illustrates the Supreme Court's position.

> X bought a cruise and other relevant tourist services from company C. When X arrived at the departure port she was refused embarkation and did not use the package of services sold to her by C. X sued C for breach of contract and claimed compensatory damages.
>
> X died before the case was decided by the court and her heirs joined the proceedings as X's legal successors. The court refused the claim, explaining that a contract for the provision of services has a close connection with the person to whom they are provided. For that reason any rights under such a contract, including the right to contractual damages, cannot pass to another person.[69]

The Supreme Commercial Court treats monetary rights from a contract for the provision of services as assignable. The position of the Supreme Court therefore

[64] CC art 58(1); Butler, above n 2, at 52.
[65] CC art 58(2); ibid 53.
[66] CC art 58(3) and (4).
[67] CC art 1112; Butler, above n 2, at 775–6.
[68] Resolution of Supreme Court of 29 May 2012 No 9 'On Court Practice on Inheritance' para 15. The court also mentioned the right to receive alimony payments, but that is already specified in CC art 1112.
[69] Ruling of Moscow City Court of 4 July 2011, case No 33-20223.

contradicts the position of the Supreme Commercial Court on what rights can and cannot be assigned. Of course, the Supreme Court will be dealing with claims from individuals, whereas the Supreme Commercial Court will be dealing with claims from legal entities (or individuals acting as individual entrepreneurs) in a commercial context; nevertheless it is unfortunate that the two leading courts have diverged in their interpretation of the law in this area.

B Transfer of Rights by a Court Decision

A court decision transferring the rights of a creditor to another person is a separate ground for assignment which can only be used in cases specified by law. However, even though CC article 387[70] lists a court decision as one of the grounds for the transfer of a right by operation of law, that designation is not exactly correct. The transfer in this case is not automatically by operation of law, it only takes place after a court decision mandating the transfer comes into force. Cases where a court decision might enforce the transfer of a right include:

- transfer to the principal of the rights of a commission agent from a contract concluded by the latter with a third party;[71]
- transfer to the pledgee of the pledged right if the pledgor does not perform his or her obligations;[72]
- transfer of the right of a seller of a share in shared property when the sale has taken place in breach of the priority rights of the other owners of the shared property;[73]
- transfer of the right of a seller of a share in a limited responsibility society (OOO)[74] or shares in a closed joint-stock society (закрытое акционерное общество; *zakrytoe aktsionernoe obshchestvo*)[75] when the sale has taken place in breach of the priority rights of other shareholders;[76] and
- transfer of the right of a lessee to the person whose priority right to rent the premises had not been respected by the lessor.[77]

To get a right transferred by a court decision the authorised person brings a relevant claim to court, which then decides about the transfer of the right and any conditions for that transfer.

[70] See above, text to n 61.
[71] CC art 993(2).
[72] Law on Pledge arts 56–7.
[73] CC art 250.
[74] See p 163 for explanation of this form of legal entity.
[75] As in CC arts 97–104.
[76] Federal Law on Limited Responsibility Societies art 21(18); Federal Law on Joint-Stock Societies art 7(3).
[77] CC art 621.

C Performance of the Debtor's Obligation by his Surety or by a Pledgor Other than the Debtor

Suretyship and pledge are both means of securing the performance of obligations, as listed in CC chapter 23 (further details on securing performance are in Chapter 9 at p 212).

CC article 361 states that 'Under a contract of suretyship the surety shall be obliged to the creditor of another person to be liable for the performance by the latter of his obligations in full or in part'.[78] The surety and the debtor become jointly and severally liable to the creditor, unless subsidiary responsibility has been provided for by a law.[79] If a surety performs the debtor's obligation, the creditor's rights with regard to this obligation pass to the surety, so that the surety becomes the new creditor to the initial obligation.[80]

As for pledge, the Civil Code allows third parties to provide pledges to secure other parties' obligations.[81] If a debtor fails to perform their obligation properly the creditor has the right to satisfy his claim from the value of the pledge.[82] If this happens, the pledgor who is not a party to the original contract becomes a creditor in respect to the initial obligation which has been satisfied at the expense of the pledge. Thus, in these cases there is an assignment of a right through the operation of the law on suretyships and pledges.

D Subrogation

The Civil Code provides that:

> to the insurer who has paid the insurance compensation shall pass within the limits of the amount paid the right of demand which the insurant [insured] (or beneficiary) has against the person responsible for the losses compensated as a result of the insurance.[83]

Here again, the operation of law assigns a right to claim compensation. However, a contract of property insurance[84] may exclude such subrogation (CC article 965(1)), except for transfer of the rights to claim as a result of intentional harm.

[78] Butler, above n 2, at 277.
[79] CC art 363(1).
[80] CC art 365(1).
[81] CC art 335(1).
[82] CC art 348(1).
[83] CC art 965(1); Butler, above n 2, at 669–70.
[84] As opposed to personal insurance.

V CONCLUSION

As this chapter has shown, assignment is an important instrument extensively used by the commercial entities in Russia to achieve their goals. It can be also seen, however, that in many cases there may be obstacles which prevent contractual parties from using assignment, these obstacles being invalidity of contract and contract being not concluded. The courts have tended to apply the rules quite rigorously, although with some lack of consistency, with the effect that the assignor, assignee and debtor may find the legal outcome is not quite what they expected.

9

Performance

I INTRODUCTION

Under Russian law the starting point and general rule for all contractual performance is that performance must be 'proper'. What constitutes 'proper performance' is dealt with in the Civil Code (CC) Part One chapter 22, and to a large extent depends on the terms of the particular contract. We discuss the elements of proper performance below.

The other important factor to note at the outset is that contract law in Russia, unlike English contract law, is oriented towards actual performance. The current Civil Code continues the general approach of the previous Soviet Civil Codes which, as a rule, did not consider payment of damages to be an appropriate remedy for improper contractual performance. As a result, the Russian Civil Code provides a contractual party to whom performance is owed – the promisee, also known as the creditor – with a number of different means to ensure their right to actual performance rather than compensation through damages (see below).

In this chapter we consider the assessment of performance, examining what factors are relevant to the decision of whether performance properly fulfils the respective contractual obligation; if not, the promisee can seek appropriate remedies, discussed in Chapter 10.

II PROPER PERFORMANCE

The Supreme Commercial Court and lower-level commercial courts often refer to the principle of proper performance of an obligation. Whether or not a contract has been performed – that is, performed properly – is probably the most frequently contested issue which the courts have to resolve. In the process of assessing performance, a court will consider two main questions:

(1) whether the action (or abstention from action) which would constitute performance was actually carried out; and
(2) if so, was it done properly.

The fact of performance is thus separated from the question of its quality. In relation to this, we discuss first the definition of performance in general and what constitutes deviation from proper performance, then move on to the elements of proper performance as understood in Russian contract law.

A Definition of Performance

The Supreme Commercial Court has defined performance of an obligation as performance by the promisor of actions which lead to the satisfaction of the promisee's needs by providing the promisee with the requirements for which he had asked in the contract: delivery of a thing, performance of work, rendering of a service, etc.[1] Of course, if performance is improper, it is unlikely to lead even to partial satisfaction of the promisee's needs. Thus, although the courts try to separate the fact of performance from its quality, the latter is inevitably an inherent characteristic of the former.

B Understanding Proper Performance

(i) Definition of Proper Performance

The principle of proper performance of an obligation is integral to the Civil Code. What this principle means is explained in general terms in CC article 309:

> Obligations must be performed in accordance with the conditions [terms] of the obligation, requirements of a law and other legal acts, and in the absence of such conditions and requirements in accordance with the customs of business turnover or other usually presented requirements.[2]

From this definition it is clear that in order for performance to be considered to be 'proper' it must comply not only with the contractual terms, but also with any relevant legislation and, possibly, trade customs. The Civil Code, both in the general Part One and in Part Two, which regulates particular contracts, provides standards for proper performance for the particular types of contracts it regulates.

(ii) Deviation from Proper Performance

Performance which deviates from the standard required for proper performance will constitute breach, and give rise to consequential obligations such as payment of a penalty (неустойка; *neustoika*) and/or damages, as discussed in Chapter 10. On the other hand, once a promisor has performed all the actions required of them under the contract, that 'proper performance' will terminate their obligation (CC article 408).

[1] Resolution of Presidium of Supreme Commercial Court of 25 July 2011 No 3108/11.

[2] WE Butler, *The Civil Code of the Russian Federation Parts 1, 2 and 3: Parallel Russian and English Texts* (Moscow, JurInfoR-Press, 2008) 243.

Russian contract law distinguishes between two different types of performance which deviate from proper performance:

(1) improper performance; and
(2) non-performance.

The distinction affects the legal consequences. According to CC article 396(1):

> The payment of a penalty and compensation of losses in the event of the *improper performance* of an obligation shall not relieve the promisor from performance of the obligation in kind unless provided otherwise by a law or by contract.[3] (emphasis added)

By contrast, under CC article 396(2):

> The compensation of losses in the event of the *failure to perform* an obligation and the payment of a penalty for the failure to perform shall relieve the debtor [promisor] from the performance of the obligation in kind unless provided otherwise by a law or by contract.[4] (emphasis added)

From these provisions the following arises:

(1) A promisor who has improperly performed an obligation, unlike one who has completely failed to perform, cannot, by paying compensation to the promisee, avoid actual performance of that obligation (for example, by eliminating any defects, or delivering the rest of the promised goods under a purchase-sale contract) unless the contract itself or a law provides otherwise.

(2) If the promisor has improperly performed their obligation, the promisee is not entitled to say that the contract has not been performed and sue for damages for breach of the whole contract, unless the contract itself or a law specifically grants him that right.

Under the general rule in the case of improper performance of a particular obligation within a contract the promisee can only claim damages for the improper performance of that obligation and also (as noted in the previous point) still require actual performance of the rest of that obligation (and any other obligations in the contract as a whole).

However, if the improper performance is sufficiently defective, the promisee can unilaterally refuse to perform their side of the contract, with the result that the whole contract will be terminated (discharged) (see Chapter 11 XI for further discussion of unilateral refusal to perform).

(3) The provisions in both CC article 396(1) and (2) can be overridden by the contract or a law. In fact, as discussed in Chapter 10, Part Two of the Civil Code provides some specific remedies for violations of particular contractual duties which make the general distinction between improper performance and non-performance irrelevant.

[3] Ibid 293.
[4] Ibid.

Given the very different legal consequences of improper performance and non-performance, it is reasonable to ask, 'How do we distinguish between them?'. Unfortunately, the Civil Code does not give any criteria applicable in all cases to decide unambiguously whether breach of a contractual obligation constitutes improper performance or non-performance.

Sometimes the distinction between improper performance and non-performance can be made clear from the terms of the contract. A good example is the contract of carriage of cargo by railroad transport, the terms of which are specified in a federal Law. According to article 45 of the Statute on Railway Transport in the Russian Federation[5] (Устав Железнодорожного Транспорта Российской Федерации; *Ustav Zheleznodorozhnogo Transporta Rossiiskoi Federatsii*) a cargo is considered lost if it has not been handed over to the recipient within 30 days of the delivery deadline, or after four months from the date where the cargo was accepted for carriage by combined transport (transport by several different means). Article 96 of the Statute then specifies that if the cargo is considered lost (ie the obligation to deliver was not performed at all) the carrier has to pay compensatory damages covering the value of the lost cargo and also the cost of its carriage. Compensation for consequential losses is not available. For late delivery of cargo (ie improper performance of the obligation to deliver it) the carrier has to pay as recompense interest of 9 per cent of the cost of carriage per day late, up to a maximum of the cost of carriage. In this way the Statute of Railway Transport explicitly provides what 'improper performance' and 'non-performance' mean in that particular context.

When the borderline between improper performance and non-performance is not laid down in legislation or the contract, the distinction between them is left to the courts. Unfortunately, however, the courts have not developed any method to distinguish between improper performance and non-performance. As a rule the courts base their conclusion merely on the judges' inner conviction and simply state that a particular breach of contract constitutes improper performance or non-performance, without further elaboration.

(iii) Elements of Proper Performance

The Civil Code includes a number of factors to consider when assessing proper performance, which we will call 'elements of proper performance'. These elements are the factors which the courts generally consider to be significant when assessing performance quality, and can be summarised as follows:[6]

(1) performance should meet the standard established in the contract and any applicable law;

[5] Federal Law of 10 January 2003 No 18-FZ.

[6] The list is based on the general understanding of scholars, court practice and the author's analysis. Although they are contained in various articles, the Civil Code does not put these factors in one list.

(2) the obligation should be performed to the right person – the promisee or person designated by the promisee;
(3) the obligation should be performed by the right person – the promisor or person designated by the promisor or who has an interest in performing the contract for the promisor;[7]
(4) the obligation should be performed by the right method;
(5) the obligation should be performed in the right place; and
(6) the obligation should be performed at the right time.

(iv) Element (1): Meeting the Standard of Proper Performance

In Russian contract law the standard of proper performance depends on the type of contract (see Chapter 2 for more details on types of contract). If the contract is of a type regulated by the Civil Code its standard of proper performance is normally established in both the Code and the contract itself.

For convenience of analysis all contracts of types regulated by Part Two of the Civil Code can be roughly divided into three main classes on the basis of their fundamental subject matter:

(1) contracts for the sale of goods (eg contracts of purchase-sale);
(2) contracts for the provision of work (eg contracts of independent work); or
(3) contracts for the provision of services (eg contracts of insurance, contracts of keeping, contracts of transfer of goods).

Each of these classes of contracts has a different method for measuring the standard of contractual performance. These are discussed in detail below.

This categorisation of contracts into three classes, however, does not reduce freedom of contract and the right of parties to conclude any contract they like within the overall legal framework. Then, unlike contracts of types regulated by the Civil Code, the standard for proper performance for these 'unregulated' contracts is solely established by the contract.

(a) Contracts for the Sale of Goods

In contracts for the sale of goods, performance is considered proper if the seller provides the buyer with goods, of which the quantity, quality and range all accord with the terms of the contract. Any deviation from this standard constitutes breach, as in the following example.

> In a case at the Supreme Commercial Court, company A as seller concluded with company C as buyer a contract for the purchase and installation of a wardrobe in a department store. The contract specified that the wardrobe should be made of solid oak. A duly supplied and installed the

[7] See below for the role of the promisee in this.

wardrobe. However, after some use, the facing material cracked and C discovered that the wardrobe was actually made of plywood covered with veneer instead of solid oak as prescribed in the contract. C regarded installation of a wardrobe made of substandard material to be a breach of contract and proposed that A reduce the price as a remedy for breach (CC article 475(1) gives a buyer in a contract of purchase-sale that option).

A objected that the contract was not purchase-sale, but an independent work contract, so C did not have a right to claim a price reduction because the Civil Code does not provide that option in relation to independent work contracts.

The Supreme Commercial Court held that the parties had actually concluded a mixed contract, both purchase-sale and independent work, and that the Civil Code provisions on purchase-sale should apply to the delivery of the wardrobe. Under CC article 456(1), 'The seller is obliged to transfer to the purchaser the good provided for by the contract of purchase-sale';[8] here, a solid oak wardrobe. Therefore C was entitled to claim the price reduction.[9]

In another case the courts' reasoning in a similar situation was not so straightforward.

Company A undertook to supply and install for F, the Federal Institute of Industrial Property, software called 'Development Environment Web Builder for UniVerse for Solaris 10 FS Prime Power'. A duly supplied some software, installed it and transferred to F the licence for its use. However, when F used the software it realised that it did not actually comply with the terms of the contract. In fact, A had supplied different software to that specified.

F sued A, demanding that A provide the correct software as well as compensatory damages. A argued that it had supplied and installed software equivalent to that specified in the contract and therefore had duly performed its contractual obligations.

The courts of the first two instances rightfully decided that A had to supply and install that exact software specified and upheld F's claim.[10] Since A had not installed the particular program, it had not performed its contractual obligation. However, the claim for compensation was rejected because F did not prove loss.

However, the Court of Cassation remanded the case back for a rehearing, calling for the first instance court to investigate (i) whether the software A actually supplied satisfied F's needs, for which the software had

[8] Butler, above n 2, at 331.
[9] Ruling of Supreme Commercial Court of 11 March 2012 No VAS-17325/11.
[10] Resolution of Ninth Appellate Commercial Court of 2 April 2010 No 09AP-5802/2010-GK.

been bought; and (ii) if the software actually installed had the same functions as the software specified in the contract. In the course of reconsideration there was a forensic examination by experts who determined that the software A installed and the software specified in the contract were not identical and required different computer specifications to function correctly. This conclusion convinced the Court of Cassation that A had breached its contractual duty so F's claim was upheld.[11]

This case shows that even though the Civil Code provides a very clear and straightforward standard of proper performance for a purchase-sale contract – to deliver the goods specified in the contract – the courts may deviate from that standard, as in the second case. There, the Court of Cassation abandoned the formal standard and evaluated A's performance not by comparison with the specific contractual terms but by investigating whether there had been satisfaction of F's actual needs, for which F had bought the software in the first place. In fact the software did not fulfil that function, so there was clear breach from the perspective of F's needs as well as from the perspective of the formal standard.

(b) Contracts for Services

A different standard of proper performance is used to evaluate performance in contracts for services.

It is important to note that in general it is very difficult to prove poor quality of service. Most court proceedings considering proper performance of services shift from a discussion about the quality of performance to the issue of whether or not the services were actually performed and accepted by the client. If so, and this is proved, most courts will reject a claim for breach of contract based on the assertion that the quality of the services provided was substandard.

In 1999, the Supreme Commercial Court in its 'Revision of court practice on contracts of compensated rendering of services'[12] noted that the provisions of CC article 779 mean that the provider of services can be considered to have properly performed their obligations if they have performed the activity specified in the contract. Refusal to pay for services which have been actually performed is not permitted. The following case provides a good illustration of this approach.

Company A, an airline, and company D, a design and engineering bureau, concluded a contract for compensated rendering of services, under which D would provide A with the service of designer supervision. D would

[11] Resolution of Federal Commercial Court of Moscow District of 14 June 2011 No KG-A40/5005-11-P.

[12] Informational Circular of Presidium of Supreme Commercial Court of 29 September 1999 No 48 'On the Particular Issues of Court Practice connected with the Disputes on Contracts for Legal Services' para 2.

supervise A's production, supply and modification of products using D's designs. The contract specified D's obligations in a very general way and did not provide any detailed description.

A only paid D less than one-third of the first fee instalment so D sued A for more payment. The lower courts rejected D's claim on the basis that it was impossible to determine exactly what services D had actually provided and hence determine what A owed. The 'notifications of services rendered' signed by both parties only indicated which services had been provided but not their price.

The Supreme Commercial Court refused to uphold the lower courts' decisions and sustained D's claim. It held that, according to CC articles 779 and 781(1) in relation to a contract of compensated rendering of services, the provider of services is obliged to provide the services in accordance with the client's designated tasks, and the client to pay for them within the contractual procedure and timeframe. The fact that D had actually carried out operational designer supervision was proved by documentation signed by both parties. Since the fact of performance had been proved, the Supreme Commercial Court concluded that D had fully and properly performed its contractual obligations so A should pay the full contract price.[13]

Russian contract law also recognises contracts for compensated rendering of services where the service is to achieve a particular outcome. Then performance is valued against that outcome; proof that the service actually led to that result might be required.

In one case the Supreme Commercial Court clarified that, under CC article 779, the obligations of a provider of services may include not only the performance of a particular activity, but also the duty to produce particular results, such as written consultations and clarifications, draft contracts, applications, appeals and other documents. These different duties involve different levels of diligence; in the first case, where the obligation is just to provide the services, the provider only has to undertake its best efforts; in the second case, where a result is specified, they must guarantee that particular outcome.

The subject matter of a contract for compensated rendering of services between service provider S and client C included activities of a legal nature (eg representation of C's interests) as well some practical processes (eg documents prepared and filed with C's debtor, insurance company, I). The particular outcome to be achieved by the services provided was to ensure payment by I of its debt to C. I did pay the debt, but C refused to pay S, claiming that the payment did not result from S's services. Since S did not provide any evidence of the preparation and filing with I of documents he

[13] Resolution of Presidium of the Supreme Commercial Court of 28 October 2010 No 15300/08.

> had prepared, and could not prove that I's payment was the result of his work, the Supreme Commercial Court concluded that S had not properly performed his obligation.[14]

It is thus clear that court interpretation of the Civil Code provisions on proper contractual performance in provision of services has put great emphasis on proof that the service was in fact provided, rather than finding a way to assess its quality. This rather formalistic approach may surprise an English lawyer.

(c) Contracts for Work

The standard of performance of an obligation to carry out work is set out in CC article 721(1); for proper performance the 'quality of work . . . must correspond with the conditions of the contract and, in the absence or incompleteness of the conditions of the contract, with the requirements ordinarily presented for work of the respective nature'.[15] CC article 721(2) provides that work must also comply with relevant legislation. The application of these standards is illustrated in the following case.

> Company A and company G concluded an independent work contract, under which A undertook to renovate the entrance hall, corridors and staircases of a building belonging to G. After the renovation works were completed G only partially paid, so A sued G for both the unpaid fee and a penalty for late payment.
>
> The Federal Commercial Court of North-Caucasian District rejected A's claim. The Court held that the particular parts renovated constituted the only emergency exit from the building. According to fire safety legislation, they therefore should have been restored using flame-resistant materials. A, as contractor, was obliged to comply with those legal requirements. However, A had used non-compliant materials, for example, flammable wall coverings and linoleum as floor covering. Therefore, the Court rightfully concluded that A's renovation works did not meet the proper performance requirements of CC article 721, so A's performance could not be qualified as proper performance. G's obligation to pay only fell due once A had provided proper performance; since that obligation had not been fulfilled, G did not have to pay for A's work.[16]

Looking more generally at the examples discussed above, it is clear that more often than not performance is evaluated against some formal standard. This can be the specification for goods to be delivered, the fact of performance of services, or a set of requirements for the result of completed work.

[14] Resolution of Presidium of the Supreme Commercial Court of 24 January 2012 No 11563/11.

[15] Butler, above n 2, at 506–7.

[16] Resolution of Federal Commercial Court of North-Caucasian District of 9 February 2010 No A63-4060/2009.

Compared to English law, the standard of exercising 'reasonable care and skill'[17] is almost never used in Russian contract law to evaluate whether there has been proper performance of an obligation by a promisor who concluded the contract in the course of carrying out entrepreneurial activity.

The reason for this is as follows. The general structure of liability for breach in Russian contract law is such that, amongst other things, as well as assessment of whether there is improper performance or non-performance, there is also assessment of fault as a separate issue. The Civil Code establishes a presumption of fault, by CC article 401 defining fault by describing the converse, the situation when a party is not at fault. CC article 401(2) states:

> The person shall be deemed to be not at fault if with that degree of concern and attentiveness which is required of him according to the character of the obligation and conditions of turnover he has taken all measures for proper performance of the obligation.[18]

The effect is that in Russian contract law the standard of 'exercising reasonable care and skill' is formulated as the issue of whether there is fault; compliance with this standard (that is, being not at fault) has to be proved by the party seeking to avoid liability for a faulty breach (CC article 401(2)).

However, unless otherwise provided by a law or by the contract, a party who has concluded a contract in the course of entrepreneurial activity is liable for breach irrespective of fault. Therefore, the standard of 'exercising reasonable care and skill' does not apply to performance by the party who concludes a contract in the course of their entrepreneurial activity; they are strictly liable.

(v) Element (2): Performance to the Right Person

Under CC article 312:

> Unless provided otherwise by agreement of the parties and does not arise from the customs of business turnover or the essence of the obligation, the debtor [promisor] shall have the right when performing the obligation to demand evidence that performance is accepted by the creditor [promisee] himself or by a person empowered by him and shall bear the risk of the consequences of the failure to present such demand.

This means that performance is only proper if it is made to the right person. The obligation to ensure this lies with the party performing. Performance to an incorrect recipient, even if otherwise meeting the appropriate standard, is not considered as proper performance, as one rather dramatic example shows.

> In accordance with a Government Decree of 2003, Ms Y was supposed to receive compensation from a bank for the loss of her house in Chechnya. In

[17] As, eg, in the Supply of Goods and Services Act 1982 s 13: 'In a contract for the supply of a service where the supplier is acting in the course of a business, there is an implied term that the supplier will carry out the service with reasonable care and skill'.

[18] Butler, above n 2, at 296.

2007 she discovered that the compensation had been obtained by another person claiming with forged documentation. Y sued the bank for the compensation to which she was entitled. The lower courts rejected her claim, however the Supreme Court overturned those decisions and allowed it.

The Supreme Court held that only performance to the correct person can be qualified as proper performance; performance to the wrong person is equal to non-performance. Therefore it does not discharge the obligation; the duty to perform subsists. Hence, the Supreme Court obliged the bank to pay Y the compensation to which she was entitled.[19] The fact that it had mistakenly but in good faith paid someone else did not discharge its duty to perform to her.

It might seem that in the this case the relations between Ms Y and the bank were not based on contract. It should be clarified that according to the relevant Government Decree a contract of bank account to the benefit of each recipient of compensation was concluded between the competent governmental authority in Chechnya and the bank designated in the Decree. Thus the provision to Ms Y of money credited to an account which had been opened in Ms Y's name would constitute the bank's performance under its contract with the competent governmental authority.

(vi) Element (3): Performance by the Right Person (and the Possibility of Vicarious Performance)

In contrast to the principle that performance must be made to the specific recipient, CC article 313 establishes the presumption that performance by a third party constitutes proper performance:

> Unless the duty of the debtor [promisor] to perform an obligation personally arises from a law, other legal acts, the conditions of the obligation, or the essence thereof . . . the creditor [promisee] is obliged to accept the performance offered by a third person for the debtor.[20]

This case from the Supreme Commercial Court gives an example of the benefit to a promisee of this rule.

Company A borrowed money from bank B under a credit contract. However, individual entrepreneur E paid A's debt to B. E did this because of a provision in a simple partnership contract between E and A; under that contract E agreed to pay off A's debt to B.

Unfortunately, the simple partnership contract was then rendered void by a court. As noted in Chapter 6 (at p 132) a void contract does not give rise to any legal consequences *ab initio*. Hence E concluded that there

[19] Ruling of Supreme Court of 12 July 2011 No 23-V11-2.
[20] Butler, above n 2, at 244.

> were no legal grounds for him to have paid off A's debt, so the money he paid to B should be qualified as unfounded enrichment and returned to him.
>
> The Supreme Commercial Court applied CC article 313 to reject E's claim. The Court held that there was no requirement that the borrower's obligation to repay should be performed personally. Here B could (and actually was obliged to) accept performance offered by E as a third party. The fact that the contract which induced E to pay A's debt to B was void did not affect B's right to accept E's performance, neither did it lead to qualification of that performance as improper.[21]

It should be noted that, instead of suing B, E could have sued A for unfounded enrichment and this claim would most probably have been upheld by the court.

In this case, performance of A's obligation by E was based on the contract between A and E. This means that A gave consent to E performing A's obligation to B. However, CC article 313(2) provides for instances when a third party may at their own expense perform the promisor's obligation without the promisor's consent. This may happen if the third party 'is subject to the danger of losing his right to the property of the debtor [promisor] (right of lease, pledge or others) as a consequence of execution being levied by the creditor [promisee] on this property'.[22] In this event the third party acquires the rights of the promisee, to whom the performance has been provided on behalf of the promisor, in accordance with the rules on assignment in CC articles 382–7. Assignment is discussed in detail in Chapter 8.

Draft Amendments to the Civil Code provide one more possibility for the performance of an obligation by a third party without the promisor's consent. The Draft Amendments suggest that:

> unless otherwise is provided for by law or contract, or arises from the essence of relations between the promisor and the third party, a third party who has a lawful interest in the performance by the promisor of a monetary obligation connected with the entrepreneurial activity of its parties may perform such obligation to the promisee without the promisor's consent.[23]

As a result, similarly to the outcome in the case just above,[24] the third party will acquire the rights of the promisee, to whom the performance on behalf of the promisor has been provided, in accordance with the rules on assignment in CC articles 382–7.

[21] Informational Circular of Presidium of the Supreme Commercial Court of 13 September 2011 No 147 'Overview of Court Practice of Resolution of Cases connected with the Application of the Norms of the Civil Code of the Russian Federation on the Credit Contract' para 14.

[22] Butler, above n 2, at 244.

[23] Draft Federal Law On Amendments to Parts One, Two, Three and Four of the Civil Code approved by the State Duma at first reading on 27 April 2012 No 47538-6 art 1 para 155 amending CC art 313.

[24] See above, text to n 21.

(vii) Element (4): Method of Performance

The method of performance – the way in which performance is made – is one of the dimensions of proper performance, provided that the contract explicitly stipulates that performance must be delivered in a specific way. In that case performance by a method other than the one specified in the contract will constitute a breach of obligation, unless the promisor is entitled by law to alter the method of performance. This is illustrated by the following example.

> Company A and bank B concluded a contract of purchase-sale of securities, that is, shares in a joint-stock society, under which B undertook to transfer the securities to A's securities account held at a depository as soon as B had received payment from A. The contract gave only the number of the account with the depository but did not indicate the depository's name.
>
> A did not pay on time. Nevertheless, B sent an instruction to transfer the securities to A's account with the depositary. This instruction was not carried out by the depository because it did not contain all the necessary details of A's securities account. Besides, in order to execute the transfer instruction the depository needed A's consent, which was also lacking.
>
> Unable to transfer the securities by the method specified in the contract, B submitted the transfer order to the registrar of securities. The registrar accordingly transferred the shares from B's account to A's personal account. Simultaneously B sued A for the payment owed.
>
> The Supreme Commercial Court held that in order to claim its payment B must first properly have performed its obligation to transfer the securities to A. The contract specified only one possible method of performance: submitting an instruction for transfer of the securities to A's securities account at the depository. Therefore, B's obligation to transfer the securities to A would only be considered to have been properly performed when a credit entry was made on A's account with the depository. No other alternative methods of performance were specified in the contract, therefore B had not properly performed its contractual obligation and was not entitled to receive payment from A for the shares.[25] It was not mentioned by the Supreme Commercial Court but in this situation B could only sue A for unfounded enrichment and claim the shares back.

The method of performance can be lawfully changed by the promisor, irrespective of what is in the contract, only in particular cases specified in the Civil Code where the obligation is to transfer money or securities. Under CC article 327(1):

[25] Resolution of Presidium of the Supreme Commercial Court of 30 November 2010 No 9217/10, case No A56-47705/2008.

> A debtor [promisor] shall have the right to place money due from him or securities on deposit with a notary, and in the instances established by a law, on deposit with a court if the obligation cannot be performed by the debtor as a consequence of:
>
> 1. the absence of the promisee or person empowered by him to accept performance at the place where the obligation must be performed;
> 2. the lack of dispositive legal capacity of the promisee and absence of his representative;
> 3. the evident lack of specificity as to who is the promisee with regard to the obligation, in particular, in connection with a dispute in this regard between the promisee and other persons; or
> 4. avoidance by the promisee of accepting performance or other delay on his part.[26]

In these circumstances using the substitute method of payment (to a notary or court), rather than the method stipulated in the contract, will be accepted as proper performance.

A joint resolution of the Plenum of the Supreme Court and Plenum of the Supreme Commercial Court[27] explained that if a promisor exercised this right to place the money or securities due from him on deposit with a notary or court within the time limit for performance specified in the contract, the obligation is considered to have been performed on time and no interest for late performance will accrue. In other words, timely use as appropriate of the provision in CC article 327(1) allows a promisor to avoid liability for both non-performance and late performance.

Although the wording of CC article 327 creates a right, and not a duty, for the promisor in the particular circumstances to place on deposit the money or securities due (for whatever reason), the courts have interpreted it as though it were an obligation on the promisor, if he or she cannot properly perform because of one of the circumstances listed. If any of these circumstances exists and the promisor fails to deposit money or securities due, they will be considered by the courts to have breached the contract, as in the following example.

> In 2005 the Commercial Court upheld that company G owed company A payment for works and services provided by A. On the basis of the court decision a writ of execution was granted to A with A named as the claimant. In 2006 A assigned to company U its right to claim the debt from G. However, a new writ of execution with U named as claimant was only issued at the end of 2008 and submitted to the Court Bailiff Service Department (служба судебных приставов; *sluzhba sudebnykh pristavov*) only in May 2009. Since G had not paid its debt by then, U sued G for interest of 1 million roubles which had accrued on G's debt. G contested

[26] Butler, above n 2, at 252.

[27] Resolution of Plenum of the Supreme Court and Supreme Commercial Court of 8 October 1998 No 13/14 'On the Court Practice of Application of the Provisions of the Civil Code of the Russian Federation on the Payment of Interest for the Use of Another Person's Monetary Means' para 8.

the amount of interest, arguing that it should not pay interest for the period from the moment of assignment to U of A's right to claim the debt from G until the date when the writ of execution naming U as claimant was submitted to the Court Bailiff Service. G believed that it could not pay the debt during this period because it was uncertain who the promisee was. The courts at all instances did not accept this argument. The courts rightfully held that, in case of evident lack of specificity as to who is the promisee with regard to a contractual obligation, the promisor could have used the right under CC article 327 and paid the debt by placing the money on deposit with a notary.[28]

(viii) Element (5): Place of Performance

Performance of an obligation cannot be considered to be proper if it were made in the wrong place. The place of performance can be specified by legislation or in the contract; it can also be established by the customs of business turnover or the essence of the obligation. If it is not possible to determine from those sources where the contract should be performed, the following general rules on the place of performance are provided by CC article 316:

> [For] a land plot, building, construction or other immovable property: at the location of the property;
>
> with regard to an obligation to transfer a good or other property providing the carriage thereof: at the place of handing over the property to the first carrier for delivery to the creditor [promisee];
>
> with regard to other obligations of an entrepreneur to transfer a good or other property: at the place of manufacture or keeping of the property if this place was known to the creditor at the moment of origin of the obligation;
>
> with regard to a monetary obligation: at the place of residence of the creditor at the moment of origin of the obligation, and if the creditor is a juridical person [legal entity] at its location at the moment of origin of the obligation; if the creditor at the moment of performance of the obligation has changed place of residence or location and notified the debtor thereof at the new place of residence or location of the creditor, relegating the expenses connected with the change of place of performance to the account of the creditor;
>
> with regard to all other obligations: at the place of residence of the debtor [promisor], and if the debtor is a juridical person at its location.[29]

The rule regarding the place of performance of a monetary obligation is clarified in the Draft Amendments to the Civil Code referred to above[30] by the indication that it will only apply to an obligation to transfer money in cash. With respect to

[28] Ruling of Supreme Commercial Court of 16 February 2010 No VAS-1688/10; Resolution of Federal Commercial Court of West-Siberian District of 28 December 2009 No A70-3036/2009.

[29] Butler, above n 2, at 246–7.

[30] See above n 23.

the place of performance of a monetary obligation to transfer finances in non-cash form, it is proposed that it should be at the location of the bank (its branch or office) where the promisee has a bank account.[31] The aim of this detailed list is clearly to forestall any unresolved issues of where performance must occur, in order to be fulfilled at the proper place.

(ix) Element (6): Time of Performance

If the contract specifies a particular date for performance, then proper performance must be on that date, or, if a period, any time during that period (CC article 314(1)). However, 'When an obligation does not provide for a period for its performance and does not contain conditions enabling this period to be determined, it must be performed within a reasonable period after the origin of the obligation' (CC article 314(2)).[32] This means that it is left to the courts to determine what is a reasonable period for performance.

(a) Determination of Period for Performance

As the courts acknowledge, a reasonable period for performance will depend on the character and circumstances of a particular contract. There are many cases when the courts have decided a reasonable period for performance for a particular contract, but unfortunately as a rule they almost never give any explanation as to why that particular period was regarded as reasonable.

The second paragraph of CC article 314(2) sets out a default position that if no period was set, and the obligation was not performed within a reasonable time, the promisor should perform:

> within a seven-day period from the day of presentation by the creditor [promisee] of the demand concerning the performance of the obligation, unless the duty to perform within another period arises from a law, other legal acts, the conditions of the obligation, the customs of business turnover, or the essence of the obligation.[33]

The same rule applies if the period of performance is determined by the point of time when a claim for performance is made. The effect of this was explained by the Nineteenth Appellate Commercial Court in one of its resolutions.[34] It said that the reasonable time for performance should be understood as a limitation preventing the promisee from presenting a demand for performance immediately after the obligation has arisen. The Court rightfully concluded that a promisor should not bear any negative consequence from the promisee failing to present a demand. If a promisor were held liable for non-performance during the reasonable time before the promisee presented a

[31] Draft Federal Law No 47538-6, above n 23 art 1 para 158(b) and (c) amending CC art 316.
[32] Butler, above n 2, at 245.
[33] Ibid 245–6.
[34] Resolution of Nineteenth Appellate Commercial Court of 7 November 2011 No A48-2031/2011.

demand, the promisor would be liable in circumstances where they were acting lawfully. Therefore, once the promisee's demand is made, the promisor is given a seven-day 'period of grace' within which to perform, before any negative consequences of non-performance arise. The court added that the provision in CC article 314(2) means that performance by a promisor at any time within seven days after the promisee has presented the demand would be proper performance.

Draft Amendments to the Civil Code change this approach to dealing with situations when the period of performance is not specified in the contract. According to the proposed amendments to CC article 314:

> in instances when an obligation does not provide for the period of its performance and does not contain terms enabling this period to be determined, as well as if the period of performance is determined by the moment of demand, *the obligation should be performed within a seven-day period from the day of presentation by the promisee of the demand* concerning the performance of the obligation, unless the duty to perform within another period arises from a law, other legal acts, the terms of the obligation, customs, or the essence of the obligation.[35] (emphasis added)

In other words, it is proposed that the current provision of CC article 314 which allows a promisee to present the demand for performance to the promisor only after a reasonable time has elapsed should be removed from the Civil Code. On the one hand, this deprives the promisor of protection from the presentation by the promisee of demand for performance immediately after the contract has been concluded. On the other hand, the proposed amendments make the rules for determining the period of performance more transparent. As mentioned above, the courts have not developed any clear criteria or approaches which could help determine what a reasonable time would be in a particular case. This has created some uncertainty for promisees as to when they might reasonably present to the promisor a demand for performance.

The Draft Amendments to the Civil Code also propose to complement CC article 314 with a provision which grants the promisor a right:

> to demand acceptance of performance by the promisee, if the promisee has not presented their demand for performance within a reasonable time, unless otherwise is provided by a law, other normative acts, terms of the contract and does not arise from customs or the essence of the obligation.[36]

Thus the risk of uncertainty inherent in the term 'reasonable time' has been shifted to the promisor. Under the proposed amendments the promisor can demand acceptance of their performance by the promisee only after a lapse of a reasonable time after the obligation has arisen.

It is important to note that this provision, if adopted, will be the only mention of the promisor's right to demand acceptance of performance by the promisee. In

[35] Draft Federal Law No 47538-6, above n 23 art 1 para 156.
[36] Ibid.

all other cases this right of the promisor to demand performance and the promisee's obligation to accept performance is merely implied.

(b) Early Performance

If at least one party is not contracting in the course of entrepreneurial activity, CC article 315 allows contractual performance earlier than originally agreed 'unless provided otherwise by a law, other legal acts, conditions of the obligation or arises from the customs of business turnover or the essence' of the contract.[37] Thus the Civil Code presumes the possibility of early performance in non-entrepreneurial contracts, unless an exception applies.

CC article 810(2) gives an example of such an exception. Under it, a loan with interest made to an individual and intended for personal, family, home or other use not connected with entrepreneurial activity may be repaid early by the borrower, in full or in part, but only provided that the lender is notified 30 days before the proposed new repayment date.[38] (The loan contract may provide for a shorter notification period.) So here the general rule allowing a promisor to perform early is restricted by the 30-day notification requirement.

If it is a business contract, that is, both parties are contracting in the course of entrepreneurial activity, early performance will only be considered proper if explicitly provided for by 'a law, other legal acts, the conditions of the obligation, the customs of business turnover or the essence of the obligation'[39] (CC article 315). Some of the provisions of Part Two of the Civil Code detailing particular types of contracts do provide the possibility of performing obligations under some commercial contracts before time. However, this possibility of early performance is conditional on the other party's prior consent, as for example, explicitly in CC article 508(3) which regulates periods for delivery of goods under a contract of delivery: 'goods may be delivered before time with the consent of the purchaser'.[40] According to CC article 711(1) relating to the procedure for payment of work under a contract of independent work 'unless preliminary payment for work fulfilled or individual stages thereof has been provided for by the contract of independent work, the customer shall be obliged to pay the independent work contractor the stipulated price . . . within the agreed period, *or with the consent of the customer before time*'[41] (emphasis added).

Court practice has revealed an interesting controversy as to when the possibility of early performance follows 'from the essence of the contract', in relation to contracts of lease. In one of its resolutions, the Federal Commercial Court of Volgo-Viatskii District concluded that the possibility of early payment of rent

[37] Butler, above n 2, at 246.
[38] CC art 810(2) as amended by the Federal Law of 19 October 2011 No 284-FZ.
[39] Butler, above n 2, at 245–6.
[40] Ibid 372.
[41] Ibid 498.

follows from the essence of a lease contract, which is the landlord's legal interest to receive rent.[42] However, in another case the Federal Commercial Court of the Far-Eastern District took a different approach.

> The tenant, T, of a plot of land paid higher rent than specified in the lease contract. T then sued the landlord, L, claiming the excess back as unfounded enrichment. L claimed that the excessive amount should be considered as early payments (pre-payments) of future rent. However, the court held that excessive payments may not be considered as pre-payments because the contract did not provide for the parties to agree on early payment. (As noted, CC article 315 says that performance of an obligation in a business contract is only considered proper if its possibility is explicitly provided for by law, other legal acts, conditions of the obligation or follows from the customs of business turnover or essence of the obligation.) Here there was no such provision so the court upheld T's claim and T recovered the excessive rent from L as unfounded enrichment.[43]

(c) 'Strict Deadlines'

There is a special category of performance periods; that is, performance within a strictly set period (the so-called 'strict deadline'), as, for example, in CC article 457(2):

> A contract of purchase-sale shall be deemed to be concluded with a condition of the performance thereof within a strictly determined period if it clearly arises from the contract that in the event of a violation of the period for the performance thereof the buyer loses interest in the contract.[44]

If a contract provides a 'strict deadline' for delivery, performance a single day later, or even a day earlier, will be considered to be no performance. The buyer need not accept either early or late performance by the seller. The Supreme Commercial Court explained that the buyer is not even obliged to inform the seller of their refusal to accept late delivery of the goods.[45] This is reminiscent of the strict approach to 'time clauses' in English commercial contracts, as for example in *Bunge v Tradax Export SA*.[46]

The provision of a 'strict deadline' can be included in any type of contract, unless disallowed by specific legislation. It is imposed by an explicit contractual

[42] Resolution of Federal Commercial Court of Volgo-Viatskii District of 12 August 2010 No A28-16266/2009.

[43] Resolution of Federal Commercial Court of Far-Eastern District of 1 December 2011 No F03-5336/2011.

[44] Butler, above n 2, at 332.

[45] Resolution of Plenum of Supreme Commercial Court of 22 October 1997 No 18 'On Particular Issues connected with the Application of Provisions of the Civil Code of the Russian Federation on Contract of Delivery'.

[46] [1981] 1 WLR 711.

term providing that violation of the performance period will lead to the promisee's loss of interest in performance, hence giving them a right to refuse to accept late performance.

III METHODS OF ENSURING PERFORMANCE

Modern Russian law has continued a practice which was an important element of the law of contract during both pre-revolutionary and Soviet times,[47] that is, having a number of procedures which can be agreed between the parties to encourage the promisor to perform. In the current Civil Code, these are set out in chapter 23, 'Securing Performance of Obligations'.

These methods of securing performance are: penalty (неустойка; *neustoika*); pledge (залог; *zalog*); withholding (удержание; *uderzhanie*); suretyship (поручительство; *poruchitel'stvo*); bank guarantee (банковская гарантия; *bankovskaia garantiia*); and deposit (задаток; *zadatok*). CC article 329(1) also allows for 'other means provided for by a law or by a contract'.[48]

Penalty (*neustoika*) is simultaneously a means to ensure actual performance and a remedy for breach of contract, and as such is extensively discussed in Chapter 10 (at p 243). Here we will not similarly go into detail for the other means to secure performance, instead will just indicate their main characteristics.[49]

Pledge is set up under a written contract ancillary to the main contract, and involves a piece of property being set aside (either literally or figuratively) and 'in the event of the failure to perform or the improper performance by the debtor [promisor] of an obligation secured by the pledge for which he is liable' (CC article 348(1))[50] execution is levied on the pledged property, that is, it is sold and the contractual debt paid out of the proceeds. The Civil Code has a number of detailed provisions in CC articles 334–58, and there is also separate legislation on pledge of real property (mortgage). According to Mozolin and Masliaev, 'A pledge is one of the most reliable means of securing the performance of obligations'.[51]

Withholding (CC articles 359–60) is the keeping by a creditor of a piece of property so long as the obligation it is securing is not performed. If necessary, execution can be levied against the object in the same way as for pledge.

Under a contract of suretyship, 'the surety shall be obliged to the creditor of another person to be liable for the performance of the last of his obligations in

[47] Soviet penalty clauses in foreign trade contracts were well known for their ferocity.

[48] Butler, above n 2, at 254.

[49] For further details, see VP Mozolin and AI Masliaev, *Russian Civil and Commercial Law, vol 2: Law of Obligations: General Provisions and Individual Types* (WE Butler (ed and trans), London, Wildy, Simmonds & Hill, 2011) ch 25, 78–127.

[50] Butler, above n 2, at 266.

[51] Mozolin and Masliaev, above n 49, at 88.

full or in part' [52] (CC article 361). In other words, an individual or legal entity stands as guarantor for the contractual obligations of another individual or legal entity. A contract of surety must be in written form. Under CC article 367, suretyship terminates with the termination of the obligation secured by it, with certain changes of circumstances, or on the expiry of a period specified in the suretyship contract.

CC article 368 sets out the concept of a bank guarantee:

> By virtue of a bank guarantee the bank, other credit institution, or insurance organisation (guarantor) gives at the request of another person (principal) a written obligation to pay to the creditor of the principal (beneficiary) a monetary amount in accordance with the conditions of the obligation given by the guarantor upon the presentation by the beneficiary of a written demand concerning the payment thereof.[53]

The detailed provisions, including the fact of the irrevocability of a bank guarantee and its non-transferability, are given in CC articles 368–79.

Deposit is 'a monetary amount issued by one of the contracting parties on the account under a contract of payment due from him to the other party as evidence of the conclusion of the contract and to secure its performance'[54] (CC article 380). 'The duty to make a deposit may be provided by agreement of the parties or by a law.'[55] So, for example, participants in a public sale are obliged to make a deposit.

Deposit must be distinguished from pre-payment (advance payment). Unlike deposit, pre-payment is merely performance of the obligation to pay a certain sum of money before the other party has provided counter-performance. If the contract is not performed, irrespective of which party is responsible, the pre-payment should be returned to the party who paid it. If money paid before counter-performance has been performed is explicitly specified in the contract to be a 'deposit', the following rules in CC article 381(2) apply:

> If for the failure to perform the contract the party which gave the deposit is responsible, it shall remain with the other party. If for the failure to perform the contract the party which received the deposit is responsible, it shall be obliged to pay the other party twice the amount of deposit.[56]

CC Article 329(3) points out that invalidity of the main obligation will invalidate an agreement setting up a method of ensuring performance, whilst invalidity of that agreement will not of itself affect the main contract.

Use within commercial contracts of an appropriate method for securing performance, mainly of penalty, suretyship and pledge, is widespread, and fits with the general characteristic of Russian law (which has been noted elsewhere in this book) of the emphasis on actual performance. Another reason for using methods

[52] Butler, above n 2, at 277.
[53] Ibid 280.
[54] Ibid 285.
[55] Mozolin and Masliaev, above n 49, at 123.
[56] Butler, above n 2, at 286.

for securing performance is that the level of contractual non-performance is, unfortunately, still rather high in Russia.

IV ALTERNATIVE OBLIGATIONS

Under Russian contract law parties can provide for alternative performance. CC article 320 states:

> The right of choice, unless it arises otherwise from a law, other legal acts, or the conditions of obligation, shall belong to the debtor [promisor] who is obliged to transfer to the creditor [promisee] one property or another or to perform one of two or several actions.[57]

In practice, this means that a contract may provide for:

(1) two alternative modes of performance, one of which is primary and the other secondary (optional obligation), so the promisor undertakes the second only if the first is not possible (that is, not practicable; strict impossibility is not required); or
(2) two alternative modes of performance without either being specified as primary (truly alternative obligation), so the promisor is free to choose which to perform.

Currently neither of these types of obligations is defined in the Civil Code. Moreover, the Civil Code does not make any distinction between the two. Performance of both types is regulated identically by a single provision in CC article 320 cited above.[58]

The following is an example of a typical optional obligation (our type 1):

> Company L contracted with company M for the purchase-sale of mineral fertilizer. Under the contract M was obliged to pay for the fertilizer by a bank transfer before a specified date. However, the contract also stipulated that if it were not possible to pay before the deadline, instead of payment M could deliver wheat to L at the market price at the time of delivery of the wheat.[59]

A truly alternative obligation (type 2) is the following.

> Company A and Municipal Administration M concluded a contract to collaborate in financing the construction of wastewater facilities in a small town. Under the contract A undertook to pay 3.3 million roubles to M. In

[57] Ibid 249.

[58] See above, text to n 57.

[59] Resolution of Federal Commercial Court of West-Siberian District of 31 October 2006 No F04-6357/2006 (26927- 70-10).

> return M was obliged either to transfer the ownership of the wastewater facilities to A or to reimburse to A 3.3 million roubles it had invested in the facilities.[60]

From the wording of the contract, the choice between one mode of performance or the other was at M's discretion.

Draft Amendments to the Civil Code[61] introduce two new articles providing for a definition of each of these two alternative types of obligation. An optional obligation (as type 1 above) is defined in draft article 308.2 as:

> an obligation according to which the promisor is granted a right to substitute the principal performance by another (optional) performance envisaged in the terms of the obligation. If the promisor is exercising his right to substitute performance specified by the terms of the obligation the promisee is obliged to accept that performance of the obligation.

Draft article 308.1 defines an alternative obligation (a truly alternative obligation, as in type 2 above) as:

> an obligation according to which the promisor is obliged to perform one of the two or several actions (or abstain from performance of an action) at his own choice. The law, other normative acts or a contract may grant the right of choice to the promisee or a third party. From the moment when the promisor (promisee, third party) has made the choice, the obligation ceases to be alternative.

Simultaneously with introducing an explicit distinction between an optional and an alternative obligation, the Draft Amendments also provide different legal consequences depending on which of the two it is, in contrast to the current state of affairs when the regulation of both types of obligations is the same.

The proposed Article 320.1[62] provides that in the case of an optional obligation, the promisee may only demand from the promisor performance of the principal obligation if the promisor has not begun to perform it by the time specified in the contract.

Under the proposed amendments to CC article 320, if the promisor with an alternative obligation does not exercise their choice, including by actually performing the obligation, within the time limit specified in the contract, the promisee may demand from the promisor performance of the promisee's choice of action.[63] So, the promisee to an optional obligation may only demand the principal performance, while the promisee to an alternative obligation can demand either performance possible under the contract, according to their own preference.

[60] Resolution of Federal Commercial Court of North-Western District of 3 July 2009 No A66-8551/2008.

[61] Draft Federal Law No 47538-6, above n 23 art 1 para 149.

[62] Ibid art 1 para 163.

[63] Ibid art 1 para 162.

The Draft Amendments to CC article 320.1(2) also establish that the rules on performance of an alternative obligation will apply to an obligation which stipulates performance by a promisor of two or more actions, unless the obligation cannot be considered to be optional.

If these proposed amendments are brought into law, they will go a long way towards tidying up a rather neglected aspect of contractual performance.

V ENTIRE AND SEVERABLE OBLIGATIONS

An obligation is entire if its partial performance would not satisfy the promisee's needs (that is, the reason they concluded the contract) at all. An obligation is severable if it can be performed in instalments and partial performance will partly satisfy the promisee's needs.

Under Russian contract law partial performance of an entire obligation constitutes non-performance of the whole obligation, and the non-performing party will have no right to claim counter-performance from the other party (as explained in Chapter 5 at p 108). The non-performing party will be liable for non-performance of the whole obligation.

By contrast, partial performance of a severable obligation will constitute improper performance, and a party who has provided partial performance will have a right to claim the other party's counter-performance in part (eg part payment) and will only themselves be liable for improper performance, not for non-performance.

An obligation may be entire because of its intrinsic characteristics (eg an obligation to deliver goods to a particular port). Alternatively, an obligation can be made entire by the particular wording in the contract. A good illustration of the latter is A's obligation in the following example.

> Company A concluded a contract with company B for A to deliver, assemble and install medical equipment for a medical centre. A delivered all the equipment but failed to assemble and install it on time. As a result the medical centre could not begin operating when planned. B sued A, claiming a penalty calculated on the basis of the whole contract price, which included the price of the equipment.
>
> A argued that it had partially performed its contractual obligation so the penalty should only be calculated on the basis of the cost of the assembly and installation, which was performed late. B responded that A's obligation under the contract was entire. Assembly and installation of the equipment was essential for B, given the contract's purpose – the medical equipment had been purchased not for storage and resale but for use at the medical centre. Thus the mere delivery of the equipment did not satisfy B's needs. Besides, the contract established a total price of all the

equipment, assembly and installation and did not provide separate prices for the equipment and each type of work.

The Federal Commercial Court of Moscow District upheld B's claim. The court agreed that A's obligation was entire and held that the penalty for late assembly and installation of the equipment should therefore be calculated on the basis of the total contract price.[64]

However, if the contract had been worded slightly differently, for example, specifying separate prices for the equipment, assembly and installation, the court might have held A's obligation to be severable, leading to a different outcome.

In another case the wording of the promisor's obligation gave serious grounds to regard it as severable. In particular, one of the classical features of a severable obligation is its performance in stages.

Company C and company D concluded a contract for the provision of consultancy services, under which D would provide legal support for the registration of C's ownership rights to a plot of land under a shop. Under the contract the consultancy services were to be provided in two stages.

At the first stage D had to negotiate with the shop's co-owner, because consent of both owners was needed for registration. At the second stage D was to prepare all the necessary documents and register C's ownership rights.

C paid D 45,000 roubles as pre-payment for all the services, whereas the remuneration for performance of the first stage was only 7,500 roubles.

D's negotiations with the co-owner failed and the latter refused the necessary consent; registration became impossible so D could not perform the second stage of the contract.

Since D did not fully perform its contractual obligations, C sued D for unfounded enrichment and demanded return of the whole pre-payment. The court held that D's obligations under the contract were severable and D had performed in part. Therefore, the part of the pre-payment which was pay for the first stage of the contract was not unfounded enrichment for D; the court recovered only 37,500 roubles from D, that is the total pre-payment (45,000 roubles) less the pay for performance of stage one (7,500 roubles).[65]

[64] Resolution of Federal Commercial Court of Moscow District of 1 June 2009 No KG-A40/4526-09.

[65] Resolution of Seventeenth Appellate Commercial Court of 19 December 2008 No A50-11198/2008.

VI PARTIAL PERFORMANCE

According to CC article 311:

> A creditor shall have a right not to accept the performance of an obligation in parts unless provided otherwise by a law, other legal acts, or by the conditions of the obligation and does not arise from the customs of business turnover or the essence of the obligation.[66]

This means that partial performance will not count as proper performance of part of an obligation unless and until it is accepted by the promisee. If they do not accept it as part-performance, the obligation will be considered to be not performed at all until it is performed fully, as in the following illustration.

> Company A concluded a contract for a direct loan from bank B, in order to buy a car. A's obligation to repay the loan was secured by surety agreements with company C and several individuals.
>
> According to CC article 367(3), 'A suretyship shall terminate if the creditor [promisee] has refused to accept proper performance offered by the debtor [promisor] or the surety'.[67] When A's outstanding debt to B still amounted to more than US$200,000, C offered B property worth approximately US$17,000 as partial performance of A's obligation. B refused.
>
> This led C to bring a case to terminate the suretyship contract. The court rejected C's claim on the following grounds. CC article 367(3) stipulates that a suretyship terminates only if the creditor has refused to accept proper performance offered by the surety. C offered only partial performance which, under the general rule, cannot be regarded as proper performance. Applying CC article 311, B was entitled to refuse to accept C's partial performance so the suretyship contract subsisted.[68]

This case also shows that a promisee's right not to accept partial performance (part payment) does not necessarily depend on the obligation being entire or severable. Even if the obligation is severable, as in the example (an obligation to pay money is always regarded as severable), a promisee/creditor still has a right under CC article 311 to refuse to accept partial performance.

VII RIGHT TO CURE BAD OR INCOMPLETE PERFORMANCE

The Russian Civil Code does not explicitly impose a general obligation on one party to accept the other's performance. However, this obligation is derived

[66] Butler, above n 2, at 244.
[67] Ibid 280.
[68] Resolution of Eleventh Appellate Commercial Court of 30 August 2011 No A55-1706/2011.

from other provisions in the Civil Code and is generally acknowledged by legal scholars.

It may surprise an English lawyer to find that the Civil Code also does not contain any general rule giving one party the right not to accept bad or incomplete performance (under Russian contract law, improper performance) nor (less surprisingly) the obligation to accept bad or incomplete performance (although special rules might apply, for example, for certain types of contract, or based on the parties' agreement). The general approach in the Civil Code, shown in its provisions on performance of particular contracts, is that a party is obliged to accept performance, whether proper or improper, unless:

(1) because of breach in relation to the time of performance, the promisee no longer has an interest in the outcome;
(2) one party has been specifically granted a right to refuse to accept bad or incomplete performance and they are exercising that right, or an equivalent right provided by law or by contract, unilaterally to refuse to accept contractual performance in full or in part; or
(3) the contract is terminated by a court due to a material breach by the other party (termination for material breach is discussed in Chapter 11 at p 269).

The absence in the Civil Code of a universal right for a promisee to refuse to accept bad or incomplete performance shows, once again, the orientation of Russian contract law towards actual performance (irrespective of quality).

A Loss of Interest in Performance

In keeping with the theme of very restricted rights to refuse performance, loss of interest in performance will only free a party from the obligation to accept bad or incomplete performance if it results from other party's performance being delayed.

According to CC article 405(2) 'If as a consequence of delay of the debtor the performance has lost interest for the promisee, he may refuse to accept performance and demand compensation of losses'.[69] In this case the promisor, in his turn, is relieved from performance of his obligation in kind (CC article 396(3)). A vivid example of the situation when the promisee is considered to have lost interest in performance is breach by the promisor of a 'strict deadline', as discussed above.

[69] Butler, above n 2, at 298.

B Explicit Right of the Promisee to Refuse to Accept Bad or Incomplete Performance

According to CC article 450(3) the right to refuse unilaterally to perform a contract in full or in part may be granted by a law or the contract itself. Such unilateral refusal to perform leads to termination of the contract, in full or in part.

Purchase-sale is a good example of a contract where one party may refuse to accept bad or incomplete performance from the other, by refusing to perform themselves or by exercising another right specifically provided by law. Under CC article 484(1), 'The purchaser shall be obliged to accept a good transferred to him except for instances when he has the right to demand the replacement of the good or to refuse performance of the contract of purchase-sale'.[70]

The buyer therefore has the right to choose either to refuse to perform the contract or to require the replacement of substandard goods by those of proper specifications, if there has been a material breach in relation to quality. Material breach of quality means the discovery of irremovable defects, defects which cannot be eliminated without incommensurate expense or expenditures of time, or manifest repeatedly, and other similar defects.

C Termination of Contract Due to Material Breach

Irrespective of the type of contract, any party may exercise their right to terminate due to a material breach by the other party. If a bad or incomplete performance meets the criteria for material breach, the non-breaching party may choose not to accept performance and apply to court for termination of the contract. Termination of contract due to material breach is further discussed in Chapter 11 at p 269.

VIII CONCLUSION

This chapter shows the extent to which the Civil Code and other laws regulate in detail proper performance and its elements. There are some general rules but what constitutes proper performance largely depends on the Civil Code provisions relating to particular types of contract. It is a peculiarity of Russian contract law that it takes a rather formalistic approach to the assessment of proper performance against the standard specified by law and/or in the contract. The standard of exercising 'reasonable care and skill' is hardly ever used in commercial contracts, because in Russian law it would only apply in consideration of

[70] Ibid 352.

the issue of fault, which does not arise in contracts linked to entrepreneurial activities.

Another interesting characteristic of Russian contract law is that it does not explicitly impose a general obligation on one party to accept the other's performance. Furthermore, the Civil Code also does not provide a general rule giving one party the right not to accept bad or incomplete performance. This feature of Russian contract law will be exemplified in greater detail in Chapter 10, on Remedies for Breach.

10

Remedies for Breach of Contract

I INTRODUCTION

It is generally accepted by Russian scholars that remedies for breach of contract are aimed to compensate the non-breaching party rather than punish the party in breach.[1] It follows that any remedies should correspond to the level of harm or loss caused. The ultimate role of liability for breach in Russian contract law is said to be restoration to the position in which the non-breaching party would have been had there been no breach in the first place. Award of remedies for breach should not lead to unfounded enrichment of the non-breaching party. These overall are the guiding principles.

However, unlike English law, Russian contract law is not always consistent with the declared fundamental compensatory principle. There are clear examples of deviation from it, including availability of a punitive penalty (штрафная неустойка; *shtrafnaia neustoika*) and also, irrespective of their actual loss, the non-breaching party's right to claim as lost revenue the amount the breaching party gained as a consequence of the breach.

Another important general principle in Russian contract law is that of full compensation for loss. This principle, unlike the general principle of the compensatory character of liability for breach, is explicitly expressed in the Civil Code (CC). CC article 15(1) declares that: 'A person whose right has been violated may demand full compensation of losses caused to him unless compensation of losses in a lesser amount has been provided for by a law or contract'.[2]

The possibility that a law or the contract itself may make an exception to the compensatory principle clearly indicates that the principle is not absolute. As shown below (at p 241), the Civil Code restricts the right to claim for full loss by limiting in some circumstances the quantum and types of losses for which damages may be claimed.

What makes Russian rules on liability for breach very unusual in comparison to English contract law – and supports the idea that the Russian legal system is

[1] See, eg MI Braginskii and VV Vitrianskii, *Договорное Право: Общая Часть* [Dogovornoe Pravo: Obshchaia Chast'; *Contract Law: General Part*] (Moscow, Statut, 2001) 610; VP Mozolin and AI Masliaev (eds), Гражданское Право. Часть Первая*:* Учебник [*Grazhdanskoe Pravo. Chast' Pervaia: Uchebnik*; *Civil Law. Part One: Text Book*] (Moscow, Iurist, 2005) 661.

[2] WE Butler, *The Civil Code of the Russian Federation Parts 1, 2 and 3: Parallel Russian and English Texts* (Moscow, JurInfoR-Press, 2008) 17.

part of the 'continental Romanist legal family' – is Russian law's focus on actual performance. In many instances the Civil Code provisions on liability for breach exemplify the fact that in Russia damages are not regarded as an equivalent substitute for proper performance, as they generally are in English law. As WE Butler succinctly put it, 'The Anglo-American concept of liquidated damages for non-performance of a contractual obligation does not exist in Russian law'.[3] We have already noted this feature of Russian contract law in our discussions on performance in Chapter 9 (at p 193). We will see, however, that in fact penalty (*neustoika*) can be somewhat analogous in effect.

Another important characteristic to note is that there are differential standards for liability for breach in Russian contract law depending on whether the parties are entrepreneurs or consumers, and their purpose in entering into the contract: whether for business or personal needs. In general Russian contract law imposes stricter requirements on entrepreneurs and is more protective of consumers.[4]

Otherwise, the different remedies for breach under Russian contract law are fairly similar to those offered by English law. The main remedies we discuss are:

- damages;
- penalty (неустойка; *neutsoika*), which despite its name is in many ways similar to liquidated damages in English law;[5] and
- required performance.

Other remedies such as restitutionary awards are not mentioned in the Civil Code nor in Russian academic commentary on contract law. Nevertheless Russian contract law does have other measures with a similar function to restitutionary awards. These will also be discussed below.

II DAMAGES

Damages are the most universal remedy for breach of contract in Russian contract law.

The right to compensation for losses suffered by the party whose rights have been breached is set out in CC article 15, quoted above;[6] Part 1 gives the right to 'demand full compensation'. The obligation of the breaching party to compensate for losses caused by the breach (by either improper performance or

[3] WE Butler, *Russian Law*, 3rd edn (Oxford, Oxford University Press, 2009) 406.

[4] See J Henderson, 'Entrepreneurs and Consumers as Subjects of Civil Law' in WB Simons (ed), *Private and Civil Law in the Russian Federation*, Law in Eastern Europe 59 (Leiden, Brill, 2009) 171.

[5] In English law, the distinction between unenforceable penalty clauses and perfectly valid liquidated damages clauses is a fine one which depends on construction of the exact contractual terms, and, in the light of the principle of freedom of contract, in recent times a 'broader approach' is prevailing; see *Murray v Leisureplay Plc* [2005] EWCA Civ 963 and discussion in E Peel, *Treitel: the Law of Contract*, 13th edn (London, Sweet and Maxwell, 2011) 1077.

[6] See above, text to n 2.

non-performance) is in CC article 393(1): 'A debtor [promisor] shall be obliged to compensate the creditor [promisee] for losses caused by the failure to perform or improper performance of an obligation'.[7] Since the obligation to compensate is specified in the Civil Code, it exists irrespective of whether or not it is mentioned in the contract.

A Conditions for Recovering Damages

Relying indirectly on CC articles 15 and 393 cited above,[8] the general rule developed through court practice for recovery of damages is that the claimant must prove:

(1) the fact of improper performance or non-performance of the contract (breach of contract) by the other party;
(2) the fact of the losses and their value; and
(3) a causal link between the breach and the losses.[9]

If any one of these elements is not proved, the court will reject the claim. These elements are considered to be absolutely necessary for liability for breach irrespective of the contract's type and purpose.

As already briefly mentioned in Chapter 9 (at p 202), there is another element for liability: fault of the breaching party. Unlike the three elements listed above as requirements, fault does not always have any legal significance in the context of liability for breach of contract. Fault is only relevant when the breach is committed by a party who has contracted other than in the course of entrepreneurial activity; if they act in the course of entrepreneurial activity, under CC article 401(3) they are subject to strict liability, so proof of any fault is not required. This is one example of the differential standards in Russian contract law depending on the purpose of the contractual relationship, whether in the course of business or not. As just noted, a party who breaches a contract concluded in the course of entrepreneurial activity is liable irrespective of fault. However, their liability is strict, not absolute. They can avoid liability, even if the party claiming damages proves all three necessary elements listed above, if they establish that proper performance was impossible as a consequence of force majeure.

Another important qualification to add in respect to the elements necessary for liability is that, in instances where fault is legally relevant, there is a presumption that it exists. It is, however, a rebuttable presumption. According to CC article 401(2), 'The absence of fault shall be proved by the person who violated the

[7] Butler, above n 2, at 290.

[8] See above, text to n 2 and n 7, respectively.

[9] See, eg Resolution of Federal Commercial Court of Volgo-Viatskii District of 4 April 2011 No 43-16599/2010; Resolution of Federal Commercial Court of Moscow District of 16 February 2011 No KG- 40/358-11,2; Ruling of Supreme Commercial Court of 27 December 2010 No VAS-17278/10.

obligation'.[10] This means that, in the case of breach of a non-entrepreneurial contract, once the claimant has satisfied the court about the three required elements, the defendant must prove their innocence of any fault to avoid liability for breach.

There is one other important element which is not traditionally considered by scholars to be necessary for the formation of liability for breach but is often treated as such by the courts: mitigation of losses by the party seeking damages. An obligation to mitigate is not explicitly provided in the Civil Code, neither is there any obligation on the claimant to prove that they have taken such measures in order to get damages for breach. Nevertheless, it is worth considering because in some cases, although the claimant has succeeded in proving all the necessary elements for other party's liability, their own failure to mitigate is taken by the court as a reason to reject their damages claim.

Each of these factors which affect a claimant's right to recover damages is discussed in more detail below.

(i) Breach

A breach of contract is any deviation from what is considered to be proper performance in a particular case. As discussed in Chapter 9 (at p 195), the Russian Civil Code distinguishes between two types of breach: non-performance and improper performance. The legal relevance of this distinction appears in the context of the Civil Code's regulation of the trade-off between the promisee's right to claim for losses and the promisor's obligation to provide actual performance. This was already briefly mentioned in Chapter 9 and is discussed below in greater detail on required performance (see p 251).

(ii) Causation

Under CC article 393(1), 'A debtor [promisor] shall be obliged to compensate the creditor [promisee] for losses caused by the failure to perform or improper performance of an obligation'.[11] This means that there must be a causal relationship between the losses and the breach.

In Russian legal theory there are a number of concepts of causation, none of which provides an 'exact formula' for establishing causation in a particular case. Legal scholars note that each of the concepts is right in its own way depending on the circumstances.[12] Thus none of them can be considered as prevailing.

The courts have not developed a single universal approach to establishing causation. Very often the courts do not refer to a particular concept of causation and simply make a statement based on the judges' inner conviction in relation to the presence or absence of causation in the case under consideration.

[10] Butler, above n 2, at 296.
[11] Ibid 290.
[12] Braginskii and Vitrianskii, above n 1, at 718; Mozolin and Masliaev, above n 1, at 667.

At the same time some courts, like their English counterparts, apply the concept of direct causation, saying that there should only be compensation of those losses which were the inevitable consequence of the breach (known in English law as the 'but for' approach).[13]

As the Seventeenth Appellate Commercial Court noted in one of its Resolutions,[14] only direct (immediate) causation between the breach and losses has legal relevance. Direct causation takes place when, in the chain of continually evolving events, there are no circumstances which have legal relevance for the purposes of civil liability between the breach and the losses; in other words, no *novus actus interveniens*.[15]

It is important to stress that the absence of proof of causation is one of the most common grounds for which Russian courts reject claims for damages. Of all the elements required for the formation of liability for breach, causation is the most difficult to prove in court. In our view the reason for this is the absence of any widely accepted rule for determining the presence or absence of causation, so that in each particular case the court proceeds from its own understanding of what causation is. Further, Russian law has not developed a concept of remoteness of damages to determine the issue of how far down the chain of causation legal liability should lie, which in English law, following *Hadley v Baxendale*[16] and later cases, depends on the foreseeability of the loss flowing from the original breach. This lack of developed sophisticated rules makes it very difficult to predict what the approach will be of a particular court defining and determining causation in a particular case. This makes it difficult to estimate the chance of recovering damages.

In some cases in the process of establishing the presence or absence of causation Russian courts apply similar reasoning to the causation and remoteness rules in English contract law, as in the following example.

> In concluding a contract to sell a plot of land to company V, City Administration A failed to inform V of an encumbrance on the plot of a public road on part of it. The purchase price for the land plot was 24,015,000 roubles. The land plot was sold at a public auction and the law requires that the auction announcement must contain information about any encumbrances on the land to be sold.
>
> Three months later V sold the plot to company S for 100,000,000 roubles on the condition that if it turned out to be encumbered in any way S could unilaterally terminate the contract and oblige V to return to them the 100,000,000 roubles and also pay a penalty of 25,000,000 roubles.
>
> S discovered that the land plot was encumbered, terminated the contract and recovered more than 125,000,000 roubles from V in court. V, in

[13] So-called because 'but for' the breach, the losses would not have occurred.
[14] Resolution of Seventeenth Appellate Commercial Court of 7 March 2012 No 17 AP-918/2012-GK.
[15] 'New intervening act'.
[16] (1854) 9 Exch 341.

turn, sued A for damages for breach of contract, claiming 108,770,416 roubles (75,985,000 lost revenue and 32,785,416 roubles 'real damage', that is, actual damage). (See below for discussion of this type of damage.)

The court rejected the claim on the grounds that, among other things, V did not prove causation. The court held that, between one party's breach and the losses of the other party whose rights have been breached, there should be direct (immediate) causation. In this case there was no direct causation because V's damages arose as a result of the sale of the land to S on conditions agreed between V and S. This contract was concluded by V in the course of entrepreneurial activity. Entrepreneurial activities are carried out at the entrepreneur's own risk. So the court concluded that V's losses were the result of entrepreneurial risk it had chosen to take and not due to A's breach. Besides, the court noted that, by the time V sold the land plot to S, V had been informed that the land plot was encumbered.[17]

Because A's failure to inform V about the encumbrance of the land plot was not the only cause of V's losses, there was no 'but for' causation in this case.

In contrast, in another case the court's reasoning, as far as causation is concerned, does not have anything to do with the concept of direct causation and seems to be somewhat random.

Company K sued an insurance company, C, for losses caused by late payment of the insurance indemnity following an occurrence of the insured event – a fire on a bus insured under the contract between K and C. The damages claimed comprised, among other things, the interest accrued on the amount of insurance indemnity as a result of its late payment, and K's lost revenue because C's late payment meant that the bus could not be repaired and used.

The court rejected the claim for damages. The court noted that K did not demonstrate how C's failure to pay the insurance indemnity had prevented K from repairing the bus. K was carrying out entrepreneurial activity as a bus company, with the intended aim of making a profit. Hence the insurance indemnity was not the only source of funds for K, and K should have been able to repair and put the bus back into use before the insurance indemnity was paid. With this in mind the court found no causation between C's failure to pay the insurance indemnity in a timely manner and K's inability to make a profit from use of the bus.[18]

[17] Resolution of Presidium of Supreme Commercial Court of 25 July 2011 No 1809/11.

[18] Resolution of Thirteenth Appellate Commercial Court of 28 January 2011 No A26-1360/2010. See also Resolution of Federal Commercial Court of the North-Western District of 26 May 2011 No A26-1360/2010.

In comparison to the previous case, here the court's focus has shifted from the causation itself to whether the claimant, K, can themselves avert the loss flowing from an event which was actually covered by K's insurance policy. As a result the court used rather perverse logic that the actual cause of K's losses was its failure to use its own funds to repair the bus. However, the whole aim of insurance is to indemnify for losses resulting from an insured event; an insurance policy is taken out specifically so that one does not have to use one's own funds to cover that event's adverse impact. It would be reasonable to foresee that, if an insurance indemnity has not been paid, the loss caused by the insured event (in this case, the bus being burnt, and therefore unusable) will not be compensated and with a high degree of probability this will lead to further losses (in this case, lost revenue because K was not able to use the bus in its business). So there is clearly a direct 'but for' causation between the delay in the insurance indemnity payment and K's losses. It appears that the court's reliance on lack of causation is difficult to sustain logically, whereas if there had been the development of a remoteness rule, then the court would have a stronger line of reasoning. Interestingly, in the leading English case of *Hadley v Baxendale* itself, Hadley's claim failed because the court decided that Baxendale would not have had in their contemplation that Hadley did not have the resources to have a spare mill-shaft, so Hadley's loss was too remote. This bears a strong analogy to the case above with K and C, where the court decided K should itself have had the resources to pay for the bus repairs.

Whilst we might find the reasoning in this case less than satisfactory, at least there was some explanation; in cases where the court concludes that actually there was causation, it frequently fails to give any reasoning at all. As a rule, the court simply states that causation was proved, without any further justification. This impedes the development of any clear basis on which to predict the outcome of cases where causation might be the main issue.

(iii) Amount of Damages

Another element in the formation of liability for breach which the claimant needs to prove is the exact value of their losses. Unlike their English counterparts, Russian courts are not entitled by law to determine the quantum of damages themselves, even when clear causation and loss have been proved. As a result the courts are forced to reject claims for damages if there is no proof of the exact value of the losses. The Supreme Commercial Court emphasised this in a case in 2011.[19] It held that where the claimant suing for damages did not prove the exact amount of loss, Russian law does not entitle the court to determine the quantum of damages at its own discretion. The fact that the exact amount of incurred losses had not been proved was grounds for rejecting the damages claim. Thus the theoretical right to compensation through damages was not protected.

[19] Ruling of Supreme Commercial Court of 14 January 2011 No VAS-17787/10.

Draft Amendments to the Civil Code contain a provision aimed at correcting this unfair situation. Under draft article 393(5),[20] the value of losses subject to compensation should be determined with a reasonable degree of certainty. However, the court may not reject a claim for damages for non-performance or improper performance of an obligation on the sole ground that the exact amount of losses cannot be determined with a reasonable degree of certainty. In that case the amount of damages 'shall be determined by the court with a view to all the circumstances of the case and proceeding from the principle of fairness and proportionality of liability to the committed breach of contract'.[21]

(iv) Fault

As mentioned above, fault only has legal relevance in the context of compensation by damages for breach of contract if:

(1) the breaching party was not contracting in the course of carrying out entrepreneurial activity; or
(2) it is explicitly provided by law or by the contract that a party is liable for breach of contract if it was at fault for committing it.

As an example of this second qualification, article 19 of the Statute on Railway Transport of the Russian Federation[22] makes consignors of cargo, recipients of cargo, carriers and owners of railway infrastructures liable for losses which arise in the process of carriage in connection with emergency situations which occur through their fault.

As noted above (at p 202) in cases where fault does have legal relevance, there is a presumption of fault in contractual breach. This presumption is set out in CC article 401(2),[23] which places the burden of proof of the fact that the breach was purely accidental on the breaching party themselves. In the light of this presumption it is logical that the Civil Code does not define fault as such, but, on the contrary, defines the absence of fault. Under CC article 401(1):

> The person shall be deemed to be not at fault if with that degree of concern and attentiveness which is required of him according to the character of the obligation and conditions of turnover he has taken all measures for proper performance of the obligation.[24]

Whether the breaching party has taken all measures for proper performance is determined by the courts on a case-by-case basis.

[20] Draft Federal Law on Amendments to Parts One, Two, Three and Four of the Civil Code No 47538-6 approved by the State Duma (lower chamber of Russian Parliament) at first hearing on 27 April 2012 art 1 para 196(c).

[21] Ibid.

[22] Federal Law of 10 January 2003 No 18-FZ on the Statute of Rail Transport of the Russian Federation.

[23] See above, text to n 10.

[24] Butler, above n 2, at 296.

The courts have developed a common approach for certain categories of cases. For example, in relation to organisations financed from the state or municipal budget which breach by failing to pay after the other party has provided contractual performance, the courts will decide if the breach was caused by the insufficiency of the funds the organisation had received from the relevant state or municipal agency. In 2006 the Supreme Commercial Court set out the approach to be taken in this type of case. The Court said that:

> applying CC Article 401 in cases where a state or municipal institution (учреждение; *uchrezhdenie*) would be held liable for the breach of a monetary obligation, courts should bear in mind that the lack of funds at the disposal of the institution cannot be considered by itself as absolving it; the institution could not have taken 'all measures for proper performance with that degree of concern and attentiveness which is required of [it] according to the character of the obligation and conditions of turnover.'[25] Therefore, lack of funding of a state or municipal institution without more would not be evidence of absence of fault so a ground for relief from its liability, following CC Article 401(1).[26]

This is a very important opinion of the Supreme Commercial Court. In Russia there are still many state or municipally owned organisations (state and municipal institutions, государственные и муниципальные учреждения; *gosudarstvennye i munitsipalnye uchrezhdeniia*) which do not themselves have ownership of their assets. Instead they have a right less than ownership ('economic jurisdiction' or 'operative management'; see chapter 19 in the Civil Code[27]) which gives them the right to use assets provided by their owner, which is the State or a municipality. Nevertheless in certain circumstances these institutions enter into commercial contracts on an equal footing to other legal entities. It has been an unfortunate but frequent occurrence that a state or municipal institution has made a contract, accepted the other party's performance but then failed to pay because it had not received the necessary funds from the state or municipal budget. When sued for damages, the institution would raise as a defence an absence of fault, saying that the processing of their state or municipal funding is beyond their control. The Supreme Commercial Court opinion is aimed at ending this practice and protecting the interests of the counterparties in these situations.

The approach to determining an absence of fault in other cases is illustrated in the following example.

> Mr A sold to Mrs B an apartment, Apartment 1, in St Petersburg. A duly transferred it to B, and B registered her ownership rights to it. At the same

[25] The wording from CC art 401(1).

[26] Resolution of Plenum of the Supreme Commercial Court of 22 June 2006 No 21 'On Some Issues of Practice of Consideration by Commercial Courts of Disputes with the Participation of State and Municipal Institutions in connection with the Application of Article 120 of the Civil Code' para 8.

[27] Butler, above n 2, at 234–9.

> time B concluded with Mr C a preliminary contract of sale of her old apartment, Apartment 2, under which she bound herself to conclude in the future a contract of sale of Apartment 2 to C.[28] However, B then in fact sold her Apartment 2 to Mr D, with the idea that she would use the proceeds of that sale to pay A for her newly purchased Apartment 1.
>
> Before D had paid B for Apartment 2, C brought court proceedings against B demanding execution of their preliminary contract. The court ruled that Apartment 2 should be sequestered pending the resolution of C's claim. As a result, B did not receive D's payment for Apartment 2, and her payment to A for Apartment 1 was seriously delayed. A sued B, seeking to terminate their contract and also claiming damages. In defence, B argued that she was not at fault for breach of contract because it was caused by D's non-performance of his obligation to pay for Apartment 2.
>
> The court concluded that B did not take all necessary 'measures for proper performance' of her obligation to pay A for Apartment 1, with 'that degree of concern and attentiveness which is required of [her] according to the character of the obligation and conditions of turnover', under CC article 401(1). In relying on receiving the money from D, B should have realised that her obligation to A was not conditional on her contractual relations with D, to which A was not privy. Moreover, B having entered into a preliminary contract with C for the future sale to him of her Apartment 2, if she acted with due concern she should have realised that C might sue to enforce the preliminary contract. Thus B took a risk when she made the contract with D and relied on its performance to be able to pay A. Taking this into account the court held that B was at fault for non-performance of her obligation to A.[29]

In a sense the court is applying the standard of a reasonably prudent person in assessing whether behaviour is free of fault. In this case, B showed unwarranted recklessness, given the overall situation.

(v) Duty to Mitigate Damages

Unlike English contract law, Russian contract law does not explicitly impose a duty on the non-breaching party to mitigate their losses. That lack sometimes allows that party to act in bad faith and not take any reasonable and practicable steps to avoid or minimise their loss. However, this deficiency in legislation has now been remedied by court practice. The courts cite a duty to mitigate as one of the necessary preconditions for a claim for damages. For example, the First Appellate Commercial Court held that a party claiming damages must prove not only the fact of breach by the counterparty, the existence and amount of

[28] For discussion of preliminary contracts, see Chapter 4 at p 105.
[29] Ruling of City Court of St Petersburg of 8 November 2011 No 33-16625/2011.

losses and the causal link between the committed breach and the losses, but also that they took all measures within their control to prevent (mitigate) losses.[30]

The courts derive the duty to mitigate from CC article 404. Part 1 of this article gives a court:

> the right to reduce the amount of responsibility of the debtor [promisor] if the creditor [promisee] has intentionally or through negligence facilitated the increase of the amount of losses caused by the failure to perform or improper performance, or has not taken reasonable measures to reduce them.[31]

This rule applies where a party by virtue of a law or the contract is liable irrespective of fault for non-performance or improper performance of an obligation.

As can be seen, the text of the article does not explicitly impose any duty on the non-breaching party to mitigate their losses, so it does not follow directly from this article that mitigation is one of the necessary preconditions to claim compensation through damages. Moreover, it only gives a court the right to reduce the level of damages but not to deprive the non-breaching party completely of the right to claim damages even though they have failed to mitigate.

The courts' reasoning applying their interpretation of CC article 404 is demonstrated in the following case.

> Company K concluded a contract of purchase-sale with a state institution, G, under which K would supply G with rye flour. Later G informed K that it wanted to terminate the contract and asked K not to deliver any more flour, because G had not received enough funding from the state budget to pay for it. As a result K did not deliver over 100 tons of flour. After the best-before date had expired and the flour was destroyed as completely unusable K sued G for damages amounting to the price of the wasted flour.
>
> The court rejected K's claim, referring to CC article 404(1). It held that G had informed K on numerous occasions of the impossibility of G's further performance. From the moment when the contract period with G ended on 30 September 2002 until the expiration of the flour's best-before date on 20 February 2003, K did not take any steps to prevent losses. K only concluded a further contract to sell flour to another buyer in May 2003. K must have known that the date of production of the flour was August 2002 and it was only good for six months. Hence, the cause of K's losses was actually its own inaction and failure to take reasonable measures to reduce the loss. On these grounds the court released G from any obligation to compensate K. In its reasoning the court also mentioned the absence of causation between G's actions and K's losses.[32]

[30] Resolution of First Appellate Commercial Court of 29 September 2011 No A43-6483/2011. See also Ruling of Supreme Commercial Court of 21 February 2012 No A40-35066/10-1-202.

[31] Butler, above n 2, at 298.

[32] Resolution of Federal Commercial Court of the Volgo-Viatskii District of 29 January 2004 No A39-1837/2003-112/8.

This example is also a good illustration of how the duty to mitigate is linked to the concept of direct causation. In order to obtain compensation the claimant had to prove direct causation between the breach and their loss, so it could be argued that the breach only caused those losses which could not be alleviated by the non-breaching party through mitigation. As the Seventeenth Appellate Commercial Court noted in one of its Resolutions, as a general rule only those losses should be compensated which could not have been prevented by the actions of the non-breaching party.[33]

However, this reasoning would not give grounds to reject completely all claims for damages. For example, if in the above case the court had based its decision only on the absence of causation it should at least have considered the price at which K could have sold its flour to a third party and the difference between that and the contract price with G. The market price of flour at the time of breach might have been lower than the contract price. The losses to K caused directly by the breach of contract would then be the difference between the two.

It is not always the case that a court referring to CC article 404 will deprive a claimant of the total sum of damages claimed if he or she has not taken measures to mitigate loss. For example, the Federal Commercial Court of Povolzhskii District in one of its Resolutions[34] held that according to CC article 404(1), failure to take reasonable steps to reduce losses may be grounds for reduction of the damages awarded, but would not completely exonerate the party in breach.

Unfortunately there is currently no consensus in the courts on the question of which party has the burden of proving whether or not there was reasonable mitigation. In the case of First Appellate Commercial Court, mentioned above,[35] the court imposed on the claimant the burden of proof that they had tried to mitigate, as did the Ninth Appellate Commercial Court in one of its Resolutions.[36] Meanwhile the Federal Commercial Court of Povolzhskii District in its Resolution[37] imposed on the defendant the burden of proving the possible reasonable measures which the claimant could have taken to reduce their loss.

B Types of Damages Claimed

Russian contract law distinguishes between two types of loss: that caused by 'real damage' (actual damage), and that caused by lost revenue. The definition of these losses as well as the difference between them is in CC article 15(2). There, real damage is defined as 'expenses which the person whose right has

33 Resolution of Seventeenth Appellate Commercial Court of 7 March 2012 No 17AP-918/2012-GK.

34 Resolution of Federal Commercial Court of Povolzhskii District of 30 October 2008 No A55-18322/07.

35 See above, text to n 30.

36 Resolution of Ninth Appellate Commercial Court of 11 October 2011 No 09AP-25477/2011-GK.

37 See above, text to n 34.

been violated made or must make in order to restore the violated right, loss or damage of his property'.[38] Lost revenue is defined as 'revenues not received which this person would have received under ordinary conditions of civil turnover if his right had not been violated (lost advantage)'.[39]

The non-breaching party may claim either or both of these types of loss; they are not mutually exclusive. The legal definition of the two types of loss along with court practice in relation to them leads to the conclusion that damages under Russian contract law in general correspond to the English concepts of the 'cost of the cure' and expectation damages, that is, the cost of restoring as far as possible to the *status quo ante* and damages to cover the loss of profit which would have been made had the contract been carried out.

As far as an equivalent of the English reliance damages, that is, losses caused by the cost of entering into the contract, is concerned, the situation is different. As we have just seen, CC article 15(2) does not explicitly assert the claimant has a right to sue for the costs to them of performing the contract in reliance on the other party's proper performance. Moreover, the literal interpretation of this article appears to say that the non-breaching party's costs in performing their side of the contract are not considered as losses at all and cannot be recovered. However, in practice the courts do consider such costs to be claimable losses. This is most commonly in cases where the non-breaching party would have been entitled by law to refuse unilaterally to perform their contractual obligations because of the other party's breach. As discussed in Chapter 11 at p 273 this would have led to discharge of the contract. The following is an example of a court allowing a claim for the cost of the contract.

> The Federal Commercial Court of North-Western District held that a contract of independent work had not been performed due to the fault of the contractor, company A, therefore the client, individual entrepreneur P, had the right under CC article 715(2)[40] to refuse to perform their own obligations under the contract and also claim for compensation. It should be noted that CC article 715 does not clarify which type of damages can be claimed as compensation and does not limit their amount.
>
> The court concluded that P's losses amounted to his costs in connection with the performance of his obligations under the contract, namely his pre-payment to A and the cost of equipment provided to A under the contract, and that he was entitled to compensation of that amount.[41]

[38] Butler, above n 2, at 17.

[39] Ibid.

[40] Ibid 500–1: 'If the independent work contractor does not embark upon the timely performance of the contract of independent work or fulfils the work so slowly that the ending thereof within the period clearly becomes impossible, the customer shall have the right to repudiate performance of the contract and require compensation of losses'.

[41] Resolution of Federal Commercial Court of the North-Western District of 25 July 2005 No 05-9678/04-24.

The following is another illustration.

> The Presidium of the Supreme Commercial Court, upholding a claim for costs incurred in the course of performance of a contract, referred to CC article 453(5), which regulates the 'Consequences of Change of and Dissolution of a Contract' but leaves unclear what type and quantum of losses can be compensated: 'If a material violation of the contract by one of the parties has served as the grounds for change or the dissolution of a contract, the other party shall have the right to demand compensation of losses caused by the change or the dissolution of the contract'.[42]
>
> The Supreme Commercial Court noted that the contract was terminated due to the contractor's late performance of his obligation to complete the construction of a heat pipeline. As a result the other party had the right to compensation for its losses caused by the termination of the contract, in this case, the money transferred as a pre-payment.[43]

Under English law, this case might be classified as 'total failure of consideration'[44] giving rise to restitution rather than damages for a reliance loss; however, in neither of the cases discussed do the Russian courts give any actual explanation of how awarding compensation for the costs to the non-breaching party of its contractual performance fits within the general definition of damages in CC article 15. The courts simply appear to decide on the basis of their inner belief and conception of justice, interpreting the rather narrowly worded Civil Code provisions on damages in a broad way.

Some of the provisions in Part Two of the Civil Code on particular types of contracts explicitly provide that, when the Civil Code grants to one party the right to terminate a contract unilaterally irrespective of whether the other party has breached, the non-breaching party is entitled to compensation for costs incurred in connection with actions relating to contractual performance.[45] For example, according to CC article 782(1), 'The customer shall have the right to refuse performance of a contract of compensated rendering of services on condition of payment to the provider of services of expenses actually incurred by him'.[46] The Supreme Commercial Court clarified that under this provision all necessary costs of the service provider should be compensated, including costs incurred in connection with services which have not yet been provided at the point the contract is terminated.[47] Such costs can, for example, include payment

[42] Butler, above n 2, at 327.

[43] Resolution of Presidium of the Supreme Commercial Court of 19 August 1997 No 2348/97. See also Resolution of Seventh Appellate Commercial Court of 29 October 2008 No 07AP-5232/08(2).

[44] As in *Fibrosa Spolka Akcyjna v Fairbairn Combe Barbour Ltd* [1943] AC 32.

[45] For further discussion of such terminations, see Chapter 11.

[46] Butler, above n 2, at 549.

[47] Informational Circular of Presidium of the Supreme Commercial Court of 21 December 2005 No 104 'Review of Practice of Application by Commercial Courts of the Norms of the Civil Code of the Russian Federation on Particular Grounds for Termination of Obligations' para 2.

to subcontractors hired to perform the contract. These costs should be distinguished from the price for services actually provided.

The costs incurred by one party in the case of a unilateral termination of the contract by the other are not mentioned in either of the Civil Code provisions dealing with damages.[48] This is logical because one of the necessary conditions for compensation for loss through damages is breach of contract. However, in these termination cases the right unilaterally to dissolve the contract is given to one party independent of any breach by the other. Therefore, there are no grounds for compensation. At the same time, it is evident that apart from the fact that they are compensated irrespective of any breach, these costs are analogous to reliance losses as recognised in English contract law.

(i) 'Real' (Actual) Damage

As mentioned above, 'real damage' constitutes 'expenses which the person whose right has been violated made or must make in order to restore the violated right, loss or damage of his property'.[49] This is similar to the 'cost of the cure' claims in English contact law.[50]

Both the Supreme Commercial Court and the Supreme Court have clarified that real damage includes not only expenses that have already been borne, but also those which the party will have to bear in the future in order to restore its violated right.[51] The claimant has to prove the necessity of these expenses, and provide a reasoned calculation to justify their estimated amount. Such proof may, for example, be provided in the form of an estimate of the cost of eliminating defects in the goods, works or services.

Unlike expenses which the non-breaching party will have to bear in the future, expenses which have already been borne cannot be proved simply by a calculation or estimate. As the Federal Commercial Court of the East-Siberian District rightfully noted, the civil law currently in force does not allow for proof of the amount of actual losses by an estimate or calculation. When a claimant provided evidence in that form, the court held that the value of the loss had not been proved.[52]

Appropriate proof of actual expenses could be, for instance, documents showing payment of the particular amount to a relevant third party, as in the following example.

[48] CC arts 15 and 393; see above, text to n 2 and n 7, respectively.

[49] See above n 38 and accompanying text.

[50] See Peel, above n 5, at 1010.

[51] Resolution of Plenum of the Supreme Court of the Russian Federation No 6; Resolution of Supreme Commercial Court No 8 of 1 July 1996 'On Particular Issues connected with Application of Part One of the Civil Code of the Russian Federation' para 10.

[52] Resolution of Federal Commercial Court of the Central District of 10 June 2010 No F10-2150/10.

> In a case adjudicated by the Federal Commercial Court of the West-Siberian District, P, an individual entrepreneur, transferred to company S his hydraulic hammer for a week of testing, with the purpose of selling it to S after the testing. However, S did not return P's hammer at the end of the week. Instead S used it, without following the rules for its operation, for four months in winter conditions. After the broken hammer was returned to P, he had it repaired and then claimed that expense from S. P successfully proved the extent of his actual expenses by documents evidencing payment to a third party for repairs, payments to the driver who transported the hammer to the repair site and postal expenses.[53]

In another case the amount of real damage in the form of the cost of replacement spare parts for a damaged excavator was proved by appropriate documents, including an inspection report and invoices covering the cost of the spare parts.[54] 'Cost of the cure' is thus quite broadly interpreted.

In certain cases the term 'real damage' is also broadly interpreted by both the courts of general jurisdiction and the commercial courts. A vivid illustration of this is the qualification of loss of commercial value (утрата товарной стоимости; *utrata tovarnoi stoimosti*) by a vehicle as real damage. The Supreme Commercial Court held that loss of commercial value is the reduction in the value of a vehicle caused by the premature deterioration of its exterior appearance and functional performance as a result of a traffic accident and subsequent repair. Hence, it can be qualified as real damage.[55] From this definition of 'loss of commercial value' it is clear that it had nothing to do with the vehicle owner's expenses in restoring the vehicle; neither did it constitute the physical damage to the vehicle. In court the measure of a vehicle's loss of commercial value can be proved by expert testimony.[56]

(ii) Lost Revenue

According to CC article 15(2), lost revenue is defined as 'revenues not received which the person whose right has been violated would have received under ordinary conditions of civil turnover if his right had not been violated (lost advantage)'.[57] CC article 393(4) specifies that 'When determining lost advantage

[53] Resolution of Federal Commercial Court of West-Siberian District of 7 June 2007 No F04-3122/2007 (34368-A45-8).

[54] Resolution of Federal Commercial Court of Volgo-Viatskii District of 12 October 2011 No A79-9077/2010.

[55] Resolution of Presidium of the Supreme Commercial Court of 19 December 2006 No 9045/06. For an example of the same approach of the Supreme Court, see para 12 of the Summary of Court Practice connected with Voluntary Insurance of Individuals' Property (approved by the Presidium of the Supreme Court on 30 January 2013).

[56] See Resolution of Federal Commercial Court of Moscow District of 16 December 2011 No A40-48079/11-43-271; Resolution of Federal Commercial Court of Povolzhskii District of 7 April 2011 No A12-17822/2010.

[57] See above n 39.

the measures undertaken by the creditor [promisee] to receive it and the preparations made for this purpose shall be taken into account'.[58]

The Supreme Court and the Supreme Commercial Court in a joint Resolution provided some additional guidelines for the determination of lost revenue.[59] The courts pointed out that the amount of profit not received (lost revenue) should be determined taking into account reasonable costs which the promisee would have borne if the obligation has been performed. In particular, in a claim for lost revenue caused by non-delivery of raw materials or component parts, the amount of such profit should be calculated on the basis of the sale price of the finished articles, as specified in any contracts with those buying them, less the price of the non-delivered raw materials or component parts, transportation costs, and other costs connected with the production of the finished articles.

Even though this joint Resolution shed further light on the meaning of lost revenue and the requirements to prove it, the uncertainty around the broad expression in article 15(2) of 'ordinary market conditions', combined with the obligation to prove the particular measures that had been and would be taken to overcome the loss, make it extremely difficult for a claimant to prove in court the fact that they have suffered lost revenue and its value, as the following case illustrates.

> In a case adjudicated by the Supreme Commercial Court, Mrs R, an individual entrepreneur, sued company B for lost revenue caused by B's late return of premises it rented from R. The court held that the person claiming lost revenue must specifically prove the fact that they had undertaken measures to obtain the supposed profit and preparations made for that purpose. Also, in evaluating the amount of lost revenue, it is of primary importance to determine the certainty of whatever profits the claimant might gain under ordinary market conditions.
>
> The courts at all instances concluded that R did not prove the amount of lost revenue. In particular, she did not provide convincing evidence of the fact that, had B vacated her premises on time, she would have *a real possibility* of gaining through her use of the premises the level of profit she was claiming from B.[60]

A good example of a rare case where the court upheld a claim for lost revenue is the following.[61]

[58] Butler, above n 2, at 291.

[59] Resolution of Plenum of the Supreme Court of the Russian Federation No 6; Resolution of Supreme Commercial Court No 8 of 1 July 1996 'On Particular Issues connected with Application of Part One of the Civil Code of the Russian Federation' para 10.

[60] Ruling of Supreme Commercial Court of 26 December 2011 No VAS-16783/11.

[61] Resolution of Federal Commercial Court of Volgo-Viatskii District of 12 October 2011 No 79-9077/2010.

> Under a contract company B undertook to provide company P with an excavator and driver to carry out work on a particular road construction site. P kept the excavator beyond the contractual period. B sued P for lost revenue caused by this unjustified retention, which lasted almost two years.
>
> The court held that in order to recover lost revenue the claimant had to prove what profits it would realistically (certainly) have received, if it had not been deprived of the possibility of renting the excavator to another company under ordinary market conditions. The court clarified that the term 'ordinary market conditions' means typical conditions in the functioning market, not affected by unforeseen circumstances or circumstances that would be force majeure. The court added that the claimant should also prove that the breach had been the only obstacle preventing them from gaining the lost revenue. In this case, following a forensic investigation initiated by the court, it accepted an independent expert's calculation as evidence of B's lost revenue.

In another case, where the claimant was not able to carry out its normal business because of the defendant's breach of contract, the quantity of lost revenue was calculated on the basis of the average monthly income for the previous eight months' business in accordance with its income and expenditure ledger as certified by the tax authority. The Federal Court of West-Siberian District upheld a claim for lost revenue calculated using this method.[62]

It is very important to stress that these cases, where claims for compensation of lost revenue were upheld by the courts, are exceptional. In most cases the courts reject without further consideration any claims for lost revenue with the justification that profit was lost and its amount had not been sufficiently proved.

(iii) Disgorgement of Profits by the Breaching Party

CC article 15(2) provides in its second paragraph that:

> If the person who has violated a right has received revenues as a consequence thereof, the person whose right was violated shall have the right to demand compensation together with the other losses, for lost advantage in an amount not less than such revenues.[63]

So, unlike English law, Russian contract law allows the non-breaching party to sue for disgorgement of any profits gained by the other party from their breach. It follows from a literal interpretation of this provision that a claimant seeking compensation for lost revenue to the extent of revenue gained by the breaching party does not have to prove that they would themselves have made that profit

[62] Resolution of Federal Commercial Court of West-Siberian District of 26 May 2010 No A45-21484/2009.

[63] Butler, above n 2, at 17–18.

had the breach not occurred. The other rules discussed in the previous section relating to proof of lost revenue also seem not to be applicable here; proving the fact that the breaching party made a certain gain is enough to sustain a claim. This position has been supported by some courts; for example, the Thirteenth Appellate Commercial Court affirmed that, if a claimant is suing for lost revenue equal to the breaching party's gain, he can establish the amount not on the basis of his own loss but as the value of the breaching party's profit; he does not have to prove that he would have been able make that amount of profit himself, nor that he took any steps towards acquiring it.[64]

However, the courts are unfortunately inconsistent in their opinions on this. In another case the Sixth Appellate Commercial Court held that the special rule of CC article 15(2) sets the minimum amount of lost revenue recoverable, provided the claimant actually proved that they incurred some lost revenue.

> Company V claimed from the Russian Railways, R, lost revenue to the amount of freight charges which R received through their illegitimate use of V's railway carriages. The court held that V did not prove that the loss of its possession of the railway carriages due to R's fault negated the possibility that it might make some profit from the use of the carriages. The fact that R received certain freight charges for carrying containers in V's railway carriages could not be evidence of the possibility that V would have made the same profit. R's receipt of the freight charges resulted from it undertaking carriage of goods by railway. However, V did not carry out such activity and so did not receive any freight charges. The court also pointed out that V did not provide any proof of the possibility that it might have made any profit from its carriages had R not been using them, including contracts with third parties, or other documents showing preparations for the carriages' use for the purpose of making a profit during the relevant period.[65]

In this case, then, the court made it clear that it required the equivalent evidence of lost revenue, as discussed above, before it would take into account any gains by R as being illegitimately acquired profits which should therefore be disgorged to V.

The courts' inconsistency in dealing with claims for lost revenue is unfortunate, especially in the light of the apparent clarity of the provision of CC article 15(2).[66]

[64] Resolution of Thirteenth Appellate Commercial Court of 6 August 2009 No A33-8599/2008-03AP-807/2009.

[65] Resolution of Sixth Appellate Commercial Court of 28 May 2010 No 06AP-2011/2010.

[66] See above, text to n 63.

C Limitation of Damages

In the Introduction to this chapter it was pointed out that one of the principles of civil liability for breach of contract in Russia is that damages should fully compensate for losses. It was also noted that the right to full compensation is not absolute and can be limited by provisions in a law or the contract. In this section we will explain these limitations in more detail.

(i) Limitation of Damages by Law

The possibility of limitation of damages by a law is provided in CC articles 15(1) and 400(1). The former allows the general possibility of limiting damages.[67] The latter explains that 'The right to full compensation of loss may be limited (limited responsibility) by a law with regard to individual types of obligations and with regard to obligations connected with the determined nature of activity'.[68]

Damages can be limited by law in two different ways. First, a cap can be set on the level of damages which can be claimed in a particular case; secondly, the law may limit the claimant to only one of the two types of damages, that is, real damage (see above).

An example of first type of limitation can be found in CC article 717, which limits the loss caused to a contractor by a client terminating a contract for independent work. According to this article, the client is obliged to compensate the contractor's losses 'within the limits of the difference between the price determined for all of the work and the part of the price paid for the work fulfilled'.[69] Thus damages may not exceed the total contract price.

A cap on the amount of damages claimed for breach may also be set at an absolute value. For example, an air carrier is liable for full or partial loss or damage to baggage, cargo and cabin luggage, up to the amount of their value but limited to 600 roubles per kilo of baggage or cargo.[70]

The second way of limiting damages – by restricting the type of claimable loss to 'real damage' (see above) – can be illustrated by the following Civil Code provisions. CC article 547(1) specifies that 'In instances of non-performance or improper performance of obligations under a contract of electric power supply, the party who has violated the obligation shall be obliged to compensate the real damage caused by this ([as defined in] article 15(2))'.[71] Similarly, under CC article 573(3), 'If the contract of gift was concluded in written form, the donor shall have the right to demand from the donee compensation of real damage

[67] See above, text to n 2.
[68] Butler, above n 2, at 295–6.
[69] Ibid 503.
[70] Air Code of the Russian Federation of 19 March 1997 No 60-FZ art 119.
[71] Butler, above n 2, at 403. See above, text to n 38 for the text of CC art 15(2).

caused by the refusal to accept the gift'.[72] CC article 692 provides that in a contract of uncompensated use, 'If the lender does not transfer a thing to the loan recipient, the last has the right to require dissolution of the contract of uncompensated use and compensation of real damage incurred by him'.[73]

The motivation for these statutorily-imposed limitations probably depends on the context. It is likely that limitation of damages in a contract of electric power supply to the amount of real damage is aimed to protect the supplier from large and unforeseeable losses which purchasers of electric power may incur; loss of profit is excluded and only the 'cost of the cure' covered. In the other two examples, of a contract of gift and a contract of uncompensated use, the limitation can be explained by the fact that both contracts are without compensation (see p 117) and have a strictly non-commercial nature so damages are kept within clear bounds.

(ii) Limitation of Damages by Contract

As noted earlier, the possibility of limiting the amount of damages by contract is specified in CC article 15(1).[74] It should be stressed that in their contract the parties may only limit the amount of damages, but are not allowed to agree to exclude completely compensation for loss. This was exemplified in a case adjudicated by the Eighteenth Appellate Commercial Court.

> The parties to a contract of independent construction work included in the contract a term excluding any liability of either party for breach of contract. The court rightly referred to CC article 9(2), under which 'The refusal of citizens and juridical persons [legal entities] to effectuate rights belonging to them shall not entail the termination of those rights except for instances provided for by a law'.[75] The court held that the parties' right to claim damages is granted to them by CC article 15; under this article they only have a right to agree on the reduction of the amount of damages, not their complete avoidance.[76]

It is relatively common to limit damages to the value of the total contract price or less, such as 10 per cent of the price.[77]

Although the Civil Code allows parties to agree to limit the amount of damages, it also imposes some restrictions. In particular, there are two very important exclusions to contractual limitation of damages:

[72] Ibid 420. As cases applying this provision would be heard at a low level in the courts of general jurisdiction, reports are unavailable and it is hard to say how often this happens.

[73] Butler, above n 2, at 486.

[74] See above, text to n 2.

[75] Butler, above n 2, at 14.

[76] Resolution of Eighteenth Appellate Commercial Court of 11 September 2009 No 18AP-7221/2009.

[77] Resolution of 28 March 2012 No 09AP-5539/2012-GK.

(1) CC article 400(2) protects a consumer who has acceded to a standard form contract (contract of adhesion) 'or other contract in which a citizen acting as a consumer is a creditor [promisee]'.[78] Such contract: 'may not limit the amount of damages for breach if the amount of responsibility for the particular type of obligations or for the particular violation has been determined by a law and if the agreement [limiting damages] was concluded before the circumstances ensue which entail responsibility for the failure to perform or the improper performance of the obligation'.[79] In other words, a dominant party contracting with a consumer is not allowed to evade their full contractual liability as set out in legislation by including a limitation clause. An agreement limiting liability of the dominant party for breach may be concluded only after the circumstances entailing such liability occur.
(2) Parties are not allowed to limit damages for intentional breach (CC article 401(4)).

In both cases, any contractual terms which purport to limit the damages available for breach are void and have no legal force.

III PENALTY (НЕУСТОЙКА; *NEUSTOIKA*)

As well as damages, in Russian contract law there is a separate head of liability for breach of contract, that is, penalty (неустойка; *neustoika*). However, unlike damages, which do not need to be mentioned in the contract in order to be available, *neustoika* can only be claimed in a particular case if the possibility to do so is specified in a law or the contract.

According to CC article 330(1):

> A penalty (fine, forfeit) [*neustroika*, штраф; *shtraf*, пеня; *penia*] . . . [is] a monetary amount determined by a law or by contract which the debtor [promisor] is obliged to pay to the creditor [promisee] in the event of the failure to perform or the improper performance of an obligation, in particular in the event of the delay of performance.[80]

Provisions on *neustoika* are included in the chapter of the Civil Code on securing performance of obligations as well as in the chapter on liability for breach (on this, see Chapter 9 at p 212). This dual placement indicates that *neustoika* is regarded as being simultaneously a means to secure performance and a form of liability for breach. The general opinion of legal scholars is that before a contract is breached *neustoika*'s function is to secure proper performance, but as soon as breach occurs, *neustoika* becomes a form of liability for that breach.

[78] Butler, above n 2, at 296.
[79] Ibid.
[80] Ibid 254.

A *Neustoika* and the Concept of Liquidated Damages

In principle *neustoika* is very close to the common law concept of liquidated damages. However, there are some differences, discussed below, the most important of which is that as noted *neustoika* may not only be compensatory but also punitive.

Neustoika is often understood by courts as a pre-estimated measure of the loss likely to be caused by a particular breach of contract. This makes it very similar to liquidated damages. This characteristic of *neustoika* is well illustrated by the courts' interpretation of contractual terms providing compensation by pre-estimated losses, as in the following example.

> The parties included in a contract of independent construction work a stipulation that, if the contractor breached the terms on construction, he should pay the client a specified fixed amount set out in the addendum to the contract as a pre-estimated measure of the loss from such a breach. Applying the rules of interpretation of contract in CC article 431, the Federal Commercial Court of Moscow District qualified these pre-estimated losses as *neustoika* and applied the Civil Code provisions on *neustoika* to them.[81]

However, this interpretation of pre-estimated losses specified in the contract as being *neustoika* is not universally accepted, as illustrated in another case.

> The parties to a contract of purchase-sale of coal specified in the contract that, if the buyer refused to accept the amount of coal designated in the contract, he should compensate the seller's losses. The parties agreed to a pre-estimate of the seller's losses as 40 roubles for each ton of coal not accepted. The contract also envisaged that even if the losses actually incurred by the seller were higher than the pre-estimate, they should be compensated at the pre-estimated amount. Even though the contractual provision defining the pre-estimated losses complied in general with the concept of *neustoika* in the Civil Code, the Federal Commercial Court of East-Siberian District held that these pre-estimated losses could not be qualified as *neustoika* and applied general rules for compensation through damages.[82]

Unfortunately there does not seem to be any clear guidance from the courts as to when they will regard pre-estimated loss clauses in a contract as setting up *neustoika*, and when they will not. Clearly in a particular case construction of

[81] Resolution of Federal Commercial Court of Moscow District of 13 March 2009 No KG-A40/1319-09. See also Resolution of Presidium of the Supreme Commercial Court of 13 September 2011 No 9899/09.

[82] Resolution of Federal Commercial Court of East-Siberian District of 15 November 2010 No 19-1828/10.

the exact wording of the contractual term will be an issue of fact at trial, but in the absence of any consistent interpretative practice, parties to contracts who attempt to pre-estimate losses must be aware of the risk of unintended consequences.

B Nature of *Neustoika*: Compensatory or Punitive?

Translation of the term *neustoika* as 'penalty' creates the impression that, as a remedy for breach, it is punitive. Even though there are indeed instances when *neustoika* does have a punitive character, as is shown below, these are more the exception than the general rule.

(i) Compensatory Nature of Neustoika

Under the general rule *neustoika*, like other remedies for breach of contract, is considered to have a compensatory nature. For example, in 2011, the Thirteenth Appellate Commercial Court held that *neustoika* is a measure of civil liability in the case of non-performance or improper performance of contractual obligations and has a compensatory character in respect to possible losses by the promisee.[83]

In another case the Eighteenth Appellate Commercial Court[84] made clear that by claiming for interest under CC article 395 (a type of *neustoika* discussed below), the promisee was restoring his violated rights, not punishing the party in breach. Application of interest under CC article 395 has a compensatory character and allows a party to compensate for losses which arose as a result of late payment of a debt. The Supreme Commercial Court noted that the proportionality of the amount of *neustoika* to the consequences of the breach is presumed.[85] Therefore a party claiming *neustoika* does not have to prove its correlation with the actual amount of loss, if any. This sounds like an irrebuttable presumption. However, it actually is not irrebuttable. Below, it will be shown that the court may reduce the amount of *neustoika* provided for in a law or contract if it is not proportionate to the amount of the actual losses suffered by the non-breaching party.

The compensatory nature of *neustoika* is also demonstrated in the general rule in the Civil Code on the interrelation between *neustoika* and damages (CC article 394(1)). According to this, 'If a penalty [*neustoika*] has been established for the failure to perform or for improper performance of an obligation, the losses shall be compensated in the part not covered by the penalty'.[86] This rule is made explicit in CC article 395(2) with respect to interest claimed under article

[83] Resolution of Thirteenth Appellate Commercial Court of 24 March 2011 No 56-57867/2010.

[84] Resolution of Eighteenth Appellate Commercial Court of 9 April 2010 No 18AP-2517/2010.

[85] Resolution of Plenum of Supreme Commercial Court of 22 December 2011 No 81 'On Particular Issues of Application of Article 333 of the Civil Code of the Russian Federation' para 1.

[86] Butler, above n 2, at 291.

395(1):

> If the losses caused to a creditor [promisee] by the unlawful use of his monetary means exceed the amount of interest due him . . . he shall have the right to demand from the debtor [promisor] compensation of losses in that part exceeding this amount.[87]

Neustoika is thus clearly part of the compensation calculation.

(ii) Punitive Component of Neustoika

The general rule just discussed governing the interrelation between *neustoika* and losses may be modified, either by a law or the contract. CC article 394(1) specifies that a law or contract may provide for circumstances where:

(1) the recovery of only *neustoika*, not losses, is permitted; or
(2) losses may be recovered in full as well as *neustoika*; or
(3) at the choice of the promisee either *neustoika* or losses may be recovered.

The second possibility supports the assertion that even though under the general rule *neustoika* is compensatory, it can in addition have a punitive character. This is the point where Russian *neustoika* and common law liquidated damages diverge. *Neustoika* claimed as well as the actual loss is nothing other than exemplary (punitive) damages prohibited under English law. Such *neustoika* is termed punitive (*shtrafnaia*) *neustoika*. This name, however, is conventional, and does not have to be used for *neustoika* to be qualified as such. As long as a provision of law or the contract specifies that *neustoika* is paid in excess of the actual losses, it is a punitive *neustoika*.

The most significant example of punitive *neustoika* in Russian contract law is in consumer protection law where both a punitive *neustoika* and a fine (paid to the Russian Federation) are imposed on the dominant party in a consumer contract, over and above the actual losses. For example, under article 28(5) of the Law on the Protection of Consumer Rights,[88] in the case of breach of the term on performance, the provider of works (or services) shall pay the consumer *neustoika* valued at 3 per cent of the price of the particular work (or services), or, if that price is not specified in the contract, 3 per cent of the total contract price, for each day of delay in performance. In addition, if the consumer wins a case in court, the court must recover from the provider of works or services a fine payable to the state budget at the level of 50 per cent of the amount successfully claimed by the consumer.

This use of contract law to protect consumer rights by a clearly punitive *neustoika* is another vivid example of differential standards in Russian contract law depending on the legal status of the parties.

[87] Ibid 292.
[88] Law of the Russian Federation of 7 February 1992 No 2300-1.

It is also interesting to note that, in contrast to normal English procedure, by offering one party an additional tool to induce the other party actually to perform the contract, Russian contract law once again displays its orientation towards performance rather than compensation for breach though damages. If punitive *neustoika* is provided in a contract or law applicable to a particular case the party due to perform has an additional incentive to fulfil their contractual obligations even though, were it not for the punitive *neustoika*, it might be more efficient to breach the contract and pay damages or even pay a compensatory *neustoika*. We can see that although there is a strong principle of freedom to contract in Russian law, there is not a corresponding freedom to breach, as arguably there is in English law based on economic efficiency arguments.

(iii) Balancing the Punitive Component: the Court's Right to Reduce the Amount of Neustoika

The possibility of recovering the clearly punitive *neustoika* (provided it is stipulated in a law or the contract) is balanced to some extent by the right given to a court by CC article 333 to reduce its value. According to this article 'If a penalty [*neustoika*] subject to payment is clearly incommensurate to the consequences of the violation of the obligation, a court shall have the right to reduce the penalty'.[89]

It should be noted, though, that this power to reduce the amount applies to all types of *neustoika*, no matter whether it exceeds the losses (so punitive *neustoika*) or not. The Supreme Commercial Court made clear that the value of *neustoika* may be reduced not only when it is specified in the contract, but also when it is provided for in a law. For instance, a court can reduce *neustoika* under the Statute on Railway Transport of the Russian Federation; Federal Law on State Material Reserve article 16; and Federal Law on Placement of Orders for Purchase of Goods, Performance of Works, Provision of Services for State and Municipal Needs article 9.[90]

In addition the Plenum of the Supreme Court acknowledged that the amount of punitive *neustoika* laid down in the consumer protection law (noted above)[91] can in exceptional cases also be reduced.[92] The Court's position here raises an interesting logical conundrum: punitive *neustoika* is punitive by default and cannot have a compensatory nature; *a priori* it is not supposed to be commensurable with the consequences of the breach. Therefore the possibility of reducing its amount raises a question about the rationale of its very existence.

[89] Butler, above n 2, at 255.

[90] Resolution of Plenum of the Supreme Commercial Court of 22 December 2011 No 81, above n 85, para 4.

[91] See above, text to n 88.

[92] Resolution of Plenum of the Supreme Court of the Russian Federation of 28 June 2012 No 17 'On the Consideration of Disputes connected with Protection of Consumer Rights by Courts' para 34.

Since that part of the Civil Code came into force, courts have actively used their right to reduce the amount of *neustoika* whenever they found it unfair and incommensurate with the consequences of the violation. In many cases they did this at their own discretion and on their own initiative.

Very often, in seeking to avoid recovery of a disproportionately high *neustoika* from a party in breach, the courts have in fact imposed a disproportionately low *neustoika*. This, in combination with the difficulties of recovering damages (as discussed above at p 228) has almost eliminated *neustoika* as an incentive for a party to perform properly their contractual obligations, as in the following example.

> In a case adjudicated by Federal Commercial Court of Moscow District company H sued company A for debt under a contract of purchase-sale, with the contract price set at 293,904 roubles with *neustoika* of 49,814 roubles for breach of the obligation to pay on time for the goods delivered. The court on its own initiative reduced the *neustoika* on the basis of CC article 333 by a factor of 10, so that, instead of the 49,814 roubles claimed, the court only awarded 4,981 roubles. At the same time the court provided no explanation whatsoever as to why it deemed the *neustoika* claimed to be incommensurate with the consequences of the breach and why the amount awarded was more appropriate.[93]

Court practice has improved to some extent after the Supreme Commercial Court formulated in 2011 general guidelines on reduction of the amount of *neustoika* under CC article 333.[94] These guidelines impose certain limitations on courts exercising their right to reduce *neustoika*. The most important of these are summarised below:

(1) The value of *neustoika* can only be reduced at the request of the defendant.
(2) The defendant must provide evidence of the obvious incommensurability of *neustoika* with the consequences of the breach. For example, the defendant may prove that the claimant's possible losses would be considerably lower than the value of *neustoika*. The claimant is allowed to bring contrary evidence.
(3) The following arguments of the defendant should not be accepted in themselves as grounds for reducing *neustoika*:
    - the impossibility of performance due to a difficult financial situation;
    - non-performance of the counterparty's obligations;
    - the existence of debts to other creditors;
    - sequestration of monetary means or other property of the defendant;

[93] Resolution of Federal Commercial Court of the Moscow District of 25 May 2006 No KG-A40/3363-06.

[94] Resolution of Plenum of the Supreme Commercial Court of 22 December 2011 No 81, above n 85.

- lack of funding from a public budget;
- voluntary payment of the debt in full or in part on the day of the court hearing;
- performance by the defendant of socially important functions; or
- the defendant's obligation to pay interest on the use of their monetary means, eg interest on a loan.

Some of these guidelines have since been included in the 2012 Draft Amendments to the Civil Code.[95] In particular, if enacted, the provisions of CC article 333 would be changed in the way that it provides the courts a right to reduce only the amount of contractual *neustoika*, but not the amount of legal (законная; *zakonnaia*) *neustoika*. The amendments would also provide that this can be done only following an application by the defendant. The new draft article 333 would also be complemented by a provision that the value of *neustoika* payable by a person carrying out entrepreneurial activity can be reduced in exceptional cases, if it can be proved that recovery of *neustoika* in the amount specified in the contract may lead to unfounded enrichment for the clamant.

This latter provision shows again the consistent pattern of the Russian legislator applying different standards to those carrying out entrepreneurial activity (whether individuals or legal entities) as compared to others – individual or legal entities – who are not acting as entrepreneurs.

C Types of *Neustoika*

It follows from the definition of *neustoika*,[96] that unlike common law liquidated damages clauses which are always contractual terms, not only can it be specified in a contract, so contractual (договорная; *dogovornaia*) *neustoika*, but also in a law, hence legal (законная; *zakonnaya*) *neustoika*.

An agreement to establish a contractual *neustoika* must be in written form, irrespective of the form of the contract setting out the primary obligations; even if the contract between the parties is concluded orally, the *neustoika* agreement must be in writing. Failure to comply with this requirement will entail its invalidity (CC article 331).

The best example of a legal *neustoika* relates to the interest specified in CC article 395 for the use of another's monetary means. For the purposes of convenience Russian lawyers call it 'interest under article 395', so we will do the same. According to CC article 395(1), 'For the use of another's monetary means as a consequence of unlawful withholding, avoidance of the return thereof, other delay in the payment thereof or the unjustified receipt or savings thereof at the expense of another person'[97] interest should be paid. The article goes on

[95] Draft Federal Law No 47538-6, above n 20 art 1 para167.
[96] See above, text to n 80.
[97] Butler, above n 2, at 292.

to set a default rate of interest, linked to the local bank rate.

Interest under CC article 395 can be claimed for any improper performance or non-performance of a monetary obligation, unless money is used not as the means of payment or settlement of a debt; examples of this exception might be an obligation to deposit money with the bank, or a carrier transferring currency notes.[98]

If *neustoika* is specified by a law the promisee has a right to claim it irrespective of whether or not the contract itself included a duty to pay *neustoika* (CC article 332(1)). Accordingly any procedures set out in the contract for settling contractual claims do not apply to recovering legal *neustoika*. Thus, if the contract provides a special complaint procedure (претензионный порядок; *pretenzionnyi poriadok*) for settling claims, this would only apply to claims for any contractual *neustoika* and damages but not to claims for legal *neustoika*.

This approach was specifically approved by the Second Appellate Commercial Court.[99] It held that the interest for the use of another's monetary means as a legal mechanism of liability for the breach of a monetary obligation has a different legal nature to contractual *neustoika*. The interest under CC article 395 is a legal *neustoika* and may be recovered from the promisor irrespective of whether or not any special complaint procedure specified in the contract was put into action before a claim was made to court.

In the case of legal *neustoika*, the law only sets its minimal amount, which can be increased by the parties' agreement unless a law explicitly prohibits this (CC article 332(2)). For example, according to CC article 395(1), the interest for the use of another's monetary means:

> shall be determined as the rate of bank interest on the day of performance of the monetary obligation or respective part thereof which existed at the place of residence of the creditor, and if the creditor is a juridical person [legal entity], at the place of its location . . . These rules shall apply unless another amount of interest has been established by a law or by the contract.[100]

D Conditions for Recovering *Neustoika*

Like damages, *neustoika* can only be claimed in the case of breach of contract: non-performance or improper performance of a contractual obligation; the claimant must prove the defendant's liability for breach in order to be able to claim *neustoika* (CC article 330(2)). This requirement was specifically affirmed by the Supreme Commercial Court: a claimant of *neustoika* must prove the

[98] Resolution of Plenum of the Supreme Court of the Russian Federation No 13; Resolution of Plenum of the Supreme Commercial Court No 14 of 8 October 1998 'On the Practice of Application of the Provisions of the Civil Code on the Interest for the Use of Another's Monetary Means'.

[99] Resolution of Second Appellate Commercial Court of 26 July 2010 No A82-17015/2009-10. See also Resolution of Federal Commercial Court of Volgo-Viatskii District of 12 November 2010 No A29-13102/2009.

[100] Butler, above n 2, at 292.

breaching party's non-performance or improper performance, which according to a law or the contract entails the obligation of the breaching party to pay the claimant a particular amount as *neustoika*.[101]

In respect to proving fault, recall from pp 202 and 229 above that where fault has legal significance for liability for breach, a presumption of fault applies, so the defendant has the burden of proving an absence of their fault.

However, unlike a claim for damages, the claimant seeking *neustoika* does not have to prove that the breach actually caused them any loss, nor establish the value of any loss that did flow from the breach (CC article 330(1)). This characteristic of *neustoika* makes it much more attractive to a claimant than damages as a form of liability for breach. As shown above (see p 226) in many instances it is difficult to prove and thus recover damages for breach. Therefore when drafting a contract parties often try to include appropriate *neustoika* for breach of different contractual obligations to guarantee their recompense in the case of breach.

IV REQUIRED PERFORMANCE

It has already been highlighted, both in Chapter 9 on Performance and elsewhere in this chapter, that Russian contract law is oriented towards securing actual performance and that as a rule damages are not considered to be a complete substitute for performance. These conclusions, however, are seldom based on any explicit provision of the Civil Code but follow from different provisions in the Code and court practice, which we will consider below. As far as the Civil Code provisions dealing with required performance are concerned, unfortunately we have to conclude that they are rather vague and at times controversial.

A General Provisions

Most importantly, the Civil Code does not explicitly give a claimant the right to demand performance in the case of non-performance or improper performance by the breaching party. On the contrary, CC article 393(1) provides a general rule under which the breaching party is obliged to compensate for losses caused by their non-performance or improper performance (see p 225 above). Based on this it could be concluded that since the breaching party is obliged to compensate for loss, the other party is entitled to claim damages from them in both the case of non-performance and improper performance of the contract; in other words, compensation through damages is accepted as a substitute for performance in Russian contract law. But this is not really so, as we shall see.

[101] Resolution of Plenum of the Supreme Commercial Court of 22 December 2011 No 81, above n 85, para 1.

The Draft Law amending the Civil Code proposes to fill the gap by providing for an explicit right of the claimant to demand performance as a remedy for breach of contract. The Draft Law introduces to the Civil Code a new article 308.4 'Protection of the Rights of the Creditor [Promisee]'. Part 1 of this article says that:

> in the case of non-performance by the debtor [promisor] of their obligation the creditor [promisee] has a right to claim for required performance in court, unless it follows otherwise from the Civil Code, other laws, the contract or the essence of the obligation.[102]

Surprisingly, this provision suggests that the promisee has a right to claim performance only in the case of non-performance by the other party of their obligation. It does not say that the promisee would have the same right in the case of improper performance by the other party. However, as we saw above, it is in cases of improper performance that the promisee is compelled by court practice to claim performance, whereas in the case of non-performance the promisee currently has the choice to claim damages, performance, or both. We believe that this inconsistency is most likely an oversight and does not have any particular rationale behind it. Paragraph 3 of the same article states that 'Protection by the creditor [promisee] of his rights in accordance with Part 1 of this Article does not relieve the promisor from liability for non-performance *or improper performance* of obligation' (emphasis added). This indicates that improper performance is also implied in Part 1 of this article and has simply been missed out at draft stage.

(i) Required Performance as a Remedy for Improper Performance

In adjudicating disputes over breaches of contract the courts tend to proceed from the principle of actual performance, which they consider to be one of the tenets of Russian contract law.[103] The courts derive this principle from CC article 396, which was discussed in Chapter 9 at p 195. This article concerns the correlation between liability for breach (compensation of damages, payment of *neustoika*) and performance. However, its interpretation has much more far-reaching consequences.

The text of CC article 396(1) is as follows:

> The payment of a penalty [*neustoika*] and compensation of losses in the event of the improper performance of an obligation shall not relieve the debtor [promisor] from performance of the obligation unless provided otherwise by a law or by contract.[104]

[102] Draft Federal Law No 47538-6, above n 20 art 1 para 149.
[103] See, eg Ruling of Supreme Commercial Court of 26 February 2007 No 1614/07.
[104] Butler, above n 2, at 293.

Part 3 of the same article provides:

> The refusal of a creditor [promisee] to accept performance which as a consequence of delay has lost interest for him (article 405(2)), and also the payment of penalty established as release-money (article 409), shall relieve the debtor [promisor] from performance of the obligation in kind.[105]

On its terms, this article does not in any way directly concern or limit a claimant's right, when there has been improper contractual performance, to demand compensation for losses instead of actual performance. However, a literal application of the provision that compensation for losses does not relieve the party in breach from the obligation to provide actual performance leads to the following situation. If a claimant applies for the full amount of damages instead of actual performance and recovers them, they will nevertheless still have the right to demand actual performance, because this is what article 396 states. As a result, the claimant can obtain both compensation in full and actual performance, so would gain an unfounded enrichment.

To avoid this clearly unfair result the courts have concluded that following breach through improper performance a claimant can in the first place claim proper performance of whatever is still due, as in the following example.

> In a case adjudicated by the Supreme Commercial Court, company B and company O concluded a contract of barter. B was obliged to transfer to O a certain amount of hard and soft wheat. O promised to transfer back to B flour ground from 51 per cent of that wheat.
>
> B fully performed its obligation, but O did not. Having received insufficient flour, B sued O for damages amounting to the value of the missing flour and interest under CC article 395.[106] The court at first instance rejected the claim on the grounds that the contract of barter had not been terminated and the method of performance of O's obligation specified in the contract had therefore not changed. The court implied that B in this case could only sue O for actual performance, not damages.
>
> Subsequently B sued O, but this time claiming for actual performance. The courts of all instances upheld the claim. The Supreme Commercial Court pointed out that O had improperly performed its obligation under the contract. The principle of performance is provided in CC article 396. Therefore, the courts reached the correct conclusion that O could not be relieved of the liability to perform its obligation in kind, that is, actually perform.[107]

The Court thus interpreted CC article 396(1) as depriving B of the right to claim damages for their loss resulting from O's partial performance and prompted B to claim instead for performance of the rest of the obligation due.

[105] Ibid 293.
[106] See above, text to n 97.
[107] Ruling of Supreme Commercial Court of 26 February 2007, above n 103.

(ii) Required Performance as a Remedy for Non-performance

A different rule applies in the case of non-performance. According to CC article 396(2):

> The compensation of losses in the event of failure to perform an obligation and the payment of a penalty [*neustoika*] for the failure to perform shall relieve the debtor [promisor] from the performance of the obligation unless provided otherwise by a law or by contract.[108]

Unlike Part (1) of the same article, this provision has not been interpreted to affect in any way the claimant's right to demand actual performance. Following breach through non-performance, a claimant is free to choose whether they sue for damages or apply for actual performance, but they cannot claim both; if they choose damages, once they are paid in full the other party is relieved of any obligation to provide actual performance. However, if the claimant demands actual performance, they can still claim damages under CC article 393 for any losses caused by the other party's failure to perform in a timely manner, and, in case of a monetary obligation, the claimant may also claim legal *neustoika* under CC article 395, as discussed above at p 249.

(iii) Feasibility of Required Performance

An important factor developed in court practice should be borne in mind in relation to required performance as a remedy for breach of contract. This is feasibility of required performance. A lack of feasibility may lead to rejection by the court of a claim for performance. From the Resolution of the Presidium of the Supreme Commercial Court which formulated this rule it follows that in deciding on required performance the courts should take into account how feasible it will be to execute a court decision requiring performance. The provisions of the Federal Law on Enforcement Proceedings (федеральный закон об исполнительном производстве; *federal'nyi zakon ob ispolnitel'nom proizvodstve*) should be taken into account when assessing the feasibility of execution.[109]

Lower courts do not always take the feasibility provision into account and make decisions on required performance which cannot be effectively executed. This is illustrated below in the discussion of required performance as a remedy for breach of contract of independent work.

B Contracts to Transfer an Individually-Specified Thing

There is one special class of contracts where the Civil Code explicitly entitles the claimant to demand required performance in case of breach. These are con-

[108] Butler, above n 2, at 293.

[109] Resolution of Presidium of the Supreme Commercial Court of 7 March 2000 No 3486/99.

tracts to transfer an individually-specified thing. As many legal systems, Russian contract law traditionally divides all things into two types:

- individually-specified things; and
- things determined by generic characteristics.

This distinction is analogous to the Roman law differentiation between '*res non fungibiles*' (unique goods) and '*res fungibiles*' (generic or replaceable goods).[110]

The Russian Civil Code itself does not explain the difference between the two types. In legal doctrine[111] an individually-specified thing is defined as a thing which has particular characteristics which are inherent only to it. Individually-specified things are always regarded legally as irreplaceable, so, for example, a piece of immovable property such as a particular house at a particular address. Things determined by generic characteristics are characterised by being quantifiable; in other words they are considered as a certain weight, measure or number of things of the same kind, for example, 10 kilograms of wheat, five trucks, 10,000 roubles, etc. Only movables can be recognised as things determined by generic characteristics; they are always regarded legally as being replaceable.

CC article 398 deals with 'Consequences of Failure to Perform Obligations to Transfer Individually-Specified Thing'. Under it, the claimant (creditor/promisee) has the right 'to demand that this thing be taken away from the debtor [promisor] and transferred to the creditor [promisee] on the conditions provided for by the obligation'.[112] There are two provisos: (i) the right 'shall disappear if the thing already has been transferred to a third person'[113] having the legal right to it (ownership or another real right); and (ii) 'The creditor [promisee] shall have the right to demand compensation of losses instead of a demand to transfer the thing to him'.[114]

It should be noted that from the theoretical point of view the remedy of transfer in CC article 398 is more than just requiring performance. It is directed at the thing itself and not at the person who is obliged to transfer it, so is conceptually very close to vindication, that is, the return of property from illegal possession. (See Chapter 6 at p 132 for problems with the overlap of vindication and restitution.)

The fact that CC article 398 explicitly provides for the alternatives, of the promisee demanding actual transfer or claiming damages, again points up, even

[110] A Clarke and P Kohler, *Property Law: Commentary and Materials* (Cambridge, Cambridge University Press, 2005) 52.

[111] See, eg, EA Sukhanov (ed), *Российское гражданское право: В двух томах. Общая часть. Вещное право. Наследственное право. Интеллектуальные права. Личине имущественные права: Учебник* [Rossiiskoe grazhdanskoe pravo: V dvukh tomakh. Obshchaia chast'. Veshchnoe pravo. Nasledstvennoe pravo. Intellektual'nye prava. Lichnie neimushchestvenne prava: Uchebnik; *General Part: Property Law, Law of Inheritance, Intellectual Property, Personal Non-Proprietary Rights, vol 1 of Russian Civil Law in 2 vols. Text book*], 2nd edn (Moscow, Statut, 2011) at 303.

[112] Butler, above n 2, at 294.

[113] Ibid.

[114] Ibid.

if indirectly, the characteristic of Russian contract law being oriented towards actual performance. If it were not, there would be no need for such a specific provision about damages in CC article 398, because CC article 393 already establishes a general rule under which the claimant has a right to seek damages for non-performance or improper performance by the other party (see p 225 above).

According to the second paragraph of CC article 398 (set out as proviso (ii) above) the promisee has the right to demand compensation through damages rather than transfer of the actual thing. This provision is sometimes mistakenly interpreted as meaning that if the promisee chooses to demand transfer, that precludes any claim for damages caused by the transfer being untimely. This is not correct. As noted in relation to article 396 (see p 252 above), a claim for actual performance does not extinguish the right to claim for losses as a consequence of that performance being late.

C Required Performance as Remedy for Breach of Contracts for Works and Services

Unlike English law Russian contract law does not expressly prohibit as a remedy the imposition of required performance of contracts for works or services.

Even though the Civil Code does not provide any explicit prohibition, it does contain two articles from which the courts have generally derived the conclusion that it is not possible to impose performance of contracts for services. These are CC articles 397 and 782. CC article 397 states:

> In the event of the failure to perform an obligation by a debtor [promisor] to manufacture and transfer [a real right to] a thing [. . .], or to transfer a thing for use to a creditor [promisee], or to fulfil specified work or to render a service for him, the creditor has the right within a reasonable period to commission the fulfilment of the obligation to third persons for a reasonable price or to fulfil it by his own efforts unless it follows otherwise from a law, other legal acts, the contract, or the essence of the obligation, and to demand from the debtor [promisor] compensation of necessary expenses and other damages incurred.[115]

As the Federal Commercial Court of the East-Siberian District acknowledged, this article does not appear to include the right to claim performance from the party in breach of a contract for services.[116] Rather, the non-breaching party may get a third party to perform and, in effect, send the party in breach the bill.

Despite the fact that CC article 397 is used by courts to justify their approach that it is not possible to oblige a party to perform a service, its literal interpretation does not actually contain any such prohibition.

[115] Ibid 293–4.

[116] Resolution of Federal Commercial Court of the East-Siberian District of 11 August 1999 No 33-1819/99-S2-F02-1320/99-S2.

This article merely enumerates the rights a party to a contact for work or service has if the other party breaches by non-performance. Since the provision is formulated in the form of a right, the non-breaching party is not obliged, but is merely empowered, to exercise it.

Another provision, CC article 782(2), specifies that the provider of services has 'the right to refuse performance of obligations under a contract of compensated rendering of services only on condition of the full compensation of losses to the customer'.[117] This provision undercuts any demand for performance by allowing a potential provider of services simply to refuse to perform the obligation under the contract without any valid reason. Of course, as the provision says, they would then have to compensate the other party for losses.

The Third Appellate Commercial Court[118] considered the situation of whether a party in a contract which combined features of a contract of independent work and a contract of compensated rendering of services could be obliged to provide performance. The Court concluded that the provisions regulating contracts of compensated rendering of services and the general provisions on contracts of independent work do not give the client a right to compel performance. If there is non-performance in relation to a contract of compensated rendering of services, the client has the right to compensation for losses but not to compel the provider to render the services specified in the contract. Any other interpretation of the legal provisions would contradict CC article 782(2), cited above.[119]

Even though providing work has a very similar nature to rendering a service, there is no provision equivalent to CC article 782(2) from which a prohibition could be derived against claiming performance of an obligation to provide work. As a result from time to time claims for performance of obligations to provide work under a contract of independent work are upheld by the courts.[120]

At the same time in certain instances the courts draw an inference from CC article 397 that it is impossible to claim performance with respect to contracts for independent work. More importantly this is where the courts also turn to the requirement of feasibility of actual performance discussed above. This recent case is an example.

> Company S, the contractor, did not perform its obligation to carry out land restoration works under a contract of independent work concluded with company G, the client. As a result G sued S for performance of the obligation. The courts at all instances rejected G's claim with a reference to CC article 397 as not giving the client in a contract of independent

[117] Butler, above n 2, at 549.

[118] Resolution of Third Appellate Commercial Court of 28 April 2012 No 33-16935/2011.

[119] See above, text to n 117.

[120] See, eg Resolution of Federal Commercial Court of North-Caucasian District of 26 March 2010 No A53-11368/2009; Resolution of Ninth Appellate Commercial Court of 31 May 2010 No 09AP-11110/2010-GK; Resolution of Federal Commercial Court of North-Western District of 29 July 2002 No 5730.

> work the right to claim performance as a remedy for non-performance of the contractor's obligation. The court at cassational instance went further and as the main ground for rejecting the claim for performance of S's obligation pointed out the lack of feasibility of execution if such a ruling were made.
>
> The court argued that civil law is based on the principle of 'the freedom of contract, inadmissibility of arbitrary interference by anyone in private matters, the necessity for the unobstructed effectuation of civil rights, ensuring the restoration of rights violated, and the judicial defence thereof'.[121]
>
> The court added that G's claim for performance by S in this particular case did not meet the general criteria of admissibility of a court claim for performance: effectiveness, appropriateness and reasonableness. Therefore, if the claim were upheld, the court decision might lead to new conflicts between the parties. This is because procedural law does not allow the possibility of direct coercion of the defendant (through an act of force) to perform the respective obligation. At the same time the court explained that rejection of G's claim for performance did not violate G's rights because CC chapter 25 and article 715 provide for other remedies G could use to protect and restore their violated rights. For example, according to CC article 715(2), in this situation G itself could refuse to perform and claim compensation for losses.[122]

In fact, the extreme difficulty or even impossibility of enforcing a court decision requiring performance of an obligation to provide work means that in practice it is comparatively rare that a party would seek that remedy following breach by improper performance and/or non-performance of a contract of independent work. Damages and, if available, *neustoika*, are much more effective as a remedy.

V SPECIFIC REMEDIES FOR BREACH OF PARTICULAR TYPES OF CONTRACTS

As well as the general remedies for breach of contract discussed above which are in Part One of the Civil Code, there are provisions in Part Two giving specific remedies for breach of particular types of contract. In some cases these provisions will override the general rules on liability; in the case of conflict, the specific rules in Part Two of the Civil Code are applied as *lex specialis* which takes priority over the *lex generalis* provisions in Part One (see Introduction at p 31 for explanation of this approach to legal sources). For example, CC article 505 sets out that:

121 CC art 1(1); Butler, above n 2, at 7.

122 Resolution of Federal Commercial Court of East-Siberian District of 10 September 2010 No 33-18907/2011.

> In the event of the failure of the seller to perform an obligation under the contract of retail purchase-sale, compensation of losses and the payment of penalty [*neustoika*] shall not relieve the seller from performance of the obligation in kind.[123]

This provision overrides the general rule of CC article 396(2), under which compensation for loss following non-performance does relieve the party in breach from actual performance unless provided otherwise by a law or contract.[124] The specific provision in CC article 505 is aimed at protecting the consumer because the buyer in a contract of retail purchase-sale is, by definition, always a consumer. This is another example of differential standards in Russian contract law depending on the legal status in the marketplace of the relevant parties.

CC article 723(1) gives an example of a specific remedy for breach of a particular type of contract, in this case, breach by the contractor of a contract of independent work:

> In instances when work is fulfilled by an independent work contractor with deviations from the contract of independent work which worsen the result of the work, or with other defects which make it unfit for the use provided for in the contract or in the event of the absence in the contract of a corresponding condition of unfitness for ordinary use, the customer shall have the right, unless established otherwise by a law or the contract, at his choice to require from the independent work contractor:
>
> - elimination of the defects without compensation within a reasonable period;
> - commensurate reduction of the price established for the work;
> - compensation of his expenses for elimination of the defects when the right of the consumer to eliminate them has been provided for in the contract of independent-work (article 397).[125]

This provision does not, however, deprive a claimant of the right additionally to demand compensation for losses caused by improper contractual performance; that remains available alongside their choice of one of the three listed remedies.

This point was specifically considered by the Federal Commercial Court of the East-Siberian District in one of its Resolutions.[126] It held that the claimant's demand that defects be eliminated without compensation within a reasonable period is a separate measure for protecting a customer's violated rights in a contract of independent work, and is applied to ensure the contractor's proper performance of his obligation. Application of this measure does not deprive the customer claimant of their right under the general Civil Code rules to claim damages for losses resulting from the contractor's improper performance (that is, the costs of eliminating the consequences of the breach). It should be noted that this provision is applicable to any customer in the contract of independent work irrespective of their legal status at the marketplace, ie to both consumers and non-consumers.

[123] Butler, above n 2, at 370.

[124] See above, text to n 108.

[125] Butler, above n 2, at 508. For CC art 397, see above, text to n 115.

[126] Resolution of Federal Commercial Court of East-Siberian District of 28 August 2006 No A33-12162/05-F02-4212/06-S2.

VI RESTITUTIONARY AWARDS

Traditionally the term 'restitution' (реституция; *restitutsiia*) is used by Russian contract law lawyers as a consequence of contractual invalidity. That right to restitution is provided in CC article 167(2):

> In the event of the invalidity of a contract, each of the parties shall be obliged to return to the other everything received according to the transaction, and if it is impossible to return that received in kind (including when that received is expressed in the use of property, work fulfilled, or service provided), to compensate its value in money, unless other consequences of the invalidity of transaction have been provided by a law.[127]

Restitution as a result of invalidity is discussed in detail in Chapter 6 at p 132.

Russian contract law does not explicitly contemplate restitutionary awards in some of the contexts where they might be awarded in English law, for example, after termination of a contract due to total failure of consideration; or for remuneration of someone who provides something used by another person outside the framework of a contract; or where the price of performance provided had not been specified (quantum meruit or quantum valebat awards). However, Russian contract law does have other provisions to resolve some of these issues addressed in English law by restitutionary awards.

A Restitutionary Awards in Case of Termination of Contract

Under the general rules governing termination of a contract, even if the termination was a result of a material breach, neither party has the right to demand the return of whatever had been performed before the point of termination, unless established otherwise by a law or by agreement of the parties (CC article 435(4)). If the termination did result from a material breach of contract by one party, the other may only claim compensation for losses caused by the termination (CC article 453(3), see p 262).

This means that in a situation where the contract was terminated at the point where one party had properly performed its obligations but the other had totally defaulted, the first party is not entitled to any remuneration under the contract. The obligation to provide such remuneration terminated simultaneously with the contract.

Of course, when parties terminate a contract by agreement they can include an obligation that the defaulting party pays some remuneration. Likewise, following termination due to material breach, the non-breaching party may claim appropriate remuneration as a part of the damages (CC article 453(5)). Unfortunately, parties do not always conclude a termination agreement and,

[127] Butler, above n 2, at 150.

even if they do, they do not always include in it any provision on remuneration, thinking that the law already provides for that. As a result, as far as the strict letter of the law is concerned, after termination of a contract in many cases a party who has properly performed their part is deprived of the possibility of any compensation from the other party.

The Presidium of the Supreme Commercial Court clarified that the provisions of CC article 453(4) do not exclude the possibility to claim any money transferred to the other party before termination of the contract as unfounded enrichment if counter-performance by the other party has not been provided and there is no longer the obligation to provide it (as the contract is terminated).[128]

It should be mentioned, though, that this clarification directly conflicts with CC article 1102. There unfounded enrichment is defined as having 'without grounds established by a law, other legal acts, or transaction acquired or saved property'.[129] Since the breaching party acquired the other party's performance under a contract, it should not be qualified as unfounded enrichment under the definition in CC article 1102.

The courts have realised the unfairness of the situation described as well as the unlawfulness of applying the rules on unfounded enrichment to it and have tried to protect the non-breaching party's position in other ways. In 2005 the Supreme Commercial Court summarised court practice in an Informational Circular.[130] There it established that, unless the parties have an agreement to the contrary, termination of a contract leads to termination of obligations only for the future (на будущее время; *na budushchee vremia*) and does not deprive a claimant of the right to sue for any debt already accumulated by the time the contract was terminated, as well as for compensation of damages or *neustoika* resulting from improper performance or non-performance of the contract. The Supreme Commercial Court illustrated its legal opinion in the following case.

> Company A (the landlord) and company B (the tenant) concluded a contract of lease for one year. After seven months the parties terminated the contract by agreement. Since at the time of termination of the contract B owed A several months' rent, A sued B claiming the debt and also a contractual *neustoika*[131] for B's late performance. The Supreme Commercial Court concluded that at the time the contract was terminated the one year rental period had not yet expired. The very fact that the contract was terminated did not eliminate B's obligation to pay rent for the time they had used the property and did not exclude the possibility that they were liable for breach. Agreement by the parties to terminate the contract did not

[128] Informational Circular of Supreme Commercial Court of 11 January 2000 No 49 'Summary of Practice in the Consideration of Disputes on Unfounded Enrichment' para 1.

[129] Butler, above n 2, at 769.

[130] Informational Circular of Supreme Commercial Court of 21 December 2005 No 104 'Overview of the Practice of Application by the Commercial Courts of the Provisions of the Civil Code on Certain Grounds for Termination of Obligations'.

[131] See p 249 above for explanation of contractual *neustoika*.

> deprive B of the obligation to pay A the accrued debt for the rent and the contractual *neustoika.*

This position of the Supreme Commercial Court allows the rights of the non-breaching party to be protected. On the other hand, it directly contradicts the provision of CC article 453(3) that:

> In the event of dissolution of a contract, the obligations shall be considered to be terminated from the moment of the conclusion of an agreement of the parties concerning the dissolution of the contract, unless it follows otherwise from the agreement of the character of the change of contract.[132]

The Supreme Commercial Court's approach also undermines the whole institution of early termination because it has made termination of a contract ineffective; in its view, even after termination, obligations remain.

Recent Draft Amendments to the Civil Code provide a different solution to the problem. CC article 453(4) is complemented with a new provision under which:

> In the case when, before dissolution or change of a contract one party, having received contractual performance from the other party, has not performed its obligation or has provided the other party with performance not having the same value, the rules on the obligations as a consequence of unfounded enrichment shall apply to the parties' relationship, unless provided otherwise in a law or contract.[133]

If these Draft Amendments to the Civil Code are adopted, they will introduce a mechanism to protect a party who has properly performed which is almost identical to restitutionary awards in English law in the form of quantum meruit and quantum valebat.[134] As with these, the obligation to compensate for unfounded enrichment does not arise directly from the contract. In Russian law, it would derive from the provisions in the Civil Code.

B Restitutionary Awards as Specific Remedies for Breaches of Particular Types of Contracts

Part Two of the Civil Code provides for some specific remedies in the provisions regulating certain types of contracts. For example, according to CC article 475(2) on the consequences of transfer of a good of improper quality under a contract of purchase-sale, 'In the event of material violation of the require-

[132] Butler, above n 2, at 328.

[133] Draft Federal Law No 47538-6 on Amendment of Part One, Two, Three and Four of the Civil Code of the Russian Federation, as well as other Legislative Acts of the Russian Federation, adopted by the State Duma in the first reading on 27 April 2012 art 1 para 238b.

[134] 'For as much as is deserved' and 'for as much as it is worth'. See further Peel, above n 5, at 1143.

ments for the quality of a good'[135] the buyer has the right to refuse to perform the contract of purchase-sale and to require the return of the money paid for the good. (See Chapter 11 at p 269 for further details of remedies for this type of breach.)

Restitutionary awards as a specific remedy may be granted not only in money but also in kind. For example, this can be done by a rent recipient in a contract of 'rent for life' (пожизненная рента; *pozhiznennaia renta*) following termination of the contract for material breach. Under this type of contract the rent-recipient transfers ownership of property to a rent-payer, and in return the rent-payer pays over to them a set sum of money or other assets during the life of the rent-recipient (CC article 583). The property can be transferred to the rent-payer either for a fee or free of charge. Under CC article 599, if the rent-recipient transferred to the rent-payer free of charge an apartment, dwelling house or other property, on condition of paying rent, the rent-recipient has the right to require the return of the property if there is material breach of contract by the rent-payer. A redemption price which is to be paid by the rent-payer to the rent-recipient in the event of termination for material breach is then set off against the value of the returned property.

C Recompense for Goods or Services

There are instances when a claim similar in effect to the English quantum meruit ('for as much as is deserved') may arise under the provisions of the Civil Code.

A suitable recompense should be paid when the contract has failed to specify the relevant remuneration. According to CC article 424(3):

> In instances when in a contract for compensation the price has not been provided for and may not be determined by proceeding from the conditions of the contract, the performance of the contract must be paid for at the price which *under comparable circumstances usually is recovered for analogous goods, work or services.*[136] (emphasis added).

An analogous claim for recompense may also arise when use of another's property creates unfounded enrichment. CC article 1105 deals with this:

> (1) In the event it is impossible to return in kind property unfoundedly received or saved, the acquirer must compensate the victim for the *real value of this property at the moment of its acquisition*, and also the losses caused by the subsequent change of the value of this property if the acquirer did not compensate its value immediately after he knew about the unfounded enrichment.
> (2) A person who unfoundedly and temporarily used another's property without the intention to acquire it or another's services must compensate the victim for that

[135] Butler, above n 2, at 345.
[136] Ibid 307.

> which he saved as a consequence of such use *at the price which existed at the time when the use ended and in that place where it occurred.*[137] (emphasis added)

The courts use the provisions in CC article 424 (see above)[138] to assist in evaluating the real value of property in order to calculate the recompense in unfounded enrichment cases, as in the following example.

> Company U sued company C claiming for unfounded enrichment as a result of C's use of U's premises to store its equipment. U argued that C received unfounded enrichment in the form of unpaid rent for the use of its premises. The Eighteenth Appellate Commercial Court agreed that there were grounds to uphold the claim. The Court also held that it would apply CC article 424(3) in determining the value of the unjustified use of the other's property, that is, to take the price which under comparable circumstances would usually be charged for analogous goods, work or services. Here the amount of recompense for the unjustified use would be determined on analogy with the value of rent, which had not been agreed by the parties, but would have been charged under comparable circumstances.[139]

This commonsense approach is encouraged by the wording of the Civil Code, appropriately applied by the courts.

VII CONCLUSION

Despite some clear differences in terminology, in general there is a remarkable similarity between the remedies for breach in Russian contract law and those offered by English contract law. The Russian concept of damages is very close to English expectation damages. Compensation for reliance losses is not provided for explicitly in the Russian Civil Code, but in some cases the courts have corrected this deficiency. In application, the Russian penalty (*neustoika*) is very similar to liquidated damages. Even though in Russian contract law there is no category of 'restitutionary awards', there are other legal tools which fulfil the same function.

At the same time the Russian approach to remedies for breach does differ to that in England in important ways. First, Russian contract law explicitly recognises punitive remedies and does not endorse the concept of efficient breach. Secondly, it specifically provides the possibility of disgorgement of profits by a breaching party. Thirdly, Russian contract law is oriented towards actual performance and does not regard damages as a complete substitute for performance.

137 Ibid 770–1.

138 See above, text to n 136.

139 Resolution of Eighteenth Appellate Commercial Court of 19 May 2010 No 18AP-1925/2010.

Another important characteristic of Russian remedies for breach which should be noted is their inefficiency as a disincentive to breach. The difficulties of proving the fact of loss, causation and value of losses, especially lost revenue, make it very problematic in practice to claim damages. Although claiming *neustoika* does not present as many problems as claiming damages, very often the courts reduce its size to negligible amounts, rendering it ineffective as a disincentive. Over and above all this, unfortunately execution of court decisions, whether for damages, *neustoika* or compelling actual performance, remains troublingly low. The combination of these factors seriously reduces the credibility of contractual promises and lowers the level of trust in contractual relations, increasing transaction costs and adversely affecting commerce.[140]

[140] See for an empirical study showing lack of institutional trust in this context, K Hendley, *Coping with Uncertainty: the Role of Contracts in Russian Industry During the Transition to the Market*, University of Wisconsin Law School Legal Studies Research Paper No 1089 (2009), available at www.papers.ssrn.com/sol3/papers.cfm?abstract_id=1458507.

11

Discharge of the Contract

I INTRODUCTION

Any contract is in some way a prediction of the future, a version of future events on which the parties to the contract hope to rely. However, it is impossible to foresee everything and frequently contractual parties (or, more usually, only one party) wish to terminate their contract because the situation has changed. This can be because, for instance, one party breaches the contract so seriously that it loses any value for the other; or the circumstances have changed so dramatically that both parties want to be discharged from their contractual obligations. In this chapter we explore the circumstances when the law allows a contract to be discharged (or terminated, the two words are used synonymously).

Russian contract law, as any other codified law, is supposed to reduce the level of uncertainty about the future by establishing rules for the various occasions when the contracting parties have themselves not provided a ready solution in their contract. However, rules of the Civil Code are interpreted by judges hearing cases, and they are not always consistent. As a result, as is seen below, it is often very hard to predict when a court will terminate a contract and when it will preserve it. This uncertainty undermines the clear principle that 'Certainty and coherence of the most obvious objects of a civil code'.[1] In this chapter we examine the rules on discharge of the contract and examples of their practical application in court.

II GENERAL RULES ON DISCHARGE

In Russian law, as in English law, discharge of a contract is normally achieved by the parties' performance in accordance with the contractual terms. However, there are other grounds for discharge under Russian contract law; these are termination by:

- agreement;
- breach;
- unilateral refusal to perform an obligation;

[1] W Snijders, 'Lessons from St Petersburg: Commerce and Civil Law' (2009) 34 *Review of Central and East European Law* 107 at 111.

- impossibility of performance; and
- material change of circumstances.

Remedies for breach are discussed in Chapter 10 (at p 222); the outline of termination by breach and details of the other factors which may discharge a contact are the topic of this chapter.

CC article 453(2) states simply that, 'In the event of the dissolution of the contract the obligations of the parties shall terminate'.[2] The following subsection defines the time of termination: if discharge by agreement, when the agreement takes effect; if by a court decision, when that decision comes into force. This has been interpreted by the courts to mean that contractual obligations terminate for the future from the moment the contract is discharged.[3] The impact of this is illustrated in the following case.

> Company A and company B signed a contract for A to sell some sunflower oil to B. Payment was to be made within 10 days of delivery. The contract also provided that ownership of the oil would only be transferred to B once A had received payment. A had the right to refuse further performance if the payment was not made on time.
>
> A delivered the oil to B and B made a partial payment. Then the parties discharged the contract by agreement but unfortunately did not define the consequences. A assigned its right to claim for unfulfilled performance and damages for breach to C. C sued B. The Court of Cassation held that although B's contractual obligations terminated at the moment of discharge, they existed up until then. Thus the discharge did not terminate B's obligation to pay for oil which had already been delivered before the discharge agreement, so B owed C the remaining payment, as well as the cost of any consequential damages A had suffered.[4] (For assignment, see Chapter 8.)

Similarly, if an insurance contract is discharged after an insured event occurs, the insurer is not relieved of the duty to pay compensation for losses which arose while the insurance subsisted.[5]

The general rule set out in CC article 453(4) is that when a contract is discharged the parties have no right to demand the return of anything provided as contractual performance before the time of the discharge. In other words, if A fulfilled its contractual obligations and B did not and then A discharged the contract, A has no right of return of whatever A performed.

[2] WE Butler, *The Civil Code of the Russian Federation Parts 1, 2 and 3: Parallel Russian and English Texts* (Moscow, JurInfoR-Press, 2008) 327.

[3] Informational Circular of Presidium of Supreme Commercial Court of 21 December 2005 No 104 'Overview of Commercial Courts Practice of Application of the Civil Code Rules on Certain Grounds for Termination of Obligations' Part 1.

[4] Resolution of Supreme Commercial Court of 16 May 2006 No 15550/05.

[5] Resolution of Federal Commercial Court of Moscow District of 19 July 2006, case No KG-A40/5901-06 26.

However, the courts have perceived this situation as being unfair and have found a way to grant recovery rights to a party which has performed its obligations. In accordance with well-established court practice, party A would have the right of recovery if A can prove that the other party B had gained unfounded enrichment from A's performance. The following is an example.

> Company A and company B had a service agreement under which A made a pre-payment. The services were not provided and the contract was subsequently discharged by agreement. A could not demand the services because the contract had now been discharged, neither could A demand return of the pre-payment. However, the pre-payment constituted unfounded enrichment for B, that is, property acquired or kept with no legal justification, so the court ruled that B had to return the payment to A on that basis.[6]

In applying the rules on unfounded enrichment the courts are basically ignoring CC article 453(4) to achieve a fairer result.

The general rule that obligations terminate on discharge only applies when the parties have not agreed to other consequences, or when the Civil Code or other legislation does not specifically regulate a particular discharge situation. Below we discuss the specific rules on the consequences of discharge for each of the five specific grounds listed above.

III DISCHARGE BY AGREEMENT

Discharge of a contract by agreement of the parties is possible 'unless provided otherwise by the present [Civil] Code, by other laws, or by contract'.[7] The discharge agreement should be in the same form as the original contract 'unless it arises otherwise from law, other legal acts, the contract, or the customs of business turnover'.[8] So, for example, if the original contract was subject to state registration, the discharge agreement must also be registered to take effect.

The discharge agreement is basically a new contract so must comply with all contractual requirements. The core of this agreement is accord of the parties' wills, with all of them wanting to be relieved of their contractual obligations. However, in exceptional circumstances the courts may impose a discharge agreement on discordant parties, as in the following example.

> Company A concluded a contract to sell company B some agricultural machines. B made a partial pre-payment. Later A notified B by letter that

[6] Informational Circular of Presidium of the Supreme Commercial Court of 11 January 2000 No 49 'Overview of Practice of Resolutions of Disputes connected with Unjust Enrichment' Part 1.

[7] CC art 450; Butler, above n 2, at 324.

[8] CC art 452; Butler, above n 2, at 327.

it was impossible for A to fulfil the contract because the manufacturer had stopped producing the particular machines. A offered to discharge the contract, promising to return the pre-payment. However, B did not accept this and demanded contractual performance. A went to court for a discharge of the contract due to a material change of circumstances; B counterclaimed, seeking discharge for material breach.

The court ruled that despite their different approaches, the will of each party was to discharge the contract, so declared that the contract was discharged by agreement.[9]

The consequences of discharge due to impossibility of performance and by breach are different, as discussed below. In this case, having said that the contract was discharged by agreement, the court left open the question of consequences. In doing so it deprived B of the right to claim damages, as the contract was discharged by agreement rather than breach.

When a contract is discharged by the parties' agreement, they are allowed to establish whatever consequences they like. They are not limited by any Civil Code provisions and can agree to consequences which are different to those normally resulting from discharge of the particular type of contract. If the parties cannot agree on the consequences, their dispute can be resolved by a court applying the general rules for discharge of such a contract.

IV DISCHARGE OF A CONTRACT BY BREACH

One very important feature of Russian law is that, unlike English law, it distinguishes between a contact being discharged by breach and being terminated as a result of one party's unilateral refusal to perform an obligation, dealt with below. Discharge by breach is only possible through a court decision, whereas unilateral refusal to perform terminates a contract without the requirement of any court process. CC article 450(2)(1) establishes that:

> Upon the demand of one of the parties a contract may be changed or dissolved by decision of the court only:
>
> (1) in the event of a material violation [breach] of the contract by the other party;
> (2) in other instances provided for by the present Code, by other laws, or by the contract.[10]

The concept of material breach in Russian law has some similarities to repudiatory breach in English law. However, the implementation is rather different.

Unlike English law, Russian contract law does not allow the non-breaching party to choose autonomously to be discharged of its contractual obligations following the other party's breach; there must be a court decision for discharge

[9] Ruling of Supreme Commercial Court of 6 March 2012 No VAS-2103/12.
[10] Butler, above n 2, at 324–5.

by breach. To achieve that decision, the claimant must prove that the breach was sufficiently material. The Civil Code defines a material breach in CC article 450(2) as a breach 'which entails for the other party such damage that it is deprived in significant degree of that which it had the right to count on when concluding the contract'.[11]

This definition is very broad and leaves a wide scope for judicial interpretation. Unfortunately, as seen below in the examples, judges in Russia have not yet developed a unified view as to what constitutes material breach.

As noted in Chapter 2 (at p 50) Russian law does not distinguish between conditions, warranties and other contractual terms. Russian law only differentiates between material terms and all other terms; the other terms are treated equally. There is a line of reasoning in discharge by breach cases where breach is considered to be material if the term breached was a material term, as illustrated in the following case.

> Company A and company B concluded an investment contract. Inter alia, B was obliged under the contract to carry out certain construction works. The works were not carried out and the court hearing the case held that the construction work was a material term of the investment contract and so breach of that term was a material breach which resulted in termination of the contract.[12]

This approach is similar to that taken in English law where any breach of a condition in a contract may be regarded as a repudiatory breach.

In many cases Russian courts consider a breach of contract to be material when one party has not provided any performance at all. In other words, non-performance is almost always considered to be a material breach, which then can lead to the contract being discharged by a court following application by the non-breaching party. In such cases the courts may not explicitly refer to the breach of a material term but this is implied.

The situation becomes more complicated when there has been partial performance, as in the following case.

> Company A concluded a contract for the sale of a building to company B. B paid part of the purchase price but refused to pay the rest. The court considered the breach material, despite the part payment already made, and discharged the contract at the request of A. The effect was that A did not have to transfer the building to B, but B could not get return of the money already paid.[13]

[11] Ibid 325.
[12] Ruling of Supreme Commercial Court of 18 June 2012 No VAS-7080/12.
[13] Ruling of Supreme Commercial Court of 12 April 2012 No VAS-3275/12.

In some cases a contract is discharged for material breach even when very substantial part performance has been provided, as in the following case.

> City Administration C signed a contract with company A for construction works. Completion was delayed and C applied to court for the contract to be discharged for material breach. The court held that even though a considerable amount of construction work had been performed, the parties had not signed any documents to evidence this, and thus the court considered the work not to have been performed. The court ignored defendant company A's objections that work had been suspended in order to get approval from the client C for additional works, which were not in the original project. The court stated that the delay in completion was a material breach for which the contract could be terminated.[14]

Compare this with another case.

> Company A assigned a right to company B. However, A failed to transfer the documents confirming the existence of the right, which were essential for its enforcement by the assignee, B. The court held that failure to transfer the documents constituted a material breach and took the decision to discharge the contract of assignment. As a result A was obliged to return the money received from B in return for the assigned right; after the discharge of the contract it constituted unfounded enrichment for A.[15]

Compared to the previous case there is some justification here for the court's position, as the particular documents were necessary for B as assignee to exercise the right they obtained under the assignment contract, so B suffered material damage as a result of this breach. However, contractual discharge has also been allowed by courts for breaches of terms which do not directly concern the subject matter of the contract.

> Bank B applied for discharge of a contract with company A which had failed to inform B of its change of address and telephone number. Immediate provision of this information to B was one of the contractual terms. The court agreed with B and considered the breach of the obligation to inform B of these changes was a material breach of contract as a result of which the contract for the provision of a bank account could be discharged.[16]

It should be noted that B did not suffer any loss from the breach, neither did it show that the breach could potentially lead to any losses. The court simply

[14] Ruling of Supreme Commercial Court of 4 April 2012 No VAS-3008/12.
[15] Resolution of Presidium of the Supreme Commercial Court of 5 April 2011 No 16002/10.
[16] Ruling of Supreme Commercial Court of 19 March 2010 No VAS-1307/10.

ignored the part of the definition of material breach in CC article 450(2) which specifies that material breach causes 'such damage that the innocent party is deprived in significant degree of that which it had the right to count on when concluding the contract'.[17] In doing this, the court followed the approach taken by most Russian commercial courts, which decide whether the breach is material or not without proper evaluation of its consequences. This approach is analogous to English law where there is no requirement to prove any actual or potential loss for breach of a condition to be considered repudiatory, but does not fit with the Russian law definition of material breach.

Interestingly, only the commercial courts commonly ignore the actual/potential damage requirement for material breach. The courts of general jurisdiction follow the law more literally. The Supreme Court stated that to have a contract discharged for material breach the claimant must prove that if the contract remained in force they would bear considerable losses which could not have been previously foreseen.[18] Generally, however, the commercial courts do not follow this approach and do not require such proof from a claimant.

One thing is clear: a breach of a contract will not be considered material if it was caused by delay by the promisee.[19] CC article 406(1) defines this as:

> if the creditor [promisee] refused to accept proper performance offered by the debtor [promisor] or did not perform actions provided for by a law, other legal acts, or by contract or arising from the customs of business turnover or from the essence of the obligation, until the performance of which the debtor [promisor] could not perform his obligation.[20]

The example below illustrates the point.

> The Committee for Property Management of the City of Saratov, S, and company A signed a contract under which A undertook to prepare three plots of land for registration in the Land Registry. Completion of A's work was delayed by three months and S considered that delay to be a material breach of contract. However, the courts found that the delay was linked to S's failure to provide A with all the relevant documentation, without which A's performance of their undertaking was impossible. The court held that S's actions constituted a delay by the promisee and thus A, the promisor, was not responsible for the subsequent breach of its own obligations.[21]

Provisions on discharge by breach for particular types of contracts can also be found in Part Two of the Civil Code. The Code frequently defines exactly what kind of breach could be grounds for termination, on the application of one of the parties. For example, CC article 619(3) stipulates that a lease agreement can

17 See above n 11.
18 Resolution of Supreme Court of 6 September 2011 No 18-B11-42.
19 Ruling of Supreme Commercial Court of 26 May 2011 No VAS-6400/11.
20 Butler, above n 2, at 299.
21 Ruling of Supreme Commercial Court of 26 May 2011 No VAS-6400/11.

be terminated by a court, on the application of the lessor, when the lessee does not 'make lease payments more than two times in succession'.[22] In such cases the courts base their decision on both the general rule in CC article 450 and the relevant special rule in Part Two of the Civil Code for the particular type of contract.[23]

When a contract is discharged for material breach the non-breaching party has the right to claim compensation for losses caused by the contract's discharge. Damages caused by discharge are considered to be the same as damages for breach[24] (which are dealt with in Chapter 10 at p 223).

V DISCHARGE AS A RESULT OF UNILATERAL REFUSAL TO PERFORM

Discharge of a contract by a court decision on application by the non-breaching party following the other party's material breach must be distinguished from discharge following one party's unilateral refusal to perform a contract. Unlike discharge for material breach, discharge through unilateral refusal to perform does not require a court ruling.

Unilateral refusal arises where one party of its own volition and within the rules established by law and by the contract decides that as a result of certain circumstances it will not perform the contract and informs the other party of that decision. It thus operates in a similar way to discharge following repudiatory breach in English law, but under Russian law the circumstances which give rise to a unilateral right to refuse to perform includes not only some breaches by the other party but also some other circumstances, as discussed below.

CC article 310 makes clear that as a general rule unilateral refusal to perform an obligation of any type is not allowed. There are two exceptions. Unilateral refusal to perform is allowed:

- in 'instances provided for by a law';[25] and
- when it is permitted by the contract, but in this case only where the obligation is 'connected with the effectuation by its parties of entrepreneurial activity' and 'unless it follows otherwise from a law or the essence of the obligation'.[26]

CC article 310 which is applicable to obligations from any type of transaction which gives rise to an obligation has its 'twin' article which specifically regulates unilateral refusal to perform contractual obligations, CC article 450(3). This article also allows unilateral refusal to perform contractual obligations when specifically allowed 'by a law or by agreement of the parties'.[27] However, it does

[22] Butler, above n 2, at 447.
[23] See, eg, Ruling of Supreme Commercial Court of 28 December 2011 No VAS-16952/11.
[24] Ruling of Supreme Court of 9 February 2010 No 9-B09-23.
[25] CC art 310; Butler, above n 2, at 243.
[26] Butler, above n 2, at 243.
[27] Ibid 325.

not have the limitation in CC article 310 that unilateral refusal to perform can only be connected 'with the effectuation . . . of entrepreneurial activity';[28] therefore under CC article 450(3) any contract can include such provisions.

One might imagine that the controversy between CC articles 310 and 450(3) is unimportant. However, the practical implications of applying one or the other are rather serious. For example, let us suppose that Mr A places a deposit in Bank B with an applicable interest rate of 10 per cent per year. The contract allows B to refuse to perform the contract unilaterally if the inflation rate falls below 4 per cent. The contract between A and B is not connected with any entrepreneurial activity by A. Thus, unilateral refusal as provided in the contract would contradict CC article 310 and be invalid. However, if CC article 450(3) is applied, the contract term would be valid because both parties agreed to include it in their contract. As yet there is no clear answer to this conundrum and the courts make different decisions.

A Discharge of a Contract Due to Unilateral Refusal Permitted by Law

Legislation which regulates particular types of contracts (including Part Two of the Civil Code) can give a non-breaching party the right to refuse to perform if a particular condition is met, for instance, when the other party breaches certain obligations specified in the legislation. For example:

(a) in a purchase-sale contract, if the seller refuses to transfer goods to the buyer, the buyer may refuse to perform;[29]
(b) likewise in a purchase-sale contract, if the buyer refuses to accept and pay for the goods, the seller may refuse to perform;[30]
(c) if the contractor in a construction contract does not start work when they should, or if they are performing the work so slowly that it becomes obvious that it cannot be finished on time, the client has a right to refuse to perform, that is, refuse to pay;[31]
(d) in a contract for storage ('keeping': хранение; *khranenie*), if a client fails to pay the custodian for more than half of the storage period, the custodian may refuse to perform the contract; they may ask the client to retrieve their goods immediately.[32]

As mentioned above, the right to refuse to perform is not always connected with the other party's breach of contract. In the following situations one or both parties have a right to refuse to perform even though no breach has occurred or is anticipated:

28 Ibid 243.
29 CC art 463(1).
30 CC art 486(4).
31 CC art 715(2).
32 CC art 896(2).

(i) in a construction contract, the customer may refuse to perform the contract when he or she does not agree with the price for additional works, the necessity of which became apparent after the original contract had been concluded;[33]
(ii) a donee can refuse to accept a gift any time before the gift has been transferred to them; [34]
(iii) any party to a contract of lease concluded for an indefinite period may refuse at any time to perform, provided they notify the other party at least one month in advance of the lease commencing;[35]
(iv) similarly, any party to a contract of uncompensated use can refuse to perform the contract, if they notify the other party at least one month in advance;[36]
(v) a customer to an independent work contract can any time before the result of the work is handed over to them refuse to perform the contract (ie pay the contractual fee), although they will have to compensate the contractor;[37]
(vi) either party to a services agreement has a right at any time to refuse to perform the contract (again, with appropriate compensation paid);[38]
(vii) a person who has taken out an insurance contract (or its beneficiary) can withdraw from it at any time before the occurrence of the insured event.[39]

This list of examples is not exhaustive; there are other situations where the law allows unilateral refusal to perform a contract.

Importantly, when legislation provides the right of one or both parties to refuse to perform, it also stipulates the consequences of that refusal. As we noted above, when unilateral refusal follows one party's breach of contract, the other may sue for damages. In situations where legislation allows unilateral refusal to perform without any breach, the consequences will depend on the nature of the contract. Generally, the law tries to compensate the other party for the negative consequences of the refusal. For example, as indicated above, if a customer to an independent work contract refuses to perform, they must pay compensation in proportion to the work already performed and also for losses caused by the early discharge. However, damages are limited to the difference between the original contract price and the sum paid for the partial performance.[40]

[33] CC art 709(5).
[34] CC art 573(1).
[35] CC art 617(2).
[36] CC art 699(1).
[37] CC art 717.
[38] CC art 782.
[39] CC art 958(2).
[40] CC art 717.

B Unilateral Refusal Allowed by Contract

The parties to a contract can agree that one (or even both) of them has a right to refuse performance. However, this is only allowed when the contract directly stipulates for it, as discussed above. The court may also decide to apply the general Code provisions on obligations and, as also discussed above, rule that only parties to an entrepreneurial contract may include a term allowing a unilateral refusal to perform (as under CC article 310).[41] Unless both parties are involved in entrepreneurial activity, such a term would be void as contradicting the law unless the court decides to apply CC article 450(3) (see the discussion of the controversy between CC articles 310 and 450(3) at p 273).

A unilateral refusal clause is normally used to replace the general Civil Code provision on termination for breach (discussed above). Parties to an entrepreneurial contract as a rule try to avoid court proceedings being lengthy so insert a unilateral refusal clause to allow a faster and less costly court process for termination for breach by providing clear evidence of the provision, as in the following example.

> City Administration C and entrepreneur E concluded a contract under which E undertook to organise regular transport services in the city. The price charged by E for passenger transportation could not exceed a maximum price set by C. The contract provided a right for C to refuse to perform the contract if within one-quarter of a year E breached three times or more the rules of passenger transportation and/or health and safety requirements. The contract had been in force for almost a year when C found that E had charged a higher price than allowed under the contract. Furthermore, in the course of additional checks, C found E had breached health and safety requirements. C sent a complaint to E demanding E eliminate the breaches. E did not comply so C sent a letter notifying E of C's unilateral refusal to perform the contract. E considered the refusal unlawful and challenged it in court. The court confirmed that C had lawfully used its right provided for in the contract and the contract was terminated.[42]

Without the contractual provision giving C the right to refuse to perform, termination would not be been possible without court procedure where C would have had to prove that the breach was sufficiently material for the contract to be terminated. As it was, in the circumstances C did end up in court, but did not have to prove the materiality of the breach.

If a contract provides a right to refuse to perform, often it also regulates the consequences. If it fails to do so, the consequences follow the general rules discussed at p 266 above.

[41] See above, text to n 26.
[42] Ruling of Supreme Commercial Court of 25 May 2012 No V S-3378/12.

VI DISCHARGE BY 'FRUSTRATION'

There is no doctrine of discharge by frustration in the Russian contract law.[43] However, there are two doctrines which deal with situations which in English law would fall under the doctrine of frustration: termination of an obligation due to impossibility of performance; and discharge of a contract due to a substantial change of circumstances. However, it should be noted that compared with English law the Russian doctrines provide the parties with a wider range of opportunities to discharge a contract when circumstances have dramatically changed.

A Impossibility of Performance

CC article 416(1) stipulates that 'An obligation shall be terminated by the impossibility of performance if it was caused by a circumstance for which none of the parties is liable'.[44] As explained in a case in 2009, CC article 416 applies to situations where rights provided in the contract cannot be used and obligations cannot be performed due to 'objective circumstances which can be described as factual'.[45] That is a general definition of impossibility of performance and any situation which fits that definition could lead to the termination of contractual obligations. We will call this situation 'general impossibility'.

The rule on 'general impossibility' in CC article 416(1) says an obligation terminates only for impossibility when none of the parties is responsible for the impossible circumstance. However, CC article 416(2) contradicts this. It states that:

> In the event of the impossibility of performance by a debtor [promisor] of an obligation caused by the guilty actions of the promisee, the latter shall not have the right to demand the return of that which has been performed under the obligation.[46]

The controversy has not yet been resolved by the courts. It seems that the most realistic interpretation is that impossibility of performance can either be caused by the guilty actions of at least one party, or not be connected with any parties' actions. If it is connected with deliberate and guilty actions, then CC article 416(2) will apply and the guilty party will have no right to demand the return of what has been performed under the contract.

One of the most common situations of termination of a contractual obligation due to impossibility of performance is when the contract's subject matter ceases to exist, as in the following case.

[43] As noted with regret by VA Rakhmilovich, 'The New Civil Code of the Russian Federation' (1996) 22(2) *Review of Central and East European Law* 135 at 152.

[44] Butler, above n 2, at 302–3.

[45] Resolution of Federal Commercial Court of Moscow District of 10 November 2009 No KG-A41/11592-09, case No 41-13282/09.

[46] Butler, above n 2, at 303.

> The Federal Property Management Agency, A, let a bus stop on the Sochi Dzhugba Highway to an entrepreneur, E. E failed to pay the rent for several months and A sued for the unpaid rent, discharge of the contract and return to its control of the bus stop. During the court hearing it became clear that the subject matter of the contract, the original bus stop, had ceased to exist. Instead E had built a new entity, a bus stop combined with a shop and café.
>
> The court ruled that the obligation to pay rent for the bus stop terminated when the original bus stop ceased to exist, due to impossibility of performance. The court also held that as the subject matter of the contract no longer existed, its return to the original owner A was impossible.[47]

The outcome of the trial may look odd and rather unfair. It should be mentioned, however, that A could bring another action against E, based either on unfounded enrichment or protection of property title, depending on which A considered more appropriate as the basis for their new claim. The following provides another illustration.

> A car which was the subject matter of a hire-purchase contract was so seriously damaged in a road accident that it could not be repaired. The court held that the obligation of the hirer to make payments under the contract terminated at the moment of the accident due to the impossibility of performance. All other obligations under the contract simultaneously terminated.[48]

One of the most common situations when the courts apply the rules on impossibility of performance is connected with transfer of building ownership. Where there is a utility service contract (for the supply of electricity, water heating and similar) to a building which has had its ownership transferred, the original owner, who was also the recipient of services under the utility service contract before the transfer of ownership, can raise the impossibility of performance to terminate their obligation to pay for utilities supplied after the ownership has been transferred.

Many residential blocks of flats formally belonged to the state, in the form of the Russian Federation. The state transferred ownership of the blocks of flats to municipalities (local government). On many occasions the courts accepted the state's argument that its obligations under utility agreements to service the blocks of flats were terminated due to impossible performance. The courts held that the state was not receiving the utilities and thus there was impossibility of performance of its obligation to pay for them.[49] Unfortunately, sometimes the

[47] Ruling of Supreme Commercial Court of 5 May 2012 No VAS-5577/12.
[48] Ruling of Supreme Commercial Court of 20 December 2011 No VAS-15941/11.
[49] Resolution of Presidium of the Supreme Commercial Court of 24 November 2009 No 9367/09.

municipalities would not pay either, so residents were deprived of water and/or heating for some periods.

The situation where the subject matter of a contract becomes unavailable for delivery is also considered to lead to impossibility of performance. This is clearly a much wider approach than that taken by the doctrine of frustration in English law, where such a change of circumstance would not be held to be a frustrating event.[50] An example of the Russian approach is in the following case.

> Mr B concluded a contract with company A, a car distributor. A undertook to deliver to B a car as described in the contract. It turned out, however, that after the contract was concluded the car manufacturer stopped producing cars of that specification. It was held that due to impossibility of performance, A's obligation to deliver the car had terminated; A was not in breach of contract.[51]

B Consequences of Impossibility

From the wording of CC article 416(2)[52] it is clear that there can be termination for impossibility even where one party, the promisee, is at fault, despite the rule on 'general impossibility' in CC article 416(1).[53] In practice the courts treat both the situations covered by CC article 416(1) and (2) as impossibility of performance leading to termination. The importance in differentiating between the two relates to the applicable consequences.

According to court practice, termination as a result of impossibility for which neither party is liable should lead, after the point of termination, to restitution as unfounded enrichment of anything provided as performance. This follows the general rules on consequences of discharge, as interpreted by the courts (see above).

> Company A signed an agreement to lease a car to company B. The car was destroyed in an accident for which neither party was liable. The court held that A was entitled to the rental payments due from B before the accident. Any sum in excess of that was considered to be unfounded enrichment and was returned to B.[54]

Sometimes performance provided before discharge may also be treated as unfounded enrichment, as in the following case.

[50] See *Blackburn Bobbin Co Ltd v T W Allen & Sons Ltd* [1918] 2 KB 467, and for a more general discussion of the impact of impracticality, *Davis Contractors Ltd v Fareham Urban District Council* [1956] AC 696.

[51] Ruling of Primorskii Krai Court of 22 September 2011, case No 33-9007.

[52] See above, text to n 46.

[53] See above, text to n 44.

[54] Ruling of Supreme Commercial Court of 20 December 2011 No BAC-15941/11.

> Company C concluded a contract for sale and delivery to entrepreneur E of a machine for the production of wire nets. E made part payment but C did not deliver the machine as delivery was only after full payment. Two years later E was deemed missing by a court decision and an administrator of his estate was appointed. The administrator demanded return of E's part payment for the machine. The courts held that the parties' contractual obligations had terminated because performance was impossible. The payment already received by C was qualified as unfounded enrichment which should be returned to E's administrator.[55]

However, occasionally the courts do not oblige either party to return what had already been provided under a contract which has become impossible to perform.

When termination of contractual obligations is caused by impossibility arising from the wilful actions of one party, the guilty party is discharged from actual performance but not from the obligation to compensate for losses caused by the termination.[56] The other party is completely excused any performance, and can claim for losses caused by the guilty party's failure to perform.

The Civil Code does not prescribe a procedure for discharge of a contract due to impossibility of performance. In practice it is sufficient for one party to notify the other of such termination. The party which takes the initiative to do this must be ready to accept the risk that the other party will not agree that performance has became impossible and will treat the situation as one of breach. Then the dispute will have to be resolved by a court decision whether indeed performance had become impossible.

It is not uncommon to include a *force majeure* clause in a contract. This defines what situations the parties agree to consider as making performance impossible. It is also not uncommon for reasonable parties to establish a procedure for termination due to impossibility of performance and to agree what consequences would follow; the law allows this and it saves time and expense.

C 'Special' Impossibility

Apart from general impossibility, the Civil Code specifies in CC articles 417–19 three situations which can be described as particular cases of impossible performance. These are (i) where there is an act of a state agency; (ii) the death of the promisor; or (iii) the liquidation of a legal entity which is the party to a contract. We now turn to these three 'special' situations.

[55] Ruling of Supreme Commercial Court of 16 January 2012 No VAS-17411/11.

[56] Informational Circular of Presidium of the Supreme Commercial Court of 21 December 2005, above n 3, Part 5.

(i) Act of State Agency

CC article 417(1) declares, 'If as a result of the issuance of an act [binding order] of a State agency the performance of an obligation becomes impossible wholly or partially, the obligation shall terminate wholly or in respective part'.[57] In this context, the term 'state agency' includes agencies of local government,[58] even though under Russian law local government is not regarded as part of the state structure. The following is an example of the rule in operation.

> Company A, an airport operator, leased a plot of land adjacent to an airport building to company B to use as a parking lot. Subsequently, the Russian Federation Ministry of Transport issued a regulation which imposed mandatory 50 metre security zones around all airports. The new zone encompassed the plot of land, so A considered the lease terminated due to impossibility of performance caused by the issuance of a legal act. A demanded that B return the plot of land. B refused, so A sued B. The courts agreed with A, holding that the parties' obligations under the lease agreement had terminated because the new regulation made performance impossible; B therefore had no right to use the land plot.[59]

For CC article 417 to be applicable, the issuance of the legal act which causes the performance to become impossible should not result from illegal actions by the promisor. If it does, the general rules on impossibility of performance apply (see p 279), as in the following case.

> Company A and company B signed a contract under which B was obliged to perform a certain activity which required a licence. After the conclusion of the contract, the relevant state licensing agency withdrew B's licence, because on a number of occasions B had broken the law in relation to it. Without a licence B could not perform its contract with A; A sued for breach. B claimed that its obligations to A were terminated due to impossibility of performance caused by the issuance of a legal act by a state agency. The courts disagreed. They held that impossibility of performance was caused by B's deliberately wrongful actions. As a result, the obligation to provide contractual performance was terminated by impossibility, but B's obligation to pay damages for breach of contract remained in force.[60]

[57] Butler, above n 2, at 303.
[58] Informational Circular of Presidium of the Supreme Commercial Court of 21 December 2005, above n 3, Part 4.
[59] Ruling of Supreme Commercial Court of 8 February 2008 No 1/08.
[60] Informational Circular of Presidium of the Supreme Commercial Court of 21 December 2005, above n 3, Part 5.

A party which incurs losses through termination as a result of an illegal or invalid act issued by a state agency may demand compensation from the agency in accordance with the Civil Code rules on 'compensation for damage caused by illegal acts and actions of state and municipal agencies', set out in CC articles 13 and 16.[61] The latter stipulates that:

> Losses caused to a citizen or juridical person [legal entity] as a result of the illegal actions (or failure to act) of state agencies, agencies of local self-government, or officials of these agencies, including issuance of an act of state agency or of agency of local self-government which does not correspond to the law or other legal act, shall be subject to compensation by the Russian Federation, respective subject of the Russian Federation or municipal formation.[62]

This, in combination with CC article 13, leads to the situation where losses can only be compensated if the act of the state agency was issued illegally and such illegality was proved in court, leading to the act being invalidated. However, in the majority of situations, legal acts which result in impossibility of performance are issued in accordance with the law and within the authority of the issuing agency. In these circumstances the parties cannot claim any compensation.

The Civil Code also stipulates that if the act of the state agency which causes the termination is deemed invalid, the obligation is restored 'unless it arises otherwise from an agreement of the parties or the essence of the obligation and performance has not lost interest for the creditor [promisee]'.[63] However, it is not clear how an obligation which has been terminated can be restored, and under what conditions. For that reason the rule is not widely applied and there is no court practice to illustrate its application.

(ii) Death of the Promisor

As a general rule death does not terminate a deceased person's obligations. The obligations pass to their heirs if they accept the inheritance. A promisor's death would only terminate an obligation if it could not be performed without their personal participation or is in some other way inextricably linked to them. This latter situation is one which commonly gives rise to termination due to impossible performance because of the promisor's death, but only of those obligations which are inextricably connected with him or her personally, for example, when the promisor had undertaken to perform at a concert or play a role in a film.

Other debts pass to the heirs who accept the inheritance. However, the heirs' liability for the deceased's debts is limited to the value of the inherited assets.

[61] CC art 417(1).
[62] Butler, above n 2, at 18.
[63] CC art 417(2); Butler, above n 2, at 303.

Any obligations in excess of that are therefore also terminated due to impossibility of performance.[64]

(iii) Liquidation of a Legal Entity

CC article 419 stipulates that the liquidation of a legal entity which is a party to a contract will terminate its contractual obligations, with one exception, noted below.

The Civil Code and other laws regulating particular types of legal entity establish the relevant liquidation process. Also, bankruptcy regulations set out the procedure for claiming against a legal entity which is in the process of being declared bankrupt. If a legal entity is liquidated as a result of bankruptcy all its obligations terminate, irrespective of whether or not they have been carried out. Liquidation of a legal entity is finalised when the completion of its liquidation is duly registered with the Unified State Registry of Legal Entities.

The exception in CC article 419 to termination by liquidation of a legal entity (either as promisor or promisee) is where 'the performance of an obligation of the liquidated legal entity is placed on another person (relating to demands concerning compensation of harm caused to life and health, and others)'[65] by 'a law or other legal acts'.[66] However, there are no such laws or other legal acts currently in force, so the exception is completely nugatory.

VII DISCHARGE OF A CONTRACT AS A RESULT OF MATERIAL CHANGE OF CIRCUMSTANCES

CC article 451(1) provides in its first paragraph that 'A material change of circumstances from which the parties proceeded when concluding a contract shall be a ground for the change or dissolution thereof unless provided by the contract or it arises from the essence thereof'.[67] This rather complexly worded provision heads a fairly long article which gives further detail of the circumstances when a material change of circumstances allows discharge.

The second paragraph of CC article 451(1) defines a material change of circumstances:

> A change of circumstances shall be deemed to be material when they have changed such that if the parties could reasonably foresee this, the contract would not have been concluded at all by them or it would have been concluded on significantly different conditions.[68]

[64] Ruling of Supreme Commercial Court of 8 February 2012 No VAS-714/12.
[65] Butler, above n 2, at 304.
[66] Ibid.
[67] Ibid 325.
[68] Ibid.

The article goes on to presume that the parties will agree to amend the contract to take the changed circumstances into account, or will agree to discharge it. However, in case agreement proves impossible, CC article 451(2) stipulates conditions when amendment or discharge is possible through a court decision. It allows an 'interested party' to apply for discharge or appropriate amendment:

> when the following [four] conditions simultaneously exist:
>
> (1) at the moment of concluding the contract the parties proceeded from the fact that such a change of circumstances would not occur;
>
> (2) the change of circumstances has been caused by reasons which the interested party could not overcome after they arose with that degree of concern and care which are required of him by the character of the contract and the conditions of turnover;
>
> (3) the performance of the contract without a change of its conditions would so violate the correlation of property interests of the parties which correspond to the contract and entail for the interested party such damage that it would be deprived to a significant degree of that which it had the right to count on when concluding the contract;
>
> (4) it does not arise from the customs of business turnover or the essence of the contract that the risk of the change of circumstances is borne by the interested party.[69]

Court practice also requires that the impact of the circumstances is such that the interested party could not and cannot eliminate the negative consequences, despite making every effort, such as would be required by a person were acting reasonably and in good faith.[70]

When courts resolve disputes arising from a material change of circumstances, they first of all determine whether the parties could foresee such change. For example, high inflation is not unforeseeable because, according to the Supreme Commercial Court, the parties 'should be able to make forecasts regarding the economic situation'.[71]

However, despite clarifications from the Supreme Commercial Court, lower courts occasionally rule that a change in market conditions can be a reason to discharge a contract, as in the following example.

> The market price for rent of commercial real property had grown five times during the five years that the contract was in force. The court decided that such a change was both material and unforeseeable.[72]

The deterioration of one party's financial situation is generally not considered to be a material change of circumstances. However, a different approach

[69] CC art 451(2); Butler, above n 2, at 326.

[70] Resolution of Federal Commercial Court of Volgo-Viatskii District of 24 August 2007, case No A79-9483/2006.

[71] Resolution of Presidium of the Supreme Commercial Court of 13 April 2010 No 1074/10.

[72] Resolution of Federal Commercial Court of Volgo-Viatskii District of 16 November 2009, case No A11-847/2009.

may be taken to the impact of a global financial crisis. There are cases where courts considered the 1998 economic crisis as a material change of consequences (see example below). However, with later financial crises the courts took a different approach.

> Company A as borrower signed a loan agreement with company B, its shareholder, in December 2004. The loan should have been repaid by December 2009. In November 2009 the parties signed an addendum changing the repayment date to December 2012. In 2012 B sued A demanding discharge of the agreement due to a material change of circumstances.
>
> The court of first instance allowed the claim but the court of appeal held that it should be dismissed. Both parties attested that in 2004 they had expected A's profits would continue increasing and it would be able to repay the loan. Against their expectation profits fell every year after 2008. The court held that 2008 was the year when the global financial crisis started. However, according to the court, economic crises are not unpredictable. The parties should have taken into consideration that they occur approximately every 10 years and they should have remembered the crisis of 1998. Therefore, as the 'dip' was foreseeable, there had been no material change of circumstances and the court refused to discharge the contract on that basis.[73]

Unfortunately, court practice on the impact of financial crises varies, with some courts considering them sufficiently material, and some not. The tendency is, however, to see subsequent crises as more predictable, as seen in the example just cited.

Sometimes the courts do find reasons why a change in circumstances arising from a financial situation can be considered sufficient reason for discharge, as in this illustration.

> Company A let a complex of buildings to company B. B undertook to use the complex as a children's summer recreational camp and any other use was only allowed if it did not affect this main purpose. B agreed to pay rent in the form of 160 tickets to the camp for children of A's employees. The duration of the contract was set at 10 years. After four years A requested discharge of the contract due to materially changed circumstances. B refused so A brought a claim to court. A stated that its financial situation had considerably worsened and many employees had been dismissed. As a result the number of children who qualified for tickets to the camp had considerably decreased; there was no need for 160 tickets. A also claimed that it could not have predicted this change.

[73] Ruling of Moscow City Court of 29 February 2012, case No 33-6512.

> The courts at first instance, appeal and cassation all agreed with A and ruled to discharge the contract as a result of a material change in circumstances. The Supreme Commercial Court took a different position. It held that A could and should have predicted a change in its financial situation and decrease in the number of employees. Thus, the change of circumstances was not unforeseeable. However, the Court found that B had been using the buildings for several years without paying the required rent. As a result A incurred losses during that time since it was still obliged to pay property tax in respect of the leased buildings. The Court held that B had created a situation of obvious disparity in the parties' material position which went against the principle of balance of the lawful interests of the participants of contractual relations. In that situation, the Court ruled, A should have a right to have the contract discharged due to a material change of circumstances.[74]

The courts may consider a change relating to the contract's subject matter, which leads to a party's loss of interest in the subject matter, to be sufficient reason to discharge a contract, as in the following case.

> Company A bought a car from company B. A properly performed all his contractual obligations: he inspected the car, paid the purchase price and registered the car with the police, as required by law. However, the registration was annulled because the car's identification data was identical to that of another, earlier registered, vehicle. A requested B to discharge the contract because the use of a car in the Russian Federation without registration is unlawful. Registration of A's car was impossible because the identification number of the car, which was assigned during manufacture and supposed to remain unchanged, had been illegally altered. Following an application by A, the courts held that the circumstances had materially changed since A could not use the car and he could not have foreseen the problem. As a result the contract was discharged by a court decision.[75]

CC article 451(1) provides that a material change of circumstances will not lead to the 'change or dissolution . . . when it is provided otherwise in the contract or it arises from the essence of the contract'.[76] In exceptional instances when there has been a material change of circumstances a court may decide to amend the contract rather than discharge it. This is only permitted when discharge is 'contrary to social interests or entails damage for the parties, which significantly exceeds the expenditures needed to perform the contract on the

[74] Resolution of Presidium of the Supreme Commercial Court of 30 November 2010 No 9600/10.
[75] Ruling of Perm Krai Court of Appeal of 4 April 2012, case No 33-2483.
[76] Butler, above n 2, at 325.

conditions changed by the court'.[77] However, cases when courts amend contractual provisions following a claim by one party are rare.

When a contract is discharged by a court at the request of one party due to a material change of circumstances, the court will determine the consequences, considering the need for 'a just distribution between the parties of the expenses incurred by them in connection with the performance of this contract'.[78]

If no contractual party has requested the court to rule on the consequences of discharge the court has no right to do so.[79] Instead, the general rules on discharge, as discussed above, apply.

Discharge of a contract due to a material change of circumstances must be distinguished from impossibility of performance. As explained in court practice, a material change of circumstances does not make performance impossible. It remains possible but because of the changed circumstances becomes exceptionally burdensome for one party, altering the parties' balance of interests, as in the following case.

> In August 1998 entrepreneur A signed a preliminary lease agreement as tenant with entrepreneur B as landlord. A intended to use the rented premises as a restaurant. He planned to finance his business with a bank loan, which had been approved, and capital from his wife, also an entrepreneur. After the contract was signed the 1998 financial crisis occurred which had a significant impact in Russia. A asked the court to discharge his contract with B as a result of changed circumstances and impossibility of performance. A claimed that because of the crisis he could not get the loan and his wife's business was not doing well so that she could not provide any capital for his business either.
>
> The court at first instance acceded to A's claim and held that the contract should be discharged due to impossibility of performance. B appealed, and the Court of Cassation explained that impossibility of performance should be distinguished from a material change of circumstances. It held that performance of the contract was still possible for both parties so the contract remained in force. However, the court went on to say that the financial crisis had made performance of the contract very burdensome for A, who could now not secure enough finance for the business he had intended to run in the rented premises. The court held that the contract should therefore be discharged as a result of this material change of circumstances.[80]

[77] CC art 451(4); Butler, above n 2, at 327.

[78] CC art 451(3); Butler, above n 2, at 326–7.

[79] Ruling of Supreme Commercial Court of 11 October 2011 No VAS-12624/11.

[80] Resolution of Federal Commercial Court of Moscow District of 10 November 2009 No KG-A41/11592-09.

Discharge as a result of a material change of circumstances should also be distinguished from discharge for material breach by one of the parties. However, the courts do not always follow that logic and on several occasions have qualified material breach by one party as a material change of circumstances.

> Company A and entrepreneur E concluded a contract under which E was obliged to transfer to A a 50 per cent share in company B in exchange for 200,000,000 roubles, to be paid in three instalments. The share was to be transferred after the final payment. In the contract E guaranteed that the value of B's capital assets would be maintained at a certain level before the share transfer to A. A paid first the two instalments to E. Then the people who controlled B decided to liquidate it. As B did not have enough assets, bankruptcy procedures were initiated. A considered the liquidation of B to be a material breach of contract and a material change of circumstances. The courts agreed with A's latter submission, holding that all four conditions needed for the discharge of a contract due to material change of circumstances discussed above were satisfied. The contract terminated due to material change of circumstances rather than due to material breach.[81]

Therefore, consequences of discharge due to change of circumstances were applied and E did not have to compensate the damages caused by the breach of contract.

VIII CONCLUSION

The rules outlined in this chapter are complex and create the situation that it is not particularly easy for a contract to be discharged when one contractual party resists that happening. The only exception is a unilateral refusal to perform a contractual obligation, and then only if the right to refuse is stipulated in the contract or is provided in the Civil Code with respect to the particular circumstances. On the one hand, this does encourage stability of contracts. On the other, it makes it difficult for a party to respond adequately to changed circumstances. It is therefore highly recommended that contracting parties include a discharge clause into their contracts otherwise they may have to bear the risk of not being able to be released from a contract which is no longer appropriate.

[81] Ruling of Supreme Commercial Court of 11 October 2011, above n 79.

12

Conclusion

We now come to the summation. What can we conclude about Russian contract law? From the outset, Russian law tries to be logical. It is inherent in having a codified system that order and categorisation are important. Russia has been able to take advantage of consideration of other twentieth-century civil law codifications, such as, for example, in the Netherlands, before taking her own decisions as to what to include and in what structure. The Russian legal draftsmen have also been able to look back to previous Russian compilations and codifications.

The result is a Civil Code (CC) with impressively detailed provisions for transactions in general; within them, the law of obligations; within that, the rules for all contracts; following that, a range of specific types of typical 'default' contracts. The fundamental guiding principle is in modern Russian contract law is freedom of contract, explicitly set out in CC articles 1 and 421. This stands in strong contrast to the situation for state-owned enterprises making contracts within the Soviet planned economy.

Under Russian law the essence of a contract is said to be the congruence of the wills of the two parties forming an agreement. Therefore, if there are factors such as delusion or infirmity of mind which undermine a party's will, the contract will be vitiated. However, clear proof is also an important feature, and in many instances written evidence (in some cases, signed by both parties, in some cases authorised by a notary) is required to substantiate a contract. Then other ways of demonstrating the parties' agreed wills will not be accepted by the court.

In general, the court has a more active role to play in relation to Russian contract law day-to-day than do, for example, courts in England. This may seem ironic, given that the majority of English contract law was actually created in the courts. However, one might generalise about English contract law to say that the formation of a contract is a comparatively simple process, and parties are given wide autonomy; the main focus of the English law is on sophisticated and transparent rules for awarding damages in the form of a sum of money in the case of contractual breach. Thus, the different heads of damage, and the rules about causation and remoteness are well-developed, and allow settlement between parties of contractual cases without resort to court. Court is an absolute last resort in England. By contrast, in Russia the main focus is on performance of the contract, and court intervention may be necessary to enforce that, or, alternatively, to declare a contract invalid and settle the consequences, including by application of the rules of unfounded enrichment. This focus on performance also gives rise to well-developed 'methods of securing performance' in chapter 23 of the Civil Code, including the possibility of a penalty (неустойка; *neustoika*) (see Chapter 9 at p 212 and Chapter 10 at p 243).

There are other clear differences between the English and the Russian approaches to contract law. Requirements of form are much more important for the latter, and this easily allows the existence of contracts without compensation, such as a contract of gift. Under English law it is not possible to have contracts without compensation; some form of consideration is always required, although it is possible to make a binding promise through the use of a particular form – a deed – to make a bare promise enforceable. As with other continental European codified legal systems, in Russia the use of a notary is mandatory to authorise certain contracts; in other instances, parties, especially private individuals, will obtain notarial certification to ensure conclusive proof of a contract. There is no direct equivalent in English contract law.

The rules on formation of a Russian contract may also have some surprises for an English lawyer. An offer may have a time limit, in which case the offeror cannot revoke it within that period. The offer will stay open for the stated time unless rejected, accepted or destroyed by a counter-offer. There is no equivalent of the English default 'postal rule' which deems acceptance to occur when the acceptance letter is put in the postal system. Under Russian law, acceptance is made when it is received by the offeror, although in some circumstances silence can be acceptance. Also, it is possible to have a binding 'agreement to agree' in the form of a preliminary contract (CC article 429; see Chapter 4 at p 105), in which case the main contract must be made within one year.

On paper, consumers are comparatively well protected under Russian law. Apart from separate specific legislation (Law of the Russian Federation on the Protection of Consumer Rights,[1] which we do not deal with in detail in this book although its effect on contract terms is described in Chapter 2 at p 73), inequality of bargaining power is dealt with through special provisions in the Civil Code such as controls on contracts of adhesion and the institution of public contracts (see Chapter 2 at p 72 and p 74, respectively). Of course, protection of the consumer does make some inroads into the principle of freedom of contract. Also, unfortunately, the courts have not yet learnt to apply these very valuable but complexly-worded Civil Code provisions.

Similarly, for many judges commercial dealings are rather alien and often they have not yet internalised the principle of freedom of contract and as a result create problems for those working in the marketplace. Contracts are quite

[1] No 2300-1 of 7 February 1992. See also J P Nehf, 'Empowering the Russian Consumer in a Market Economy' (1992–93) 14 *Michigan Journal of International Law* 739 and P Jordan, 'Russian Lawyers as Consumer Protection Advocates, 1992–1995' (1996) 4–5 *Parker School Journal of East European Law* 486.

frequently invalidated by courts, or deemed to be not concluded; an unfortunate everyday reality for Russian lawyers.

The Russian legislature does accept the importance of civil law to a well-functioning market economy. A large draft reform to the Civil Code was undertaken, with a draft bill published in 2012.[2] Since then some shorter individual pieces of amending legislation have been enacted; we have tried wherever possible to include both actual and proposed changes to our topics of discussion.

The role of Russian courts has already been noted as frequently having importance for the resolution of individual contractual disputes. There is another dimension, however. As will be very apparent from our citation throughout this book of case examples, the role of the courts, and particularly the commercial courts headed by the Supreme Commercial Court, is instrumental in the development of Russian contract law in practice. Despite some resistance by Russian legal theoreticians, it is clear that case law is a source of law in Russia, and the Supreme Commercial Court, particularly under its current Chairman, Anton Aleksandrovich Ivanov, has been trying to clarify and systematise the use of the Civil Code, and sensibly fill any gaps. Sometimes the Supreme Commercial Court is not consistent in its compulsory explanations and legal opinions, which gives rise to unfortunate inconsistencies. However, it is still early days. In the modern era, Russia has only had a market economy for just over two decades. Judicial experience of resolving entrepreneurial disputes is barely out of its infancy. This stands in strong contrast to the English experience, where orderly development of commercial law can be dated back to the days of Lord Mansfield as Lord Chief Justice in the eighteenth century, if not earlier. We should not be surprised that there are areas within Russian contract law, and its practical application, where further improvement is clearly necessary, but suggest that Russian contract law should be understood in the context of recently developing codes of law, and not judged too harshly in contrast to other legal systems which have had much longer gestation.

[2] Draft Federal Law on Amendments to Parts One, Two, Three and Four of the Civil Code of the Russian Federation and certain other legal acts of the Russian Federation No 47538-6 approved by the State Duma at first reading on 27 April 2012.

Index